CHILTON'S
REPAIR & TUNE-UP GUIDE
TOYOTA
TRUCKS
1970-86

All U.S. and Canadian models of Pick-ups, Land Cruisers
and 4Runner; including 4-wheel drive and diesel engines

President LAWRENCE A. FORNASIERI
Vice President and General Manager JOHN P. KUSHNERICK
Executive Editor KERRY A. FREEMAN, S.A.E.
Senior Editor RICHARD J. RIVELE, S.A.E.

CHILTON BOOK COMPANY
Radnor, Pennsylvania
19089

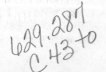

SAFETY NOTICE

Proper service and repair procedures are vital to the safe, reliable operation of all motor vehicles, as well as the personal safety of those performing repairs. This book outlines procedures for servicing and repairing vehicles using safe, effective methods. The procedures contain many NOTES, CAUTIONS and WARNINGS which should be followed along with standard safety procedures to eliminate the possibility of personal injury or improper service which could damage the vehicle or compromise its safety.

It is important to note that repair procedures and techniques, tools and parts for servicing motor vehicles, as well as the skill and experience of the individual performing the work vary widely. It is not possible to anticipate all of the conceivable ways or conditions under which vehicles may be serviced, or to provide cautions as to all of the possible hazards that may result. Standard and accepted safety precautions and equipment should be used when handling toxic or flammable fluids, and safety goggles or other protection should be used during cutting, grinding, chiseling, prying, or any other process that can cause material removal or projectiles.

Some procedures require the use of tools specially designed for a specific purpose. Before substituting another tool or procedure, you must be completely satisfied that neither your personal safety, nor the performance of the vehicle will be endangered.

Although information in this guide is based on industry sources and is as complete as possible at the time of publication, the possibility exists that the manufacturer made later changes which could not be included here. While striving for total accuracy, Chilton Book Company cannot assume responsibility for any errors, changes, or omissions that may occur in the compilation of this data.

PART NUMBERS

Part numbers listed in this reference are not recommendations by Chilton for any product by brand name. They are references that can be used with interchange manuals and aftermarket supplier catalogs to locate each brand supplier's discrete part number.

SPECIAL TOOLS

Special tools are recommended by the vehicle manufacturer to perform their specific job. Use has been kept to a minimum, but where absolutely necessary, are they referred to in the text by the part number of the tool manufacturer. These tools can be purchased, under the appropriate part number, from Kent-Moore Corporation, 29784 Little Mack, Roseville, Michigan 48066. For Canada, contact Kent-Moore of Canada, Ltd., 2395 Cawthra Mississauga, Ontario, Canada L5A 3P2 or an equivalent tool can be purchased locally from a tool supplier or parts outlet. Before substituting any tool for the one recommended, read the SAFETY NOTICE at the top of this page.

ACKNOWLEDGMENTS

The Chilton Book Company expresses appreciation to Toyota Motor Sales, U.S.A., Inc., 2055 W. 190th Street, Torrance, California 90504, Biscotte Toyota, 2062 W. Main Street, Norristown, Pennsylvania 19401 and Mainlane Toyota, Devon, Pennsylvania 19333 for their generous assistance.

Chilton's Repair & Tune-Up Guide: Toyota Trucks 1970–86
ISBN 0-8019-7661-8 pbk.
Library of Congress Catalog Card No. 85-47962

CONTENTS

 **1 General Information and Maintenance**

1 How to Use this Book
1 Tools and Equipment
4 Routine Maintenance and Lubrication

2 Tune-Up and Performance Maintenance

25 Tune-Up Procedures
27 Tune-Up Specifications

3 Engine and Engine Rebuilding

40 Engine Electrical System
48 Engine Service and Specifications

 **4 Emission Controls and Fuel System**

82 Emission Control System and Service
96 Gasoline Engine Fuel System
109 Diesel Engine Fuel System

5 Chassis Electrical

112 Heater and Accessory Service
117 Instrument Panel Service
118 Lights, Fuses and Flashers

 6 Clutch and Transmission

121 Manual Transmission
124 Clutch
129 Automatic Transmission

7 Drive Train

135 Driveshaft and U-Joints
137 Front Drive Axle
144 Rear Drive Axle

8 Suspension and Steering

147 Front Suspension
156 Rear Suspension
158 Steering

9 Brakes

167 Front Brakes
172 Rear Brakes
175 Brake Specifications

10 Troubleshooting

180 Problem Diagnosis

213 Mechanic's Data
215 Index

92 Chilton's Fuel Economy and Tune-Up Tips

188 Chilton's Body Repair Tips

8702148

Quick Reference Specifications For Your Vehicle

Fill in this chart with the most commonly used specifications for your vehicle. Specifications can be found in Chapters 1 through 3 or on the tune-up decal under the hood of the vehicle.

Tune-Up

Firing Order_____

Spark Plugs:

    Type_____

    Gap (in.)_____

Torque (ft. lbs.)_____

Idle Speed (rpm)_____

Ignition Timing (°)_____

    Vacuum or Electronic Advance (Connected/Disconnected)_____

Valve Clearance (in.)

    Intake_____   **Exhaust**_____

Capacities

Engine Oil Type (API Rating)_____

    With Filter Change (qts)_____

    Without Filter Change (qts)_____

Cooling System (qts)_____

Manual Transmission (pts)_____

    Type_____

Automatic Transmission (pts)_____

    Type_____

Front Differential (pts)_____

    Type_____

Rear Differential (pts)_____

    Type_____

Transfer Case (pts)_____

    Type_____

FREQUENTLY REPLACED PARTS

Use these spaces to record the part numbers of frequently replaced parts.

PCV VALVE	**OIL FILTER**	**AIR FILTER**	**FUEL FILTER**
Type_____	Type_____	Type_____	Type_____
Part No._____	Part No._____	Part No._____	Part No._____

General Information and Maintenance

1

HOW TO USE THIS BOOK

Chilton's Repair & Tune-Up Guide for Toyota Trucks is intended to teach you more about the inner workings of your truck and save you money on its upkeep. The first two chapters will be used the most, since they contain maintenance and tune-up information and procedures. The following chapters concern themselves with the more complex systems of your truck. Operating systems from engine through brakes are covered to the extent that we feel the average do-it-yourselfer should get involved. This book will not explain such things as rebuilding the differential for the simple reason that the expertise required and the investment in special tools make this task uneconomical. We will tell you how to change your own brake pads and shoes, replace points and plugs, and many more jobs that will save you money, give you personal satisfaction, and help you avoid problems.

A secondary purpose of this book is as a reference for owners who want to understand their car and/or their mechanics better. In this case, no tools at all are required.

Before removing any parts, read through the entire procedure. This will give you the overall view of what tools and supplies will be required.

The sections begin with a brief discussion of the system and what it involves, followed by adjustments, maintenance, removal and installation procedures, and repair or overhaul procedures. When repair is not considered feasible, we tell you how to remove the part and then how to install the new or rebuilt replacement. In this way, you at least save the labor costs. Backyard repair of such components as the alternator is just not practical.

Two basic mechanic's rules should be mentioned here. One, whenever the left side of the truck or engine is referred to, it is meant to specify the driver's side to the truck. Conversely, the right side of the truck meant the passenger's side. Secondly, most screws and bolts are removed by turning counterclockwise, and tightened by turning clockwise. Safety is always the most important rule. Constantly be aware of the dangers involved in working on an automobile and take the proper precautions. Use jackstands when working under a raised vehicle. Don't smoke or allow an exposed flame to come near the battery or any part of the fuel system. Always use the proper tool and use it correctly; bruised knuckles and skinned fingers aren't a mechanic's standard equipment; once you have some experience, working on your truck will become an enjoyable hobby.

TOOLS AND EQUIPMENT

It would be impossible to catalog each and every tool that you may need to perform all the operations included in this book. It would also not be wise for the amateur to rush out and buy an expensive set of tools on the theory that he may need one of them at some time. The best approach is to proceed slowly, gathering together a good quality set of those tools that are used most frequently. Don't be misled by the low cost of bargain tools. It is far better to spend a little more for quality, name brand tools. Forged wrenches, 10 or 12 point sockets and fine-tooth ratchets are by far preferable to their less expensive counterparts. As any good mechanic can tell you, there are few worse experiences than trying to work on a car or truck with bad tools. Your monetary savings will be far outweighed by frustration and mangled knuckles.

Begin accumulating those tools that are used most frequently; those associated with routine maintenance and tune-up. In addition to the normal assortment of screwdrivers and pliers, you should have the following tools for routine maintenance jobs:

1. Metric wrenches, sockets and combination open end/box end wrenches
2. Jackstands for support
3. Oil filter wrench
4. Oil filler spout or funnel
5. Grease gun for chassis lubrication
6. Hydrometer for checking the battery
7. A low flat pan for draining oil
8. Lots of rags for wiping up the inevitable mess.

In addition to the above items, there are several others that are not absolutely necessary, but are handy to have around. These include oil drying compound, a transmission funnel, and the usual supply of lubricants, antifreeze and fluids, although these can be purchased as needed. This is a basic list for routine maintenance, but only your personal needs can accurately determine your list of tools.

The second list of tools is for tune-ups. While the tools involved here are slightly more sophisticated, they need not be outrageously expensive. There are several inexpensive tach/dwell meters on the market that are every bit as good for the average mechanic as a $100.00 professional model. Just be sure that it goes to at least 1200–1500 rpm on the tach scale, and that it works on 4,6, and 8 cylinder engines. A basic list of tune-up equipment could include:

1. Tach/dwell meter
2. Spark plug wrench
3. Timing light (preferably a DC light that works from the truck battery)
4. A set of flat feeler gauges
5. A set of round wire spark plug gauges.

In addition to these basic tools, there are several other tools and gauges you may find useful. These include:

1. A compression gauge. The screw-in type is slower to use, but eliminates the possibility of a faulty reading due to escaping pressure
2. A manifold vacuum gauge
3. A test light
4. An induction meter. This is used for determining whether or not there is current in a wire. These are handy for use if a wire is broken somewhere in a wiring harness. As a final note, you will probably find a torque wrench necessary for all but the most basic work. The beam type models are perfectly adequate, although the newer click type are more precise.

SPECIAL TOOLS

Normally, the use of special factory tools is avoided for repair procedures, since these are not readily available for the do-it-yourself me-

chanic. When it is possible to perform the job with more commonly available tools, it will be pointed out, but occasionally, a special tool was designed to perform a specific function and should be used. Before substituting another tool, you should be convinced that neither your safety nor the performance of the vehicle will be compromised.

Some special tools are available commercially from major tool manufacturers. Others for your Toyota can be purchased from your dealer or from Owatonna Tool Co., Owatonna, Minnesota 55060.

SERVICING YOUR VEHICLE SAFELY

It is virtually impossible to anticipate all of the hazards involved with automotive maintenance and service but care and common sense will prevent most accidents.

The rules of safety for mechanics range from, don't smoke around gasoline, to, use the proper tool for the job. The trick to avoiding injuries is to develop safe work habits and take every possible precaution.

DO

• Do keep a fire extinguisher and first aid kit within easy reach.

• Do wear safety glasses or goggles when cutting, drilling, grinding or prying. If you wear glasses for the sake of vision, then they should be made of hardened glass that can serve also as safety glasses, or wear safety goggles over your regular glasses.

• Do shield your eyes whenever you work around the battery. Batteries contain sulphuric acid; in case of contact with the eyes or skin, flush the area with water or a mixture of water and baking soda and get medical attention immediately.

• Do use safety stands for any under-truck service. Jacks are for raising vehicles; safety stands are for making sure the vehicle stays raised until you want it to come down. Whenever the vehicle is raised, block the wheels remaining on the ground and set the parking brake.

• Do use adequate ventilation when working with any chemicals. Asbestos dust resulting from brake lining wear can cause cancer.

• Do disconnect the negative battery cable when working on the electrical system. The primary ignition system can contain up to 40,000 volts.

• Do follow manufacturer's directions whenever working with potentially hazardous materials. Both brake fluid and antifreeze are poisonous if taken internally.

• Do properly maintain your tools. Loose hammerheads, mushroomed punches and chisels, frayed or poorly grounded electrical cords, excessively worn screwdrivers, spread wrenches (open end), cracked sockets, slipping ratchets, or faulty droplight sockets can cause accidents.

• Do use the proper size and type of tool for the job being done.

• Do when possible, pull on a wrench handle rather than push on it, and adjust your stance to prevent a fall.

• Do be sure that adjustable wrenches are tightly adjusted on the nut or bolt and pulled so that the face is on the side of the fixed jaw.

• Do select a wrench or socket that fits the nut or bolt. The wrench or socket should sit straight, not cocked.

• Do strike squarely with a hammer to avoid glancing blows.

• Do set the parking brake and block the drive wheels if the work requires that the engine be running.

DON'T

• Don't run an engine in a garage or anywhere else without proper ventilation—EVER! Carbon monoxide is poisonous; it is absorbed by the body 400 times faster than oxygen; it takes a long time to leave the human body and you can build up a deadly supply of it in your system by simply breathing in a little every day. You may not realize you are slowly poisoning yourself. Always use power vents, windows, fans or open the garage doors.

• Don't work around moving parts while wearing a necktie or other loose clothing. Short sleeves are much safer than long, loose sleeves. Hard-toed shoes with neoprene soles protect your toes and give a better grip on slippery surfaces. Jewelry such as watches, fancy belt buckles, beads or body adornment of any kind is not safe working around a car. Long hair should be hidden under a hat or cap.

• Don't use pockets for toolboxes. A fall or bump can drive a screwdriver deep into your body. Even a wiping cloth hanging from the back pocket can wrap around a spinning shaft or fan.

• Don't smoke when working around gasoline, cleaning solvent or other flammable material.

• Don't smoke when working around the battery. When the battery is being charged, it gives off explosive hydrogen gas.

• Don't use gasoline to wash your hands; there are excellent soaps available. Gasoline may contain lead, and lead can enter the body through a cut, accumulating in the body until you are very ill. Gasoline also removes all the natural oils from the skin so that bone dry hands will absorb oil and grease.

• Don't service the air conditioning system unless you are equipped with the necessary tools and training. The refrigerant, R-12, is extremely cold and when exposed to the air, will instantly freeze any surface it comes in contact with, including your eyes. Although the refrigerant is normally non-toxic, R-12 becomes a deadly poisonous gas in the presence of an open flame. One good whiff of the vapors from burning refrigerant can be fatal.

HISTORY

The Toyota Truck is the refinement of a light-duty, multi-purpose vehicle, manufactured by the world's third largest producer of commercial vehicles, the Toyota Motor Company. It is a rugged, but comfortable, half-ton truck which easily doubles as around town transportation.

In 1933 the Toyoda Automatic Loom Works started an automobile division. Serious automobile production did not begin until 1937, when the Toyota Motor Co., Ltd. was founded. A numerologist suggested changing the family name Toyoda, to Toyota because it was favored in this type of endeavor. The numerologist must have been right because by 1947 Toyota had produced 100,000 vehicles. Today Toyota Motor Co. is Japan's largest automotive manufacturer.

Toyotas were not imported until the late 1950s and Americans were generally not impressed by the heavy, underpowered cars. Toyota scored a major breakthrough in the American economy in 1965 with the introduction of the Corona sedan.

The earliest recollection of a Toyota truck being imported to this country is around 1966. It was called a Stout and was powered by a 1900cc overhead valve engine.

SERIAL NUMBER IDENTIFICATION

Vehicle

1970–81

The vehicle serial number is stamped on the left side of the frame behind the front wheel. It consists of a four digit model number and a six digit production number.

1982–86

The number is located both on the right fender apron in the engine compartment, and on the driver's side door pillar.

ENGINE

The engine serial number consists of an engine series identification number followed by a six digit production number.

On 8R-C and 2F engines, the serial number is stamped on the right side of the engine block beside the fuel pump.

The 2000cc model 18R-C engine has its serial number stamped on the left side of the engine below the number one spark plug.

On later engines the serial number is stamped on the left side of the cylinder block, behind the alternator.

ROUTINE MAINTENANCE

Air Cleaner

Dry Type

The paper element of the air filter assembly should be blown clean with compressed air every 6 months or 6,000 miles under normal driving conditions. For 1970–78 the filter element should be changed every 24,000 miles. 1979–85 filters should be changed every 30,000 miles. Advance the cleaning and replacement schedule when the vehicle is operated in dusty areas.

To remove the paper element, unscrew the wing nut on the air filter assembly and unlatch the clamps securing the cover. Make sure that the gaskets on the case and cover are in place before reassembling. 20R engines have a hose connected to the top cover. This will have to be disconnected before removing the cover. After removing the paper element, wipe out the cover and case with a soft rag to remove any accumulated dust. Match up the arrows on the cover and case when reassembling.

NOTE: *Do not operate the engine without the air filter element in place.*

Oil Bath Type

Clean the element and replace the oil in the oil bath type air cleaner every 3,000 miles or sooner in dusty areas.

Remove the air cleaner assembly from the vehicle and disassemble the various parts. Remove any rubber or plastic hoses that are connected to the air cleaner. Remove the oil from the oil cup and scrape out all the dirt inside and on the bottom. Wash the cup with a safe sol-

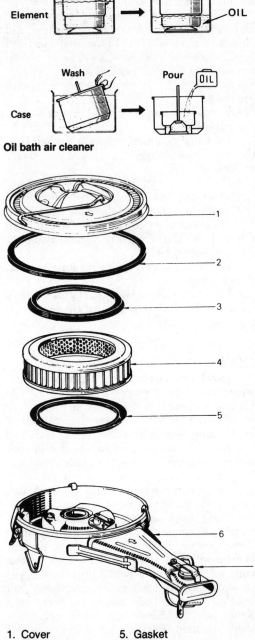

Oil bath air cleaner

1. Cover
2. Gasket
3. Gasket
4. Cleaner element
5. Gasket
6. Case
7. Hot air intake diaphragm

20R air cleaner element and case. Other models are similar. Check the gasket for a tight seal before replacing the cover

vent, such as kerosene. Refill the oil cup to the level mark with the same weight (SAE) oil as is being used in the engine at that particular time. If it is cold and you are using a light viscosity oil in the engine, use a light viscosity oil in the air filter. If you are using a heavier oil in the crankcase for warm weather, use the same, heavier oil in the oil bath air cleaner. Soak the filter element in the same safe solvent as the oil cup. Agitate the element thoroughly in the cleaning solution to remove all dirt particles. Dry the element thoroughly with compressed air. Reassemble the air cleaner assembly and reinstall it on the engine in the reverse order of disassembly and removal.

PCV Valve

The operation of the positive crankcase ventilation system should be checked every 12,000 miles. To do this remove the hose from the valve located at the top of the valve cover. Remove the valve and shake it. If it rattles, it's okay. If not, replace it. Wash the valve with kerosene or other suitable solvent and blow clean with compressed air. Clean the hose which goes from the valve to the intake manifold by running a solvent soaked rag through the hose. If it shows signs of wear, replace it with a hose of equal quality.

Replace the PCV valve every 12,000 miles for 1970–78 and 30,000 miles for 1979 and later.

NOTE: *The PCV system will not function properly unless the oil filler cap is tightly sealed. Check the gasket on the cap and be certain it is not leaking. Replace the cap or gasket or both if necessary to ensure proper sealing.*

Evaporative Emission Control Canister

Late 1971 and later models use a charcoal canister. It can be found on the front of the left fender on late 1971 through 1974 trucks and at the rear of the engine compartment, on or near the firewall on 1975 and later trucks.

Clean and inspect the canister for damage every 12,000 miles, (1970–78), 30,000 miles (1979–and later). Every 50,000 miles it should be replaced (1970–78). It is not necessary to replace this canister on 1979 and later models.

Case Storage System

1970–71 trucks use a case storage system in lieu of the charcoal canister. This system's basic function is to prevent the escape of fuel vapors by routing them into a storage case for later combustion. The only scheduled maintenance for this system is the replacement of the system's air filter every 12,000 miles. The filter is located above the fuel vapor storage case, next to the fuel filler cap. Unplug the old filter from the hose, discard it, and insert the new filter.

Drive Belts

The fan belt should be checked for cracks and wear periodically, and especially before going on any long distance trip. Check the belt tension regularly in the following manner. Depress the belt midway between the fan and alternator pulleys. The belt should have about ⅛ in. by ½ in. slack. If the belt is too loose, tighten it by loosening the alternator bracket bolt and the bolt on the adjusting bar; then, using a long piece of wood or a hammer handle, pry the alternator away from the engine until the proper tension is achieved.

CAUTION: *Do not use a screwdriver or other metal device to pry the alternator as damage to the alternator may result.*

Tighten the alternator and adjusting bar bolts securely. If a new belt is installed, the tension should be checked again after about 1,000 miles of operation.

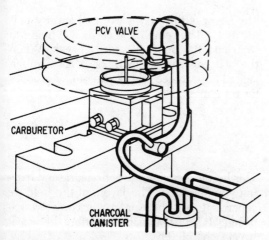

Typical PCV valve and Charcoal Canister installation. On 20R engines, the PCV valve is under the second hose, in the center of the valve cover

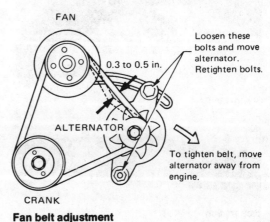

Fan belt adjustment

HOW TO SPOT WORN V-BELTS

V-Belts are vital to efficient engine operation—they drive the fan, water pump and other accessories. They require little maintenance (occasional tightening) but they will not last forever. Slipping or failure of the V-belt will lead to overheating. If your V-belt looks like any of these, it should be replaced.

Cracking or weathering

This belt has deep cracks, which cause it to flex. Too much flexing leads to heat build-up and premature failure. These cracks can be caused by using the belt on a pulley that is too small. Notched belts are available for small diameter pulleys.

Softening (grease and oil)

Oil and grease on a belt can cause the belt's rubber compounds to soften and separate from the reinforcing cords that hold the belt together. The belt will first slip, then finally fail altogether.

Glazing

Glazing is caused by a belt that is slipping. A slipping belt can cause a run-down battery, erratic power steering, overheating or poor accessory performance. The more the belt slips, the more glazing will be built up on the surface of the belt. The more the belt is glazed, the more it will slip. If the glazing is light, tighten the belt.

Worn cover

The cover of this belt is worn off and is peeling away. The reinforcing cords will begin to wear and the belt will shortly break. When the belt cover wears in spots or has a rough jagged appearance, check the pulley grooves for roughness.

Separation

This belt is on the verge of breaking and leaving you stranded. The layers of the belt are separating and the reinforcing cords are exposed. It's just a matter of time before it breaks completely.

HOW TO SPOT BAD HOSES

Both the upper and lower radiator hoses are called upon to perform difficult jobs in an inhospitable environment. They are subject to nearly 18 psi at under hood temperatures often over 280°F., and must circulate nearly 7500 gallons of coolant an hour—3 good reasons to have good hoses.

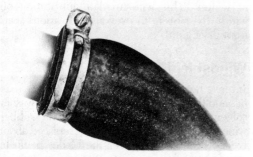

A good test for any hose is to feel it for soft or spongy spots. Frequently these will appear as swollen areas of the hose. The most likely cause is oil soaking. This hose could burst at any time, when hot or under pressure.

Swollen hose

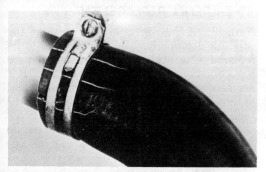

Cracked hoses can usually be seen but feel the hoses to be sure they have not hardened; a prime cause of cracking. This hose has cracked down to the reinforcing cords and could split at any of the cracks.

Cracked hose

Weakened clamps frequently are the cause of hose and cooling system failure. The connection between the pipe and hose has deteriorated enough to allow coolant to escape when the engine is hot.

Frayed hose end (due to weak clamp)

Debris, rust and scale in the cooling system can cause the inside of a hose to weaken. This can usually be felt on the outside of the hose as soft or thinner areas.

Debris in cooling system

Belt adjustments for the air pump and air conditioning compressor are made in the same way. Be careful not to pry against the cast housing of the air pump, as it is brittle and subject to breakage.

Be certain when making these adjustments not to overtighten. Overtight drive belts will lead to bearing failure.

Air Conditioning System Check

Toyota units have a sight glass for checking the refrigerant charge. This is on top of the receiver dehydrator, alongside the radiator.

CAUTION: *Do not attempt to charge or discharge the refrigerant system unless you are thoroughly familiar with its operation and the hazards involved. The compressed refrigerant used in the air conditioning system expands and evaporates (boils) into the atmosphere at a temperature of $-21.7°F$ ($-29.8°C$) or less. This will freeze any surface, including your eyes, that it contacts. In addition, the refrigerant decomposes into a poisonous gas in the presence of flame.*

NOTE: *If your truck is equipped with an aftermarket air conditioner, the following system check may not apply. You should contact the manufacturer of your unit for instructions on system checks.*

1. Start the engine and set it on fast idle.

2. Set the controls for maximum cold with the blower on high.

3. If bubbles are present in the sight glass, the system is low on charge. If no bubbles are present, the system is either fully charged or empty.

4. Feel the high and low pressure lines at the compressor. The high pressure lines should be warm and the low pressure line should be cool. If no appreciable temperature difference is felt, the system is empty, or nearly so.

Even if there is a noticeable temperature difference, there is a possibility of overcharge. Disconnect the compressor clutch wire. If the refrigerant in the sight glass remains clear for more than 45–60 seconds before foaming and then settling away from the sight glass, an overcharge is indicated. If the refrigerant foams and then settles away from the sight glass in less than 45–60 seconds, it can be assumed that the system is properly charged.

The air conditioning system should be operated for about five minutes each week, even in winter. This will circulate lubricating oil within the system to prevent the various seals from drying out.

Windshield Wipers

Intense heat from the sun, snow and ice, road oils and the chemicals used in windshield washer solvents combine to deteriorate the rubber wiper refills. The refills should be replaced about twice a year or whenever the blades begin to streak or chatter.

WIPER REFILL REPLACEMENT

Normally, if the wipers are not cleaning the windshield properly, only the refill has to be replaced. The blade and arm usually require replacement only in the event of damage. It is not necessary (except on new Tridon® refills) to remove the arm or the blade to replace the refill (rubber part), though you may have to position the arm higher on the glass. You can do this by turning the ignition switch on and operating the wipers. When they are positioned where they are accessible, turn the ignition switch off.

There are several types of refills and your vehicle could have any kind, since aftermarket blades and arms may not use exactly the same refill as the original equipment.

Most Trico® styles use a release button that is pushed down to allow the refill to slide out of the yoke jaws. The new refill slides in and locks in place. Some Trico® refills are removed by locating where the metal backing strip or the refill is wider. Insert a small screwdriver blade between the frame and metal backing strip. Press down to release the refill from the retaining tab.

The Anco® style is unlocked at one end by squeezing 2 metal tabs, and the refill is slid out of the frame jaws. When the new refill is installed, the tabs will click into place, locking the refill.

The Polycarbonate® type is held in place by a locking level that is pushed downward out of the groove in the arm to free the refill. When the new refill is installed, it will lock in place automatically.

The Tridon® refill has a plastic backing strip with a notch about an inch from the end. Hold the blade (frame) on a hard surface so that the frame is tightly bowed. Grip the tip of the

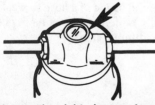

Arrow points to the sight glass on top of the air conditioner's receiver dehydrator, located next to the radiator. Although the sight glass is very small, any bubbles in the refrigerant should be readily apparent in strong light

backing strip and pull up while twisting counterclockwise. The backing strip will snap out of the retaining tab. Do this for the remaining tabs until the refill is free of the arm. The length of these refills is molded into the end and they should be replaced with identical types.

No matter which type of refill you use, be sure that all of the frame claws engage the refill. Before operating the wipers, be sure that no part of the metal frame is contacting the windshield.

Fluid Level Checks

Engine Oil

The oil level in the engine should be checked as the last step in a fuel stop. The check should be made with the engine warm and switched off for a period of about one minute so that the oil can drain down into the crankcase. Pull out the dipstick, wipe it clean, and reinsert it. The level of the oil should be kept between the minimum and maximum marks at all times. If the oil level is kept above the maximum mark, heavy oil consumption will result. If the level remains below the minimum mark, severe engine damage will result. When topping off the crankcase oil be sure to add oil of the same viscosity rating as the oil in the crankcase.

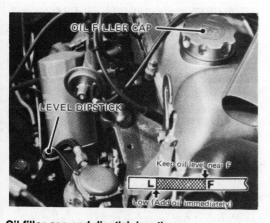

Oil filler cap and dipstick location

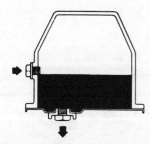

Oil level should reach the bottom of the filler plug hole in the manual transmission

Manual Transmission Fluid

Park the truck on level ground and using a 17mm wrench, loosen the filler plug. The lubricating oil should reach the bottom of the filler plug hole. If it does not, fill to the proper level with SAE 90 weight gear oil meeting the API service GL-4 specification. Perform this check every 6 months or 7500 miles. If operating in deep water, change the fluid as soon as possible.

Automatic Transmission Fluid

It is best to check the fluid level of an automatic transmission when the engine and transmission are warm. A transmission is warm after it has been driven 6 or 7 miles. Park the truck on level ground and set the parking brake firmly. Shift the transmission through all gear ranges at idle speed. Use the transmission dipstick to check the fluid level with the transmission in the Neutral range. Pull the dipstick, wipe it clean, reinsert it, making sure it is fully seated, then pull it out again and check the level of the fluid. It should be within the Hot range marked on the dipstick. If additional fluid is required, add Type F fluid only through the dipstick tube. Stop and check the fluid level frequently as you add; overfilling will cause foaming, fluid loss, and slippage.

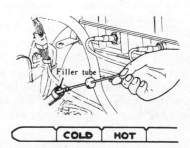

Checking automatic transmission fluid level

Transfer Case and Power Take-Off

Check both the transfer case and the power take-off lubricant levels every 6,000 miles. The oil level should be up to the filler plug in each case. Replenish the supply with SAE 90 gear oil, if necessary.

Brake and Clutch Master Cylinders

The reservoirs must be kept ¾ full at all times. It is best to check the level weekly. When adding fluid take care to prevent foreign material from entering the cylinder. Use DOT 3 classification brake fluid.

NOTE: *It is normal for the fluid level to fall as the disc brake pads wear. However, if the*

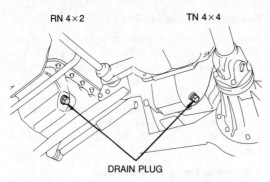

Transmission and transfer case drain plugs

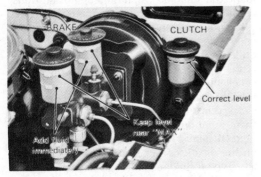

Brake and clutch master cylinder reservoirs

Radiator cap and coolant reservoir

master cylinder requires filling frequently, you should check the system for leaks in the hoses, master cylinder, or wheel cylinders. Brake fluid dissolves paint. It also absorbs moisture from the air; never leave a container or the master cylinder or the clutch cylinder uncovered any longer than necessary. The clutch master cylinder uses the same fluid as the brakes, and should be checked at the same time as the brake master cylinder.

Cooling System

Dealing with the cooling system can be a dangerous matter unless the proper precautions are exercised. It is best to check the coolant level in the radiator when the engine is cold by simply removing the radiator cap and seeing that the coolant reaches the bottom of the filler neck. On newer trucks the cooling system has, as one of its components, an expansion tank in which case the radiator cap need not be removed if coolant is visible in the expansion reservoir. Always make certain that the filler caps on both the radiator and the reservoir are tightly closed. In the event that you must check the coolant level when the engine is warm, proceed in this manner: place a thick rag over the radiator cap and slowly turn the cap to the detent. This will allow the pressure to drop gradually, preventing an explosion of hot coolant. When the steam

has escaped, remove the cap the rest of the way.

CAUTION: *When draining the coolant, keep in mind that cats and dogs are attracted by the ethylene glycol antifreeze, and are quite likely to drink any that is left in an uncovered container or in puddles on the ground. This will prove fatal in sufficient quantity. Always drain the coolant into a sealable container. Coolant should be reused unless it is contaminated or several years old.*

NOTE: *When adding cold coolant to a hot radiator, always do so with the engine running. If the coolant level is low, add equal amounts of antifreeze and clean water. On models without an expansion tank, add coolant through the radiator filler neck. Add coolant to the recovery tank on trucks equipped with that system.*

If the coolant level is chronically low, refer to the Troubleshooting Chapter for diagnosis of the problem. Refer to Chapter Three for coolant draining and refilling, which should be done every 24 months or 24,000 miles for 1970–78, and 24 months or 30,000 miles on 1979 and later.

Drive Axles

The lubricant in the differential housing must reach the bottom of the filler plug hole. To see if it does, remove the filler plug with a 24mm wrench and use your finger to check the level. If you must add fluid it should be SAE 90 weight gear oil meeting the API service GL-5 classification. If the truck is to be operated in temperatures under −10°F (−23°C), use SAE 80W or

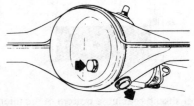

Position of the differential fill and drain plugs

85W GL-5 gear oil. You should check the fluid level every 6 months or 6,000 miles.

Steering Gear

Every year you should check the steering gear housing lubricating oil. The housing should be full of SAE 90 weight gear oil meeting API service GL-4 classification. The filler plug is on top of the housing and requires a 14mm wrench for removal.

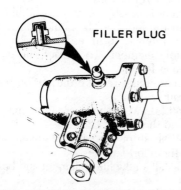

Steering gear housing filler plug

Steering Knuckle

4-WHEEL DRIVE

Check the amount and condition of the lubricant in the steering knuckle every 6 months or 12,000 miles, whichever comes first. The steering knuckle should be packed with multipurpose grease (NLGI No. 2).

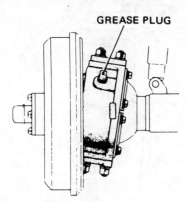

Steering knuckle filler plug

Battery Electrolyte

At every fuel stop the level of the battery electrolyte should be checked. The level should be maintained between the upper and lower levels marked on the battery case or the bottom of the vent well in each cell.

If the electrolyte level is low, distilled water should be added until the proper level is

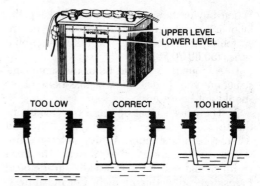

Black battery case fluid level

reached. Each cell is completely separate from the others, so each must be filled individually. It is a good idea to add the distilled water with a squeeze bulb to avoid having electrolyte splash out. If water is frequently needed, the most likely cause is overcharging, caused by a faulty voltage regulator. If any acid solution should escape, it can be neutralized with a baking soda and water solution, but don't let the stuff get in the battery. In winter, add water only before driving to prevent the battery from freezing and cracking. When replacing a battery, it is important that the replacement have an out put rating equal to or greater than original equipment. See Chapter Three for details on battery replacement.

CAUTION: *If you get acid on your skin or in your eyes, rinse it off immediately with lots of water. Go to a doctor if it gets in your eyes. The gases formed inside the battery cells are highly explosive. Never check the level of the electrolyte in the presence of flame or while smoking.*

Tires

The importance of proper tire inflation cannot be overemphasized. A tire employs air under pressure as part of its structure. It is designed around the supporting strength of a gas at a specified pressure. For this reason improper inflation drastically reduces the tire's ability to perform as it was intended. Tire pressures should be checked regularly with a reliable pressure gauge. Too often the gauge on the end of the air hose at your corner garage is not accurate enough because it suffers too much abuse.

Always check tire pressure when the tires are cold as pressure increases with temperature. If you must move the vehicle to check the tire inflation, do not drive more than a mile before checking. A cold tire is one that has not been driven on for a period of about three hours.

CAUTION: *Never exceed the maximum tire pressure marked on the tire.*

When buying new tires, you should keep the following points in mind, especially if you are switching to larger tires or a different profile series (50,60,70,78):

1. All four tires should be of the same construction type. Radial, bias, or bias-belted tires should not be mixed.

2. The wheels must be the correct width for the tire. Tire dealers have charts of tire and wheel rim compatibility. A mismatch can cause sloppy handling and rapid tread wear. The tread width should match the rim width (inside bead to inside bead) within an inch. For radial tires, the rim width should be 80% or less of the tire (not tread) width.

3. The height (mounted diameter) of the new tires can change speedometer accuracy, engine speed per given road speed, fuel mileage, acceleration, and ground clearance. Tire manufacturers furnish full measurement specifications.

4. The spare tire should be usable, at least for low speed operation, with the new tires.

5. There shouldn't be any body interference when the truck is loaded, on bumps or in turning.

TIRE ROTATION

So that the tires wear more uniformly, it is recommended that the tires be rotated every 6,000 miles. This can be done when all four tires are of the same size and load rating capacity.

Radial tires should not be cross-switched; they'll last longer if their direction of rotation is not changed. Truck type tires sometimes have directional tread, indicated by arrows molded into the sidewalls; the arrow shows the direction of rotation. They will wear very rapidly if reversed. Studded snow tires will lose their studs if their direction of rotation is reversed.

All season tires are preferable to snow tires in areas which receive moderate snowfalls and areas prone to ice and sleet storms. Snow tires work better in deep snow, but lose traction on ice.

NOTE: *Mark the wheel position or direction of rotation on radial tires or studded snow tires before removal. Avoid overtightening*

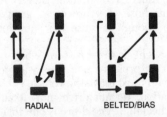

RADIAL   BELTED/BIAS

These patterns should be followed when rotating tires; however, the spare tire can be bypassed, if desired

the lug nuts or the brake disc or drum may become permanently distorted. Alloy wheels canbe cracked by overtightening. Always tighten the nuts in a crisscross pattern.

Fuel Filter
REPLACEMENT
F Series

The Land Cruiser uses a cartridge type fuel filter with a disposable element. The filter is located in the fuel line. It should not be necessary to remove it in order to change the disposable element. To replace the element, proceed as follows:

1. Loosen and remove the nut on the filter bowl bail.

2. Withdraw the bowl, element spring, element and the bowl gasket.

3. Wash all of the parts in solvent and examine them for damage.

4. Install a new filter element and bowl gasket.

5. Install the components in the reverse order of removal. Do not fully tighten the bail nut.

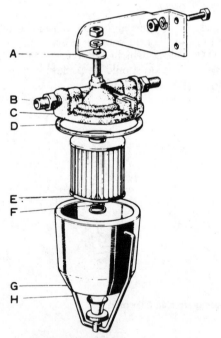

A. Fuel filter bracket
B. Fuel line fitting
C. Mounting boss
D. Filter bowl gasket
E. Filter element
F. Filter element positioning spring
G. Fuel filter bowl
H. Bowl retaining bail

Early Land Cruiser fuel filter

6. Seat the bowl by turning it slightly. Tighten the bail nut fully and check for leaks.

The above procedure should be performed if the clear glass bowl fills up with water or every 1,200 miles.

CAUTION: *Do not have any open flame nearby while servicing the fuel filter because of the presence of flammable gasoline vapors.*

8R-C ENGINES

It is not necessary to remove the filter unit to replace the element.

1. Loosen and remove the nut on the filter bowl bail.

2. Take out the bowl, element spring, element, and bowl gasket.

3. Wash the parts (except for the element—discard that) in solvent and inspect for damage. Install a new filter element, and if its condition warrants, a new gasket.

4. After reinstalling the parts, do not fully tighten the bail nut.

5. Seat the bowl by turning it slightly, pressing gently against the gasket. Tighten the bail nut fully and check for leaks.

18R-C ENGINES

The entire fuel filter is replaced on these engines.

1. Unfasten the fuel intake hose. Use a wrench to loosen the attachment nut, and another wrench on the opposite side to keep the filter from turning.

2. Remove the flexible fuel line from the other side of the filter. Unfasten the attaching screws from the filter bracket.

3. Install the new filter and reconnect the fuel lines. Start the engine and check for leaks.

20R, 22R and 22R-E Engines

The entire fuel filter is replaced on these engines.

1. Using a pair of pliers, expand the hose clamp on one side of the filter, and slide the clamp further down the hose, past the point to which the filter pipe extends. Remove the other clamp in the same manner.

2. Grasp the hoses near the ends and twist them gently to pull them free from the filter pipes.

3. Pull the filter from the clip and discard.

4. Install the new filter into the clip. The arrow must point towards the hose that runs to the carburetor. Push the hoses onto the filter pipes, and slide the clamps back into position. Start the engine and check for leaks.

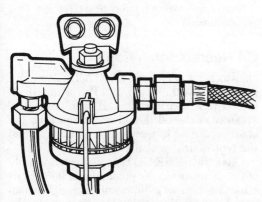

Only the bottom nut need be unbolted on the 8R-C fuel filter

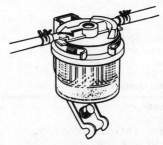

The arrow on the 20R fuel filter must point toward the carburetor line

The fuel filter on 18R-C engines will either have two nuts, as illustrated here, or a nut on one side and a clamp on the other. Be sure you get the correct replacement filter for your truck

LUBRICATION

Fuel Recommendations

Octane rating is based on the quantity of antiknock compounds added to the fuel and determines the speed at which the fuel will burn; the lower the octane rating, the faster it burns. The higher the numerical octane rating, the slower the fuel burns and the greater the percentage of compounds in the fuel to prevent knock and preignition. As the temperature of the engine increases, the air/fuel mixture shows a tendency to ignite before the spark plug is

Preventive Maintenance Schedule*

	1970–78	1979–86
ENGINE		
Valve Clearance	6	15
Drive Belts	12	30
Engine Oil	6 ①	10 ②
Oil Filter	6 ①	10 ②
Coolant	24	30
Inspect Cooling System Hoses	12	60
Inspect Exhaust Pipes and Mountings	12	15
Engine Idle	6	15
Choke Mechanism and Linkage	12	15
Replace Fuel Filter	24	60
Replace Air Filter Element	24	30
Check Timing and Dwell	12	30 ③
Replace Points	12	—
Replace Spark Plugs	12	15
Inspect PCV Valve	6	30
Replace PCV Valve	12	30
CHASSIS		
Inspect Brake Lining and Drums	12	15
Inspect Brake Lines and Hoses	6	7.5
Steering Gear Oil Level	12	15
Ball Joint and Dust Cover	6	7.5
Check Transmission Oil Level	6	7.5
Replace Transmission Oil	24	30
Check Automatic Transmission Fluid Level	6	7.5
Replace Automatic Transmission Fluid	24	30
Wheel Bearing and Ball Joint Greasing	24	30
Grease Driveshaft	6	15
Grease Control Arm Shaft Bushings	6	7.5
Check Brake Fluid	Weekly	Weekly
Check Clutch Master Cylinder	Weekly	Weekly

*The numerals refer to months or mileage whichever comes first.
① The oil should be changed more frequently under severe service conditions.
② 2 Wheel Drive 10,000 miles or 18 months; 4 Wheel Drive 10,000 miles or 8 months.
③ Ignition timing only.

fired and the exhaust valve is opened. This is especially important in high compression engines (compression ratio of 9.0:1 or greater), where the use of low octane gas will cause combustion to occur before the piston has completed its compression stroke, thereby forcing the piston down while it is still traveling up. Fuel of the proper octane rating for the compression ratio of your engine will allow the combustion process to occur at precisely the right time thereby producing efficient, and complete burning.

The Toyota 1900 8R-C engine in the 1970–71 Hi-Lux trucks has a compression ratio of 9.0:1 and therefore requires premium grade fuel. The 2000cc 18R-C engine has a compression ratio of 8.5:1 and runs at peak efficiency on regular grade gasoline. The 2200cc 20R engine, with a compression ratio of 8.4:1, uses regular gas. However, some 1976 models, and all 1977 and later trucks must use unleaded gas, whether catalyst equipped or not. If knocking occurs in these engines, try changing brands of gasoline. Some brands have slightly higher octane ratings than others. It is recommended that all 1985 trucks use a premium grade unleaded fuel with a minimum octane rating of 90. All 1981 and later diesels require the use of No. 2 diesel fuel.

NOTE: *Your engine's fuel requirement can change with time, mainly due to carbon buildup, which changes the compression ratio. If your engine pings, knocks, or runs on, switch to a higher grade of fuel, if possible, and check the ignition timing. If it is necessary to retard timing from specifications, don't change it more than about four degrees. Retarded timing will reduce power output and fuel mileage, and will increase engine temperature. Toyota distributors have an octane selector which allows you to change the timing for this purpose. See Chapter Two for details.*

Oil Recommendations

Oil which has been rated SE/SF/CD heavy duty detergent by the American Petroleum Institute is best to use under all conditions. The viscosity of the oil should be chosen from the chart according to temperature conditions and the type of driving done.

Oil of the SE/SF/CD type performs a variety of functions inside the engine in addition to its basic function as a lubricant. Through a balanced system of metallic detergents and polymeric dispersants, the oil prevents the formulation of high temperature and low temperature deposits and also keeps sludge and dirt particles in suspension. Acids, particularly sulfuric acid as well as other by-products of combustion, are neutralized. These acids, if permitted to concentrate, cause corrosion and rapid wear of internal parts.

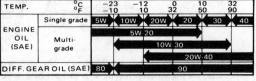

Recommended lubricant viscosities for the engine and rear axle

Engine Oil and Filter Changing

**All Except 1970–72 Land Cruiser with
Canister Type Filter and 4 Runner**

If you purchased your Toyota Truck new, the engine oil should be changed at the end of the first 1,000 miles. The oil should then be changed again at the 6,000 mile mark (1970–1978) and each 6,000 miles thereafter. The 1979 and later at 10,000 miles. You should also make it a practice to change the filter at every oil change.

These intervals ought to be halved when the truck is operated under severe conditions, such as dusty conditions, trailer towing, prolonged high speeds, off-road driving, or repeated short trips in freezing temperatures.

To change the oil:

1. Operate the truck until the engine is at normal operating temperature. A run to the parts store for oil and a filter will accomplish this. If the engine is not hot when the oil is changed, most of the acids and contaminants will remain inside the engine.

2. Shut off the engine, and slide a pan of at least six quarts capacity under the oil pan. Throw away aluminum roasting pans can be used for this.

3. Remove the drain plug from the engine oil pan, after wiping the plug area clean. The drain plug is the bolt inserted at a sight angle into the lowest point of the oil pan.

Removing oil filter cartridge

4. The oil from the engine will be HOT. It will probably not be possible to hold onto the drain plug. You may have to let it fall into the pan and fish it out later. Allow all the oil to drain completely. This will take a few minutes.

5. The drain plug is magnetic. Wipe it off

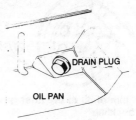

Typical oil pan drain plug location

Capacities

Model	Year	Crankcase (Qt.) w/filter	Crankcase (Qt.) w/o filter	Transmission (Qt.) Manual	Transmission (Qt.) Automatic	Trans. Case	Drive Axle Front	Drive Axle Rear	Fuel Tank	Cooling System
Hi Lux 1900 (8R-C) and 2000 (18R-C)	70–73	5.3	4.3	1.8	7.4	—	—	1.1	12.1	7.8
2000 (18R-C)	74	5.3	4.3	2.0	6.8	—	—	1.6	13.7	9.0
2200 (20R)	75–78	4.8	3.9	2.0①	7.0④	—	—	1.6	12.1②	8.5③
2200 (20R)	79	4.9	4.0	2.0	6.7	1.7	2.0	2.1	—	7.4
2200 (20R)	80	4.9	4.0	2.0	6.7	1.7	2.4	2.3	—	8.9
2400 (22R)	81–82	4.9	4.0	2.1⑥	6.7	1.7	2.4	1.8⑦	13.7⑤	8.9
Diesel	1981–82	6.1	5.1	2.3	—	—	—	1.8	16.0	11.1
Land Cruiser	70–74	8.46	6.56	⑧	—	1.8⑪	2.6	2.6	16.5⑫	17.7
	75–83	8.4	7.4	⑧	—	3.6	5.2	5.2	22.2⑨	17.5⑩
22R-22RE	1984–85	4.9	4.0	4.1⑮	—	1.7	2.4	2.3	17.2⑬	8.9
Diesel	1983–85	6.1	5.1	4.1⑮	—	1.7	2.4	2.3	17.2⑬	10.4
4 Runner	1985	4.9	4.0	4.1⑮	—	1.7	2.4	2.3	14.8⑭	8.9

① 5 Speed: 2.8
② Long Bed 1976–78: 16.1
③ 7.4 1978 only
④ 6.7 1978 only
⑤ 16.1 Long Bed
⑥ 2.7 5 speed

⑦ 1.9 qt ¾ ton-2.3 qt. 4x4
⑧ 3-sp.: 1.8; 4-sp.: 3.3
⑨ Sta. Wgn.: 21.7
⑩ 78–82: 19.9
⑪ W/P.T.O.: 2.2
⑫ Sta. Wgn.: 23.8

⑬ Large Type 19.3
⑭ Large Type 17.2
⑮ 22R Engine only, all others 3.2

thoroughly, removing any traces of metal particles. Pay particular attention to the threads. Replace it, and tighten it snugly. Every fourth oil change, replace the drain plug gasket.

6. The oil filter is on the right side of the engine. Use a filter wrench to loosen it. These are available at auto parts stores, among other sources. Place the drain pan on the ground under the filter. Unscrew and discard the old filter. It will be HOT, so be careful.

7. If the oil filter is on so tightly that it collapses under pressure from the wrench, drive a long punch or a screwdriver through it, across the diameter and as close to the base as possible, and use this as a lever to unscrew it. Make sure you are turning it counterclockwise.

8. Clean off the oil filter mounting surface with a rag. Apply a thin film of clean engine oil to the filter gasket.

Apply a thin film of oil to the filter gasket to prevent it from buckling

9. Screw the filter on by hand until the gasket makes contact. Then tighten it by hand an additional ½ to ¾ of a turn. Do not overtighten.

10. Remove the filler cap on the rocker (valve) cover, after wiping the area clean.

11. Add the correct number of quarts of oil specified in the Capacities Chart (approximately 5 quarts). If you don't have an oil can spout, you will need a funnel. Be certain you do not overfill the engine, which can cause serious damage. Replace the cap.

12. Check the oil level on the dipstick. It is normal for the level to be a bit above the full mark. Start the engine and allow it to idle for a few minutes.

CAUTION: *Do not run the engine above idle speed until it has built up oil pressure, indicated when the oil light goes out.*

13. Check around the filter and drain plug for any leaks. Shut off the engine, allow the oil to drain for a minute, and check the oil level.

After completing this job, you will have several quarts of filthy oil to dispose of. The best thing to do with it is to funnel it into old plastic milk containers or bleach bottles. Then you can either pour it into the recycling barrel at the gas station (if you're on good terms with the attendant), or put the containers into the trash.

1970–72 Land Cruiser w/Canister type Oil Filter

The oil filter on the earlier models is a replaceable element type of oil filter. Change this type of filter along with the oil in the crankcase as follows:

1. Drain the oil as outlined previously.

2. Place the drain pan under the drain plug on the filter case and remove the plug. Allow all of the oil to drain from the oil filter case.

3. Remove the two oil lines from the filter case.

4. Unfasten the mounting bolts which attach the filter bracket to the intake manifold. Remove the entire filter assembly.

5. Unscrew the securing bolt from the cap.

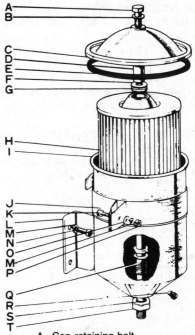

A. Cap retaining bolt
B. Gasket
C. Cap
D. Upper spacer
E. Cap gasket
F. Upper spacer washer
G. Washer
H. Filter element
 I. Filter case
J. Filter case retaining clamp
K. Clamp bolt
L. Mounting bracket
M. Mounting bolt
N. Washer
O. Nut
P. Nut
Q. Filter element support ring
R. Drain plug
S. Gasket
T. Filter element guide

Early Land Cruiser oil filter cartridge

Remove the large cap gasket, collar, small gasket and the filter element.

6. Remove the gasket, element support spring, and washer from the element guide.

7. Clean the sludge out of the bottom of the case with solvent. Allow the case to dry completely.

8. Replace the element and all of the gaskets with new ones.

9. Assemble the filter assembly and install it in the reverse order of removal.

10. Make sure that the crankcase drain plug is installed and fill the crankcase with the proper amount and type of oil.

1985 4 Runner

1. Remove the oil drain plug and drain oil into a container.

2. Remove the oil filter (located on the right side of the engine block) using a filter wrench.

3. Inspect and clean the surface where the oil filter is to be mounted.

4. Apply clean engine oil to the gasket of the new filter.

5. Lightly screw in the filter to where you feel resistance.

6. Then, using a filter wrench, tighten the oil filter an extra ¾ turn.

7. Clean and install the drain plug with a new gasket, then fill the engine with new oil.

8. Start the engine and check for leaks. Then, with the engine OFF, recheck the oil level.

Changing Transmission Fluid

Manual w/2-Wheel Drive

Once every 24,000 miles (1970–78) and once every 30,000 miles (1979 and later) the oil in the manual transmission should be changed.

1. The transmission oil should be hot before it is drained. If the engine is at normal operating temperature, the transmission oil should be hot enough.

2. Raise the truck and support it properly on jackstands so that you can safely work underneath. You will probably not have enough room to work if the truck is not raised.

3. The drain plug is located on the bottom of the transmission. It is on the passenger side on four speeds, and on the bottom center of five speeds. Place a pan under the drain plug and remove it.

CAUTION: *The oil will be HOT. Be careful when you remove the plug so that you don't take a bath in hot gear oil.*

4. Allow the oil to drain completely. Clean off the plug and replace it, tightening it until it is just snug.

5. Remove the filler plug from the side of

the transmission case. It is on the driver's side of four speeds, and on the passenger side on five speeds. There will be a gasket underneath this plug. Replace it if damaged.

6. Fill the transmission with gear oil through the filler plug hole. The proper oil to use is SAE 90 weight oil, API service GL-5. This oil usually comes in a plastic squeeze bottle, with a long nozzle. If yours isn't, or if the nozzle isn't long enough, you can use a rubber squeeze bulb of the type sold for kitchen use to squirt the oil in. This will come in handy for other uses as well, notably the differential. Refer to the Capacities Chart for the amount of oil needed to refill your transmission.

7. The oil level should come right up to the edge of the hole. You can stick your finger in to verify this. Watch out for sharp threads.

8. Replace the filler plug and gasket, lower the truck, and check for leaks. Dispose of the old oil in the same manner as old engine oil.

Manual Transmission and Transfer Case w/4-Wheel Drive

1. Park the car on a level surface and put on the parking brake.

2. Remove the oil filler (upper) plug.

3. Place a container, of a large enough capacity to catch all of the oil, under the drain (lower) plug. Use the proper size wrench to loosen the drain plug slowly, while maintaining a slight upward force to keep the oil from running out. Once the plug is removed, allow all of the oil to drain from the transmission.

4. Install the drain plug and its gasket, if so equipped.

5. Fill the transmission to capacity. (See the Capacities Chart above.) Use API grade SAE 90 gear oil. Be sure that the oil level reaches the bottom of the filler plug.

6. Remember to install the filler plug when finished.

7. Repeat Steps 1–6 in order to change the oil in the transfer case.

Automatic

Automatic transmission fluid should be changed every 24,000 miles (1970–78). In 1979 and later models it should be changed every 30,000 miles. It should also be changed every 12,000 miles if a lot of stop-start driving, extended high speed cruising, or trailer towing is done, or if the truck is normally operated in a heavily loaded condition.

1. The transmission fluid must be hot before it is changed. Drive the truck for ten or fifteen minutes, making a number of stops and starts. Park the truck on a level surface.

2. Get out the drain pan used for oil changes, and place it under the transmission. The drain

plug is easy to spot. It is the only bolt on the flat bottom surface of the fluid pan. It is in the front corner of the pan on the passenger side until 1978. Remove the bolt to drain the fluid. Be careful—the fluid will be HOT.

3. Replace the drain plug and its gasket, after cleaning both thoroughly.

4. Since the fluid in the torque converter will not drain completely, it is a good idea to measure the volume of fluid that does drain out. This will give you a good indication of how much fluid must be replaced.

5. The transmission is refilled through the dipstick tube. You will probably need a funnel and a long tube. Use Type F automatic transmission fluid only.

6. It is important that the transmission is not overfilled. As you add fluid, stop the process from time to time, allow the fluid to drain for a minute, and check the level. When it reaches the top of the Cold level on the dipstick, stop filling.

7. Start the engine, let it idle, and shift slowly through all the gear ranges. Do not race the engine. Shut it off and check the fluid level again. If necessary, add fluid to bring it up to the cold level.

8. Now start the engine again, and take a short drive to bring the transmission to operating temperature. Drive at a high enough speed to engage third gear, but no faster. Stop on a level surface and check the fluid level once more. It should be at the top of the Hot range on the dipstick. Make certain that the transmission is not overfilled. Overfilling will cause slippage, fluid loss, and seal damage.

Changing Differential Oil

Once every 24,000 miles (1970–79), 30,000 miles (1979–later), the differential oil should be changed. You may also want to change it if you have bought the truck used, or if the truck has been driven in water over the axle vent.

1. Park the truck on the level with the axle at normal operating temperature.

2. Place the pan used for oil changes underneath the drain plug on the differential housing.

3. Remove the filler plug. This will provide an additional vent to speed the draining process.

4. Remove the drain plug. See the illustration earlier in the chapter under Fluid Level Checks for the location of these plugs.

5. After all the oil has drained out, clean the drain plug and its gasket, and replace it.

6. Fill the differential through the filler hole with SAE 90 GL-5 gear lubricant. This usually comes in a plastic squeeze bottle with a nozzle.

If not, use a squeeze bulb to squirt in the oil.

7. Fill the differential right up to the edge of the filler hole. To verify this, insert a finger, watching out for sharp threads.

8. Clean the filler plug, replace it, and check both plugs for leaks.

Chassis Greasing

Complete chassis greasing should include an inspection of all rubber suspension bushings, lubrication of all body hinges, as well as proper greasing of the front suspension upper and lower ball joints and control arm bushings. To provide correct operation, the chassis should be greased every 6 months or 6,000 miles on 1970–78 trucks. The 1979 and later trucks should be greased every 7,500 miles.

If you wish to perform this operation yourself you should purchase a cartridge type grease gun and several cartridges of multipurpose lithium base grease. You will also need to purchase grease fittings from your Toyota dealer, as the front end components are fitted with screw-in plugs to prevent entry of foreign material.

Remove the plug, using a 10mm wrench and install the grease fitting. Push the nozzle of the grease gun down firmly onto the fitting and while applying pressure, force the new grease into the boot. Force sufficient grease into the fitting to cause the old grease to be expelled. When this has been accomplished, remove the

Recommended Lubricants

Lubricants:	Classifications:
Engine Oil	API service SE classification
Gear Oil (Transmission and Steering Gear Box)	API service GL-4 classification
Gear Oil Differential	API service GL-5 classification
Automatic Transmission	ATF Type F
Chassis Grease (Ball Joint Arm bushing)	NLGI No. 1 or No. 2
Driveshaft (Long Bed only)	NLGI No. 1 or No. 2
Wheel Bearing Grease	NLGI No. 2
Brake Fluid	DOT 3
Antifreeze	Anti-rust type ethylene glycol base coolant

fitting and replace the plug. Follow this procedure on each front suspension lubrication point.

Long Bed pick-ups have a two piece driveshaft which must be greased at the same 6 month/7,500 mile interval. The driveshaft is equipped with a grease fitting, located on the shaft just behind the center support bearing. Simply wipe off the fitting and pump in two or three shots of grease. There is no built in escape hole for the old grease to exit, so don't keep pumping in grease until the seal gives way. The factory recommends 5–10 grams of lithium base grease at the specified interval.

Wheel Bearings

ADJUSTMENT AND LUBRICATION

Only the front wheel bearings require periodic service. The lubricant to use is high temperature disc brake wheel bearing grease meeting NLGI No. 2 specifications. (This grease should be used even if the truck is equipped with drum brakes; it has superior protection characteristics.) This service is recommended at the specified period in the Maintenance Intervals chart or whenever the truck has been driven in water up to the hub.

Before handling the bearings there are a few things that you should remember to DO the following:

1. Remove all outside dirt from the housing before exposing the bearing.

2. Treat a used bearing as gently as you would a new one.

3. Work with clean tools in clean surroundings.

4. Use clean, dry canvas gloves, or at least clean, dry hands.

5. Clean solvents and flushing fluids are a must.

6. Use clean paper when laying out the bearings to dry.

7. Protect disassembled bearings from rust and dirt. Cover them up.

8. Use clean rags to wipe bearings.

9. Keep the bearings in oil-proof paper when they are to be stored or are not in use.

10. Clean the inside of the housing before replacing the bearings. Do NOT do the following:

1. Don't work in dirty surroundings.

2. Don't use dirty, chipped, or damaged tools.

3. Try not to work on wooden work benches or use wooden mallets.

4. Don't handle bearings with dirty or moist hands.

5. Do not use gasoline for cleaning; use a safe solvent.

6. Do not spin dry bearings with compressed air. They will be damaged.

7. Do not spin unclean bearings.

8. Avoid using cotton waste or dirty cloths to wipe bearings.

9. Try not to scratch or nick bearing surfaces.

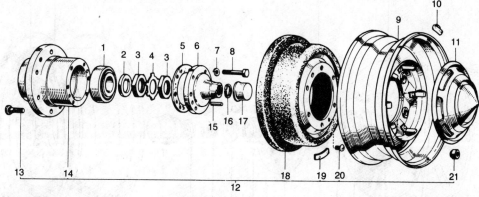

1. Outer bearing
2. Claw washer
3. Wheel bearing adjusting nut (inner) and locknut (outer)
4. Lockwasher
5. Drive flange gasket
6. Drive flange
7. Lockwasher
8. Drive flange-to-hub attaching bolt
9. Wheel
10. Balance weight
11. Hub cap
12. Front axle hub and brake drum assembly
13. Lug bolt
14. Hub
15. Locating pin
16. Axle shaft snap-ring
17. Outer axle shaft flange cap
18. Brake drum
19. Balance weight
20. Brake drum set screw
21. Lug nut

Early Land Cruiser front hub assembly

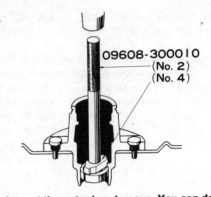

The numbers in this photograph refer to the factory tool number for the claw puller, used to remove the inner bearing on drum brakes. You can get a similar tool from a parts store or rental agency. Just make sure the fingers are thin enough to slip under the grease seal

Driving out the outer bearing cup. You can do this job with a socket or pipe, or a soft brass drift, instead of the factory tool illustrated here

10. Do not allow the bearing to come in contact with dirt or rust at any time.

2-Wheel Drive

You will need a special claw type puller for this job to remove the inner bearing and the steering knuckle grease retainer if your truck has drum brakes.

Procedures are basically the same for either disc or drum brakes.

1. Remove the brake drum or brake caliper, following the procedure outlined in Chapter 9.

2. It is not necessary to remove the drum or disc from the hub. The outer wheel bearing will come off with the hub. Simply pull the hub and disc or drum assembly towards you off the spindle. Be sure to catch the bearing before it falls to the ground.

3. Drum brakes: The inner bearing and grease retainer must be pulled from the spindle with the claw puller. Be sure that the fingers of the tool pull on the seal, and not on the bearing itself. Discard the grease retainer.

Disc brakes: The inner bearing will have to be driven from the hub along with the oil seal. Use a brass rod as a drift and carefully drive the inner bearing cone out. Remove the bearing and the oil seal. Discard the seal.

4. Clean the bearings in solvent and allow to air dry. You risk leaving bits of lint in the races if you dry them with a rag. Clean the bearing cups in the hub.

5. Inspect the bearings carefully. If they are

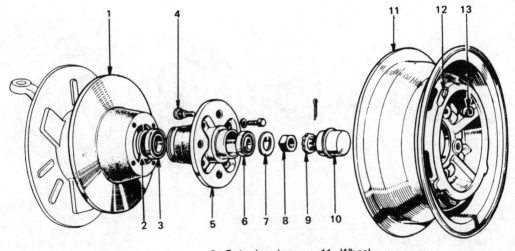

1. Disc	6. Outer bearing	11. Wheel
2. Oil seal	7. Lock washer	12. Balance weight
3. Inner bearing	8. Nut	13. Lug nut
4. Hub bolt	9. Adjusting cap	
5. Hub	10. Grease cap	

Exploded view of the front disc and hub assembly. Drum brakes are similar, but have only one castellated nut between the lock washer and grease cap

worn, pitted, burned, or scored, they should be replaced, along with the bearing cups in which they run.

6. You can use a brass rod as a drift, or a large socket or piece of pipe to drive the inner and outer bearing cups out of the hub.

7. Install the new inner cup, and then the outer cup, in that order, into the hub, using either the brass drift or socket method outlined earlier.

NOTE: *Use care not to cock the bearing cups in the hub. If they are not fully seated, the bearings will be impossible to adjust properly.*

8. Drum brakes: Press a new grease retainer onto the spindle. Place a large glob of grease into one palm and force the edge of the inner bearing into it so that the grease fills the bearing. Do this until the whole bearing is packed. Press the inner bearing into the spindle, seating it firmly against the grease retainer.

Disc brakes: Coat the inner bearing cup with grease. Pack the inner bearing with grease as outlined for drum brakes, and press the inner bearing into the cup. Press a new oil seal into place on top of the bearing. You may have to give the seal a few gentle raps with a soft drift to get it to seat properly.

9. Install the hub and drum or disc assembly onto the spindle. With drum brakes, first thoroughly coat the inner cup with grease.

10. Coat the outer bearing cup with grease. Pack the outer bearing with grease and install into the cup.

11. Pack the grease cap with grease and set it aside. It will be replaced last, after the preload adjustment. You can put the grease away now.

12. Install the lock washer, and castellated nut (lock washer, nut, and adjusting castle nut with disc brakes) loosely, and go on to the preload adjustment following.

BEARING PRELOAD ADJUSTMENT

1. While turning the hub forward, tighten the castellated nut (plain nut on disc brakes) to 35 ft. lb. (21 ft. lb. with disc brakes).

2. Rotate the hub a few more times to snug down the bearings.

3. Retighten the nut to the above specification. Unscrew it 1/6 of a turn and lock it in place with a new cotter pin. On disc brakes, snug the adjusting nut up against the nut and then back it off the required distance to insert a new cotter pin. You should not have to back it off more than 1/6 of a turn.

4. Install the grease cap, and wipe off any grease that oozes out.

5. Install the front wheel and a couple of lug nuts. Check the axial play of the wheel by shaking it back and forth; the bearing freeplay should feel close to zero, but the wheel should spin freely. With drum brakes, be sure that the shoes are not dragging against the drum.

6. If the bearing play is correct with drum brakes you can install the rest of the lug nuts. With disc brakes, remove the wheel, replace the caliper, then install the wheel.

4-Wheel Drive

NOTE: *The following applies to early models without free wheeling hubs. For models with free wheel hubs, see the front drive axle part of Chapter 7.*

The front wheel bearings should be repacked every 12,000 miles, or once a year, whichever comes first.

REMOVAL

1. Remove the hub cap and loosen the lug nuts.

2. Raise the front of the Cruiser and support it with jackstands.

3. Remove the lug nuts and the wheel.

4. Remove the cap from the axle shaft outer flange. Remove the snapring from the shaft.

5. Remove the bolts which secure the axle shaft outer flange to the hub.

6. Install two service bolts into the holes provided in the flange. Tighten the bolts evenly in order to loosen the flange. Withdraw the flange and the sealing gasket.

NOTE: *The flange should never be removed by prying it off; damage to the sealing surface could result in oil leaks.*

7. Remove the set screws and remove the brake drum.

8. Straighten out the lockwasher and remove the adjusting nut, using a spindle nut wrench.

NOTE: *Removing the adjusting nut with a hammer and chisel will result in damage to the nut and the spindle threads.*

9. Remove the hub assembly, complete with the washer, bearings and oil seal.

10. Remove the bearings from the hub.

CLEANING, INSPECTION, AND PACKING

Place all of the bearings, nuts, washer, and dust caps in a container of solvent. Cleanliness is basic to wheel bearing maintenance. Use a soft brush to thoroughly clean each part. Make sure that every bit of dirt and grease is rinsed off, then place each cleaned part on an absorbent cloth and let them dry completely.

Inspect the bearings for pitting, flat spots, rust, and rough areas. Check the races on the hub and the spindle for the same defects and rub them clean with a rag that has been soaked in solvent. If the races show hairline cracks or worn, shiny areas, they must be replaced with new parts. Replacement seals, bearings, and other required parts can be bought at an auto parts store. The old parts that are to be replaced should be taken along to be compared with the replacement part to ensure a perfect match.

Pack the wheel bearings with grease. There are special devices made for the specific purpose of greasing bearings, but, if one is not available, pack the wheel bearings by hand. Put a large dab of grease in the palm of your hand and push the bearing through it with a sliding motion. The grease must be forced through the side of the bearing and in between each roller. Continue until the grease begins to ooze out the other side and through the gaps between the rollers; the bearing must be completely packed with grease.

INSTALLATION

1. Install the inner bearing cone and the oil seal.
2. Pack the hub with grease, and install the outer bearing cup.
3. Assemble the brake drum to the hub.
4. Install the hub and drum assembly over the spindle and then install the outer bearing.
5. Install the claw washer and adjusting nut with the spindle nut wrench.
6. Adjust the bearing preload in the following manner:

    a. After tightening the adjusting nut with the spindle nut wrench, rotate the wheel back-and-forth in order to seat the bearing.

    b. Loosen the adjusting nut 1/8 to 1/6 of a turn.

    c. Check the brake drum for free rotation.

    d. Install the lockwasher and the locknut. Use the spindle nut wrench to tighten the locknut.

    e. Bend up the tabs on the lockwasher.

7. Install the axle shaft flange and gasket. Tighten the retaining bolts to 11–16 ft.lb.
8. Install the bolt on the end of the outer shaft. Pull out on the shaft while installing the snapring.
9. Install the flange cap.
10. Install the wheel and the hub cap. Lower the vehicle.

PUSHING AND TOWING

As long as your pick-up is equipped with a manual transmission, you won't have any prob-

Proper places to attach towing apparatus

lem towing the vehicle without the use of a wrecker. Simply attach the tow chain or cable to the towing hook at the right front of the frame, place the transmission in Neutral, and release the emergency brake. If the truck is equipped with a steering column lock device, the ignition switch must be in the ACC position.

Under emergency conditions the engine can be started by pushing. Turn the ignition switch to the ON position and place the transmission in Third gear. Depress the clutch pedal fully and when the vehicle is moving, gradually release the clutch pedal until the engine turns over. As soon as the engine catches, depress the clutch pedal again and throttle the engine gradually into life.

CAUTION: *Never under any circumstances attempt to tow or start the engine in this manner if the vehicle is equipped with an automatic transmission.*

Should you wish to tow another vehicle, attach the towing chain or cable to the rear spring hanger.

If your vehicle is equipped with an automatic transmission, the driveshaft must be disconnected from the differential if the vehicle is being towed on the rear wheels. It is not permissible to move the vehicle even the shortest distance if the driveshaft has not been disconnected.

If the rear axle of the vehicle is inoperative or if for any reason the vehicle is to be towed

JUMP STARTING A DEAD BATTERY

The chemical reaction in a battery produces explosive hydrogen gas. This is the safe way to jump start a dead battery, reducing the chances of an accidental spark that could cause an explosion.

Jump Starting Precautions

1. Be sure both batteries are of the same voltage.
2. Be sure both batteries are of the same polarity (have the same grounded terminal).
3. Be sure the vehicles are not touching.
4. Be sure the vent cap holes are not obstructed.
5. Do not smoke or allow sparks around the battery.
6. In cold weather, check for frozen electrolyte in the battery.
7. Do not allow electrolyte on your skin or clothing.
8. Be sure the electrolyte is not frozen.

Jump Starting Procedure

1. Determine voltages of the two batteries; they must be the same.
2. Bring the starting vehicle close (they must not touch) so that the batteries can be reached easily.
3. Turn off all accessories and both engines. Put both cars in Neutral or Park and set the handbrake.
4. Cover the cell caps with a rag—do not cover terminals.
5. If the terminals on the run-down battery are heavily corroded, clean them.
6. Identify the positive and negative posts on both batteries and connect the cables in the order shown.
7. Start the engine of the starting vehicle and run it at fast idle. Try to start the car with the dead battery. Crank it for no more than 10 seconds at a time and let it cool off for 20 seconds in between tries.
8. If it doesn't start in 3 tries, there is something else wrong.
9. Disconnect the cables in the reverse order.
10. Replace the cell covers and dispose of the rags.

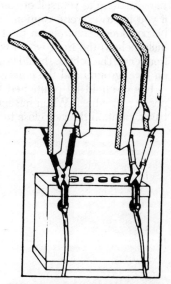

Side terminal batteries occasionally pose a problem when connecting jumper cables. There frequently isn't enough room to clamp the cables without touching sheet metal. Side terminal adaptors are available to alleviate this problem and should be removed after use.

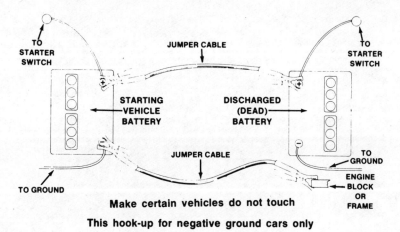

TO STARTER SWITCH

JUMPER CABLE

TO STARTER SWITCH

STARTING VEHICLE BATTERY

DISCHARGED (DEAD) BATTERY

TO GROUND

JUMPER CABLE

TO GROUND

ENGINE BLOCK OR FRAME

Make certain vehicles do not touch

This hook-up for negative ground cars only

with the rear end elevated, the front wheels must be supported in a suitable carriage. The steering wheel locking mechanism will not keep the front wheels in position while being towed.

JACKING AND HOISTING

It is imperative that strict safety precautions be observed when raising your truck with a jack and in the subsequent supporting of the vehicle. Severe damage to the vehicle may result, not to mention the possible physical harm that may be done to yourself or some other person if you fail to exercise caution. The jack should be positioned squarely on the frame of the vehicle behind the front wheel when raising the front end. The vehicle should be parked, in gear, on level ground and the emergency brake set. A block should be positioned behind the opposite rear wheel. When raising the rear of the truck, position the jack close to the inside edge of the rear leaf spring on the rear axle housing. Again, a block should be placed at the opposite front wheel.

Whenever you plan to work under the car you must support it on jackstands. Never use cinder blocks or stacks of wood to support a vehicle which you will be underneath for even a few minutes. Small hydraulic, screw, or scissors jacks are satisfactory for raising the truck. Drive-on trestles, or ramps, are also a handy and safe way to raise the truck. These can be bought or constructed from suitable heavy timbers or steel.

If the vehicle is to be raised with a hoist such as those used at service stations, the pads of the hoist should be positioned on the frame rails of the truck and never on any suspension member or underbody panel.

Whatever method you use to raise the vehicle, always be absolutely certain that it is firm in its support. When you are satisfied that it is solid, proceed with your work.

Tune-Up and Performance Maintenance

2

TUNE-UP PROCEDURES

In order to extract the full measure of performance and economy from your engine it is essential that it be properly tuned at regular intervals. A regular tune-up will keep your engine running smoothly and will prevent the annoying minor breakdowns and poor performance that are associated with an untuned engine.

A tune-up restores the power and performance which can be lost as parts wear or fall out of adjustment through normal use. You can save time and money and achieve positive results by following an exact and methodical plan for analyzing and correcting malfunctions.

The manufacturer's recommended tune-up interval is every 12,000 miles, or twelve months, whichever comes first. This interval should be shortened if the truck is operated under severe conditions such as trailer towing, or if started and running problems are noticed. It is assumed that the routine maintenance described in Chapter 1 has been kept up, as this will have an effect on the results of a tune-up. All the applicable steps of a tune-up should be followed, as the result is a cumulative one. If the specifications on the tune-up sticker in the engine compartment disagree with the Tune-Up Specifications chart in this Chapter, the figures on the sticker must be followed. The sticker often reflects changes made during the production run. This sticker is usually found on the side of the air cleaner or at the rear of the engine compartment.

Spark Plugs

Check, clean, and adjust the spark plugs every 6,000 miles (1970–78) and at 15,000 miles (1979 and later).

1. The distributor cap and the spark plug wires are usually numbered at the factory.

However, if yours are not, it is a good idea to number each spark plug wire to make reinstallation easier. This can be done with pieces of adhesive tape.

2. Disconnect each spark plug wire at the plug by twisting and pulling on the rubber boot, not on the wire itself.

3. If the wires are dirty or oily, wipe them clean with a cloth dampened in kerosene and then wipe them dry. If the wires are cracked, they should be replaced. Make sure to get the radio noise suppression type. Spark plug wires normally last about 35,000 miles. If your engine is reluctant to start in wet weather, they may be the cause.

4. Blow or brush the dirt away from each spark plug. This can also be accomplished by loosening each spark plug about two turns and cranking the engine with the starter.

5. Remove each spark plug with the socket that came with the truck. Make sure that the socket is all the way down on the plug, to prevent it from slipping and cracking the porcelain insulator.

6. Refer to the color insert section for an analysis of spark plug condition. Generally speaking, a tan or medium grey color (rust red with some unleaded fuels) on the plug tip indicates normal combustion conditions. Spark plugs normally last about 12,000 miles. It isn't worth the time it takes to clean and gap them after that point, as they will have to be replaced shortly anyway.

7. If the plugs are to be reused (after a 6,000 mile check) 1970–78 only file the center and side electrodes flat with a small, fine points file. Heavy or baked on deposits can be scraped off with a penknife. Check the gap between the two electrodes with a spark plug gap gauge. Do not use a flat feeler gauge; an inaccurate reading will result. If the gap is not as specified (0.031 in most cases), use the bending tool on the gap gauge to gently bend the outside

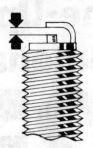

Adjust the spark plug gap to 0.031 in. with a wire gauge

Pull on the rubber boot, not on the plug wire

electrode to the correct setting. Always check the gap on new plugs.

NOTE: *Never bend the center electrode. Be careful not to bend the side electrode too far or too often; this could cause it to break off and fall into the combustion chamber, with severe consequences, including broken piston rings and valves.*

8. Clean the plug threads with a wire brush. Lubricate them with a drop of oil.

9. Screw the plugs back into the cylinder head finger tight. Then, using the socket wrench, tighten them against their seats. Do not use the same amount of force you would apply to a bolt, just snug them in. The cylinder head is made from aluminum, and the spark plug threads in it can be quite easily stripped.

10. Push the spark plug wires back onto their respective plugs, pushing on the boots. You will be able to feel them click into place.

Breaker Points and Condenser

The ignition distributor breaks the primary current, distributes the high voltage surges induced in the coil secondary winding to the spark plugs according to the firing order, and sets the ignition timing in relation to engine rpm and load. The engine output, to a large extent, is governed by the ignition timing. Maximum engine output is obtained when the combustion process is well under way as the piston starts down on the power stroke. If the spark is too far advanced the engine knocks, which causes a drop in engine power output as well as overheating. If the spark is retarded part of the energy developed during combustion is wasted, resulting in poor fuel economy and reduced power output. These factors are extremely relevant in the maintenance, removal and installation of the contact points. Each time the points are reset, the ignition timing is changed.

NOTE: *If you adjust the point gap or install new breaker points, you must adjust the basic engine timing.*

There are two basically similar ignition systems used in the 1970–77 Toyota trucks. The first is a conventional ignition which uses points, condenser, coil and distributor. The other, used from 1975–77, is a semi-transistorized unit which eliminates the condenser but includes a transistorized igniter. This igniter contains two transistors and an assortment of resistors which together serve as a switching device to turn the coil primary current on and off. The advantage of this type of circuitry is a reduced current through the distributor breaker points, thus prolonging their expected life and reducing scheduled maintenance.

The transistorized igniter is found next to the coil on the right fender panel (as you face the truck) in 1975, and mounted on top of the coil in the same location in 1976–77. We will consider the two systems together for tune-up purposes. Igniter troubleshooting will be found following Octane Selector adjustments.

REPLACEMENT

1. The distributor cap is held to the distributor body by two clips. Insert a screwdriver under their ends and release them. Lift off the distributor cap with the wires attached.

2. Wipe the inside of the cap with a clean rag. Check it for cracks and carbon tracks. A carbon track shows as a dark line running from one terminal to another. If it cannot be successfully removed, replace the cap and rotor. Generally, a cap and rotor will last for about 36,000 miles.

3. Pull the distributor rotor and dust cover straight up and off the distributor shaft. Inspect the rotor for wear. You can clean off the metal tip of the rotor but don't file it. Replace the rotor as necessary, or if a new one came with your tune-up kit.

4. The points will have to be removed whether or not they are to be reused. On some 20R engines there is dust cover over the points which must be pulled off first. Use a magnetic screwdriver when working on the points. If a screw falls into the works, the distributor will probably have to be removed to fish it out. Unfasten the wire running from the points to the distributor. There are two screws holding the points; one also locates the ground wire. Remove the screws and the points.

Year	Engine Type	Spark Plugs Type	Spark Plugs Gap (in.)	Distributor Point Dwell (deg)	Distributor Point Gap (in.)	Ignition Timing (deg)▲ MT	Ignition Timing (deg)▲ AT	Fuel Pump Pressure (psi)	Manifold Vacuum at Idle* In. Hg	Compression Pressure (psi) @ 250 rpm**	Idle Speed (rpm) MT	Idle Speed (rpm) AT	Valve Clearance‡ (in.) In	Valve Clearance‡ (in.) Ex
1970	8R-C	W20 EP	0.031	52	0.018	TDC	TDC	2.8–4.3	15.7	164	650	650	0.008	0.014
1971	8R-C	W20 EP	0.031	52	0.018	10B	10B	2.8–4.3	15.7	164	650	650	0.008	0.014
1972–1973	18R-C	W20 EP	0.031	52	0.018	7B	7B	2.8–4.3	15.7①	164	650	650	0.008	0.014
1974	18R-C	W20 EP	0.031	52	0.018	7B	7B	2.8–4.3	15.7①	164	800	800	0.008	0.014
1975–1978	20R	W16 EP	0.031	52	0.018④	8B③	8B③	2.1–4.3	16.5	156	850②	850②	0.008	0.012
1979–1980	20R	W16 EX-U	0.031	52	0.018	8B	8B	2.1–4.3	15.75	156	850	850	0.008	0.012⑤
1981–1982	22R	W16 EXR-U	0.031	Electronic		8B	8B	2.1–4.3	15.8	156	700	750	0.008	0.012
1970–1974	F series	B5-ES	0.030	41	0.018	—	—	3.4–4.8	15.8	150	650	—	0.008	0.014
1975–1977	2F	W14 EX	0.037	41	0.018	—	—	3.4–4.8	15.8	150	650	—	0.008	0.014
1978–1983	2F	⑥	⑦	Electronic		—	—	3.4–4.8	15.8	150	⑧	—	0.008	0.019
1983	22R	W16 EXR-U	0.031	Electronic		5B	5B	2.1–4.3	15.8	171	700	750	0.008	0.012
1984–1985	22R	W16 EXR-U	0.031	Electronic		5B	5B	2.1–4.3	15.8	171	700	750	0.008	0.012
1985	22RE	W16 EXR-U	0.031	Electronic		5B	5B	2.1–4.3	15.8	171	750	750	0.008	0.012

▲With automatic transmission in D (drive) and manual transmission in Neutral
*These are the minimum readings you must obtain
**Look for uniformity among cylinders rather than specific pressure
‡When assembling engine cold valve clearance is Intake 0.007 and Exhaust 0.013, 1970–74 only
① 18R-C engine/manual transmission—17.7
② 800—1977–78 only
③ 13B with High Altitude Compensation—see text
④ Distributor Air Gap 0.008–0.016 in.—1978–80

⑤ 1979 20R Exhaust Valve 0.01 in.
⑥ '78–'79: W14-EX
  '80: W14-EXU
  '81–'83: W14-EXR-U
⑦ '78–'79: 0.039
  '80–'83: 0.031
⑧ '78–'80: 800
  '81–'83: 650

NOTE: If these figures do not correspond to information given on the engine compartment decal, use the figures found on the decal. They are current for the engine in your truck.

Diesel Engine Tune-Up Specifications

Injector Opening Pressure (psi)	Idle Speed (rpm)	Valve Clearance (in.)		Cranking Compression Pressure @ 250 rpm	Maximum Compression Variance ③	Firing Order
		Intake	Exhaust			
1636–1778 ① 1493–1777 ②	700	.010	.014	284–455 psi	71 psi	1-3-4-2

① New
② Used
③ Between highest & lowest readings

5. Inspect the points for wear. If they are pitted, burned, or rough, replace them. They can be reused if they are only slightly worn. File them flat with a special points file. Do not use an emery board or sandpaper, as a residue will remain that will cause arcing across the point gap.

6. Remove the condenser if it is to be replaced. It is recommended that whenever the points are replaced, the condenser be replaced as well. It is attached to the outside of the distributor body with a single screw on all engines except the 2F. The 2F has the condenser inside the distributor. Its wire is attached with a nut, a lockwasher, and a washer.

7. Lubricate the distributor cam with grease. There may be a small tube of this with your tune-up kit. If not, just place a matchhead sized dab of grease on the cam and smooth it around evenly. Don't use oil; this will get on the points and cause them to burn.

8. Install the points and leave the screws slightly loose. Install the new condenser if used. Make certain that all the wires (ground, points and condenser) are properly routed around the works.

9. Check that the points meet squarely. If not, the fixed point arm can be bent slightly with gentle force and needlenosed pliers.

10. Check the operation of the centrifugal advance mechanism by turning the rotor clockwise. Release the rotor; it should return to its

original position. If it doesn't, check for binding parts.

11. Check the vacuum advance unit by removing the clear plastic cap over the octane selector. Press in the octane selector and release. It should return to its original position. If not, check for binding.

12. To set the points on their proper gap, the rubbing block on the point set must rest on the high point of a cam lobe. You can rotate the engine by hand if the spark plugs are removed by moving the fan belt. Otherwise, you can bump the engine around using the ignition key or a remote starter. The important thing

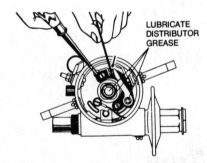

LUBRICATE DISTRIBUTOR GREASE

Adjustment of the points and lubrication of the distributor cam

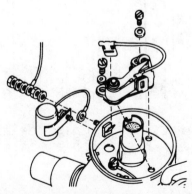

Location of points and condenser. The screw below the points wire clip also serves to locate the ground wire, seen attached incorrectly here. For an exploded view of the entire distributor, see Chapter 3

Pull straight up on the rotor to remove. When replacing, make certain that it is fully seated. The flying saucer shaped thing below the rotor is the dust cover; wipe it off thoroughly before replacing

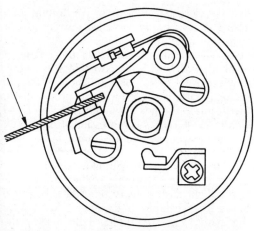

The arrow indicates the feeler gauge used to set the point gap. Make certain that the rubbing block rests on the high spot of the cam, as shown here

here is to make sure that the rubbing clock is on one of the four high spots of the cam.

13. Insert a 0.018 in. flat feeler gauge between the contact points. A slight drag should be felt. If no drag can be felt, or the gauge cannot be inserted at all, adjustment is made with a screwdriver inserted into the slot cut into the end of the points base next to the fixed point. There are two raised bumps on the advance mechanism base against which to lever the screwdriver. Adjust the points to the proper gap.

14. When the points are set, tighten the point screws, and then recheck the gap. Sometimes it takes three or four tries to get the points set correctly, so don't feel frustrated if they seem to move around on you a little. It is not always easy to feel the correct gap, either. Use gauges 0.002 in. larger and smaller than 0.018 as a test. If the points are spread slightly by a 0.020 in. gauge and not touched at all by a 0.016 in. gauge, the setting should be fine.

15. Most distributors have a damping spring located in the distributor body opposite the points. It resembles the arm and rubbing block of the points. It must be adjusted so that there is 0.002–0.018 in. clearance between its rubbing point and the flat side of the cam.

16. After all the adjustments are complete, pull a white business card between the points to clear any traces of oil or grit. It is particularly important that the points be scrupulously clean on 20R engines. The current through the points is very low and can be stopped by any slight trace of oil.

17. Replace the points cover, if so equipped, the dust shield, and the rotor. The rotor has a tab which fits in a slot cut into the distributor shaft. Reinstall the rotor. Replace the distrib-

utor cap, and snap on the clips. If you have a dwell meter, you should next set the dwell. Otherwise, go on to the ignition timing.

Dwell Angle

The dwell angle is the number of degrees of distributor cam rotation through which the contact points remain closed (conducting electricity). Increasing the point gap decreases dwell while decreasing the point gap increases the dwell.

1. Connect a dwell meter to the ignition system, according to the manufacturer's instructions.

   a. When checking the dwell on a conventional ignition system, connect one meter lead (usually black) to a metallic part of the truck to ground the meter; the other lead (usually red) is connected to the coil primary post (the one with the small lead which runs to the distributor body);

   b. When checking the dwell on a model with transistorized ignition (20R engines), ground one meter lead (usually black) to a metallic part of the truck; hook up the other lead (usually red) to the negative (–) coil terminal. Under no circumstances should the meter be connected to the distributor or the positive (+) side of the coil. Damage to the switching transistor will result if the meter is connected in the usual manner.

2. If the dwell meter has a set line, adjust the needle until it rests on the line.

3. Start the engine. It should be warmed up and running at the specified idle speed.

CAUTION: *Be sure to keep your fingers, tools, clothes, hair, and wires clear of the engine fan. The transmission should be in Neutral (Park with automatic), parking brake set, front wheels blocked. Run the engine only in a well ventilated area.*

4. Check the reading on the dwell meter. If

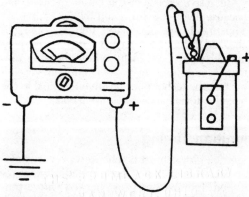

Dwell meter connections with transistorized ignition

your meter doesn't have a four cylinder scale, multiply the eight cylinder reading by two.

5. If the meter reading is within the range specified in the Tune-Up Specifications chart, shut off the engine and disconnect the meter.

6. If the dwell is not within specifications, shut the engine off and remove the distributor cap. Adjust the point gap as previously outlined. Increasing the point gap will decrease the dwell, and vice versa.

7. Adjust the points until dwell is within specifications, then disconnect the dwell meter. Adjust the timing; see the following section.

Fully Transistorized Ignition

1978 and Later

A fully transistorized ignition system, utilizing an ignition signal generating device rather than ignition points and condenser, was first used on trucks in 1978. Located in the distributor, in addition to the normal ignition rotor, is a four spoke timing rotor which rests on the distributor shaft where the cam is found on earlier systems, a magnet, and a pick-up coil. The system also uses a transistorized igniter mounted on the top of the ignition coil, found on the fender.

When a rotor spoke is not lined up with the pick-up coil, it generates large lines of flux between itself, the magnet, and the pick-up coil. This large flux variation results in high generated voltage in the pick-up coil, preventing battery current from flowing to the pick-up coil. When a rotor spoke lines up with the coil, the flux variation is low. Thus, zero voltage is generated in the pick-up coil, allowing current to flow in. Ignition primary current is then cut off by the igniter, causing high voltage to be induced in the ignition coil secondary windings. The high voltage flows through the distributor to the spark plug.

Because no points or condenser are used, and because dwell is determined by the igniter, no adjustments are necessary. Ignition timing is checked in the usual way, but it is not likely to ever change very much. When checking timing, be sure to observe the caution about connecting the tachometer positive terminal to the negative terminal of the ignition coil.

Ignition Timing

Ignition timing must be checked at every tune-up and whenever the points are adjusted or replaced. Ignition timing is checked with a timing light. This instrument is connected to the number one spark plug of the engine, which is the one closest to the front. The timing light flashes every time an electrical current is sent from the distributor through the No. 1 spark plug. The crankshaft pulley of the engine is notched, and the front cover of the engine (timing cover) has a point (or line). When the timing pointer is aligned with the proper mark, the piston in the no. 1 cylinder is at Top Dead Center (TDC) of its compression stroke. With the engine running, and the timing light aimed at the timing pointer, the stroboscopic flashes from the timing light will allow you to check the ignition timing setting of the engine. The timing light flashes every time the spark plug in the No. 1 cylinder of the engine fires. Since the flash from the timing light makes the crankshaft seem stationary for a moment, you will be able to read the exact position of the piston by observing the marks.

There are three basic types of timing light available. The first is a simple neon bulb with two wire connections. One wire connects to the spark plug terminal and the other plugs into the end of the spark plug wire for the no. 1 cylinder, thus connecting the light in series with the spark plug. This type of light is very dim and must be held closely to the timing marks in order to illuminate them. It has the advantage of low price. A second type operates from the truck battery. Two alligator clips connect to the battery terminals, while an adapter enables the third wire to be connected to the no.1 spark plug and wire. This type is more expensive, but it provides a nice bright flash that you can even see in daylight. The third type replaces battery current with 100 volt house current.

1. Clean off the timing marks. On the 2F, the timing marks are a ball on the flywheel and a pointer on the bellhousing. On all other engines, the marks are on the crankshaft pulley and timing cover. The timing notches in the

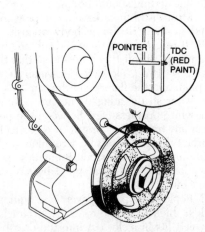

Timing marks 8R-C and 18R-C engines

crankshaft pulley are normally marked at the factory with red or white paint. You may want to retouch them if they are dark, using chalk or paint. Fluorescent (dayglow) paint is excellent for this purpose. You might have to bump the engine around with the starter to find the pulley marks.

2. Warm the engine to operating temperature. Connect a tachometer and check the engine idle speed to see that it is within the range found in the Tune-Up Specifications chart. Adjust it, if necessary, according to the procedure found at the end of this Chapter.

CAUTION: *On 20R, 22R and 22R-E engines, connect the positive (+) tachometer terminal to the negative (–) ignition coil terminal. Do NOT connect it to the distributor side. Improper connections will damage the transistorized igniter.*

3. Shut off the engine and connect a timing light according to the manufacturer's directions.

4. Disconnect the vacuum hose from the distributor vacuum unit. Plug the hose with a pencil, golf tee, or the like, being careful not to split the hose.

NOTE: *On 20R, 22R and 22R-E engines with HAC (High Altitude Compensation system) there are two vacuum hoses which connect to the distributor. Both must be disconnected and plugged. These systems require an extra step in the timing procedure, found at the end of this section. You can obtain more information about the HAC in Chapter 4.*

5. Be sure that the timing light wires are clear of the fan and pulleys, and start the engine

CAUTION: *Keep fingers, clothes, hair, tools, and wires clear of the fan and fan belts. They appear to be standing still when illuminated by the strobe light. Run the engine only in a well ventilated area.*

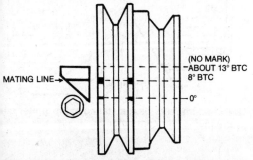

MATING LINE→

(NO MARK) –ABOUT 13° BTC 8° BTC

0°

20R engine timing marks. The 8° notch is the larger and deeper of the two cut into the pulley, and must align with the mating line at idle for proper timing. The 13° indication is only for 1977–78 trucks with HAC

6. Allow the engine to run at the specified idle speed with the gearshift in Neutral, or Drive with automatics as the case may be. Be certain that the parking brake is set, the front wheels blocked, and don't stand in front of the truck when making adjustments with the engine running.

7. Point the timing light at the marks on the timing cover. With the engine at the specified idle, the marks should line up.

8. If the timing is incorrect, loosen the bolt at the base of the distributor just enough so that the distributor can be turned. Hold the distributor by its base and turn it slightly to advance or retard the timing as required. Once the marks are seen to align properly, tighten the bolt. If only minor corrections in the timing are necessary, adjustment can be made with the octane selector, rather than by moving the distributor. See the 'Octane Selector section following for information.

9. After tightening the bolt, or moving the octane selector, recheck the timing. It is not unusual for it to change during the tightening process. It may take two or three tries to get it perfect. Shut off the engine, disconnect the timing light, and connect the vacuum line at the distributor, except on engines with HAC.

10. On engines with HAC (identified in the Note earlier) after setting the initial timing, reconnect the vacuum hose at the distributor. Recheck the timing. It should now be about 13° BTC.

11. If the advance is still about 8° pinch the hose between the HAC valve and the three way connector. It should now be about 13°. If not, the HAC valve should be checked for proper operation.

TROUBLESHOOTING

Troubleshooting this system is easy; but you must have an accurate ohmmeter and voltmeter. The numbers in the diagram correspond to the numbers of the following troubleshooting steps. Be sure to perform each step in order.

1. Check for a spark at the spark plugs by hooking up a timing light in the usual manner. If the light flashes, it can be assumed that voltage is reaching the plugs, which should then be inspected, along with the fuel system. If no flash is generated, go on to the following ignition checks.

2. Check all wiring and plastic connectors for tight and proper connections.

3. With an ohmmeter, check between the positive (+) and negative (–) primary terminals of the ignition coil. The resistance (cold) should be $1.3–1.7\Omega$. Between the (+) primary terminal and the high tension terminal, the resis-

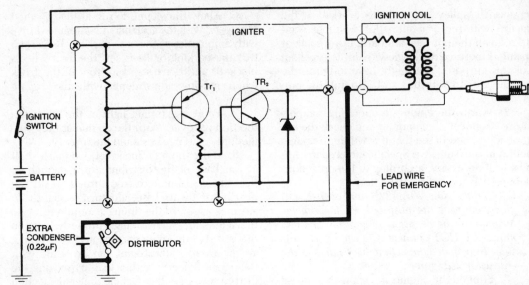

The igniter can be bypassed, if necessary, by disconnecting it entirely, and installing an automotive condenser across the points and a wire from the negative coil terminal to the positive points terminal. This only works on 1975–77 semitransistorized models

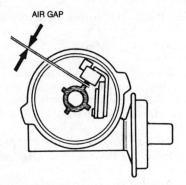

Check the air gap between the timing rotor and the pick-up coil

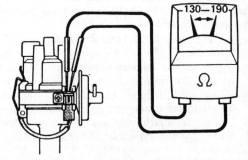

Measure the signal generator (pick-up coil) resistance at the pink and white wires

tance (cold) should be 12–16 KΩ. The insulation resistance between the (+) primary terminal and the ignition coil cases should be infinite.

4. The resistor wire (brown and yellow) resistance should be 1.2Ω (cold). To measure, disconnect the plastic connector at the igniter and connect one wire of the ohmmeter to the yellow wire and one to the brown.

5. Remove the distributor cap and ignition rotor. Check the air gap between the timing rotor spoke and the pick-up coil. When aligned, the air gap should be 0.008–0.016 in. You will probably have to bump the engine around with the starter to line up the timing rotor. Unplug the distributor connector at the distributor. Connect one wire of the ohmmeter to the white wire, and one wire to the pink wire. The resistance of the signal generator should be 130–190Ω.

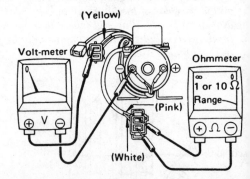

Use the ohmmeter as resistance at the igniter end of the distributor connector

6. Checking the igniter last, connect the (–) voltmeter wire to the (–) ignition coil primary terminal, and the (+) voltmeter wire to the yellow resistor at the connector unplugged in

Step 4. With the ignition switch turned to ON, not START, the voltage should measure 12 volts. Check the voltage between the (–) ignition coil primary terminal and the yellow resistor wire again, but this time use the ohmmeter as resistance. Using the igniter end of the distributor connector unplugged in Step 5, connect the positive (+) ohmmeter wire to the pink distributor wire, and the negative (–) ohmmeter wire to the white wire.

NOTE: *Do not intermix (+) and (–) terminals of the ohmmeter.*

Select either the 1 ohm or 10 ohm range of the ohmmeter. With the voltmeter connected as in Step 6 (1), and the ignition switch turned to ON, not START, the voltage should measure nearly zero.

Octane Selector

The octane selector is used as a fine adjustment to match the ignition timing to the grade of gasoline being used. It is located near the distributor vacuum advance unit, under a plastic cover. Normally the octane selector should not require adjustment; however, adjustment is as follows:

1. Align the setting line with the threaded end of the housing and then align the center line with the setting mark on the housing.
2. Drive the truck at 16–22 mph in high gear on a level road.
3. Depress the accelerator pedal all the way to the floor. A slight pinging sound should be heard. As the vehicle accelerates, the sound should go away.
4. If the pinging sound is loud, or if it fails to disappear as the vehicle accelerates, retard the timing by turning the knob toward R (retard).
5. If there is no pinging sound at all, advance the timing by turning the knob toward A (advance).
6. When the adjustment is completed, replace the dust cover.

NOTE: *One graduation of the octane selector is equal to about 10° of crankshaft angle.*

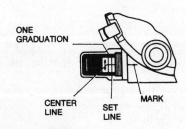

Octane selector setting

Igniter

TROUBLESHOOTING

1975–77

If the igniter in the 1975–77 semi-transistorized ignition is suspected as faulty, it may be checked as follows.

1. Check the coil beforehand, using the methods outlined in the Troubleshooting section at the end of this Book.
2. Check to see if there is a battery voltage at the resistor terminal. Connect a test light between igniter side ballast resistor terminal and the ground bolt at the igniter, or any suitable ground. With the ignition on, the test light should indicate a complete circuit there.
3. Remove the coil primary wire from the distributor and hold it next to a ground. Disconnect the thin secondary wire from the side of the distributor. Make intermittent contacts with suitable ground point with the secondary distributor wire. You may need an extra length of wire to do this on later models with piggyback oil and igniter assemblies. With the ignition on, sparks should be produced from the coil primary wire.
4. If no spark is produced the igniter is probably bad and should be replaced. If a spark is produced, the problem is in the points. Make certain that they are clean and properly adjusted.

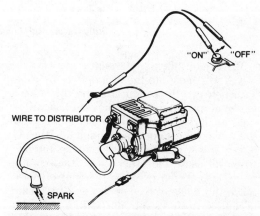

Troubleshooting the igniter. Later models have a snap connector in the wire between the igniter and the distributor. On trucks with separate coil and igniter, you will not need the extra wire shown here

Valve Lash Adjustment

As part of every major tune-up or once every 6,000 miles (1970–74) 12,500 miles (1975–78 20R engine), and 15,000 miles (1979 and later) the valve clearance should be checked and adjusted if necessary.

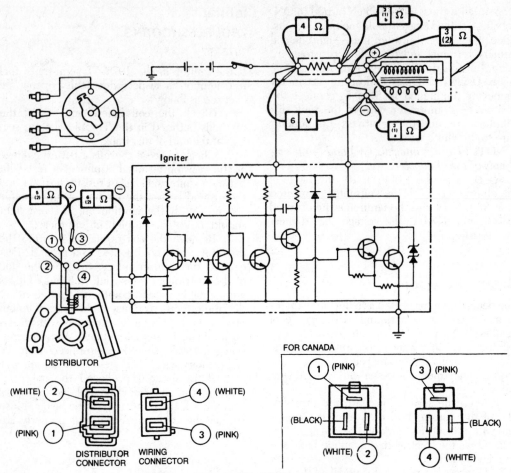

Fully transistorized ignition troubleshooting

Valve adjustment determines how far the valves will open into the cylinder. If the clearance between the rocker arm and the valve is too great, part of the lift of the camshaft will be used up in removing the excess clearance; thus the valve will not open far enough into the cylinder. This will cause the valve to tap and likewise will cause the other valve train components to make an excessive amount of noise. Since the intake valves open less, the quality of air/fuel mixtures introduced into the cylinder will be less and the less the exhaust valves open, the greater the exhaust backpressure. These factors add up to a significant loss of power.

If the valve clearance is too small, the intake and exhaust valves will not fully seat on the cylinder head valve seats when they close. When the valve is tight against the valve seat it performs two functions: it seals the combustion chamber so that none of the gases in the cylinder can escape and the valve is cooled by the transference of heat to the cylinder head, which is in turn cooled by the cooling system of the engine. Therefore, if the valve clearance is too small the engine will run poorly due to the escape of gases from the combustion chambers on the compression and power strokes of the engine and the valves will overheat and burn because they cannot transfer heat properly.

Valve adjustments must be made as accurate as possible, however, it is better to have the valve clearance somewhat larger than smaller if there is any doubt.

All except 2F and Diesel

1. Start the engine and allow it to reach normal operating temperature (above 175°F).

2. Stop the engine. Remove the air cleaner assembly, its hoses, and bracket. Remove any other cables, hoses, wires, etc., which are attached to the valve cover. Remove the valve cover.

3. Check the torque of the valve rocker shaft bolts and the camshaft bearing bolts; they should be 12–17 ft. lb.

4. Check the torque specification of the

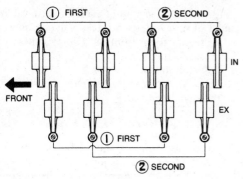

Valve clearance adjustment sequence—20R engine

bearing cap union bolts. They should be torqued to 11–16 ft. lbs.

5. Set the No. 1 cylinder to TDC on its compression stroke. To do this, remove the spark plugs and turn the engine with a wrench applied to the crankshaft bolt. Place a finger on the no.1 spark plug hole. When pressure is felt on your finger and the TDC line on the crankshaft pulley is aligned with the timing pointer (or line), the engine is at TDC. The rocker arms on cylinder No. 1 should be loose, and the rocker arms on cylinder No. 1 should be loose, and the rocker arms on cylinder No. 4 should be tight if the engine is at TDC. Note that the timing mark you are watching is not the same one used for engine timing. That notch indicates a certain number of degrees before TDC.

NOTE: *Do not start the engine. Valve clearances are checked with the engine stopped to prevent hot oil from being splashed out by the timing chain.*

6. Check the clearance (see the Tune-Up Specifications chart) and adjust the first set of valves to the proper specifications, if necessary. See the illustrations for the proper adjusting sequence.

NOTE: *The clearance is measured with a feeler gauge between the valve stem and the air adjusting screw.*

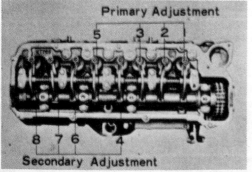

Valve clearance adjustment sequence—8R-C and 18R-C

7. To adjust the valve clearance, loosen the locknut and turn the adjusting screw until the specified clearance is obtained. Tighten the locknut and check the clearance again.

8. Crank the engine one revolution (360°) and perform Steps 6 and 7 for the second set of valves in the illustration. Crank the engine in a clockwise direction (to the right as you face the engine), passing the timing mark just before reaching TDC mark.

9. Install the spark plug in the no.1 cylinder. Install the valve cover, air cleaner assembly, and any other components which were removed.

NOTE: *If you are assembling the engine after it has been dismantled, the valves must be adjusted with the engine cold. Do not start the engine before performing a valve adjustment with all the components cold. Use the clearance valve for cold valves from the Tune-Up Specifications chart in this chapter. After adjusting the valves to their cold value, run the engine and see if the valves have the proper hot clearance. Readjust as necessary. Damage may result to the rocker arms if the valves are not adjusted to the cold valve during assembly. See Chapter 3.*

2F Engines

1. Start the engine and allow it to reach normal operating temperature (above 165°F).

2. Stop the engine. Remove the air cleaner assembly with related components. Remove any cables, hoses, wires, etc., which are attached to the valve cover and remove the valve cover.

3. Following the Torque Sequence and Torque Specification charts at the beginning of this section, retorque the cylinder head bolts. On 2F engines, also torque the manifold attaching nuts to 28–37 ft. lb. for trucks outside of California, or 37–51 ft. lb. for California trucks, and the rocker support fasteners to 15–21 ft. lb. on 8mm bolts and 22–32 ft.lb. on 10mm bolts.

4. Start the engine and adjust the idle speed as described in the following procedure.

5. Check the clearance between each of the rocker arms and valve stems while the engine is at slow idle, using a feeler gauge of the proper size (See the Tune-Up Specifications chart).

6. If the clearance is incorrect, loosen the locknut and turn the adjusting screw as required. Tighten the locknut and recheck the clearance.

7. After adjusting all of the valves, install the valve cover and any other components which were removed during step 2.

8. Recheck the engine idle speed and adjust if necessary.

Diesel Engine

The valves are adjusted in basically the same manner as the 20R, 22R and 22R-E engines, in that the engine must be off during the adjustment and that the clearance is checked with a feeler gauge between the rocker arm and the valve stem end.

NOTE: *The engine must be at normal operating temperature to obtain the proper valve clearances.*

1. Remove the valve cover and rotate the crankshaft to align the TDC mark on the crankshaft pulley with the corresponding pointer. The valves of the number one cylinder should be closed (rocker arms should feel loose). If the rocker arms of the number one cylinder are tight, rotate the engine another 360° and again align the TDC marks.

2. Adjust the clearances of the following valves:
   - Number one cylinder: intake and exhaust
   - Number two cylinder: intake
   - Number three cylinder: exhaust

3. Rotate the crankshaft 360° and adjust the remaining valves:
   - Number two cylinder: exhaust
   - Number three cylinder: intake
   - Number four cylinder: intake and exhaust

Remember that the cylinder numbering from the front of the engine to the rear is #1 through #4, and that the valve arrangement from the front of the engine is E-I-E-I-E-I-

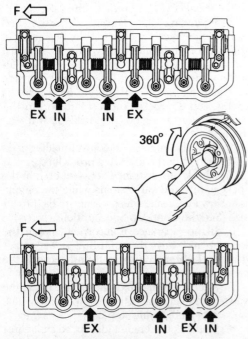

Diesel valve adjustment sequence

E-I, with E designating each exhaust valve and I designating each intake valve. Choose your specifications from the Diesel Tune-Up Chart accordingly.

4. Reinstall the valve cover.

NOTE: *Never operate the engine with the valve cover removed.*

Carburetor

Carburetor adjustments should be performed as the last phase of a major engine tune-up. Adjusting the carburetor when you are uncertain of the other tune considerations will lead to trouble requiring professional correction. Adjusting the carburetor and the procedures involved can be simplified if you understand how the carburetor functions.

The sole function is to mix liquid fuel with air in the correct proportions to provide a combustion mixture for the engine. A partial vacuum is created by the downward movement of the pistons on their intake stroke. This vacuum draws a stream of air through the carburetor into which a jet of fuel is introduced; the air/fuel mixture is drawn into the engine by the action of that same vacuum. The amount of this mixture which enters the engine is controlled by the throttle plates in the bottom of the carburetor. When the engine is not running, these plates are completely closed. The plates are connected by various kinds of linkage to the accelerator pedal inside the vehicle. When you depress the accelerator pedal, you are opening the throttle plates and allowing more of the air/fuel mixture to be drawn into the engine, thus increasing the engine speed.

When the engine is idling, the throttle plates are kept open a specified amount by the idle speed screw which contacts the throttle lever on the outside of the carburetor.

Since it is difficult for the engine to draw a sufficient supply of mixture when the throttle plates are only slightly open at idle, an internal idle mixture passage is provided. This passage delivers air/fuel mixture to the engine through a hole located at the bottom of the carburetor below the throttle plates. This passage has an adjustment screw to regulate the flow.

Basic carburetor adjustment involves the accurate adjustment of these two devices to provide adequate, but not excessive, air/fuel mixture at idle. The method used on 8R-C and 18R-C engines is called the maximum boot method and requires the use of a vacuum gauge.

IDLE SPEED AND MIXTURE ADJUSTMENT
8R-C and 18R-C

NOTE: *See Chapter 4 for further information and adjustments. Perform all adjust-*

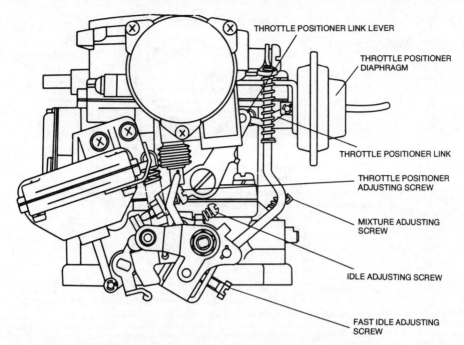

THROTTLE POSITIONER LINK LEVER

THROTTLE POSITIONER DIAPHRAGM

THROTTLE POSITIONER LINK

THROTTLE POSITIONER ADJUSTING SCREW

MIXTURE ADJUSTING SCREW

IDLE ADJUSTING SCREW

FAST IDLE ADJUSTING SCREW

Location of carburetor adjustment screws—8R-C and 18R-C

ments with the engine at the operating temperature and the air cleaner assembly in place. Vehicles equipped with automatic transmission should have these adjustments performed with the transmission in Drive range. Be certain that the emergency brake is firmly set and that the front wheels are blocked.

1. Connect a tachometer to the engine as detailed in the manufacturer's instructions.

2. Remove the plug in the intake manifold vacuum port and connect a vacuum gauge by using a suitable metric adapter.

3. Start the engine and let it run at idle speed.

4. Turn the mixture screw in or out to obtain the lowest idle speed at which the engine will not stall.

5. Turn the idle speed screw to obtain the highest vacuum reading at the specified idle speed.

6. Race the engine momentarily by manipulating the throttle linkage to verify that the engine will return to the correct idle speed.

NOTE: *If the engine will not idle smoothly at this point, perform the adjustment again.*

7. Remove the tachometer and the vacuum gauge. Install the plug in the intake manifold and road test the vehicle.

20R,22R, 22R-E and 2F

The idle speed and mixture should be adjusted under the following conditions: air cleaner on,

choke fully opened, transmission in Neutral (all transmissions), all accessories turned off, all vacuum lines connected, all previous adjustments (timing, dwell, etc.) made.

1. Start the engine and allow it to reach operating temperature.

2. Check the float setting on the carburetor. The fuel level should be just about even with the spot on the sight glass. If it is too high or too low, the float level will have to be adjusted following the procedure in Chapter 4.

3. Connect a tachometer to the engine. Connect the tachometer positive (+) lead to the coil negative (–) terminal. Do NOT hook it up to the distributor or positive side; damage to the transistorized ignition will result. See the illustration earlier in the Chapter concerning dwell meters, for proper connections.

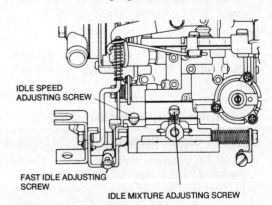

IDLE SPEED ADJUSTING SCREW

FAST IDLE ADJUSTING SCREW

IDLE MIXTURE ADJUSTING SCREW

20R carburetor adjusting screws

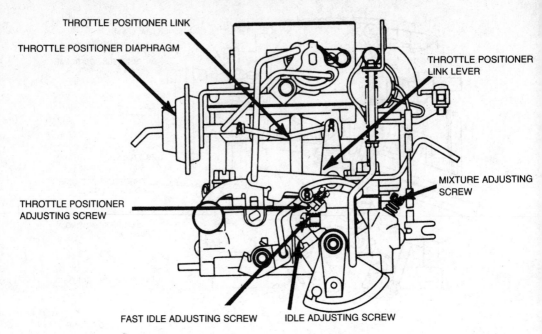

THROTTLE POSITIONER LINK

THROTTLE POSITIONER DIAPHRAGM

THROTTLE POSITIONER LINK LEVER

MIXTURE ADJUSTING SCREW

THROTTLE POSITIONER ADJUSTING SCREW

FAST IDLE ADJUSTING SCREW

IDLE ADJUSTING SCREW

Carburetor adjustment on the F series engine

4. Adjust the engine speed to the highest rpm it will attain with the idle mixture adjusting screw.

5. Set the rpm to the idle mixture speed of 900 rpm by turning the idle speed adjusting screw. You may have to repeat Steps 4 and 5 a few times until the highest idle reached in Step 4 will go no further.

6. Now set the speed to the initial idle speed of 850 rpm by turning the idle mixture adjusting screw in (clockwise).

7. Disconnect the tachometer.

NOTE: *On later model carburetors the limiter caps are designed to limit the adjustment. These can be removed and adjusted, but this should be done only by a professional mechanic with an exhaust analyzer machine to set the emissions at the proper limits. The 1981 carburetors cannot be adjusted. They are preset at the factory.*

22R, 22R-E

There is no adjustment needed on the idle mixture screw. It has been preset at the factory.

Electronic Fuel Injection (EFI)

Electronic Control System

The 22R-EC engine is equipped with a Toyota Computer Control System (TCCS) which centrally controls the EFI, ESA, Diagnostic systems, etc. by means of an Electronic Control Unit (ECU—formerly EFI computer) employing a microcomputer. By means of the ECU, the TCCS controls the following functions.

1. Electronic Fuel Injection (EFI).
2. Electronic Spark Advance (ESA).
3. Diagnostics.
4. Fail Safe Function.

The Electronic Fuel Injection and Electronic Control Systems are extremely complicated and require special tools for diagnosis and repair. For these reasons all maintenance and adjustments to these systems should be referred to a qualified technician.

Diesel Fuel System

IDLE AND MAXIMUM SPEED ADJUSTMENTS

NOTE: *The following adjustments are made with the transmission in neutral and the parking brake applied fully.*

1. Warm the engine to normal operating temperature and allow it to idle.

2. Turn the idle adjuster knob counterclockwise; the knob should return to its unlocked position.

3. Turn the engine off and remove the accelerator connection rod.

4. Connect a tachometer to the engine according to the tachometer manufacturer's instructions.

5. Start the engine and check the engine rpm at idle. The idle rpm should be 700 rpm.

6. If adjustment is necessary, turn the idle adjusting screw on the fuel injection pump as

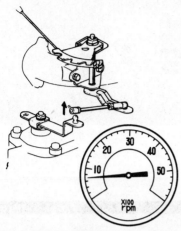

After making speed adjustments on the diesel, attach the accelerator cable and adjust it to remove all slack

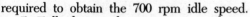

Diesel idle speed adjustment with the accelerator rod disconnected at the pump lever

required to obtain the 700 rpm idle speed.

7. Fully depress the injection pump lever, note the maximum engine speed and release the accelerator pedal immediately. The maximum rpm should be 4900.

8. If adjustment is necessary:

a. Remove the wire seal of the maximum speed adjusting screw, if so equipped.

b. Using Toyota special service tool #09275-54020 or its equivalent, loosen the locknut of the maximum speed adjusting screw.

c. Turn the maximum speed adjusting screw until the proper maximum rpm is obtained.

9. Install the accelerator connecting rod and adjust its length so that there is no slack in the accelerator cable.

10. Check that the idle speed increases as the idle adjuster knob is pulled outward. Then turn the knob counterclockwise so that the rpm returns to the idle specifications.

11. Turn the engine off and disconnect the tachometer from the engine.

Engine and Engine Rebuilding

3

ENGINE ELECTRICAL

Distributor

REMOVAL

1. Mark the position of the spark plug wires on the distributor cap and remove the wires from the spark plugs.

2. Remove the coil primary wire and the vacuum line from the distributor. Remove the distributor cap with plug wires attached.

3. Using a dab of paint, mark the distributor housing and the block so the distributor may be relocated. Also mark the position of the rotor on the distributor housing.

4. Remove the distributor clamp, bolt on the clamp (bolt only on 20R). Pull the distributor from the block.

NOTE: *It is easier to install the distributor if the engine timing is not disturbed while it is removed. Do not turn the engine over with the distributor removed.*

INSTALLATION—TIMING NOT DISTURBED

1. Lubricate the drive gear with engine oil. Insert the distributor in the block and align the paint marks made during removal.

2. Engage the distributor drive with the oil pump driveshaft.

3. Install the distributor clamp, cap primary wire and vacuum line.

4. Install the spark plug wires. Be sure to check the positioning against the wiring diagram supplied in this chapter.

5. Start the engine. Check the timing and adjust the octane selector as outlines in Chapter 2.

INSTALLATION—TIMING LOST

If the engine has been cranked, dismantled, or the timing otherwise lost, proceed as follows:

1. Remove the no. 1 spark plug and place a finger over the hole. Crank the engine until the compression pressure builds up. When the timing marks are exactly aligned the no. 1 piston will be at top dead center (TDC).

2. From the Tune-Up Specifications chart in Chapter 2, determine the correct setting for your engine.

3. Temporarily install the rotor on the distributor shaft without the dust cover. Turn the distributor shaft until the rotor is pointing to the no. 1 firing position. The points should be just about to open.

4. Use a thin screwdriver to align the slot on the distributor drive (the oil pump driveshaft) with the key on the bottom of the distributor shaft.

5. Install the distributor in the block by moving it slightly (no more than one gear tooth in either direction) until the driven gear meshes with the drive.

NOTE: *Oil the distributor spiral gear and the oil pump driveshaft before installing the unit.*

6. Rotate the distributor, once it is installed, so that the points are just about to open. This can be determined by inserting a thin piece of paper between the points. Rotate the distributor housing and the points will grasp the paper. Rotate the housing the other way until you

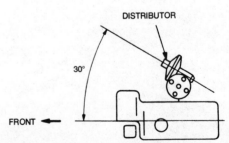

Installed position of the distributor—8R-C and 18R-C

feel the points begin to release the paper, then temporarily tighten the hold down bolt.

7. Remove the rotor. Install the dust cover. Reinstall the rotor, distributor cap, primary wire, vacuum line and all spark plugs and wires.

8. Start the engine and follow the instructions given in Chapter 2 for adjusting the timing, dwell angle, and the octane selector.

FIRING ORDER

To avoid confusion replace spark plug wires one at a time.

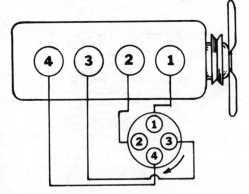

8R-C and 18R-C

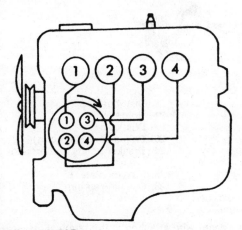

20R and 22R

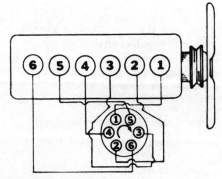

F series firing order

Alternator

The alternator converts the mechanical energy supplied by the drive belt into electrical energy by a process of electromagnetic induction. When the ignition switch is turned on, current flows from the battery through the charging system light (or ammeter) to the voltage regulator, and finally to the alternator. When the engine is started, the drive belt turns the rotating field (rotor) in the stationary windings (stator), inducing alternating current. This alternating current is converted into usable direct current by the diode rectifier. Most of this current is used to charge the battery and to supply power for the vehicle's electrical accessories. A small part of this current is returned to the field windings of the alternator enabling it to increase its power output. When the current in the field windings reaches a predetermined level, the voltage regulator grounds the circuit preventing any further increase. The cycle is continued so that the voltage supply remains constant.

The alternator is a 40 amp Nippondenso® unit with six integral silicone diodes.

On 1979 and later models there was an optional 55 ampere alternator available. The regulator is attached directly to the back of the alternator. There is no adjustment that is necessary to this regulator. It must be replaced as a complete unit.

ALTERNATOR PRECAUTIONS

1. If the battery is removed be sure to observe the proper polarity when reinstalling. Failure to do so will result in damage to the one-way rectifiers.

2. Make sure that the battery, alternator, and regulator leads are not disconnected when the engine is running.

3. Never attempt to polarize an alternator. Never operate on an open circuit.

4. When charging a battery be sure to disconnect the output cable.

5. Always remove the ground cable when replacing any electrical component.

6. If arc welding equipment is used on the vehicle, the alternator must be disconnected.

7. Never subject the alternator to extreme temperature or dampness when steam cleaning the engine.

REMOVAL AND INSTALLATION

NOTE: *On some models, the alternator is mounted very low on the engine. On these models, it may be necessary to remove the gravel shield and work from beneath the car in order to gain access to the alternator.*

1. Disconnect the negative battery cable.

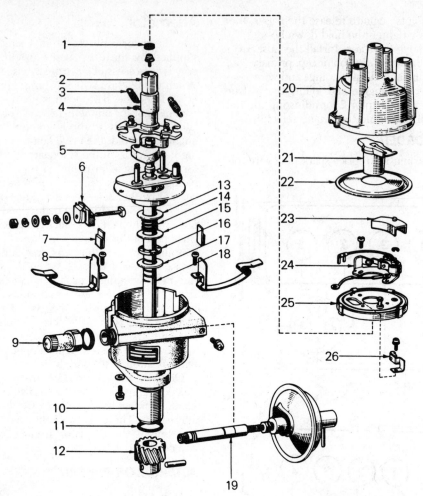

1. Grease stopper
2. Cam
3. Governor spring
4. E-ring
5. Governor weight
6. Terminal insulator
7. Rubber plug
8. Hold-down clip for cap
9. Octane selector cap
10. Distributor housing

11. O-ring
12. Drive gear
13. Washer
14. Spring (20R only)
15. Washer (20R only)
16. Bearing (20R only)
17. Washer (20R only)
18. Distributor shaft
19. Vacuum advance and oc-
    tane selector assembly

20. Distributor cap
21. Rotor
22. Dust cover
23. Points cover (20R only)
24. Breaker points and ground
    wire
25. Breaker plate
26. Damping spring

20R points-type distributor. Earlier models have the condenser wire attached to the terminal insulator screw (#6 in this diagram)

2. Loosen the alternator adjusting arm bolt and move the alternator so that the drive belt may be removed.

3. Remove the wiring connections to the alternator, and tag them for assembly.

4. Remove the adjusting bolt and the attaching bolt and remove the alternator.

5. Install in reverse order and adjust the drive belt tension as follows: Push down on the alternator belt at a point midway between the fan and alternator pulleys. There should be about ⅜–½ in. of deflection in the belt. To adjust,

simply loosen the adjusting bolt and move the alternator in the desired direction.

NOTE: *Never pry on the alternator with a metal instrument. If you must use a pry bar, use a wooden hammer handle.*

1979 and Later 55 Ampere Regulator

1. Disconnect the negative battery terminal.

2. Remove the mounting bolts and remove the alternator.

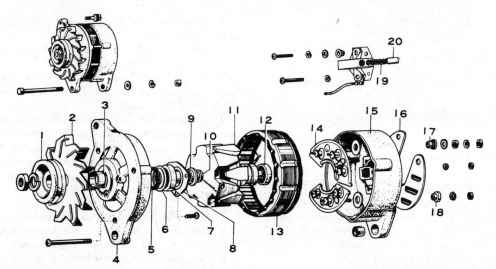

1. Alternator pulley
2. Alternator fan
3. Space collar
4. Drive end frame assembly
5. Felt
6. Felt cover
7. Bearing

8. Bearing retainer plate
9. Space ring
10. Snap-ring
11. Alternator rotor assembly
12. Bearing
13. Alternator stator assembly
14. Holder with rectifiers

15. Rectifier end frame assembly
16. Rear end cover
17. B terminal insulator
18. Insulator
19. Brush spring
20. Alternator brush

Alternator components

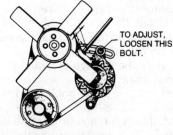

TO ADJUST,
LOOSEN THIS
BOLT.

Belt tension adjustment

3. Disconnect the electrical wires on the alternator.

4. Remove the end cover screws and cover.

5. Remove the three screws on the terminals inside the regulator.

6. Remove the two screws from the top of the regulator and pull the regulator out.

NOTE: *This regulator can't be repaired. It must be replaced.*

7. Installation is the reverse of removal.

Voltage Regulator

REMOVAL AND INSTALLATION

NOTE: *On Land Cruisers, disconnect the leads from their screw terminals after noting their positions.*

1. Disconnect the negative battery cable.

2. Disconnect the wiring harness.

3. Remove the retaining hardware and remove the regulator.

4. To install, attach the new regulator to the compartment panel, replace the wiring harness, and connect the battery cable.

VOLTAGE ADJUSTMENT

NOTE: *Only external units are adjustable.*

1. Connect a voltmeter to the battery terminals.

2. Start the engine and gradually increase the engine speed to about 1,500 rpm.

3. At this speed, the voltage reading should be 13.8–14.8 volts.

4. If the voltage does not fall within this range, a minor adjustment may be made to the adjusting arm. Disconnect the ground cable of the battery and remove the regulator cover. Bend the adjusting arm very slightly with a pair of needlenosed pliers. Replace the cover and battery cable.

5. Repeat the voltage test and if the voltage cannot be brought within specifications, proceed to the mechanical adjustments listed next.

MECHANICAL ADJUSTMENTS

Field Relay

1. Remove the cover from the regulator.

2. Depress the armature and check the contact spring deflection. It should be 0.008–0.018 in.

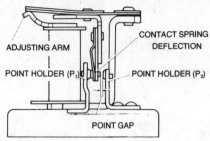

Field relay internal parts

3. Correct the deviations by bending the point holder marked P_2 in the illustration.

4. Check the point gap with a feeler gauge. It should fall somewhere between 0.016–0.047 in. If it does not, adjust by bending the point holder marked P_1 in the illustration.

5. The points can be cleaned with emery paper and solvent.

Voltage Regulator

1. The air (armature) gap must measure 0.008 in. If it does not, adjust by bending the low speed point holder.

2. Measure the point with a feeler gauge. It should be 0.010–0.018 in. If it is not, bend the high speed point holder to correct the adjustment. Clean the points with emery paper and use a solvent to remove dust.

3. Check the contact spring deflection with the armature depressed. It should measure between 0.008–0.018 in. as it does on the field relay. If it does not, REPLACE the regulator.

4. Perform the voltage test again. If the voltage reading cannot be brought to specification, replace the voltage regulator. If this fails to correct the situation, the alternator then must be suspected as the defective unit.

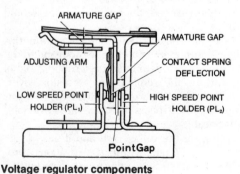

Voltage regulator components

Starter
REMOVAL AND INSTALLATION

NOTE: *On some models with automatic transmission, it may be necessary to disconnect the throttle rod.*

1. Disconnect the positive (+) battery cable at the battery, then at the starter.

2. Disconnect the remaining electrical connections at the starter solenoid.

3. Remove the two nuts holding the starter to the bell housing and pull the starter toward the front of the vehicle.

4. To install the unit, insert the starter into the bell housing being sure that the starter drive is not jammed against the flywheel. Tighten the attaching nuts and replace all electrical connections making the battery connection the last.

OVERHAUL

NOTE: *The following instructions cover all starter components. If you are having trouble with the starter motor it is advisable to inspect the entire unit while it is out of the vehicle.*

Disassembly

1. Remove the starter from the vehicle.

2. Disconnect the field coil wire from the solenoid.

3. Remove the two solenoid retaining screws and remove the solenoid by tilting it upward to unhook the moving stud from the drive lever spring.

4. Remove the bearing cover screws and cover. Pull out the armature shaft lockplate, plate washer, seal washer and brake spring. The 20R does not have the spring.

5. Remove the through-bolts and the commutator end frame.

6. Pull out the brush holder and remove the brushes.

   a. At this point the brushes should be inspected. Their minimum length must be 0.47 in. If they require replacement, be sure to dress the ends of the new brushes with emery paper. This will ensure good contact on the commutator.

7. Remove the yoke from the drive housing.

Remove the starter solenoid in the direction of the arrow

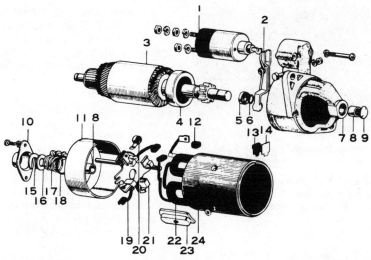

1. Solenoid
2. Engagement lever
3. Armature
4. Overrunning clutch
5. Clutch stop
6. Snap-ring
7. Drive housing
8. Bushing
9. Bearing cover
10. Bearing cover
11. Commutator end frame
12. Rubber bushing
13. Rubber grommet
14. Plate
15. Lockplate
16. Washer
17. Brake spring
18. Gasket
19. Brush
20. Brush spring
21. Brush holder
22. Field coil
23. Pole shoes
24. Field yoke

Starter motor components—8R-C and 18R-C. others similar

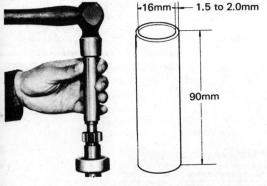

Removing the starter drive thrust collar

8. Remove the shift lever fulcrum bolt, the rubber piece and the plate from the drive housing.

9. Remove the armature and the drive lever from the drive housing.

10. To remove the drive unit from the armature shaft you will need a tool similar to the one pictured. (A piece of ½ in. pipe coupling will work here).

11. Place the cylinder over the shaft to bear against the pinion stop retainer. Drive the retainer down to expose the snapring. Remove the snapring from the groove in the shaft and slide the starter drive mechanism off the armature shaft. On 20R starters, there is a center bearing, a spring, and a spring holder behind the drive mechanism. These will slide off the armature shaft.

Assembly

1. Lubricate the armature shaft. Install the drive assembly with the pinion outward. Install the spring holder, spring, and center bearing onto the armature shaft first on 20R starters.

2. Slide the pinion stop retainer down over the shaft with the recessed side outward.

3. Place a new snapring on the drive end of the shaft and hold it in place with a block of hardwood. Strike the block with a hammer to force it over the end of the shaft. Slide the ring down into the groove on the shaft.

4. Place the thrust collar on the shaft with the shoulder next to the snapring and move the retainer into contact with the ring. Using pliers on opposite sides of the shaft, squeeze the retainer and the thrust collar together until the collar surrounds the ring. Pinch the collar in several places to lock the ring in place.

5. Install the drive lever onto the clutch as shown in the illustration.

NOTE: *Be sure that the steel washer is located on the clutchside.*

6. Lubricate the drive housing bushing and install the armature and drive unit in the housing.

7. Install the plate and the rubber piece in the drive housing. Install the shift lever fulcrum bolt being certain that it is lubricated with

Correctly installed starter drive lever. The 20R model is shown here; the center bearing is to the right of the drive lever. Earlier models do not have this bearing

multipurpose lubricant. Assemble the yoke in the drive housing.

8. Install the field frame.

9. Install the brush holder and brushes.

10. Install the commutator end frame. Be sure to coat the bushing with multipurpose grease.

11. Install the through-bolts. Inspect the thrust clearance of the armature. The clearance should be between 0.002–0.014 in. Add washers if needed.

12. Install the seal washer, brake spring, plate washer, and lock plate.

13. Pack the bearing cover with grease and install it on the end frame.

14. Hook the moving stud of the solenoid from under the spring. Install the solenoid retainers.

15. Check the clearance between the pinion and the pinion retainer. It should be 0.04–0.16 in. on earlier models, and 0.008–0.157 on 20R trucks. To adjust the clearance, the moving stud of the solenoid may be lengthened or shortened accordingly.

Testing

A simple no-load test should be performed before installing the starter in the vehicle. Use a fully charged battery to perform the test. Hook the test leads up as shown in the illustration. The negative side of the battery should be grounded on the starter drive housing. The positive side should run to an ammeter and then to the battery cable connection on the solenoid. The starter should rotate smoothly within the given specifications.

Battery

Refer to Chapter One for details on battery maintenance.

REMOVAL AND INSTALLATION

1. Disconnect the negative (ground) cable from the terminal, and then the positive cable. Special pullers are available to remove the cable clamps.

NOTE: *To avoid spark, always disconnect the ground cable first, and connect it last.*

2. Remove the battery holddown clamp.

3. Remove the battery, being careful not to spill the acid.

NOTE: *Spilled acid can be neutralized with*

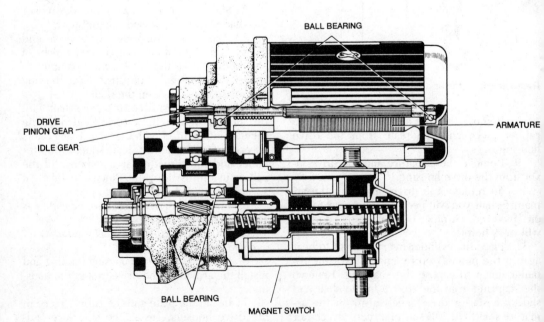

Cross-section of the reduction gear starter motor

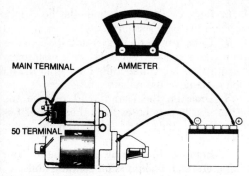

MAIN TERMINAL   AMMETER

50 TERMINAL

Simplified no-load test

a baking soda/water solution. If you some-how get acid in your eyes, flush it out with lots of water and get to a doctor.

4. Clean the battery posts thoroughly be-fore reinstalling, or when installing a new bat-tery.

5. Clean the cable clamps, using a wire brush, both inside and out.

6. Install the battery and the holddown clamp or strap. Connect the positive, and then the negative cable. Do not hammer them in place. The terminals should be coated lightly (exter-nally) with grease to prevent corrosion. There are also felt washers impregnated with an an-ticorrosion substance which are slipped over the battery posts before installing the cables; these are available in auto parts stores.

CAUTION: *Make absolutely sure that the battery is connected properly before you turn on the ignition switch. Reversed polarity can burn out your alternator and regulator within a matter of seconds.*

Radiator

REMOVAL AND INSTALLATION

CAUTION: *When draining the coolant, keep in mind that cats and dogs are attracted by the ethylene glycol antifreeze, and are quite likely to drink any that is left in an uncov-ered container or in puddles on the ground. This will prove fatal in sufficient quantity. Always drain the coolant into a sealable con-tainer. Coolant should be reused unless it is contaminated or several years old.*

1. Drain the cooling system completely by removing the lower and then the upper radia-tor hoses.

2. If the vehicle is equipped with an auto-matic transmission, remove the cooling lines from the bottom of the radiator.

NOTE: *Use care when removing the cooling lines; the compression fittings are easily damaged as is the radiator. If available use special flare nut wrenches on the fittings.*

CAUTION: *Do not allow dirt or water to enter the cooling lines!*

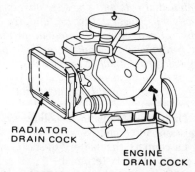

RADIATOR DRAIN COCK

ENGINE DRAIN COCK

Location of 20R drain plugs—other trucks similar

Battery and Starter Specifications

All cars use 12 volt, negative ground electrical systems

Year	Engine Type	Battery Amp Hour Capacity	Starter Lock Test Amps	Lock Test Volts	Torque (ft/lbs)	No Load Test Amps	No Load Test Volts	RPM	Brush Spring Tension (oz)	Min. Brush Length (in.)
1970–74	8R-C and 18R-C	50	550	7.7	10	45	11	6,000	21	0.47
1975–80	20R	60	Not Recommended			50	11.5	5,000	21	0.47
1981 and later	22R 22R-E	60	Not Recommended			90	12.0	3,500	64	0.39
1981 and later	Diesel	60	Not Recommended			180	11	3,500	84–96	0.47
1970 and later	2F	50	Not Recommended			50	11.5	5,000	64	0.39

3. Detach the hood lock cable and remove the hood lock from the radiator upper support. It may be necessary to remove the grille in order to gain access to the hood lock/radiator support assembly.

4. Remove the fan shroud.

5. Remove the radiator upper support.

6. Unfasten the retaining bolts and remove the radiator.

CAUTION: *Do not damage the cooling fans on the radiator when withdrawing it from the engine compartment.*

7. Reverse the procedure to install. Make sure that you check the fluid level of the automatic transmission before using the vehicle. See Chapter 1 for applicable procedures.

Engine

REMOVAL AND INSTALLATION

Two Wheel Drive Pick-Ups

GASOLINE ENGINES

CAUTION: *When draining the coolant, keep in mind that cats and dogs are attracted by the ethylene glycol antifreeze, and are quite likely to drink any that is left in an uncovered container or in puddles on the ground. This will prove fatal in sufficient quantity. Always drain the coolant into a sealable container. Coolant should be reused unless it is contaminated or several years old.*

1. Drain the radiator, cooling system, transmission, and engine oil.

2. Disconnect the battery-to-starter cable at the positive battery terminal.

3. Scribe marks on the hood and its hinges to aid in alignment during installation.

4. Remove the hood supports from the body. Remove the hood.

NOTE: *Do not remove the supports from the hood.*

5. Remove the headlight bezel and the radiator grille.

Removing the camshaft

6. Remove the fan shroud, the hood lock base and the base support.

7. Detach both the upper and lower hoses from the radiator. On cars with automatic transmissions, disconnect the lines from the oil cooler. Remove the radiator.

8. Unfasten the clamps and remove the heater and bypass hoses from the engine. Remove the heater control cable from the water valve.

9. Remove the wiring from the coolant temperature and oil pressure sending units.

10. Remove the air cleaner from its bracket, complete with its attendant hoses.

11. Unfasten the accelerator torque rod from the carburetor. On models equipped with automatic transmissions, remove the transmission linkage as well.

12. Remove the emission control system hoses and wiring, as necessary.

13. Remove the clutch hydraulic line support bracket.

14. Unfasten the high tension and primary wires from the coil.

15. Mark the spark plug cables and remove them from the distributor.

16. Detach the right hand front engine mount.

17. Remove the fuel line at the pump.

18. Detach the downpipe from the exhaust manifold.

19. Detach the left hand front engine mount.

20. Disconnect all the wiring harness multiconnectors.

Perform the following steps on models with manual transmission.

21. Remove the center console if so equipped.

22. Remove the shift lever boot(s).

23. Unfasten the four shift lever cap retaining screws. Remove the cap and withdraw the shift lever assembly.

Perform the following steps on models equipped with automatic transmission:

24. Remove the transmission selector linkage:

   a. On models equipped with a floor mounted selector, disconnect the control rod from the transmission.

   b. On column mounted gear selection models, remove the shifter rod.

25. Disconnect the neutral safety switch wiring connector.

26. Raise the rear of the vehicle with jacks and support it on jack stands.

27. Remove the retaining screws and remove the parking brake equalizer support bracket. Disconnect the cable which runs between the lever and the equalizer.

28. Remove the speedometer cable from the

ENGINE OVERHAUL

Most engine overhaul procedures are fairly standard. In addition to specific parts replacement procedures and complete specifications for your individual engine, this chapter also is a guide to accepted rebuilding procedures. Examples of standard rebuilding practice are shown and should be used along with specific details concerning your particular engine.

Competent and accurate machine shop services will ensure maximum performance, reliability and engine life. Procedures marked with the symbol shown above should be performed by a competent machine shop, and are provided so that you will be familiar with the procedures necessary to a successful overhaul.

In most instances it is more profitable for the do-it-yourself mechanic to remove, clean and inspect the component, buy the necessary parts and deliver these to a shop for actual machine work.

On the other hand, much of the rebuilding work (crankshaft, block, bearings, pistons, rods, and other components) is well within the scope of the do-it-yourself mechanic.

Tools

The tools required for an engine overhaul or parts replacement will depend on the depth of your involvement. With a few exceptions, they will be the tools found in a mechanic's tool kit (see Chapter 1). More indepth work will require any or all of the following:

• a dial indicator (reading in thousandths) mounted on a universal base
• micrometers and telescope gauges
• jaw and screw-type pullers
• scraper
• valve spring compressor
• ring groove cleaner
• piston ring expander and compressor
• ridge reamer
• cylinder hone or glaze breaker

• Plastigage®
• engine stand

Use of most of these tools is illustrated in this chapter. Many can be rented for a one-time use from a local parts jobber or tool supply house specializing in automotive work.

Occasionally, the use of special tools is called for. See the information on Special Tools and the Safety Notice in the front of this book before substituting another tool.

Inspection Techniques

Procedures and specifications are given in this chapter for inspecting, cleaning and assessing the wear limits of most major components. Other procedures such as Magnaflux and Zyglo can be used to locate material flaws and stress cracks. Magnaflux is a magnetic process applicable only to ferrous materials. The Zyglo process coats the material with a flourescent dye penetrant and can be used on any material. Check for suspected surface cracks can be more readily made using spot check dye. The dye is sprayed onto the suspected area, wiped off and the area sprayed with a developer. Cracks will show up brightly.

Overhaul Tips

Aluminum has become extremely popular for use in engines, due to its low weight. Observe the following precautions when handling aluminum parts:

• Never hot tank aluminum parts (the caustic hot-tank solution will eat the aluminum)
• Remove all aluminum parts (identification tag, etc.) from engine parts prior to hot-tanking.
• Always coat threads lightly with engine oil or anti-seize compounds before installation, to prevent seizure.
• Never over-torque bolts or spark plugs, especially in aluminum threads.

Stripped threads in any component can be repaired using any of several commercial repair kits (Heli-Coil, Microdot, Keenserts, etc.)

When assembling the engine, any parts that will be in frictional contact must be prelubed to provide lubrication at initial start-up. Any product specifically formulated for this purpose can be used, but engine oil is not recommended as a pre-lube.

When semi-permanent (locked, but removable) installation of bolts or nuts is desired, threads should be cleaned and coated with Loctite® or other similar, commercial non-hardening sealant.

Repairing Damaged Threads

Several methods of repairing damaged threads are available. Heli-Coil® (shown here), Keenserts® and Microdot® are among the most widely used. All involve basically the same principle—drilling out stripped threads, tapping the hole and installing a prewound insert—making welding, plugging and oversize fasteners unnecessary.

Two types of thread repair inserts are usually supplied—a standard type for most Inch Coarse, Inch Fine, Metric Coarse and Metric Fine thread sizes and a spark plug type to fit most spark plug port sizes. Consult the individual manufacturer's catalog to determine exact applications. Typical thread repair kits will contain a selection of prewound threaded inserts, a tap (corresponding to the outside diameter threads of the insert) and an installation tool. Spark plug inserts usually differ because they require a tap equipped with pilot threads and a combined reamer/tap section. Most manufacturers also supply blister-packed thread repair inserts separately in addition to a master kit containing a variety of taps and inserts plus installation tools.

Before effecting a repair to a threaded hole, remove any snapped, broken or damaged bolts or studs. Penetrating oil can be used to free frozen threads; the offending item can be removed with locking pliers or with a screw or stud extractor. After the hole is clear, the thread can be repaired, as follows:

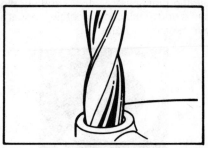

Drill out the damaged threads with specified drill. Drill completely through the hole or to the bottom of a blind hole

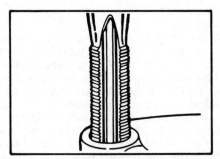

With the tap supplied, tap the hole to receive the thread insert. Keep the tap well oiled and back it out frequently to avoid clogging the threads

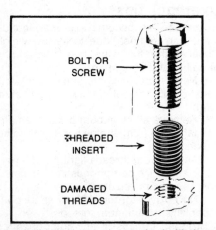

Damaged bolt holes can be repaired with thread repair inserts

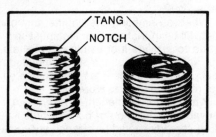

Standard thread repair insert (left) and spark plug thread insert (right)

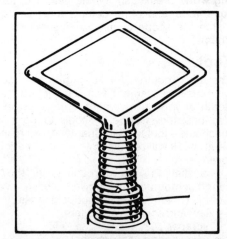

Screw the threaded insert onto the installation tool until the tang engages the slot. Screw the insert into the tapped hole until it is ¼–½ turn below the top surface, After installation break off the tang with a hammer and punch

Standard Torque Specifications and Fastener Markings

In the absence of specific torques, the following chart can be used as a guide to the maximum safe torque of a particular size/grade of fastener.

- There is no torque difference for fine or coarse threads.
- Torque values are based on clean, dry threads. Reduce the value by 10% if threads are oiled prior to assembly.
- The torque required for aluminum components or fasteners is considerably less.

U.S. Bolts

SAE Grade Number	1 or 2			5			6 or 7		
Number of lines always 2 less than the grade number.									
Bolt Size (Inches)—(Thread)	**Maximum Torque**			**Maximum Torque**			**Maximum Torque**		
	Ft./Lbs.	Kgm	Nm	Ft./Lbs.	Kgm	Nm	Ft./Lbs.	Kgm	Nm
¼—20	5	0.7	6.8	8	1.1	10.8	10	1.4	13.5
—28	6	0.8	8.1	10	1.4	13.6			
5/16—18	11	1.5	14.9	17	2.3	23.0	19	2.6	25.8
—24	13	1.8	17.6	19	2.6	25.7			
3/8—16	18	2.5	24.4	31	4.3	42.0	34	4.7	46.0
—24	20	2.75	27.1	35	4.8	47.5			
7/16—14	28	3.8	37.0	49	6.8	66.4	55	7.6	74.5
—20	30	4.2	40.7	55	7.6	74.5			
½—13	39	5.4	52.8	75	10.4	101.7	85	11.75	115.2
—20	41	5.7	55.6	85	11.7	115.2			
9/16—12	51	7.0	69.2	110	15.2	149.1	120	16.6	162.7
—18	55	7.6	74.5	120	16.6	162.7			
5/8—11	83	11.5	112.5	150	20.7	203.3	167	23.0	226.5
—18	95	13.1	128.8	170	23.5	230.5			
¾—10	105	14.5	142.3	270	37.3	366.0	280	38.7	379.6
—16	115	15.9	155.9	295	40.8	400.0			
7/8— 9	160	22.1	216.9	395	54.6	535.5	440	60.9	596.5
—14	175	24.2	237.2	435	60.1	589.7			
1— 8	236	32.5	318.6	590	81.6	799.9	660	91.3	894.8
—14	250	34.6	338.9	660	91.3	849.8			

Metric Bolts

Relative Strength Marking	4.6, 4.8			8.8		
Bolt Markings						
Bolt Size Thread Size x Pitch (mm)	**Maximum Torque**			**Maximum Torque**		
	Ft./Lbs.	Kgm	Nm	Ft./Lbs.	Kgm	Nm
6 x 1.0	2–3	.2–.4	3–4	3–6	.4–.8	5–8
8 x 1.25	6–8	.8–1	8–12	9–14	1.2–1.9	13–19
10 x 1.25	12–17	1.5–2.3	16–23	20–29	2.7–4.0	27–39
12 x 1.25	21–32	2.9–4.4	29–43	35–53	4.8–7.3	47–72
14 x 1.5	35–52	4.8–7.1	48–70	57–85	7.8–11.7	77–110
16 x 1.5	51–77	7.0–10.6	67–100	90–120	12.4–16.5	130–160
18 x 1.5	74–110	10.2–15.1	100–150	130–170	17.9–23.4	180–230
20 x 1.5	110–140	15.1–19.3	150–190	190–240	26.2–46.9	160–320
22 x 1.5	150–190	22.0–26.2	200–260	250–320	34.5–44.1	340–430
24 x 1.5	190–240	26.2–46.9	260–320	310–410	42.7–56.5	420–550

CHECKING ENGINE COMPRESSION

A noticeable lack of engine power, excessive oil consumption and/or poor fuel mileage measured over an extended period are all indicators of internal engine wear. Worn piston rings, scored or worn cylinder bores, blown head gaskets, sticking or burnt valves and worn valve seats are all possible culprits here. A check of each cylinder's compression will help you locate the problems.

As mentioned in the "Tools and Equipment" section of Chapter 1, a screw-in type compression gauge is more accurate than the type you simply hold against the spark plug hole, although it takes slightly longer to use. It's worth it to obtain a more accurate reading. Follow the procedures below for gasoline and diesel-engined cars.

Gasoline Engines

1. Warm up the engine to normal operating temperature.
2. Remove all spark plugs.

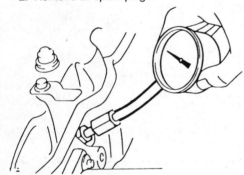

The screw-in type compression gauge is more accurate

3. Disconnect the high-tension lead from the ignition coil.
4. On carbureted cars, fully open the throttle either by operating the carburetor throttle linkage by hand or by having an assistant "floor" the accelerator pedal. On fuel-injected cars, disconnect the cold start valve and all injector connections.
5. Screw the compression gauge into the No. 1 spark plug hole until the fitting is snug.
   NOTE: *Be careful not to crossthread the plug hole. On aluminum cylinder heads use extra care, as the threads in these heads are easily ruined.*
6. Ask an assistant to depress the accelerator pedal fully on both carbureted and fuel-injected cars. Then, while you read the compression gauge, ask the assistant to crank the engine two or three times in short bursts using the ignition switch.

7. Read the compression gauge at the end of each series of cranks, and record the highest of these readings. Repeat this procedure for each of the engine's cylinders. Compare the highest reading of each cylinder to the compression pressure specifications in the "Tune-Up Specifications" chart in Chapter 2. The specs in this chart are maximum values.

A cylinder's compression pressure is usually acceptable if it is not less than 80% of maximum. The difference between each cylinder should be no more than 12–14 pounds.

8. If a cylinder is unusually low, pour a tablespoon of clean engine oil into the cylinder through the spark plug hole and repeat the compression test. If the compression comes up after adding the oil, it appears that that cylinder's piston rings or bore are damaged or worn. If the pressure remains low, the valves may not be seating properly (a valve job is needed), or the head gasket may be blown near that cylinder. If compression in any two adjacent cylinders is low, and if the addition of oil doesn't help the compression, there is leakage past the head gasket. Oil and coolant water in the combustion chamber can result from this problem. There may be evidence of water droplets on the engine dipstick when a head gasket has blown.

Diesel Engines

Checking cylinder compression on diesel engines is basically the same procedure as on gasoline engines except for the following:

1. A special compression gauge adaptor suitable for diesel engines (because these engines have much greater compression pressures) must be used.
2. Remove the injector tubes and remove the injectors from each cylinder.
   NOTE: *Don't forget to remove the washer underneath each injector; otherwise, it may get lost when the engine is cranked.*

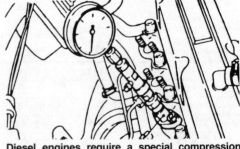

Diesel engines require a special compression gauge adaptor

3. When fitting the compression gauge adaptor to the cylinder head, make sure the bleeder of the gauge (if equipped) is closed.
4. When reinstalling the injector assemblies, install new washers underneath each injector.

transmission. Disconnect the back-up wiring.

29. Detach the driveshaft from the rear of the transmission.

NOTE: *If oil runs out of the transmission, an old U-joint yoke sleeve makes an excellent plug.*

30. Detach the clutch release cylinder assembly, complete with hydraulic lines. Do not disconnect the lines.

31. Unbolt the rear support member mounting insulators.

32. Support the transmission and detach the rear support member retaining bolts. Withdraw the support member from the car.

33. Install lifting hooks on the engine lifting brackets. Attach a suitable hoist to the engine.

34. Remove the jack from under the transmission.

35. Raise the engine and move it toward the front of the car. Use care to avoid damaging the components which remain on the car.

36. Support the engine in the reverse order of removal. Adjust all of the linkages as detailed in the appropriate section. Install the hood and adjust it. Replenish the fluid levels in the engine, radiator and transmission.

DIESEL ENGINE

1. Make accurate marks on the body to indicate the relationship between the hood supports and the body. Unbolt the hood support at the body and remove the hood.

2. Disconnect and remove both batteries from the vehicle.

CAUTION: *When draining the coolant, keep in mind that cats and dogs are attracted by the ethylene glycol antifreeze, and are quite likely to drink any that is left in an uncovered container or in puddles on the ground. This will prove fatal in sufficient quantity. Always drain the coolant into a sealable container. Coolant should be reused unless it is contaminated or several years old.*

3. Drain the cooling system and remove the radiator, shroud, and radiator hoses.

4. If the vehicle is equipped with air conditioning, remove the compressor drive belt, unbolt the compressor and tie the compressor out of the way. Do not disconnect the refrigerant lines from the compressor.

5. Remove the engine cooling fan, pulley, and drive belt.

6. Disconnect the two heater hoses from the left side of the engine.

7. Disconnect the vacuum reservoir hose from the rear of the alternator.

8. Disconnect the vacuum hose from the idle-up unit, if the vehicle is equipped with air conditioning.

9. Disconnect the fuel hoses from the fuel pump return connection and the sedimenter inlet connection.

10. Disconnect the wiring from the following components:
   a. Alternator
   b. Thermo-switch
   c. Oil preessure switch
   d. No.1 glow plug relay (terminal + B)
   e. Starter

Mark these wires and tie them out of the way.

11. Disconnect the wiring from the left fender and the injection pump (accelerator wire). Also mark and tie these wires out of the way.

12. Using Toyota special service tool #09305-20012 or its equivalent, remove the transmission lever from inside the vehicle.

13. Raise the vehicle and support it safely.

14. Drain the engine oil.

15. Remove the engine under cover and remove the backup light switch wire.

16. Remove the engine shock absorber.

17. Remove the propeller (drive) shaft from the vehicle. Mark the propeller shaft and the companion flange so that the shaft may be reinstalled in its original position.

18. Disconnect the speedometer cable from the transmission.

19. Disconnect the exhaust pipe clamp from the transmission housing and the exhaust pipe mounting nuts from the exhaust manifold.

20. Unbolt the clutch release cylinder and lay the cylinder alongside the frame.

21. Remove the engine mounting bolts from each side of the engine.

22. Place a jack under the transmission so that it just touches the transmission.

23. Unbolt the transmission mounting bracket from the transmission and the crossmember. Remove the bracket.

24. Attach the engine lifting equipment to the engine.

25. Check that all wiring and hoses air clear of the engine and transmission.

26. Carefully raise the engine and transmission assembly out of the engine compartment, being especially careful not to damage the air conditioning compressor, if so equipped.

27. Remove the starter, and with the help of an assistant, disconnect the transmission from the engine. Mount the engine securely in a workstand and service the engine as necessary, according to the appropriate sections of this book.

28. Reverse the previous steps to install the engine. Replenish the fluids in the engine, cooling system, and transmission if required.

Four Wheel Drive Pick-Ups

CAUTION: *Be sure to support the rear of the engine with a jack to avoid damage to the front motor mounts while performing engine removal procedures.*

1. Set the engine to top dead center according to the marks on the vibration damper and timing cover pointer.

2. Remove the transmission and transfer case according to the procedures found in the appropriate sections.

3. Make accurate marks on the body to indicate the relationship between the hood supports and the body. Unbolt the hood supports at the body and remove the hood.

4. Remove the battery and the air cleaner assembly. Mark the hoses from the air cleaner to simplify installation.

CAUTION: *When draining the coolant, keep in mind that cats and dogs are attracted by the ethylene glycol antifreeze, and are quite likely to drink any that is left in an uncovered container or in puddles on the ground. This will prove fatal in sufficient quantity. Always drain the coolant into a sealable container. Coolant should be reused unless it is contaminated or several years old.*

5. Drain the cooling system and remove the radiator hoses.

6. Remove the radiator fan shroud and disconnect the heater outlet hose at the radiator.

7. Remove the radiator.

8. If the vehicle is equipped with air conditioning, remove the compressor drive belt, unbolt the compressor and tie it out of the way. It is not necessary to disconnect the refrigerant lines.

9. Remove the water pump drive belt, pulley and cooling fan.

10. Disconnect the heater inlet hose, brake booster hose and emission control hoses. Move the hoses out of the way and tie if necessary. Mark the hose locations to simplify installation.

11. Disconnect the two fuel hoses from the pipes beneath the intake manifold.

12. Disconnect all wiring attached to the engine. Mark the wire locations to simplify installation.

13. Remove the high voltage wiring from the spark plugs, distributor and ignition coil. Be sure to mark the spark plug wire locations.

14. Disconnect the accelerator linkage at the carburetor.

15. Attach an engine hoist to the engine but do not raise the hoist.

16. Remove the two engine mount-to-frame bolts from each side of the engine.

17. Be sure that all wires and hoses are clear of the engine.

18. Carefully raise the engine out of the engine compartment, being especially careful not to damage the air conditioning condenser, if so equipped.

19. Securely mount the engine on a workstand.

20. Perform the necessary service(s) to the engine according to the appropriate sections of the book.

21. Reverse the previous steps to install the engine. Replenish the fluids in the engine, cooling system, and transmission.

Land Cruiser and Wagon

1. Scribe marks on the hood and hinges to aid in alignment during installation. Remove the hinge bolt from the hood and then remove the hood.

CAUTION: *When draining the coolant, keep in mind that cats and dogs are attracted by the ethylene glycol antifreeze, and are quite likely to drink any that is left in an uncovered container or in puddles on the ground. This will prove fatal in sufficient quantity. Always drain the coolant into a sealable container. Coolant should be reused unless it is contaminated or several years old.*

2. Drain the cooling system and engine oil.

3. Unfasten the radiator grille mounting bolts and remove the grille.

NOTE: *On station wagon models, remove the parking light assembly and wiring first.*

4. Remove the hood latch support rod. Detach the hood latch assembly from the radiator upper bracket. Remove the bracket.

5. Disconnect the heater hose from the radiator.

6. Detach the upper radiator hose at the water outlet housing and the lower hose at water pump.

7. Remove the six bolts which secure the radiator and lift the radiator out of the vehicle.

8. Remove the heater hoses from the water valve and heater box. Disconnect the temperature control cable from the water valve.

9. Detach both the battery cables and remove the battery.

10. Remove the wires from the starter solenoid terminal.

11. Detach the fuel lines from the pump and remove the fuel filter assembly.

12. Disconnect the primary wire from the ignition coil.

13. Detach both of the intermediate rods from the shifter shafts (column shift models only).

14. Remove the air cleaner assembly, complete with hoses, from its bracket.

15. Remove the emission control system cables and hoses as necessary.

16. Disconnect the alternator multiconnector.

17. Disconnect the hand throttle, accelerator, and choke linkage from the carburetor.

General Engine Specifications

Year	Engine Type	Engine Displacement Cu. In. (cc)	Carburetor Type	Horsepower (@ rpm) ▲	Torque @ rpm (ft. lbs.) ▲	Bore x Stroke (in.)	Compression Ratio	Oil Pressure @ rpm (psi)
1970–74	F	236.7 (3878)	2-bbl	135 @ 4000	213 @ 2000	3.54 x 4.00	7.8:1	60 @ 2000
1975–83	2F	257.9 (4200)	2-bbl	125 @ 3600	200 @ 1800	3.70 x 4.00	7.8:1	60 @ 2000
1970–71	8R-C	113.4 (1858)	2-bbl	108 @ 5500	113 @ 3800	3.38 x 3.15	9.0:1	56.9 @ 2500
1972–74	18R-C	123.0 (1980)	2-bbl	97 @ 5500	106 @ 3600	3.48 x 3.15	8.5:1	54.0 @ 2500
1975–78	20R	133.6 (2189)	2-bbl	95 @ 4800	122 @ 2400	3.48 x 3.50	8.4:1	64.0 @ 2500
1979–80	20R	133.6 (2189)	2-bbl	90 @ 4800	122 @ 2400	3.48 x 3.50	8.4:1	64.0 @ 2500
1981–85	22R 22R-E	156.4 ② (2563)	2-bbl ①	96 @ 4800	129 @ 2800	3.62 x 3.50	9.0:1	64.0 @ 2500
1981–85	Diesel	133.5 ③ (2188)	—	62 @ 4200	93 @ 2400	3.54 x 3.38	21.5:1	11.4 @ 700

▲ 1972 and later figures are SAE net ratings.
① 84–85 models may have Electronic Fuel Injection Systems.
② 84–85   144.4   ③ 84–85   149.3

Torque Specifications
All readings in ft. lbs.

Year	Engine Type	Engine Displacement Cu. In. (cc)	Cylinder Head Bolts	Rod Bearing Bolts	Main Bearing Bolts	Crankshaft Pulley Bolt	Flywheel-to-Crankshaft Bolts	Manifolds Intake	Manifolds Exhaust
1970–74	F	236.7 (3878)	83–98	35–55	90–108 ②	116–145	43–51	14–22 ①	
1975–83	2F	257.9 (4200)	83–98	35–55	90–108 ②	116–145	59–62	28–37	
1970–71	8R-C	113.4 (1858)	75.0–85.0	42.0–48.0	72.0–80.0	43.0–51.0	42.0–49.0	20.0–25.0 ①	
1972–74	18R-C	123.0 (1980)	72.0–82.0	39.0–48.0	69.0–83.0	43.0–51.0	51.0–58.0	30.0–35.0 ①	
1975–79	20R	133.6 (2189)	52.1–63.7	39.1–47.7	68.7–83.2	79.6–94.0	61.5–68.7	10.6	28.9–36.2
1980	20R	133.6 (2189)	53–63	40–47	69–83	120–130	73–86	13–19	29–36
1981–85	22R 22R-E	156.4 (2563)	53–63	40–47	69–83	120–130	73–86	13–19	29–36
1981–85	Diesel	133.5 (2188)	84–90	37–43	71–81	69–75	84–90	8–11	11–15

① Intake and exhaust manifolds combined
② Rear bearing: 76–94

Crankshaft and Connecting Rod Specifications

All measurements are given in inches

Year	Engine Type	Crankshaft				Connecting Rod		
		Main Brg Journal Dia	Main Brg Oil Clearance	Shaft End-Play	Thrust on No.	Journal Diameter	Oil Clearance	Side Clearance
1970–71	F	①	0.0012–0.0018	0.0024–0.0065	3	2.1252–2.1260	0.0008–0.0024	0.0040–0.0090
1972–74	F	①	0.0014–0.0018	0.0024–0.0065	3	2.1252–2.1260	0.0008–0.0024	0.0040–0.0090
1975–83	2F	②	0.0008–0.0017	0.0024–0.0063	3	2.1252–2.1260	0.0012–0.0028	0.0031–0.0079
1970–71	8R-C	2.3613–2.3622	0.0008–0.0020	0.0020–0.0100	3	2.0857–2.0866	0.0008–0.0020	0.004–3 0.0097
1972–74	18R-C	2.3613–2.3622	0.0008–0.0020	0.0008–0.0080	3	2.0857–2.0866	0.0010–0.0021	0.0060–0.0100
1975–80	20R	2.3614–2.3622	0.0010–0.0022	0.0007–0.0079	3	2.0862–2.0866	0.0010–0.0022	0.0063–0.0102
1981–85	22R	2.3614–2.3622	0.0006–0.0020	0.0008–0.0089	3	2.0862–2.0866	0.0008–0.0020	0.0008–0.0087
1981–85	Diesel	2.4402–2.4409	0.0012–0.0028	0.0016–0.0098	3	2.0858–2.0866	0.0012–0.0028	0.0031–0.0079

① #1: 2.6366–2.6378
　#2: 2.6957–2.6969
　#3: 2.7547–2.7559
　#4: 2.8138–2.8150

② #1: 2.6367–2.6376
　#2: 2.6957–2.6967
　#3: 2.7548–2.7557
　#4: 2.8139–2.8148

Piston and Ring Specifications

(All measurements in inches)

Year	Engine Type	Piston Clearance 68°F	Ring Gap			Ring Side Clearance (Ring to Land)		
			Top Compression	Bottom Compression	Oil Control	Top Compression	Bottom Compression	Oil Control
1970–71	F	0.0012–0.0020	0.006–0.016	0.006–0.016	②	0.0016–0.0031	0.0016–0.0031	①
1972–74	F	0.0012–0.0020	0.008–0.016	0.006–0.014	0.006–0.014	0.0012–0.0028	0.008–0.0024	0.0008–0.0026
1975–83	2F	0.0012–0.0020	0.008–0.016	0.008–0.016	snug	0.0012–0.0024	0.0008–0.0024	snug
1970–71	8R-C	0.0010–0.0020	0.004–0.012	0.004–0.012	0.004–0.012	0.0012–0.0028	0.0012–0.0028	0.0008–0.0028
1972–74	18R-C	0.0020–0.0030	0.004–0.012	0.004–0.012	0.004–0.012	0.0012–0.0028	0.0012–0.0028	0.0008–0.0028
1975–80	20R	0.0012–0.0020	0.004–0.012	0.004–0.012	0.004–0.012	0.0012–0.0028 ①	0.0012–0.0028 ①	snug
1981–85	22R 22R-E	0.0020–0.0028	0.0094–0.0142	0.0071–0.0154	snug	0.008	0.008	snug
1981–85	Diesel	0.0014–0.0022	0.008–0.0157	0.0118–0.0197	0.0118–0.0197	0.0024–0.0039	0.0016–0.0031	0.0012–0.0028

① Limit—0.008
② Top: 0.006–0.018
Bottom: 0.006–0.016
③ Top: 0.0016–0.0031
　Bottom: 0.0016–0.0033

Valve Specifications

Year	Engine Type	Seat Angle (deg)	Face Angle (deg)	Spring Test Pressure (lbs) ②		Spring Installed Height (in.)		Stem-to-Guide Clearance (in.) ▲		Stem Diameter (in.)	
				Inner	Outer	Inner	Outer	Intake	Exhaust	Intake	Exhaust
1970–71	F	45	45	—	150	—	1.324	0.0010–0.0026	0.0014–0.0028	0.3141	0.3137
1972–74	F	45	45	—	71.5	—	1.693	0.0010–0.0026	0.0014–0.0028	0.3141	0.3137
1975–83	2F	45	44.5	—	71.6	–	1.693	0.0012–0.0024	0.0016–0.0028	0.3140	0.3137
1970–74	8R-C and 18R-C	45	45	15.2	50.6	1.480	1.640	0.0010–0.0022	0.0014–0.0030	0.3140	0.3136
1975–77	20R	45	45	—	60 ①	—	1.594	0.0006–0.0024	0.0012–0.0026	0.3138–0.3144	0.3136–0.3142
1978–80	20R	45	44.5	—	55.1	—	1.594	0.0008–0.0024	0.0012–0.0026	0.3138–0.3136	0.3136–0.3142
1981–85	22R 22R-E	45 ③	44.5	—	55.1	—	1.594	0.0008–0.0024	0.0012–0.0026	0.3188–0.3145	0.3136–0.3142
1981–85	Diesel	45 ③	44.5	—	56	—	1.547	0.0008–0.0024	0.0016–0.0030	0.3340	0.0330

▲ Valve Guides Are Removable
① Limit—54 lbs.
② At installed height
③ Blend with 30′ & 60′ cuttens to center the 45° part on the valve face

18. On models equipped with vacuum assisted 4WD engagement, remove the control unit vacuum hose from its manifold fitting.

19. Disconnect the oil pressure and water temperature gauge sender's wiring.

20. Unfasten the downpipe from the exhaust manifold.

21. Detach the parking brake cable from the intermediate lever.

22. Unbolt the front driveshaft from the flange on the transfer case output shaft.

23. Remove both the left and right engine stone shields. Remove the transmission skidplate.

24. Remove the cotter pin and disconnect both the high- and low-range shifter link lever and the high/low shift rod.

25. Remove the high/low range shifter link lever and the high/low shift rod.

26. Disconnect the clutch release fork spring. Remove the clutch release cylinder from its mounting bracket at the rear of the engine.

27. Unfasten the clamp screws and withdraw the vacuum lines from the transfer case control unit vacuum chamber (only on models with vacuum assist 4WD engagement).

28. Remove the 4WD indicator switch assembly.

29. Unfasten the speedometer cable from the transmission.

30. Disconnect the rear driveshaft from the transmission.

31. Detach the gearshift rod and gear selector rod from the shift outer lever and the gear selector outer lever respectively.

32. Unbolt the rear engine mounts from the frame.

33. Perform Step 32 to the front engine mounts.

34. Install lifting hooks on the engine lift points and connect a hoist.

35. Lift the engine slightly and toward the front, so the engine/transmission assembly clears the front of the vehicle.

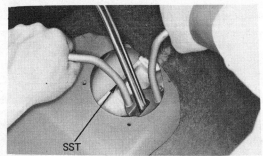

You should be able to remove the manual transmission shift lever with a pair of channel lock pliers, rather than the special service tool indicated here

Engine installation is performed in the reverse order of its removal. Refill the engine with coolant and lubricant. Check and adjust all linkages, as outlined in the appropriate section. Install the hood and align the matchmarks.

Water Pump

REMOVAL AND INSTALLATION

1. Drain the cooling system.

CAUTION: *When draining the coolant, keep in mind that cats and dogs are attracted by the ethylene glycol antifreeze, and are quite likely to drink any that is left in an uncovered container or in puddles on the ground. This will prove fatal in sufficient quantity. Always drain the coolant into a sealable container. Coolant should be reused unless it is contaminated or several years old.*

2. Remove the fan shroud.

3. Loosen the alternator adjusting link and remove the drive belt.

4. Remove the drive belt from the air pump if so equipped.

5. Remove the by-pass hose from the water pump.

6. Take the retaining bolts out of the water pump and remove the pump with the fan.

NOTE: *If the fan is equipped with a fluid coupling be careful not to tip the assembly as the fluid will spill out.*

7. Use a new gasket between the water pump and the block when installing the unit. Try not to get a lot of sealer behind the pump.

Thermostat

REMOVAL AND INSTALLATION

1. Partially drain the cooling system.

CAUTION: *When draining the coolant, keep*

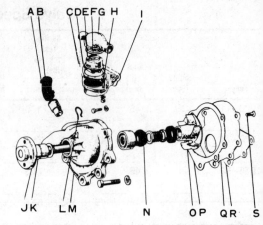

A. Hose clamp	K. Water pump bearing
B. By-pass hose	L. Bearing retaining win
C. Water outlet	M. Water pump body
D. Gasket	N. Shaft seal
E. Thermostat	O. Water pump rotor
F. Gasket	P. Gasket
G. Water outlet housing	Q. Seat plate
H. Stud bolt	R. Gasket
I. Gasket	S. Screw
J. Pulley seat	

F series engine water pump

in mind that cats and dogs are attracted b the ethelyne glycol antifreeze, and are qui likely to drink any that is left in an uncov ered container or in puddles on the ground This will prove fatal in sufficient quantity Always drain the coolant into a sealable cor tainer. Coolant should be reused unless it contaminated or several years old.

2. Unless the upper radiator hose is pos tioned over one of the thermostat housing (wate outlet) bolts, it is not necessary to detach th hose.

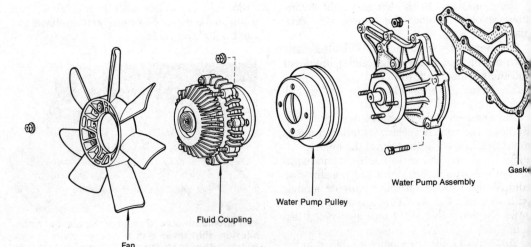

Fan

Fluid Coupling

Water Pump Pulley

Water Pump Assembly

Gask

Water pump for all exc. F series and diesel

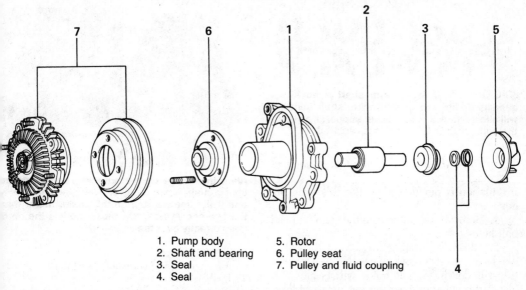

1. Pump body
2. Shaft and bearing
3. Seal
4. Seal
5. Rotor
6. Pulley seat
7. Pulley and fluid coupling

Diesel engine water pump

3. Remove the bolts and remove the water outlet.

4. When installing a new thermostat always use a new gasket. Be sure that the thermostat is positioned with the spring down. The factory recommended thermostat temperature is 180° for all engines.

Cylinder Head

REMOVAL AND INSTALLATION

3R-C and 18R-C

CAUTION: *Do not perform this operation on a warm engine.*

1. Disconnect the negative battery cable and drain the cooling system.

CAUTION: *When draining the coolant, keep in mind that cats and dogs are attracted by the ethelyne glycol antifreeze, and are quite likely to drink any that is left in an uncovered container or in puddles on the ground. This will prove fatal in sufficient quantity. Always drain the coolant into a sealable container. Coolant should be reused unless it is contaminated or several years old.*

2. Remove the air cleaner assembly.

3. Detach the throttle cable from its support on the cylinder head as well as the carburetor.

4. Remove the water hose bracket from the valve cover.

5. Remove any cooling system hoses which are in the way.

6. Disconnect the PCV hose from the valve cover.

7. Remove the vacuum lines from the distributor advance unit. Remove the lines which run from the vacuum switching valve to the various emission control systems on the engine.

8. Remove the fuel and vacuum lines from the carburetor.

9. Remove the automatic choke stove pipe.

10. Remove the spark plug wires. Remove the combination intake and exhaust manifold.

11. Remove the valve cover screws and the valve cover.

NOTE: *Be sure not to let anything fall into the timing case opening.*

12. Remove the thermostat housing complete with thermostat and upper radiator hose.

13. Remove the rocker arm assembly and oil delivery pipes.

CAUTION: *When loosening the bolts on the rocker arm assembly, loosen them in the order shown in the illustration. They should be removed gradually and evenly in three states. Reduce the torque on each bolt in sequence. Use a torque wrench!*

14. Remove the bolts securing the timing gear to the camshaft. Support the chain so that it does not fall inside the cover.

15. Remove the crankshaft bearing caps and remove the crankshaft.

NOTE: *Temporarily assemble the caps on their respective saddles. Keep the bearings in their proper order. These parts must be reassembled in their original order!*

16. Loosen the cylinder head bolts in three stages in the sequence illustrated. Lift the cylinder head off the block.

NOTE: *Do not attempt to slide the cylinder head as it is positioned with dowels. Never*

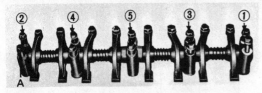

8R-C and 18R-C rocker arm shaft removal sequence. Pulling out of the rocker shaft bolts (A) will allow removal of the rocker supports, so leave the bolts in place unless this is required

Align the marks on the sprocket, camshaft and timing chain. Some early 8R-C engines have only one white line painted on the chain, rather than the two shown here. On those models the mark goes directly over the dowel pin

pry under the head with any tool as you will damage the surface.

Installation is performed in the following order:

1. Remove any water from the cylinder head bolt holes.

2. Clean the mating surfaces of the cylinder head and the block. Coat the area around the cylinder head bolt holes with sealer and install the cylinder head gasket on the block. Be certain that all the oil and coolant holes are open and not covered by some part of the gasket.

3. Lower, do not attempt to slide, the cylinder head onto the block.

4. Clean the threads of the cylinder head bolts thoroughly and give them a light coat of oil. Insert all of the bolts and tighten them in three or four stages to 75–85 ft. lb.

CAUTION: *The head bolts must be tightened in the proper sequence and they must be tightened in several stages. Not following this procedure exactly will result in damage to the cylinder head.*

5. Install each camshaft bearing lower half into the saddle from which it was removed. Coat the bearing surface with oil. Place the camshaft into the cylinder head. Then insert each camshaft upper bearing half into the bearing cap from which it was removed and install the bearing caps on the saddles.

CAUTION: *It cannot be overemphasized that the parts must be replaced in their original positions. Damage to the camshaft bearing surfaces and the entire valve train may result otherwise.*

6. Tighten the camshaft bearing caps to 12–17 ft. lb.

7. In order to reestablish the correct engine timing it is necessary to align three timing marks located on the timing chain, timing sprocket, and the camshaft. Crank the engine until the No. 1 cylinder is at top dead center of the compression stroke. The mark on the timing chain must align with the dowel hole on the camshaft timing gear and the mark on the camshaft must align with the same dowel hole on the sprocket. When the marks have been aligned in this manner, install the timing gear on the camshaft.

NOTE: *All three marks should align so that they are facing upward.*

8. Install the rocker arm assembly and tighten the attaching bolts to 12–17 ft. lb. according to the sequence illustrated.

NOTE: *Be sure that you tighten the bolts in several stages thus avoiding damage to the assembly.*

9. Install the oil delivery pipe.

10. Install all other external components removed to gain access to the cylinder head.

11. Adjust the valves as outlined in Chapter

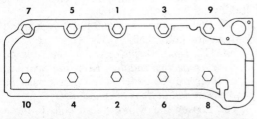

Tightening sequence for 8R-C and 18R-C cylinder head bolts. Tighten to specified torque in three passes. Loosen the bolts in the reverse of the order shown here, in two passes

8R-C and 18R-C rocker arm shaft tightening sequence

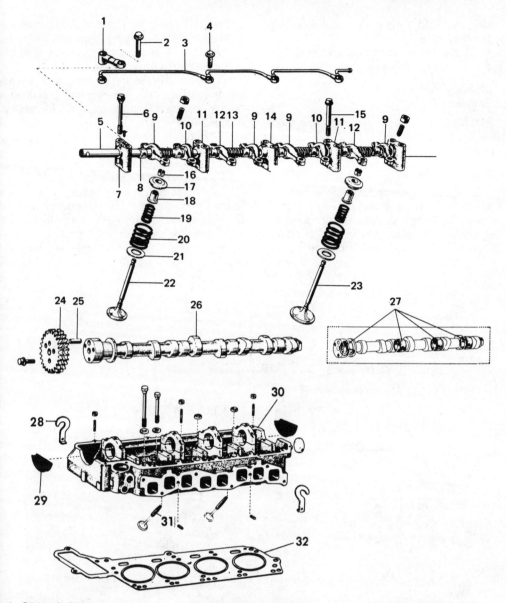

1. Oil banjo fitting
2. Bolt
3. Oil pipe assembly
4. Bolt
5. Valve rocker shaft
6. Bolt
7. Valve rocker support type #1
8. Bushing
9. Rocker arm type #1
10. Rocker arm type #2
11. Valve rocker support type #2
12. Rocker arm type #3
13. Spring
14. Valve rocker support type #3
15. Bolt
16. Valve keeper
17. Spring retainer
18. Valve stem oil seal
19. Inner valve spring
20. Outer valve spring
21. Spring seat
22. Exhaust valve
23. Intake valve
24. Camshaft sprocket
25. Dowel pin
26. Camshaft
27. Camshaft bearing set
28. Engine lifting hook
29. Half circle cam seal
30. Cylinder head
31. Valve guide
32. Head gasket

8R-C and 18R-C cylinder head components

2, using the cold valves from the Tune-Up Specifications chart.

CAUTION: *Do not start the engine until the valves have been adjusted properly.*

20R Engines

CAUTION: *Do not perform this operation on a warm engine.*

1. Disconnect the battery, negative cable first.

2. Remove the three exhaust pipe flange nuts and separate the pipe from the manifold.

CAUTION: *When draining the coolant, keep in mind that cats and dogs are attracted by the ethelyne glycol antifreeze, and are quite likely to drink any that is left in an uncovered container or in puddles on the ground.*

This will prove fatal in sufficient quantity. Always drain the coolant into a sealable container. Coolant should be reused unless it is contaminated or several years old.

3. Drain the cooling system, both the radiator and the block. The engine block drain is on the driver's side of the engine. The coolant, if good, may be reused.

4. Remove the air cleaner assembly complete with hoses, from the carburetor.

NOTE: *Cover the carburetor with a clean cloth so that nothing can fall into it.*

5. Tag all the various vacuum and emission hoses for reassembly and disconnect them at the engine or carburetor. Remove all linkages, fuel lines, coolant lines, etc., from the carburetor, cylinder head and manifolds. Remove the wire supports.

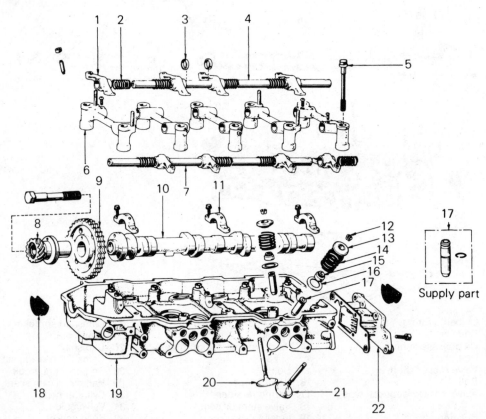

1. Rocker arm
2. Spring
3. Spacer
4. Rocker shaft (intake)
5. Head bolt
6. Rocker stand
7. Rocker shaft (exhaust)
8. Distributor drive gear
9. Cam sprocket
10. Camshaft
11. Camshaft bearing cap
12. Valve keeper
13. Spring retainer
14. Valve spring
15. Valve seal
16. Spring seat
17. Valve guide
18. Half circle cam seal
19. Cylinder head
20. Intake valve
21. Exhaust valve
22. Rear cover (EGR cooler)

Supply part

20R, 22R and 22R-E cylinder head components

6. Mark the spark plug leads and disconnect them from the plugs.

7. Matchmark the distributor housing and the engine block. Disconnect the high tension wire and the primary lead and remove the distributor. Installation will be easier if you leave the cap and spark plug wires in place.

8. Remove the four nuts which secure the valve cover.

9. Remove the rubber half circle cam seals. Remove the cam sprocket bolt. Slide the distributor drive gear off the camshaft and wire the cam sprocket in place to the timing chain.

10. Remove the timing chain cover bolt at the front of the head. This must be done before the head bolts are loosened.

11. Remove the cylinder head bolts in the order shown. Note that the numerical order in the illustration is for tightening, and must be reversed for loosening. Loosen the bolts in two or three stages.

NOTE: *Improper removal of the cylinder head bolts can cause head warpage.*

12. Using pry bars applied evenly at the front and rear of the valve rocker assembly, pry the assembly off its mounting dowels.

13. Lift the head straight up off its dowels. Do NOT pry it off, or attempt to slide it off.

14. Drain the engine oil from the crankcase after the head has been removed, because the oil will become contaminated with coolant when the head is removed.

Installation is as follows:

1. Clean off the top of the cylinder block and the head, using a scraper or a razor blade. Be careful not to gouge the aluminum head. You may also want to clean off the tops of the pistons, but as this requires rotation of the crankshaft, you must be careful to keep sufficient tension on the cam chain to prevent it from slipping a tooth. Vacuum out any bits which have fallen into the cylinders, being careful not to nick the cylinder walls.

2. Apply a liquid sealer to the front corners of the block and install a new head gasket.

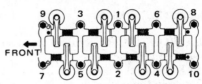

20R, 22R and 22R-E head bolt tightening sequence

3. Lower the head over the locating dowels. Do not attempt to slide it into place.

4. Rotate the camshaft so that the sprocket aligning pin is at the top. Remove the wire and hold the cam sprocket tight against the chain. Manually rotate the engine so that the cam sprocket hole is also at the top. Wire the sprocket in place again.

5. Install the rocker arm assembly over its positioning dowels.

6. Clean the threads of the cylinder head bolts thoroughly and give them a light coat of oil. Install them and tighten evenly, in three stages, in the sequence shown. Torque them to 52–63 ft. lb.

7. Install the timing chain cover bolt and tighten it to 7–12 ft. lb.

8. Remove the wire and fit the sprocket over the camshaft dowel. If the chain won't allow the sprocket to reach, rotate the crankshaft back and forth, while lifting up on the chain and sprocket.

9. Install the distributor drive gear and tighten the sprocket bolt to 51–65 ft. lb.

10. Adjust the valves as outlined earlier. After completing the adjustment, rotate the crankshaft 352°, so that the 8° BTDC mark on the pulley aligns with the timing mark on the block.

11. Install the distributor, as outlined earlier.

12. Install the spark plugs and leads.

13. Make sure the oil drain plug is installed. Install the rubber half circle cam seals and fill the engine with oil. Pour the oil over the top of the head, onto the distributor drive gear and the valve rockers.

14. Install the rocker cover and tighten the nuts to 7–12 ft. lb.

15. Connect all the vacuum hoses and electrical leads which are removed during disassembly. Reconnect the fuel line. Install the spark plug lead clips onto the rocker cover. Fill the cooling system. Install the air cleaner.

16. Tighten the exhaust pipe manifold nuts to 25–33 ft. lb.

17. Reconnect the battery, negative cable last. Start the engine and allow it to reach normal operating temperature. Check the timing and adjust the idle speed and mixture. Shut off the engine and reset the valves.

Rotate the 20R, 22R and 22R-E camshaft so that the pin is at the top

22R-E and 22R Engines

CAUTION: *Do not perform this operation on a warm engine.*

1. Disconnect the negative battery cable.
2. Drain the coolant from the radiator and the engine block.

CAUTION: *When draining the coolant, keep in mind that cats and dogs are attracted by the ethelyne glycol antifreeze, and are quite likely to drink any that is left in an uncovered container or in puddles on the ground. This will prove fatal in sufficient quantity. Always drain the coolant into a sealable container. Coolant should be reused unless it is contaminated or several years old.*

3. Drain the engine oil.
4. Remove the air cleaner hose.
5. Disconnect the exhaust pipe from the exhaust manifold. Disconnect the Ox sensor wire. Then remove the three nuts holding the exhaust manifold to the exhaust pipe.
6. Disconnect the upper radiator hose from the thermostat housing.
7. Disconnect the two heater hoses.
8. Disconnect the accelerator cable and the throttle cable (for the automatic transmission) from the bracket.
9. Disconnect the following parts on the 22R-E.
 a. PCV hoses No. 1 and No. 2.
 b. Brake booster hose.
 c. Air control valve hoses.
 d. EVAP hose from canister.
 e. Actuator hose (if equipped with cruise control).
 f. EGR vacuum modulator hose.
 g. Air valve hose No. 1 from the throttle body.
 h. Air valve hose No. 2 from the chamber.
 i. Water bypass hoses No. 2 and No. 3 from the throttle body.
 j. Air control valve from actuator.
 k. Pressure regulator hose from the chamber.
 l. Cold start injection pipe.
 m. BVSV hoses.
10. Disconnect the following parts on the 22-R.
 a. Charcoal canister hose.
 b. Brake booster hose.
 c. Fuel main hose from the fuel inlet pipe.
 d. Fuel return hose from the fuel return pipe.
 e. HAC from the bracket (Exc. Calif.).
 f. Vacuum switch, EBCV (For Calif.) and VSV with the bracket.
11. Disconnect the following wires.
 a. Cold start injection wire.
 b. Throttle position wire.
 c. Air valve wire.
12. Remove the bolt holding the EGR valve to the chamber.
 a. Disconnect the chamber and retainer.
 b. Remove the bolts and nuts holding the chamber to the intake manifold.
 c. Remove the chamber with the throttle body.
13. Disconnect and mark the following wires
 a. Water temperature sender gauge wire.
 b. Temperature sensor wire.
 c. Start ignition time switch wire.
 d. Overdrive thermo switch wire (with automatic transmission).
 e. Injection wires.
14. Remove the pulsation damper. Remove the bolt holding the fuel hose to the delivery pipe and disconnect the fuel hose.
15. Disconnect the No. 4 bypass hose and remove the air valve from the intake manifold.
16. Disconnect the bypass hose from the intake manifold.
17. Remove the distributor and the spark plugs.
18. Disconnect the bond cable from the vane pump bracket.
19. Disconnect the vacuum hose from the air control valve. Loosen and remove the drive belt. Then move the vane pump to one side without disconnecting the hoses.

NOTE: *If the vehicle has power steering, remove the vane pump with the bracket.*

20. Remove the bond cable from the body. Remove the four nuts and seals. Then remove the head cover.

NOTE: *Cover the oil return hole with a rag to prevent objects from falling in.*

21. Turn the crankshaft until the No. 1 cylinder position is set at T.D.C. compression. Place matchmarks on the sprocket and the chain. Remove the semicircular plug and the cam sprocket bolt.
22. Remove the distributor drive gear and fuel pump drive cam (22R) or the camshaft thrust plate (22R-E).
23. Remove the cam sprocket and chain from the camshaft. DO NOT REMOVE THE VIBRATION DAMPER.
24. Remove the bolt at the front of the head before the other head bolts are removed.
25. Carefully remove the head bolts in the proper sequence.

CAUTION: *Head warpage or cracking could result from removing in incorrect order.*

26. Remove the rocker arm assembly by applying pressure to the front and rear simultaneously with pry bars.
27. Remove the cylinder head.

CAUTION: *Be careful not to damage the cylinder head or the block surface.*

28. Installation is the reverse of the removal procedure.

Diesel Engine

1. Disconnect the cables from both batteries.

2. Remove the air cleaner assembly.

3. Drain the cooling system and remove the radiator, shroud, and radiator hoses.

CAUTION: *When draining the coolant, keep in mind that cats and dogs are attracted by the ethelyne glycol antifreeze, and are quite likely to drink any that is left in an uncovered container or in puddles on the ground. This will prove fatal in sufficient quantity. Always drain the coolant into a sealable container. Coolant should be reused unless it is contaminated or several years old.*

4. If the vehicle is equipped with air conditioning, remove the compressor drive belt and unbolt the compressor from its mounting

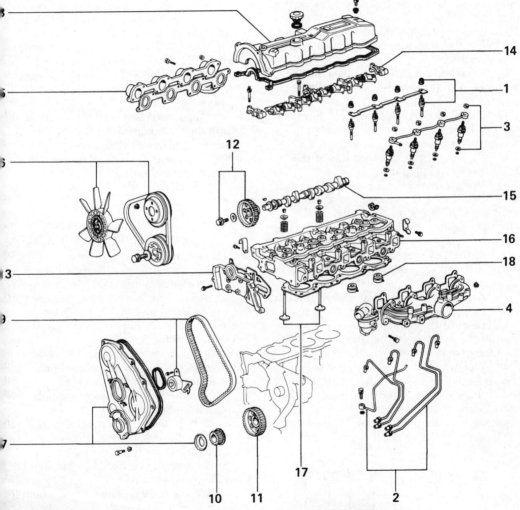

1. Glow plug
2. Injection pipe and fuel pipe
3. Injection nozzle holder and linkage pipe
4. Intake manifold
5. Exhaust manifold
6. Fan, fan pulley and crankshaft pulley
7. Timing gear cover and belt guide
8. Cylinder head cover
9. Idle pulley and timing belt

10. Crankshaft timing pulley
11. Pump drive pulley
12. Camshaft timing pulley
13. No. 2 oil seal retainer
14. Valve rocker shaft assembly
15. Camshaft
16. Cylinder head
17. Valve and compression spring
18. Combustion chamber subassembly

Diesel cylinder head

brackets. Tie the compressor out of the way. Do not remove the refrigerant lines.

5. Remove the engine cooling fan, pulley, and drive belt.

6. Disconnect the heater hoses at the engine and move the hoses aside.

7. Disconnect the cables which are positioned above the valve cover and move the cables aside.

8. Remove the valve cover and upper front engine cover.

9. Disconnect and remove the glow plugs.

10. Disconnect the fuel injection lines at the injectors and the injection pump. Remove the lines.

11. Remove the fuel injectors. Arrange the injectors so that they may be reinstalled in their original locations.

12. Unbolt and remove the intake manifold assembly. Also remove the water outlet housing from the cylinder head.

13. Unbolt the exhaust manifold from the cylinder head. Secure the manifold in a position away from the cylinder head.

14. Disconnect the fuel feed line at the injection pump and plug the line.

15. Using a wrench on the center crankshaft pulley bolt, rotate the engine (clockwise only) until the TDC mark on the pulley is aligned with the pointer. Check that the valves on the number one cylinder are closed (rocker arms loose). If the valves are not closed, rotate the engine 360° and again align the TDC mark with the pointer.

16. Remove the crankshaft pulley using a puller.

17. Remove the timing belt cover from the front of the engine and the timing belt guide from the front of the crankshaft timing gear.

18. Remove the timing belt idler pulley. If the timing belt is to be reused, mark the belt and all timing gears to indicate their relationships. Remove the timing belt.

19. Remove the timing gear from the camshaft, using a puller.

20. Remove the camshaft oil seal retainer.

21. Gradually loosen the rocker shaft support nuts, working from the ends towards the center. Remove the rocker shaft and arms as an assembly.

22. Gradually remove the cylinder head bolts in the reverse order of the installation torque sequence.

23. Remove the cylinder head from the engine.

24. Installation of the cylinder head is basically the reverse of the previous steps. Note the following points.

   a. Clean the mating surfaces of the cylinder block and head, and use a NEW head gasket during installation.

   b. DO NOT rotate the engine while the cylinder head is removed.

   c. Torque the cylinder head bolts gradually, following the head bolt tightening sequence.

   d. Align the timing marks according to the illustration accompanying the Timing Belt Removal and Installation procedure.

   e. Replenish the cooling system with the proper type and quantity of coolant.

   f. Check for leaks after the engine has been started.

2F Engine

1. Disconnect the battery and drain the cooling system.

CAUTION: *When draining the coolant, keep in mind that cats and dogs are attracted by the ethelyne glycol antifreeze, and are quite likely to drink any that is left in an uncovered container or in puddles on the ground. This will prove fatal in sufficient quantity. Always drain the coolant into a sealable container. Coolant should be reused unless it is contaminated or several years old.*

2. Remove the air cleaner assembly from its bracket, complete with its attendant hoses.

3. Detach the accelerator cable from its support on the cylinder head cover and also from the carburetor throttle arm.

4. Remove the choke cable and fuel lines from the carburetor.

5. Remove the water hose bracket from the cylinder head cover.

6. Unfasten the water hose clamps and remove the hoses from the water pump and the water valve. Detach the heater temperature control cable from the water valve.

7. Disconnect the PCV line from the cylinder head cover.

8. Disconnect the vacuum lines, which run from the vacuum switching valve, at the various components of the emission control system.

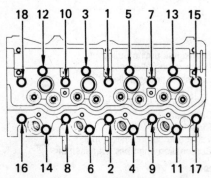

Diesel engine head bolt tightening sequence

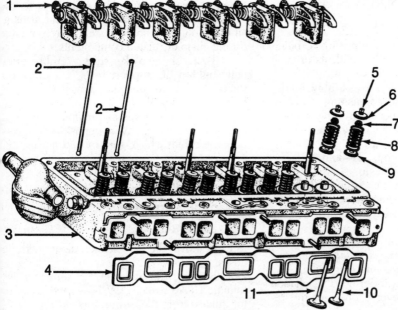

1. Rocker arm and shaft assembly
2. Pushrods
3. Cylinder head
4. Intake and exhaust manifold gasket
5. Valve keepers
6. Valve spring retainer
7. Valve seal
8. Valve spring
9. Valve spring seat
10. Exhaust valve
11. Intake valve

F series cylinder head

9. Drain the engine oil. Unfasten the oil lines from the oil filter and remove the filter assembly from the manifold.

10. Detach the vacuum valve solenoid wire from the coil.

11. Disconnect any remaining lines from the carburetor and remove the carburetor from the manifold.

12. Unfasten the alternator adjusting link and then remove the drive belt and the alternator.

13. Disconnect the distributor vacuum line from the distributor. Remove the wire from its supports on the head.

14. Disconnect the carburetor fuel line from the fuel pump. Remove the line.

15. Disconnect the spark plug and coil cables, after marking their respective locations.

16. Unfasten the primary wire from the distributor. Remove the distributor clamp bolts and withdraw the distributor.

17. Remove the oil gauge sending unit.

18. Remove the coil from its bracket on the cylinder head.

19. Remove the fuel pump.

20. Remove the oil filter tube clamping bolt from the valve lifter (side) cover. Drive the oil filler tube out of the cylinder block.

21. Remove the combination intake/exhaust manifold from the cylinder block.

22. Take off the cylinder head cover and its gasket.

23. Unfasten the oil delivery union, spring, and sleeve from the valve rocker shafts.

24. Unfasten the securing nuts and bolts from the valve rocker shaft supports. Withdraw the rocker assembly.

25. Withdraw the pushrods from their bores. Be sure to keep them in the same order in which they were removed.

26. Remove the valve lifter (side) cover and gasket.

27. Withdraw the valve lifters from the block. NOTE: *The valve lifters should be kept, with their respective pushrods, in the sequence in which they were removed.*

28. Unfasten the oil delivery union from the oil feed pipe.

29. Loosen the cylinder head bolts in two or three stages and in the order illustrated above.

30. Lift off the cylinder head and the gasket.
Installation of the cylinder head is performed in the following order:

1. Clean the gasket mounting surfaces of both the cylinder head and block.

2. Place a new head gasket over the dowels on the block.

3. Lower the cylinder head on to the block.

4. Tighten the bolts, in stages, and in the sequence illustrated, to the specified torque.

5. Install the oil feed pipe.

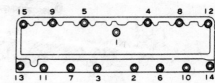

F series cylinder head bolt tightening sequence

6. Place each valve lifter in the original position from which it came.

NOTE: *Do not interchange valve lifters.*

7. Perform step 6 for the pushrods, being careful to mate each pushrod with its original lifter.

8. Install the valve rocker assembly, oil delivery union, spring and connecting sleeve in the head. Tighten the rocker assembly support nuts and bolts to the following torque specifications, in several stages:

- 10mm nuts and bolts: 24–30 ft. lb.
- 8mm bolts: 14–22 ft. lb.

9. Adjust the valves, as outlined above, to the following cold specifications (each piston TDC of its compression stroke):

- Intake: 0.008 in.
- Exhaust: 0.014 in.

NOTE: *Adjust the valve clearance again after the engine is assembled and warmed up.*

10. The rest of the cylinder head installation is performed in the reverse order of the removal procedure.

Valve Rocker Shafts
REMOVAL AND INSTALLATION
Gasoline Engines

Valve rocker shaft removal and installation is given as part of the cylinder head removal and installation procedure. Perform only the steps of the appropriate procedure necessary to remove or install the rocker shafts.

Note that on the 20R, 22R and the 22R-E engines all rocker arms are the same, but all rocker stands are different. If the parts are disassembled on any of the engines, they must be put back together in exactly the same order as removed. Lubricate all parts with engine oil before assembly.

Diesel Engine

1. Disconnect the cables which are positioned above the valve cover and move the cables aside.

2. Remove the valve cover.

3. Gradually loosen the rocker shaft support fasteners, working from the ends towards the center. Remove the rocker shaft and arms as an assembly. It is not necessary to remove the timing chain or related components.

4. To install the rocker shaft assembly, gradually tighten the support bolts, working from the center towards the ends. Finally tighten the bolts to 11–15 ft. lb.

5. Adjust the valves as previously outlined and install the valve cover. Reposition and connect the cables which were moved during step 1.

Intake and Exhaust Manifolds
REMOVAL AND INSTALLATION
8R-C and 18R-C

1. Remove the air cleaner along with its hoses.

2. Remove the fuel line, vacuum line, automatic choke stove, PCV hose, and accelerator linkage from the carburetor.

3. Remove the carburetor from the manifold.

4. Use a jack to raise the front end of the truck and support it firmly on jackstands.

5. Remove the exhaust pipe from the manifold.

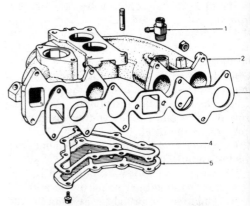

1. Vacuum fitting 4. Gasket
2. Intake manifold 5. Cover
3. Gasket

20R intake manifold components, 22R similar

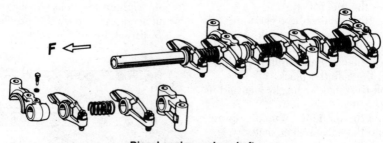

Diesel engine rocker shaft

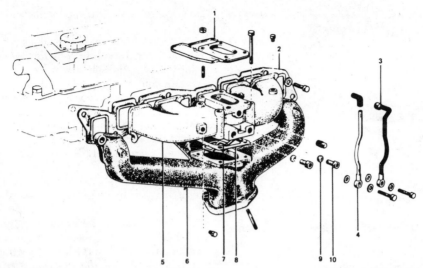

1. Heat insulator
2. Manifold gasket (manifold-to-head)
3. Choke stove outlet pipe
4. Choke stove intake pipe
5. Intake manifold
6. Exhaust manifold
7. Choke stove pipe
8. Manifold gasket (intake-to-exhaust)
9. Sleeve
10. Union

Manifold components—8R-C and 18R-C

6. Remove the manifold bolts. To do this correctly you should start with the bolts at the center of the manifold and gradually loosen the bolts in three stages. Undue stress will be placed on the manifold if one bolt is completely removed while another remains installed at its maximum strength.

7. Always use new gaskets when installing the manifold. Tighten the bolts to 20–25 ft. lb. and be sure to increase torque in states working from the center.

20R, 22R and 22R-E Intake Manifold

1. Disconnect the battery, negative cable first.

2. Drain the cooling system.

CAUTION: *When draining the coolant, keep in mind that cats and dogs are attracted by the ethelyne glycol antifreeze, and are quite likely to drink any that is left in an uncovered container or in puddles on the ground. This will prove fatal in sufficient quantity. Always drain the coolant into a sealable container. Coolant should be reused unless it is contaminated or several years old.*

3. Remove the air cleaner assembly, complete with hoses.

4. Disconnect the vacuum lines from the EGR valve and the carburetor. Tag them for assembly.

5. Remove the fuel line, accelerator linkage, electrical leads, and coolant hose from the carburetor.

6. Remove the coolant bypass hose from the manifold.

7. Unbolt and remove the intake manifold, complete with carburetor and EGR valve.

8. Cover the cylinder head intake ports with a clean cloth.

9. Installation is the reverse of the removal. Use a new gasket, and torque the mounting nuts to 11–15 ft. lb. Tighten the bolts in several stages, working from the inside bolts outward. Refill the cooling system.

20R, 22R and 22R-E Exhaust Manifold

CAUTION: *Do not perform this operation on a warm or hot engine.*

1. Remove the three exhaust pipe-to-manifold nuts and disconnect the pipe.

2. Remove the hot air intake tube from the heat stove. Remove the outer part of the heat stove.

3. Remove the manifold nuts.

4. Remove the exhaust manifold, complete with air injection tubes and the inner portion of the heat stove. It may be necessary to remove the heater hose that plugs into the driver's side of the firewall to provide space to remove the manifold. In this case the cooling system will have to be drained.

CAUTION: *When draining the coolant, keep in mind that cats and dogs are attracted by the ethelyne glycol antifreeze, and are quite likely to drink any that is left in an uncovered container or in puddles on the ground. This will prove fatal in sufficient quantity. Always drain the coolant into a sealable container. Coolant should be reused unless it is contaminated or several years old.*

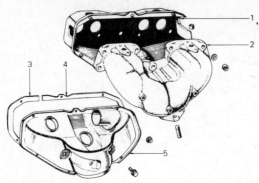

1. Inner heat stove
2. Exhaust manifold
3. Gasket
4. Gasket
5. Outer heat stove

20R, 22R and 22R-E exhaust manifold components

5. Installation is the reverse of removal. Tighten the nuts to 29–36 ft. lb., working from the inside out, and in several stages. Tighten the exhaust pipe nuts to 30–36 ft. lb.

Combination Manifold

REMOVAL AND INSTALLATION

2F Engine

1. Remove the air cleaner assembly, complete with hoses.
2. Disconnect the accelerator and choke linkages from the carburetor, as well as the fuel and vacuum lines. Remove the hand throttle linkage.
3. Remove, or move aside, any of the emission control system components which are in the way.
4. Disconnect the oil filter lines and remove the oil filter assembly from the intake manifold. Unfasten the solenoid valve wire from the ignition coil terminal. Remove the EGR pipes from the exhaust gas cooler, if so equipped.
5. Unfasten the retaining bolts and remove the carburetor from the manifold.
6. Loosen the manifold retaining nuts, working from the inside out, in two or three stages.
7. Remove the intake/exhaust manifold assembly from the cylinder head as a complete unit.
8. Installation is performed in the reverse order of removal. Always use new gaskets. Tighten the bolts, working from the inside out.

NOTE: *Tighten the bolts in two or three stages.*

Diesel Manifolds

Removal of the intake manifold of the diesel engine requires removal of the air cleaner assembly, injection lines, and related hoses and bracketry. If you are in doubt during the disconnection of any item, be sure to mark the item so that it may be properly reinstalled. Before installing the manifold, be sure to clean the cylinder head and manifold mating surfaces of the old gasket material, and use a new gasket when installing the manifold.

The exhaust manifold is retained to the cylinder head with eight fasteners. Disconnect the

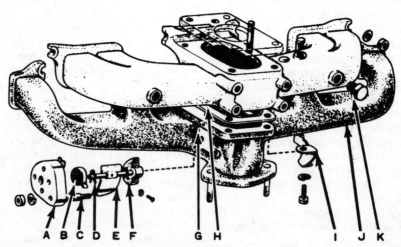

a. Heat control valve bimetal case
b. Valve coil
c. Bolt
d. Retaining spring
e. Heat control valve
f. Heat control valve shaft
g. Dowel
h. Manifold gasket
i. Counter weight stop
j. Exhaust manifold
k. Screw plug

F series combination manifold

exhaust pipe from the manifold and remove these fasteners. Disconnect the exhaust pipe from the manifold and remove these fasteners to remove the exhaust manifold. On models with air conditioning, it may be necessary to remove the air conditioning compressor from the mounting bracket (without disconnecting the refrigerant lines) and tie the compressor out of the way. Also remove the compressor mounting bracket(s) if interference is encountered. Be sure that the manifold and cylinder head mating surfaces are clean, and install a new exhaust manifold gasket during manifold installation.

Refer to the torque specifications listed at the beginning of this section to determine the required tightening torque of the fasteners.

Oil Pan
REMOVAL AND INSTALLATION
Pick-Ups and 4Runner

1. Raise the hood and leave it open for the duration of this repair.
2. Drain the engine oil.
3. Raise the front end of the truck and support it on jackstands.
4. Remove the steering relay rod and the tie rods from the idler arm, pitman arm, and steering knuckles as outlined in Chapter 8.
5. Remove the engine stiffening plates.
6. Remove the splash pans from under the engine.
7. Support the front of the engine with a jack and remove the front motor mount attaching bolts.
8. Raise the front of the engine slightly with the jack.
9. Remove the oil pan bolts and remove the oil pan.
10. The installation process is the reverse of removal. Apply gasket sealer to the oil pan when installing a new gasket. The oil pan bolts should be tightened to 3–5 ft. lb., 8R-C and 18R-C engines; 33–70 in.lb. for 20R engines. Tighten the bolts in a circular pattern, starting in the middle of the pan and working out towards the ends.

Land Cruiser

1. Remove the engine skid plates.
2. Remove the flywheel side cover and skid plate.
3. Disconnect the front driveshaft from the engine.
4. Drain the engine oil.
5. Remove the bolts which secure the oil pan. Remove the pan and its gasket.
6. Installation is performed in the reverse order from removal. Always use a new pan gasket.

Timing Chain Cover
REMOVAL AND INSTALLATION
8R-C, 18R-C, 20R, 22R and 22R-E

1. Remove the cylinder head.
2. After draining oil, remove the oil pan and its gasket.
3. Remove the radiator.
4. Remove the fan and drive belts.
5. Remove the air pump, hoses, and bracket, if so equipped.
6. On 8R-C and 18R-C engines, remove the alternator and its bracket. Tag the wires for assembly. On 20R, 22R and 22R-E engines remove the alternator adjuster bracket and move it towards the alternator.
7. On 8R-C and 18R-C engines only remove the fan and water pump as an assembly.
NOTE: *To prevent the fluid from running out of the fan coupling, do not tip the unit on its side.*
8. Remove the center bolt on the crankshaft pulley. Using a gear puller, remove the crankshaft pulley.
NOTE: *Do not remove the 10mm bolt from the hole in the pulley, if present. It has been installed to correctly balance the engine.*
9. On 8R-C and 18R-C engines, remove the cover. On 20R, 22R and 22R-E engines, remove the 2 water bypass tube bolts, the one bolt at the rear of the cover on the left side (behind the coolant inlet pipe), and the six bolts on the front of the timing cover. Gently tap the timing cover off with a plastic faced hammer. If removal is difficult, there is probably a bolt still in place.
10. When installing, use a new gasket on the timing cover and oil pan. Use sealer at the corners of the oil pan. Tighten the timing cover bolts to 11–15 ft. lb. on 8R-C and 18R-C engines, 7–12 ft. lb. on 20R, 22R and 22R-E engines. Tighten the oil pan bolts to 35–70 in.lb.
11. Install the crankshaft pulley. On 8R-C and 18R-C engines, it will probably have to be

Remove the six bolts indicated on the 20R & 22R engines

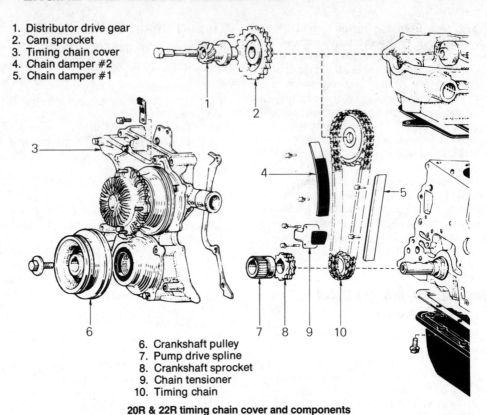

1. Distributor drive gear
2. Cam sprocket
3. Timing chain cover
4. Chain damper #2
5. Chain damper #1

6. Crankshaft pulley
7. Pump drive spline
8. Crankshaft sprocket
9. Chain tensioner
10. Timing chain

20R & 22R timing chain cover and components

driven on with a large socket or pipe. Make certain that the pulley TDC groove is aligned with the timing cover pointer. Tighten the pulley bolt to 43–51 ft. lb. on the 8R-C, and 54–80 ft. lb. on the 18R-C. On 20R, 22R and 22R-E engines, install the crankshaft pulley over the key. Tighten the bolt to 80–94 ft.lb.

NOTE: *Do not allow the pulley to rotate when tightening the pulley bolt.*

12. Further installation is the reverse of removal.

Diesel Engine

Refer to steps 1–8, then 15–17 of the Cylinder Head Removal and Installation procedure.

Torque the timing belt cover fasteners to 3–5 ft. lbs., and the crankshaft pulley center bolt to 69–75 ft. lb.

2F Engines

1. Drain the cooling system and the crankcase.

CAUTION: *When draining the coolant, keep in mind that cats and dogs are attracted by the ethelyne glycol antifreeze, and are quite likely to drink any that is left in an uncovered container or in puddles on the ground. This will prove fatal in sufficient quantity. Always drain the coolant into a sealable con-*

Removing the crankshaft pulley and the timing chain cover—8R-C and 18R-C

Installing the timing case cover oil seal

tainer. Coolant should be reused unless it is contaminated or several years old.

2. Disconnect the battery.

3. Remove the air cleaner assembly, complete with hoses, from its bracket.

4. Remove the hood latch as well as its brace and support.

5. Remove the headlight bezels and grille assembly.

6. Unfasten the upper and lower radiator hose clamps and remove both of the hoses from the engine.

7. Unfasten the radiator securing bolts and remove the radiator.

NOTE: *Take off the shroud first, if so equipped.*

8. Loosen the drive belt adjusting link and remove the drive belt. Unfasten the alternator multiconnector, withdraw the retaining bolts, and remove the alternator.

9. Perform step 8 to the air injection pump, if so equipped. Disconnect the hoses from the pump before removing it.

10. Remove the fan and water pump as an assembly.

11. Remove the crankshaft pulley with a gear puller.

12. Remove the gravel shield from underneath the engine.

13. Remove the front driveshaft.

14. Remove the front oil pan bolts, to gain access to the bottom of the timing chain cover.

NOTE: *It may be necessary to insert a thin knife between the pan and the gasket in order to break the pan loose. Use care not to damage the gasket.*

15. Installation is the reverse of removal. Be sure to adjust the drive bolts.

Oil Seal Replacement

1. Remove the timing chain cover.

2. Pry the old seal out, using a large, flat-bladed screwdriver. Be careful not to damage the lip of the cover.

3. Place the cover on a flat surface, face up. Lubricate the new seal with grease, and drive it into place with a large socket, pipe, or block of wood. The seal can be damaged easily so work carefully. Install the seal so that it is flush with the front of the cover.

4. Install the timing chain cover as previously outlined.

Timing Chain and Tensioner

REMOVAL AND INSTALLATION

8R-C and 18R-C

1. Remove the timing chain cover and the cylinder head as outlined earlier in this chapter.

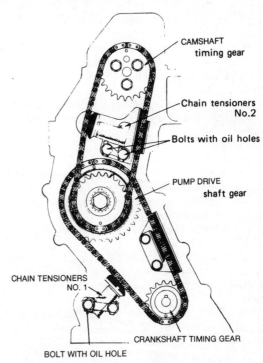

Timing chain and gear relationship—8R-C and 18R-C

2. Remove the chain tensioners (numbered 1 and 2 in the drawing). Keep the parts separate to avoid intermixing.

3. The upper timing chain and camshaft sprocket are removed with the cylinder head. Remove the camshaft drive gear next, using a gear puller. This is the gear in front of the pump drive shaft gear.

4. Remove the pump drive shaft gear, crankshaft timing gear, and chain as a unit, by using a gear puller alternately on the gears, working them evenly off the shafts.

NOTE: *Both timing chains are identical. They should be tagged so that they may be installed correctly.*

5. Inspect the chains and sprockets for wear

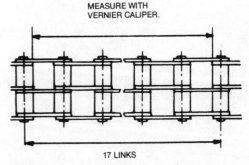

Timing chain stretch measurement—8R-C and 18R-C

or damage. Clean the chains thoroughly with solvent.

6. Use a vernier caliper to measure the amount of stretch in both chains. Measure a span of any 17 links while the chain is pulled taut.

7. Repeat Step 5 at two other places along the chains. If any of the 17 link measurements exceeds 5.792 in. or if the difference between the maximum and minimum reading is greater than 0.0078 in., the chain should be replaced.

8. Remove the plunger and spring from one of the chain tensioners. Inspect all of the parts of the tensioner mechanism for wear or damage. If there are no defective parts, fill the nut with oil and reassemble it. Perform this inspection on both tensioners.

NOTE: *Do not get the parts from the two tensioners mixed.*

Installation is performed in the following manner:

1. When the keyway in the crankshaft is pointing straight up and is perpendicular to the cylinder head, the No. 1 piston is at top dead

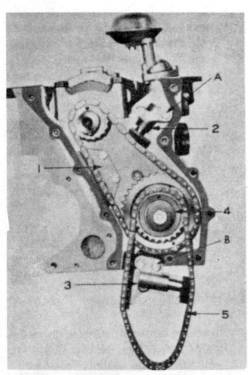

A. Chain tensioner bolt
B. Chain tensioner bolt
1. Chain vibration damper
2. Chain tensioner (oil pump drive chain)
3. Chain tensioner (camshaft timing chain)
4. Camshaft drive sprocket
5. Camshaft timing chain

Timing chain installation (engine inverted)—8R-C and 18R-C

center (TDC). Turn the engine by hand to achieve this configuration.

2. Align the oil pump jackshaft so that its keyway is facing in the same direction as that on the crankshaft.

3. Align the marks on the timing sprocket and the oil pump drive sprocket with each of the marks on the chain.

4. Install the chain and sprocket assembly over the keyways, while retaining alignment of the chain/sprocket timing marks.

NOTE: *Use care not to disengage the plug at the rear of the oil pump driveshaft, by forcing the sprocket over its keyway.*

5. Install the oil pump drive chain vibration damper.

6. Install the gasket for the timing chain cover.

NOTE: *Use liquid sealer on the gasket before installation.*

7. Install both the tensioners in their respective places, being careful not to mix them up. Tighten their securing bolts to 12–17 ft. lb. for 8R-C engines. On 18R-C engines, tighten No. 1 to 15–22 ft. lb., and No. 2 to 22–29 ft. lb. Use liquid sealer on the threads of the bolts without drilled oil holes.

NOTE: *Use care when installing the chain tensioner bolts; they have oil hoses taped in them. If oil remains in the body of tensioner no.2, it will be difficult to install the camshaft timing gear. If the plunger does not sink when pressed, loosen the bolts holding the vibration damper and drain out the oil.*

8. Fit the camshaft drive sprocket over the keyway on the oil pump driveshaft. Tighten its securing nut to 58–72 ft. lb.

9. Install the camshaft drive chain over the camshaft drive sprocket. Align the mating marks on the chain and sprocket.

10. Apply tension to the chain by tying it to the chain tensioner. This will prevent it from falling back into the timing chain cover once it is installed.

11. Install the timing chain cover and cylinder head as outlined above.

20R, 22R and 22R-E

1. Remove the cylinder head and timing chain cover as previously outlined.

2. Remove the chain from the dampers and remove the chain and cam sprocket together.

3. If the chain and sprocket are worn, they will have to be replaced, along with the crankshaft sprocket. Pull the crankshaft sprocket and pump drive spline as a unit, using a gar puller.

4. Measure the chain tensioner for wear. If it is worn below 0.43 in., replace it as a unit.

5. Measure the chain dampers for wear. If

either is visibly worn or measures below the limit, replace as a unit.

- Damper #1 0.20 in.
- Damper #2 0.18

To install:

1. After installing any necessary dampers or new tensioner, turn the crankshaft by hand until the key is at TDC. If removed, slide the crankshaft sprocket over the key. Place the chain on the sprocket so that the single bright link is over the mark on the sprocket.

2. Position the cam sprocket in the chain so that the timing mark on the sprocket is located between the two bright links of the chain.

3. Install the oil pump drive spline over the crankshaft key, if removed.

4. After cleaning the old gasket surface thoroughly, install a new cover gasket over the locating dowels.

5. Turn the camshaft sprocket counterclockwise to take any slack out of the chain.

6. Install the timing chain cover and cylinder head as previously outlined.

Timing Belt

REMOVAL AND INSTALLATION

Diesel Engine

The diesel timing belt may be removed by following steps 1–8, then 15–18 of the Cylinder Head Removal and Installation procedure. To install the belt:

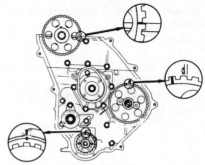

Preliminary timing gear positioning on the diesel engine

1. Temporarily install the idler pulley and check that the pulley bracket can be moved to the left and right by hand.

2. Align each timing gear according to the accompanying illustration. Note that the injection pump gear is positioned in a slightly retarded manner.

3. Install the timing belt without altering the position of any timing gear.

4. Install the idler pulley spring.

5. Temporarily install the crankshaft timing gear center bolt and turn the crankshaft timing gear center bolt and turn the crankshaft exactly two revolutions (clockwise). As you turn the crankshaft, you should notice movement of the idler pulley bracket.

6. Each timing gear should now align as shown in the accompanying illustration. Note that the injection pump gear marking should

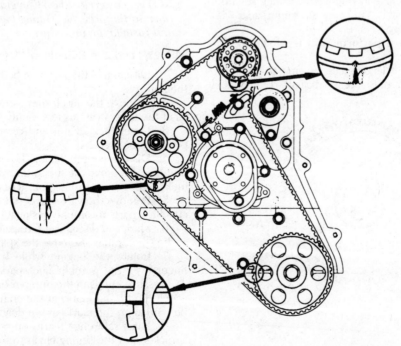

Final view of the timing marks on the diesel engine, after the crankshaft is turned twice

now be aligned with the corresponding diamond mark on the engine.

7. Tighten the idler pulley bolts to 1–15 ft. lb.

8. Install the crankshaft belt drive pulley. Dip the pulley retaining bolt in engine oil, install the bolt and tighten to 69–75 ft. lbs. WITHOUT turning the engine.

9. Assemble the remaining engine components by reversing the disassembly steps.

Timing Gears
REMOVAL AND INSTALLATION
2F Engines

NOTE: *This procedure contains camshaft removal and installation.*

1. Perform the cylinder head and timing cover removal procedures, as previously outlined.

2. Slip the oil slinger off the crankshaft.

3. Remove the camshaft thrust plate retaining bolts by working through the holes provided in the camshaft timing gear.

4. Remove the camshaft through the front of the cylinder block. Support the camshaft while removing it, so as not to damage its bearings or lobes.

NOTE: *The timing gear is a press-fit and cannot be removed without removing the camshaft.*

5. Inspect the crankshaft timing gear. Replace it if it has worn or damaged teeth.

6. To remove it, remove the sliding key from the crankshaft. Withdraw the timing gear with a gear puller.

Installation is performed in the following order:

1. Use a large piece of pipe to press the timing gear onto the crankshaft. Lightly and

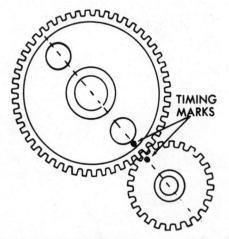

F series timing gear alignment

evenly tap the end of the pipe until the gear is in its original position.

2. Apply a coat of engine oil to the camshaft journals and bearings.

3. Insert the camshaft into the block.

NOTE: *Use care not to damage the camshaft lobes, bearings, or journals.*

4. Align the mating marks on each of the gears as illustrated.

5. Slip the camshaft into position. Tighten the camshaft thrust plate bolts to 14.5 ft. lb.

6. Check the gear backlash with a feeler gauge, inserted between the crankshaft and the camshaft timing gears. The backlash should be no more than 0.002–0.005 in. If it exceeds this, replace one or both of the gears, as required.

7. Check the gear runout with a dial indicator. Runout, for both gears, should not exceed 0.008 in. If it does, replace the gear.

8. Install the oil nozzle, if it was removed, by screwing it in place with a screwdriver and punching it in two places, to secure it.

NOTE: *Be sure that the oil hole in the nozzle is pointed toward the timing gear before securing it.*

9. Install the oil slinger on the crankshaft.

10. Install the timing gear cover and cylinder head, as outlined above.

Camshaft
REMOVAL AND INSTALLATION
2F Engines

NOTE: *To service the 2F engine camshaft, refer to the previous Timing Gear Removal and Installation procedure.*

20R, 22R and 22R-E Engines

1. Disconnect the negative battery cable at the battery.

2. Remove the air cleaner assembly. Mark all of the hose locations to simplify installation.

3. Drain the radiator and remove the upper radiator hose.

4. Disconnect the flexible hoses at the fuel pump and remove the fuel pump. Replace the fuel gasket during installation, if necessary.

5. Remove the valve cover. Mark all of the attaching parts to simplify installation.

6. Mark and disconnect the spark plug wires at the spark plugs. Remove the spark plugs.

7. Rotate the engine while holding your finger over the number one spark plug hole. As pressure builds in the number one cylinder, watch the timing marks at the crankshaft damper and align the marks at top dead center.

8. Paint reference marks on both the cam sprocket and the timing chain to indicate their relationship for installation.

9. Remove the distributor cap (with wires intact) and move it out of the way.

10. Mark the position of the distributor housing and the cylinder head, indicating the relationship between these two components.

11. Disconnect the distributor primary wire and remove the distributor.

12. Remove the half circle seal from the cylinder head.

13. Remove the cam sprocket bolt, the distributor drive gear and the fuel pump eccentric.

14. Remove the rocker shafts as previously outlined.

15. Measure the camshaft thrust clearance using a feeler gauge inserted between the thrust bearing and the cylinder head. If the clearance is greater than 0.0098 in., the cylinder head must be replaced.

16. Remove the camshaft journal caps.

NOTE: *The camshaft may now be lifted out of the cylinder head but it is recommended that you continue with the following checking procedures.*

17. Check the camshaft journal caps for damage. Clean all of the bearing surfaces, including the caps, cam journal, and the cylinder head.

18. With the camshaft in place on the cylinder head, lay small strips of Plastigage® on each of the camshaft journals (at the tops of the journals, facing front-to-rear).

19. Reinstall the journal caps in their original locations (arrows facing forward), and torque the caps to 13–16 ft. lbs.

20. Remove the journal caps and gauge the width of the Plastigage® against the chart on the Plastigage® package. Maximum journal clearance is 0.004 in. If the journal clearance is greater than specified, measure the cam journal diameters with a micrometer (or have a professional machine shop do so). If the diameter of any cam journal is less than specified obtain a new camshaft and recheck the journal clearance. If the clearance is still excessive, the cylinder head must be replaced.

To install the camshaft, position it in the cylinder head, install the journal caps (torque to specification), and reverse steps 1–15. Be sure to align all the reference marks made during removal. Replenish the cooling system. If a new cam is installed, use an assembly lube (available at most auto stores) on the cam lobes and engine oil on the journals. If the old cam is damaged excessively (lobes worn round, etc.) change the engine oil and filter.

NOTE: *If any of the reference marks made during removal will not align during assembly, remove the timing chain and retime the engine as previously outlined.*

Diesel Engine

Refer to step 1–8, then 15–21 of the Cylinder Head Removal and Installation procedure. The journal clearances are checked in the same manner as the 20R, 22R and 22R-E engines. During installation, note the following fastener torque values:

- Rocker shaft supports: 11–15 ft. lb.
- Oil seal retainer: 8–12 ft. lb.

Refer to the Timing Belt Removal and Installation procedure to properly install the timing belt.

Rear Main Oil Seal
REPLACEMENT

NOTE: *This procedure should not be attempted on trucks equipped with an automatic transmission.*

1. Refer to Chapter 6 for instructions on removal of the transmission. Remove the transmission.

2. Remove the clutch cover assembly and the flywheel. This procedure is also covered in Chapter 6.

3. Remove the oil seal retaining plate along with the seal.

4. Pry or drive the old seal from the retaining plate. Be careful not to damage the retaining plate.

5. Install a new oil seal using either a block of wood or a seal driver to firmly seat the new seal.

6. Lubricate the lips of the seal with multipurpose grease.

7. Install the retaining plate and seal. Install the flywheel, clutch cover assembly, and transmission.

8. Adjust the clutch.

Oil Pump
REMOVAL AND INSTALLATION
8R-C and 18R-C

1. Remove the oil pan.

2. Unbolt the oil pump attaching bolts and remove the entire assembly.

3. Installation requires no special procedures. Simply position the pump and reinstall the attaching bolts. Replace the oil pan.

4. Fill the engine with clean engine oil.

20R, 22R and 22R-E

1. Drain the oil, and remove the oil pan and the oil strainer and pick-up tube.

2. Remove the drive belts from the crankshaft pulley.

3. Remove the crankshaft bolt, and remove

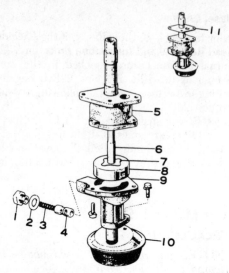

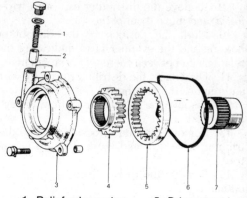

1. Relief valve spring   5. Driven gear
2. Relief valve   6. O-ring
3. Pump body   7. Drive spline
4. Drive gear

20R oil pump, 22R similar

1. Relief valve plug   7. Drive rotor
2. Gasket   8. Driven rotor
3. Relief valve spring   9. Pump cover
4. Relief valve   10. Strainer
5. Pump body   11. Gasket
6. Pump shaft

8R-C and 18R-C oil pump

the pulley with a gear puller, as outlined in the timing chain cover section.

4. Remove the five bolts from the oil pump and remove the oil pump assembly.

Inspect the drive spline, driven gear, pump body, and timing chain cover for excessive wear or damage. If necessary, replace the gears or pump body or cover. Unbolt the relief valve (the vertical bolt on the pump body) when attached to the engine and check the pistons, oil passages, and sliding surfaces for burrs or scoring. Inspect the crankshaft front oil seal and replace if worn or damaged.

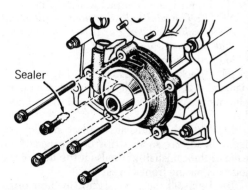

Apply sealer to the upper bolt on the 20R oil pump

When installing, use a new O-ring if necessary. Apply a sealer to the upper bolt and install the five bolts. Install the crankshaft pulley as outlined in the timing cover section, and use

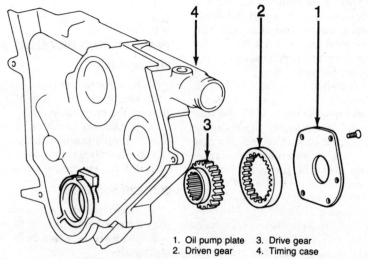

1. Oil pump plate   3. Drive gear
2. Driven gear   4. Timing case

Diesel oil pump

Oil Pump Clearance Specifications
(All measurements in inches)

Engine	Maximum Gear Tip Clearance ①	Maximum Gear Backlash ②	Side Clearance ③	Cover Wear ④	Body Clearance ⑤
2F	0.008	0.037	0.006	0.006	—
all exc 2F	0.012	—	0.006	—	0.008

① 2F Engines: Measured between the gear teeth of each gear and the pump body
  20R, 22R and L Engines: Measured between the gear teeth of each gear and the crescent
② Measured between the gear teeth with the gears meshed together
③ Measured between a straightedge positioned across the oil pump body and the gear faces
④ Measured between a straightedge positioned across the cover and the cover wear (gear contact) surface
⑤ Measured between the oil pump driven gear and the pump body

a new gasket on the oil strainer and oil pan. Be sure to apply sealer to the corners of the oil pan gasket before installing the pan.

Diesel Engine

1. Disconnect the cables which are positioned above the valve cover and move the cable aside. Remove the valve cover.

2. Disconnect the cables from both batteries.

3. Using a wrench on the center crankshaft pulley bolt, rotate the engine (clockwise only) until the TDC mark on the pulley is aligned with the pointer. Check that the valves of the number one cylinder are closed (rocker arms loose). If the valves are not closed, rotate the engine 360° and again align the TDC mark with the pointer.

4. Remove the following components as previously outlined:
   a. Oil pan and pump strainer assembly
   b. Timing cover and belt.

5. Disconnect the wiring from the alternator. Remove the alternator and the mounting brackets.

6. If equipped with air conditioning, unbolt the air conditioning compressor and tie it out of the way (without disconnecting the refrigerant hoses). Also remove the compressor bracketry.

7. Refer to the Diesel Fuel System section and remove the fuel injection pump.

8. Remove the crankshaft timing gear, using a puller.

9. Unbolt and remove the water pump.

10. Unbolt and remove the timing case assembly.

11. Remove the oil pump cover plate from the rear of the timing case assembly to gain access to the oil pump. Clearances are checked in the same manner as the pump used in the 20R, 22R and 22R-E engines.

12. Remove the pump gears and check the

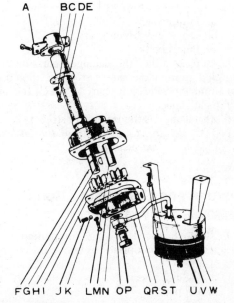

A. Oil pump supporter
B. Body thrust ring
C. Lockwasher
D. Bolt
E. Oil pump body
F. Oil pump shaft
G. Oil pump shaft key
H. Oil pump drive gear
I. Oil pump cover gasket
J. Valve spring
K. Valve ball
L. Oil pump driven shaft
M. Oil pump driven gear
N. Gasket
O. Union bolt washer
P. Suction pipe union bolt
Q. Oil pump inlet pipe
R. Oil pump cover
S. Bolt
T. Lockwasher
U. Rubber washer
V. Oil strainer
W. Oil strainer shell

F series oil pump

gears and timing case gear surfaces for damage or excessive wear.

13. Install the gears with the triangular markings of each gear facing the pump plate side of the timing case. Install the pump cover plate.

14. Reverse steps 1–10 to complete the installation. Note that all gasket surfaces must be

cleaned, and that damaged gaskets must be replaced. Be sure to follow the specific procedures concerning timing belt installation and fuel injection pump installation, as outlined previously and in the Diesel Fuel System section.

2F Engines

1. Remove the oil pan as previously outlined.

2. Remove the oil strainer and unfasten the union nuts on the oil pump pipe.

3. Remove the lock wire and the oil pump retaining bolt and pipe from the engine.

4. Remove the oil pump cover and inspect the following parts for nicks, scoring, grooving, etc.:

    a. Pump cover
    b. Drive and driven gears
    c. Pump body

5. Replace either the damaged parts or the complete pump if damage is excessive. See the Oil Pump Specification chart to check the oil pump clearance.

6. Installation is the reverse of steps 1–3.

NOTE: *Be sure to check all of the gaskets and replace if necessary.*

Pistons and Connecting Rods

REMOVAL AND INSTALLATION

1. Remove the following components as outlined in the appropriate section of this chapter:

    a. Cylinder head
    b. Oil pan
    c. Oil pump (not necessary on 20R, 22R and 22R-E engines)
    d. Oil strainer

2. Remove the cylinder ridges with a ridge reamer.

3. Mesure the connecting rod side clearance.

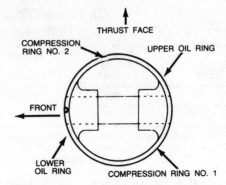

Mandatory piston ring positioning on the F series engine

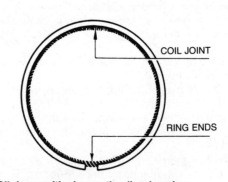

Mandatory piston ring positioning on the Diesel engine

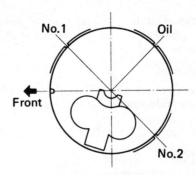

Oil ring positioning on the diesel engine

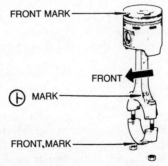

Piston and connecting rod installation on the diesel engine

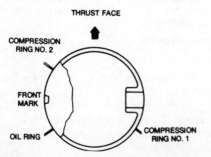

Mandatory piston ring positioning on the 20R and 22R engines

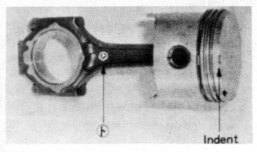

Piston and connecting rod assembly marks

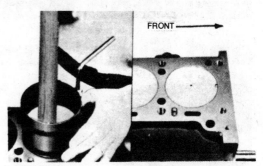

Piston installation. The notch on top of the piston faces front

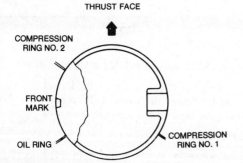

Ring gap positioning on 8RC & 18RC engines

4. Mark the connecting rods and caps.

5. Remove the connecting rod cap of the number one cylinder and check the oil clearance with Plastigage®. Record the clearance and compare with the specification chart. Repeat this step for each connecting rod.

6. With the number one connecting rod cap removed, install a short piece of rubber hose onto each connecting rod bolt (the hose must completely cover the bolt).

7. Using a wood or plastic handle (an old hammer handle works well), carefully tap the piston/connecting rod assembly out of the cylinder. Do not use excessive force as this could damage the connecting rods. Repeat this step for each cylinder.

8. Reinstall the oil strainer, oil pumps, oil pan and cylinder head following the appropriate procedures.

Emission Controls and Fuel Systems

EMISSION CONTROLS

According to Federal law, motor vehicles must be equipped with pollution control devices which limit the quantities of harmful pollutants emitted into the atmosphere. Toyota has been successful in developing various emission control systems which minimize atmospheric pollution without seriously limiting the overall performance of the engines.

There are three major sources of vehicle emissions: exhaust gas, blow-by gases, and fuel evaporation. Exhaust gases contain unburned hydrocarbons (HC), carbon monoxide (CO), and oxides of nitrogen (NO). Blow-by gases are high pressure exhaust gases which force their way past the piston rings and enter the crankcase. Evaporation of gasoline from the fuel tank and carburetor also allows unburned hydrocarbons to enter the atmosphere.

Toyota trucks are equipped with systems to control emissions from all these sources.

Positive Crankcase Ventilation System

A positive crankcase ventilation (PCV) system is used on all engines. Blow-by gases are routed from the crankcase to the carburetor where they are combined with the air/fuel mixture and burned in the cylinder.

A valve is used to prevent the gases in the crankcase from being ignited in the event of a backfire. The quantity of blow-by gases is also regulated by the PCV valve which is spring loaded and has a variable orifice. The valve is mounted on the valve cover of the engine and should be replaced every 24,000 miles, on 1970–78 trucks, and 30,000 miles on 1979 and later trucks.

REMOVAL AND INSTALLATION

To remove the valve simply disconnect the hose from the top of the valve and remove the valve from the rubber grommet in the valve cover.

TESTING

Check the PCV system hoses and connections to determine that there are no leaks, then tighten or replace as necessary.

To check the operation of the valve, remove it and blow through both of its ends. When blowing through the end which goes toward the intake manifold, very little air should pass through the valve. When blowing from the valve cover side, the air should pass freely.

If the valve does not perform in this manner, replace it with a new valve.

NOTE: *Toyota does not recommend cleaning of the PCV valve or any adjustments.*

Evaporative Emission Control System

To prevent hydrocarbon emissions from entering the atmosphere due to the evaporation of fuel in the tank and carburetor, Toyota pick-up trucks are equipped with evaporative emission control (EEC) systems. Between 1970 and 1971 the case storage system was used. Later models use the charcoal canister storage system.

The major components of the case storage system are a vacuum switching valve, a fuel vapor storage case, an air filter, a thermal expansion tank, and a special fuel tank.

When the vehicle is stopped or the engine is running at low speed, the vacuum switching valve is closed; fuel vapor travels only as far as the case where it is stored. At cruising speed the vacuum switching valve opens and the stored vapors are drawn into the intake manifold along with fresh air drawn through the air filter.

The charcoal storage system functions in a

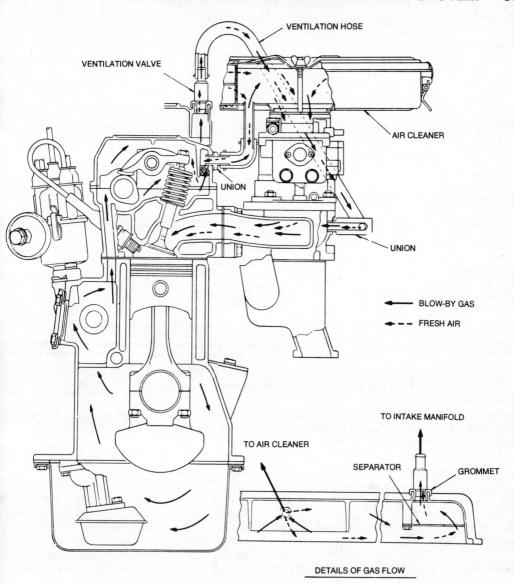

VENTILATION HOSE

VENTILATION VALVE

AIR CLEANER

UNION

UNION

◄─── BLOW-BY GAS

◄- - - FRESH AIR

TO AIR CLEANER

TO INTAKE MANIFOLD

SEPARATOR

GROMMET

DETAILS OF GAS FLOW

Diagram of the positive crankcase ventilation system—8R-C and 18R-C

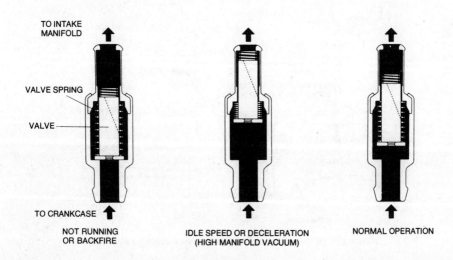

TO INTAKE
MANIFOLD

VALVE SPRING

VALVE

TO CRANKCASE

NOT RUNNING
OR BACKFIRE

IDLE SPEED OR DECELERATION
(HIGH MANIFOLD VACUUM)

NORMAL OPERATION

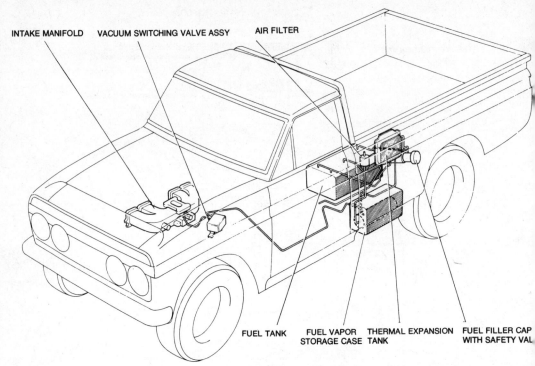

INTAKE MANIFOLD   VACUUM SWITCHING VALVE ASSY   AIR FILTER

FUEL TANK   FUEL VAPOR STORAGE CASE   THERMAL EXPANSION TANK   FUEL FILLER CAP WITH SAFETY VAL

The case storage system for evaporation control

similar manner except that the vapors are stored in a canister filled with activated charcoal. The air filter is an integral part of the charcoal canister.

Required maintenance includes replacement of the air filter at regular intervals for the case storage system, and replacement of the charcoal canister at 50,000 mile intervals for the later system. Both maintenance procedures are covered in Chapter One.

NOTE: *On 1979 and later models the charcoal canister should be checked at 30,000 and 60,000 miles. It is not necessary to replace the canister.*

Throttle Positioner

During rapid deceleration large volumes of fuel/air mixture are drawn into the cylinders due to high manifold vacuum. If the throttle plates close completely there is not sufficient oxygen to permit complete combustion. Therefore a throttle positioner is installed to

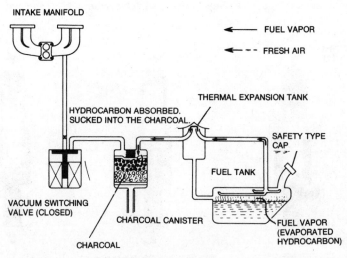

INTAKE MANIFOLD

FUEL VAPOR

FRESH AIR

THERMAL EXPANSION TANK

HYDROCARBON ABSORBED. SUCKED INTO THE CHARCOAL.

SAFETY TYPE CAP

FUEL TANK

VACUUM SWITCHING VALVE (CLOSED)

CHARCOAL CANISTER

CHARCOAL

FUEL VAPOR (EVAPORATED HYDROCARBON)

Schematic of the charcoal canister vapor storage system

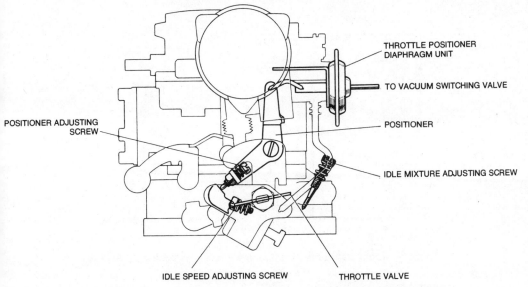

POSITIONER ADJUSTING SCREW

THROTTLE POSITIONER DIAPHRAGM UNIT

TO VACUUM SWITCHING VALVE

POSITIONER

IDLE MIXTURE ADJUSTING SCREW

IDLE SPEED ADJUSTING SCREW

THROTTLE VALVE

Components of the throttle positioner—8R-C engine. Other models similar

keep the throttle plates slightly open during deceleration. Vacuum is reduced under the throttle valve which, in turn, acts on the retard chamber of the distributor vacuum unit. This ignition retard compensates for the loss of engine braking caused by the partially opened throttle.

NOTE: *See the appropriate section in this chapter for a description of the dual diaphragm distributor.*

Once the vehicle drops below a predetermined speed, the vacuum switching valve provides vacuum to the throttle positioner diaphragm. The throttle positioner then retracts allowing the throttle valve to close completely. The distributor also returns to normal operation.

ADJUSTMENT

1. Start the engine and allow it to reach normal operating temperature.

2. Adjust the engine idle speed as outlined in Chapter 2. Leave the tachometer connected.

3. Detach the vacuum line from the throttle positioner diaphragm and plug the line.

4. Accelerate the engine slightly to set the throttle positioner.

5. Check the engine speed with a tachometer when the positioner is in place.

6. The engine should run at 1,400 rpm (1,050 with automatic transmission and all 1978 and later trucks) with the positioner set. If it does not, adjust the throttle positioner adjusting screw.

7. Connect the vacuum hose to the positioner diaphragm.

8. The throttle lever should be freed from

the positioner as soon as the vacuum line is connected. Engine idle should return to normal.

9. If the throttle positioner fails to perform properly, check the linkage and the diaphragm unit. If there are no defects in these components the problem probably lies in the vacuum switching valve or in the speed marker unit.

Dual Diaphragm Distributor

Some Toyota half-ton pick-ups with an 8R-C engine are equipped with a dual diaphragm distributor unit. This distributor has a retard diaphragm as well as an advance diaphragm.

Retarding the timing helps to reduce exhaust emissions as well as compensating for the lack of engine braking caused by the activation of the throttle positioner.

TESTING

NOTE: *Check all the vacuum hoses for leaks, kinks, or improper connections before making any test, and install replacements where necessary.*

1. Connect the timing light to the engine. Check the ignition timing as outlined in Chapter 2.

NOTE: *Before proceeding with the test, disconnect any spark control devices, distributor vacuum valves, etc. If these are left connected, inaccurate results may be obtained.*

2. Remove the retard hose from the distributor and plug it. As the engine speed increases, the timing should advance. If it does not, the vacuum unit is faulty and should be replaced.

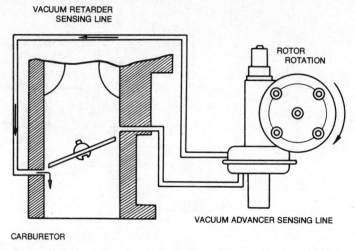

VACUUM RETARDER
SENSING LINE

ROTOR
ROTATION

VACUUM ADVANCER SENSING LINE

CARBURETOR

Dual diaphragm distributor—without the vacuum switching valve (VSV)

3. Check the ignition timing with the engine running at idle speed. Connect the retard hose to the vacuum unit; the timing should instantly be retarded 4–10°. If this does not occur, the retard diaphragm has a leak and the vacuum unit must be replaced.

Transmission Controlled Spark (TCS) System

The TCS system alters the distributor advance curve under certain operating conditions, thereby reducing emissions of oxide of nitrogen (NO).

When the system is operational, the computer closes the vacuum switching valve (VSV) ground circuit. The valve in the VSV closes the passage between the distributor advance side and the carburetor advancer port. In this manner, advance of the engine timing is stopped.

The computer receives its messages from the speed sensor unit and the thermal sensor which only operates when the coolant temperature is between 140–210°F. 1975 and 1976 trucks use a TVSV (thermostatic vacuum switching valve) in addition to the VSV, computer, and speed sensor, to provide normal vacuum advance at engine temperatures below 122°F.

Spark Control (SC) System

A modified TCS system called Spark Control is used on 1977 and later trucks. The principle of delayed vacuum advance to minimize HC and NO emissions remains the same, but the system is simplified by elimination of the computer control, VSV, and TVSV. Instead, a vacuum transmitting valve (VTV) is placed in the vacuum hose between the distributor diaphragm and the carburetor. Vacuum is delayed to the diaphragm by the closing of a check valve within the VTV. When intake vacuum drops (at wide throttle openings) the check valve opens and faster transmission vacuum is allowed, thus advancing the distributor timing. The VTV is coded in a dark blue color in automatic transmission trucks, and brown in all manual transmission equipped trucks.

Exhaust Gas Recirculation System (EGR)

Oxides of nitrogen can only be formed under conditions of high pressure and high temperature. Elimination of one of these conditions reduces their production. A reduction of peak combustion temperature is accomplished by exhaust gas recirculation into the carburetor.

1974 California trucks, and all 1975 and later trucks are equipped with an EGR system. 1974 18R-C engines have a tube running from the exhaust manifold to the EGR valve, and a tube from the valve to the carburetor above the throttle plates. 1975–80 20R engines are similar, with the addition of an exhaust gas cooler cast into the rear of the cylinder head. 1974–76 systems use a thermo switch, computer speed sensor, EGR valve and a vacuum switching valve (VSV). In addition, 1974 18R-C engines have a temperature switch at the carburetor flange. When the speed sensor and thermo switch are both within their operating ranges, the computer turns the VSV on, which in turn, opens the EGR valve, allowing a proportion of the exhaust gases to re-enter the engine through the carburetor. 1977–78 EGR systems eliminate all but the EGR valve, and add a TVSV (thermostatic VSV). At coolant temperatures above 50°F, the TSVS opens allowing engine vacuum to open the EGR valve. This permits a recirculation of exhaust gases.

TESTING

1974–77

1. Check all vacuum hoses for breaks, kinks, and improper connections. Repair or replace as necessary.

2. After warming the engine to operating temperature, remove the air cleaner lid.

3. With the engine idling, connect the EGR valve and the intake manifold together with a length of vacuum hose. This should cause the carburetor to make a bubbling noise. On the 1974 18R-C, disconnect the EGR valve sensing hose from the VSV, and connect this to the EGR valve at the fitting normally connected to the white hose. Connected , the carburetor should produce a bubbling noise.

4. The noise should disappear when the vacuum hose is disconnected from the EGR valve. If the carburetor fails to make the noise in Step 3, or if the noise does not stop when the hose is disconnected in Step 4, the EGR valve can be considered to be bad and should be replaced.

1978 and Later

1978 and later engines have a vacuum modulator attached to the EGR valve, and a VCV (except on those with automatic transmission) in the vacuum hose between the carburetor and vacuum modulator. To test the system:

1. Check and clean the filter in the EGR vacuum modulator.

2. Disconnect the vacuum hose from the EGR port of the carburetor, and connect it to the intake manifold. The other end of this hose should remain attached to the BVSV.

3. Disconnect the vacuum hose from the EGR valve, and connect a vacuum gauge to the hose.

4. If your truck has a manual, pinch off the vacuum hose between the VCV and the carburetor.

5. Start the engine and allow it to idle. The vacuum gauge reading should be zero at 2000 rpm if the engine is cold.

6. Allow the engine to warm up. The vacuum gauge should indicate a low vacuum at 2000 rpm. If it still reads zero, check the BVSV and modulator.

7. Release the pinched hose. The vacuum gauge should indicate low vacuum at 2000 rpm. If not check the VCV.

8. Pinch off the hose between the VCV and the carburetor. Disconnect the vacuum gauge. Remove the hose which runs from the BVSV to the front of the vacuum modulator, and connect it directly to the EGR valve, bypassing the modulator. The engine should die. If so the EGR valve is working properly. Reconnect the hoses and release the pinched hose.

EGR WARNING LIGHT (1975 ONLY)

1975 trucks have an EWGR warning light on the instrument panel above the windshield wiper switch. The light remains on until the switch is reset. The switch should not be reset until all required maintenance on the EGR and other emission systems has been performed. To reset the switch:

1. Remove the lockscrew from the switch cover. This screw requires a tool with two prongs.

2. Remove the cover. Reset the switch by moving it to the position opposite its present position.

3. Replace the cover and lockscrew, and check to see that the light turns on when the ignition switch is turned to the Start position.

Air Injection (AI) System

The air injection system is used on all 20R trucks 1975 and later.

Because of the many variables under which the engine operates, some hydrocarbons and carbon monoxide gases escape unburnt from the combustion chamber. To burn these gases more thoroughly, a belt driven air pump is used to supply fresh air to an air injection manifold located just beyond the exhaust valves. The injection of fresh air causes more complete combustion of the hot unburned HC and CO gases. An air bypass valve (air switching valve in 1977 and later) is used to control the flow of air from the pump to prevent backfiring, which results from an overly rich mixture under closed throttle conditions.

A check valve prevents hot exhaust gas backflow into the pump and hoses, in case of a pump failure, or when the air bypass valve is not in operation. In trucks equipped with a catalytic converter, the air blown into the exhaust system is also used as the oxygen source for the oxidizing reaction. The system also includes an air switching valve (ASV). On trucks without catalytic converters, the ASV is used to stop air injection when the engine is in a constant heavy load condition. On engines with catalytic converters, the ASV is also used to prevent converter overheating, by diverting the injected air necessary for converter operation. The air pump relief valve is built into the ASV.

Other components of the 1975 and later system include a vacuum switching valve (VSV), a thermo switch and a speed sensor. The com-

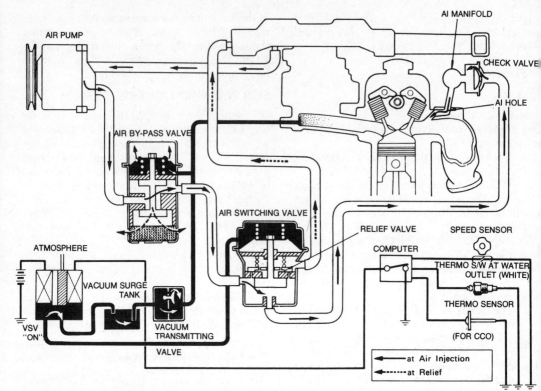

Components of the Air Injection system 1975–1976. This illustration shows the path of air from the pump both when injected and when diverted

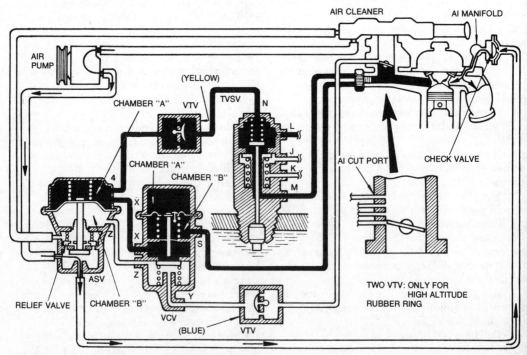

Components of the 1977 and later Air Injection system, shown here in the hot engine-low speed mode

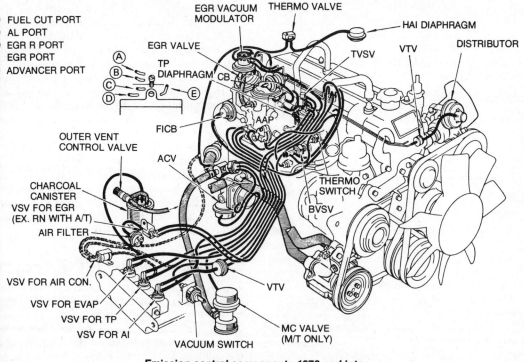

- FUEL CUT PORT
- AL PORT
- EGR R PORT
- EGR PORT
- ADVANCER PORT

Ⓐ
Ⓑ
Ⓒ
Ⓓ   Ⓔ

EGR VACUUM MODULATOR

THERMO VALVE

HAI DIAPHRAGM

DISTRIBUTOR

EGR VALVE

TVSV

VTV

TP DIAPHRAGM CB

FICB

AAP

OUTER VENT CONTROL VALVE

ACV

THERMO SWITCH

BVSV

CHARCOAL CANISTER
VSV FOR EGR
(EX. RN WITH A/T)
AIR FILTER

VSV FOR AIR CON.

VSV FOR EVAP

VSV FOR TP

VSV FOR AI

VACUUM SWITCH

VTV

MC VALVE (M/T ONLY)

Emission control components 1979 and later

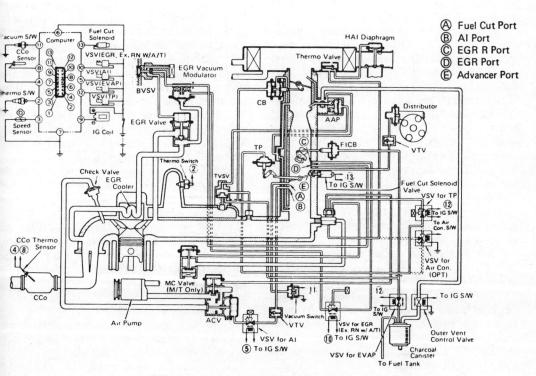

Ⓐ Fuel Cut Port
Ⓑ AI Port
Ⓒ EGR R Port
Ⓓ EGR Port
Ⓔ Advancer Port

Emission control schematic 1979 and later

puter acts directly on the VSV. 1977–78 trucks eliminate the computer, speed sensor, thermo switch, and VSV, and add a vacuum control valve (VCV), and a thermostatic VSV (TVSV). High altitude trucks have two vacuum transmitting valves (VTV). One, coded yellow, is placed in the line between the ASV and the TVSV, and delays the closing of the ASV during hot engine/heavy load conditions. The other VTV, coded blue delays the bypass of air for a few moments during high speed/hot temperature conditions, and is placed between the VCV and the carburetor.

MODES OF OPERATION

The Air Injection System normally operates in the hot engine/low speed mode outlined here. However, certain conditions cause the system to divert the air flow from the pump, to prevent problems such as backfiring, overheating, and poor cold engine performance. These conditions and the systems operation are as follows:

• Cold engine: During cold engine operation, air is diverted by the ASV to the air cleaner, rather than to the AI manifold. This is accomplished on 1975 and later trucks by the thermo switch, which signals the computer to turn off the VSV, which in turn causes the ASV to divert the air to the air cleaner. On 1977 and later trucks, the TVSV closes the vacuum passage between the ASV and the intake manifold. This closes the ASV, diverting the air to the air cleaner.

• Hot engine/low speed: At engine temperatures above 55°F on 1975–76 trucks, the computer is signaled by the thermo switch and speed sensor to turn the VSV on, which causes the intake manifold vacuum to open the ASV, which in turn then allows air to flow from the pump to the AI manifold, where it ignites the hot HC and CO gases. This is the normal operating mode for the AI system. On 1977 and later trucks, the TVSV opens the vacuum passage between the intake manifold and the ASV, with the same results as in the earlier system. In both cases, if the air pump pressure rises above a predetermined level, the ASV relief valve opens, venting that air through the VSV to the air cleaner.

• Hot engine/high speed: The speed sensor in 1975 and later trucks causes the computer to turn the VSV off, which in turn causes the ASV to divert the pumped air to the air cleaner. On later trucks the vacuum from the AI ports in the carburetor acts on the ASV bottom chamber, while intake manifold vacuum acts on the ASV top chamber. This results in an equal vacuum on both sides of the ASV diaphragm. The equilibrium is overcome by a spring on the diaphragm located in the upper chamber, which closes the ASV, diverting the pumped air to the air cleaner. On high altitude trucks, this action is delayed by the blue VTV.

• Hot engine/sudden deceleration: The sudden increase of vacuum from the intake manifold, caused by the closed throttle, opens the air bypass valve, which vents the pumped air to the atmosphere on 1975–76 trucks. On 1977 and later models, the sudden closing of the throttle and subsequent loss of vacuum from the carburetor to the VCV allows the ASV to close, diverting the air to the air cleaner.

• Hot engine/heavy load: On all trucks, the decrease in intake manifold vacuum causes the ASV to close, diverting the air to the air cleaner. On 1977 and later high altitude trucks, this action is delayed by the yellow VTV.

Catalytic Converter (CCO) System

Catalytic converters are used on 1976 and later trucks sold in California, and 1977 and later trucks sold in high altitude areas. The converter is a muffler shaped device, located in the exhaust system between the manifold and the muffler. Its purpose is to oxidize hydrocarbons (HC) and carbon monoxide (CO).

The catalyst is made of noble metals (platinum and palladium) bonded to pellets of granular alumina. These catalysts cause the HC and CO to break down into water and carbon dioxide (CO_2) without taking part in the reaction; thus, it is reasonable to expect a catalyst life of 50,000 miles in normal use. The air pump used in the air injection system also supplies fresh air to the catalyst via the exhaust pipe; this fresh air is used to supply oxygen for the reaction. A thermosensor, inserted into the body of the converter, shuts off air supply if catalyst temperatures become excessive.

The same sensor circuit also causes an instrument panel warning light labeled EXH TEMP to come on when the temperature rises beyond the predetermined level.

NOTE: *It is normal for the light to come on temporarily if the truck is driven down hill for a long period of time (such as when descending a mountain).*

The light will come on and stay on if the air injection system is malfunctioning or if the engine is misfiring, both of which will cause the catalyst temperature to rise.

PRECAUTIONS

1. Use only unleaded fuel.
2. Avoid prolonged idling; the engine should run no longer than 20 minutes at curb idle, no longer than 10 minutes at fast idle.
3. Reduce fast idle speed, by quickly depressing and releasing the accelerator pedal, as soon as the coolant temperature reaches 120°F.

4. Do not disconnect any spark plug leads while the engine is running.

5. Make engine compression checks as quickly as possible.

6. Do not dispose of the catalyst in a place anything coated with grease, gas, or oil is present.

CATALYST TESTING

At the present time there is on known way to reliably test catalytic converter operation in the field. The only reliable test is a 12 hour and 40 minute soak test (CVS) which must be done in a laboratory.

An infrared HC/CO tester is not sensitive enough to measure the higher tail pipe emissions from a partially failed converter. Thus, a bad converter may allow enough HC and CO emissions to escape, so that the truck is not in compliance with Federal (or state) standards, but still will not cause the needle on the HC/CO tester to move off zero.

A completely failed converter should cause the tester to show a slight reading. As a result, it should be possible to spot one of these.

As long as you avoid severe overheating or use of leaded fuels and the truck has less than 50,000 miles on it, it is safe to assume that the converter is working.

If you are in doubt about the converter, take your truck to diagnostic center which has an infrared tester.

WARNING LIGHT CHECKS

NOTE: *The warning light will come on when the ignition switch is turned to the Start position, as a means of checking its operation.*

1. If the warning light illuminates and remains on, check the components of the air injection system. If these are not defective, check the ignition system for faulty leads, plugs, points or igniter.

2. If no problems can be found in Step 1, check the warning light wiring for short or open circuits.

3. If nothing can be found in Steps 1 or 2, check the operation of the emission control system vacuum switching valve or the computer, either by substitution of a new unit, or by taking the truck to a service facility which has Toyota's diagnostic emission control system checker.

CONVERTER REMOVAL AND INSTALLATION

CAUTION: *Do not perform this operation on a hot (or even warm) engine. Catalyst temperatures may go as high as 1,700°F, so that any contact with the catalyst could cause severe burns.*

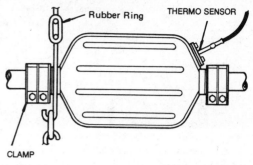

Typical catalytic converter installation

1. Disconnect the lead from the converter thermosensor.

2. Remove the wiring shield.

3. Unfasten the pipe clamp, securing bolts at either end of the converter. Remove the clamps.

4. Push the tail pipe rearward and remove the converter, complete with thermosensor.

5. Carry the converter with the thermosensor upward to prevent the catalyst from falling out.

6. Unfasten the screws and take out the thermosensor and gasket.

Installation is as follows:

1. Place a new gasket on the thermosensor. Push the thermosensor into the converter and secure it with its two bolts. Be careful not to drop the thermosensor.

NOTE: *Service replacement converters are provided with a plastic thermosensor guide. Slide the sensor into the glide to install it. Do not remove the guide.*

2. Install new gaskets on the converter mounting flanges.

3. Secure the converter with its mounting clamps.

4. If the converter is attached to the body with rubber O-rings, install the O-rings over the body and converter mounting hooks.

5. Install the wire protector and connect the leads to the thermosensor.

Automatic Hot Air Intake (HAI)

All 1975 and later trucks are equipped with the HAI system, which consists of a heat stove around the exhaust manifold, a thermostatically controlled door (air control valve) in the air cleaner horn, and a length of insulated flexible pipe connecting the two. The purpose of the system is to keep the temperature of the air drawn into the carburetor as constant as possible. It directs a hot air supply to the carburetor in cold weather to provide faster engine warming and to reduce the possibility of

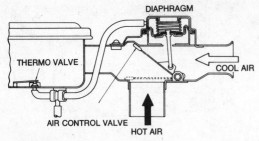

20R HAI system—later models have a slightly different thermo valve

carburetor icing. By providing the cold engine with warmer air, the choke stays on for a shorter length of time, thus reducing fuel consumption and the rich mixture condition. Leaner combustion mixtures are inherently lower in HC and CO emission.

The air control valve in the air cleaner horn is controlled by a vacuum diaphragm. The vacuum hose is connected at one end to the diaphragm, and to both a thermo valve and intake manifold at the other. Initially, when cold, the thermo valve is closed. Intake manifold vacuum therefore causes the diaphragm to rise, opening the door in the air horn to admit preheated air drawn from the heat stove around the exhaust manifold. As the engine temperature rises, the thermo valve opens, thus reducing the intake manifold vacuum, allowing the diaphragm to lower, which in turn closes the door in the air horn to admit cool outside air.

INSPECTION

With the engine idling and warm, connect the diaphragm hose directly to the intake manifold, and plug the thermo valve hose end. The air control valve should rise to admit hot air.

As with all vacuum operated systems, the hoses should be checked for any kinks, breaks, or improper connections. If none are found and the air valve does not work properly, the diaphragm and the thermo valve must be checked. Suction applied to the vacuum hose should cause the diaphragm to raise the door. If it does, the thermo valve can be considered faulty. If not, the diaphragm should be replaced.

Auxiliary Acceleration Pump (AAP) System

To reduce emissions, carburetor air/fuel mixtures are calibrated to be as lean as possible. Although a lean mixture will burn readily at hotter temperatures, it is reluctant to ignite when cold, not because of the mixture as such, but because fuel vaporizes less readily when cold. Thus, increasing the amount of fuel in a cold air/fuel mixture increased the amount of vaporized fuel available.

The problem of a poor air/vaporized fuel mixture in a cold engine is accentuated when accelerating. Although the carburetor is equipped with an acceleration pump for normal accelerating engine demands, its capacity is insufficient for a cold engine. The auxiliary acceleration pump (AAP) is designed to send additional fuel into the acceleration nozzle in the carburetor independent of the regular acceleration pump. All 1975 and later trucks are equipped with the AAP system.

The AAP itself is an integral part of the carburetor. It consists of two check valves controlled by springs, and a diaphragm controlled by both a spring and engine vacuum obtained from the intake manifold. At constant speeds, intake manifold vacuum draws the AAP Diaphragm back, enlarging the AAP chamber and thus allowing gasoline to enter. When the engine is accelerated, intake manifold vacuum drops, allowing the AAP diaphragm to be pushed back by the spring. The resultant reduction in chamber volume forces the gasoline out through the other check valve, into the acceleration nozzle. Thus, the engine gets a needed squirt of gasoline.

AAP operation is governed by the same TVSV described in the AI section earlier. At cold coolant temperatures, the TSVS allows intake manifold vacuum to reach the AAP diaphragm. At approximately 122°F, the TSVS closes off the passage to vacuum, thus shutting off the AAP.

INSPECTION

The vacuum hose should be checked for leaks, kinks, or improper connection.

1. With the engine cold (below 75°F) and idling (front wheels blocked, parking brake on, transmission in neutral) remove the air cleaner cap and look into the carburetor. At the instant the vacuum hose is removed from the AAP, gasoline should squirt from the nozzle.

2. If it does not, check for vacuum in the hose. If present, the AAP diaphragm may be defective, the nozzle may be blocked, the check valves may be stuck, or gasoline may not be flowing into the chamber.

3. If there is no vacuum in the line, either the line has an air leak or the TSVS is defective.

4. After warming the engine to operating temperature, perform the same test as in Step 1. If gasoline spurts out, the TSVS is defective

Choke Breaker (CB) System

All 20R and 22R engines use an automatic choke consisting of a thermostatic bimetal spring which expands and contracts in response to cold and

CHILTON'S
FUEL ECONOMY
& TUNE-UP TIPS

Tune-up • Spark Plug Diagnosis • Emission Controls

Fuel System • Cooling System • Tires and Wheels

General Maintenance

CHILTON'S FUEL ECONOMY & TUNE-UP TIPS

Fuel economy is important to everyone, no matter what kind of vehicle you drive. The maintenance-minded motorist can save both money and fuel using these tips and the periodic maintenance and tune-up procedures in this Repair and Tune-Up Guide.

There are more than 130,000,000 cars and trucks registered for private use in the United States. Each travels an average of 10-12,000 miles per year, and, and in total they consume close to 70 billion gallons of fuel each year. This represents nearly ⅔ of the oil imported by the United States each year. The Federal government's goal is to reduce consumption 10% by 1985. A variety of methods are either already in use or under serious consideration, and they all affect you driving and the cars you will drive. In addition to "down-sizing", the auto industry is using or investigating the use of electronic fuel delivery, electronic engine controls and alternative engines for use in smaller and lighter vehicles, among other alternatives to meet the federally mandated Corporate Average Fuel Economy (CAFE) of 27.5 mpg by 1985. The government, for its part, is considering rationing, mandatory driving curtailments and tax increases on motor vehicle fuel in an effort to reduce consumption. The government's goal of a 10% reduction could be realized — and further government regulation avoided — if every private vehicle could use just 1 less gallon of fuel per week.

How Much Can You Save?

Tests have proven that almost anyone can make at least a 10% reduction in fuel consumption through regular maintenance and tune-ups. When a major manufacturer of spark plugs sur

TUNE-UP

1. Check the cylinder compression to be sure the engine will really benefit from a tune-up and that it is capable of producing good fuel economy. A tune-up will be wasted on an engine in poor mechanical condition.

2. Replace spark plugs regularly. New spark plugs alone can increase fuel economy 3%.

3. Be sure the spark plugs are the correct type (heat range) for your vehicle. See the Tune-Up Specifications.

Heat range refers to the spark plug's ability to conduct heat away from the firing end. It must conduct the heat away in an even pattern to avoid becoming a source of pre-ignition, yet it must also operate hot enough to burn off conductive deposits that could cause misfiring.

The heat range is usually indicated by a number on the spark plug, part of the manufacturer's designation for each individual spark plug. The numbers in bold-face indicate the heat range in each manufacturer's identification system.

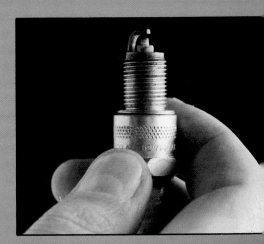

Periodically, check the spark plugs to be sure they are firing efficiently. They are excellent indicators of the internal condition of your engine.

Manufacturer	Typical Designation
AC	R **45** TS
Bosch (old)	WA **145** T30
Bosch (new)	HR **8** Y
Champion	RBL **15** Y
Fram/Autolite	4**15**
Mopar	P-**62** PR
Motorcraft	BRF-**42**
NGK	BP **5** ES-15
Nippondenso	W **16** EP
Prestolite	14GR **5** 2A

On AC, Bosch (new), Champion, Fram, Autolite, Mopar, Motorcraft and Prestolite, a higher number indicates a hotter plug. On Bosch (old), NGK and Nippondenso, a higher number indicates a colder plug.

4. Make sure the spark plugs are properly gapped. See the Tune-Up Specifications in this book.

5. Be sure the spark plugs are firing efficiently. The illustrations on the next 2 pages show you how to "read" the firing end of the spark plug.

6. Check the ignition timing and set it to specifications. Tests show that almost all cars have incorrect ignition timing by more than 2°.

veyed over 6,000 cars nationwide, they found that a tune-up, on cars that needed one, increased fuel economy over 11%. Replacing worn plugs alone, accounted for a 3% increase. The same test also revealed that 8 out of every 10 vehicles will have some maintenance deficiency that will directly affect fuel economy, emissions or performance. Most of this mileage-robbing neglect could be prevented with regular maintenance.

Modern engines require that all of the functioning systems operate properly for maximum efficiency. A malfunction anywhere wastes fuel. You can keep your vehicle running as efficiently and economically as possible, by being aware of your vehicle's operating and performance characteristics. If your vehicle suddenly develops performance or fuel economy problems it could be due to one or more of the following:

PROBLEM	POSSIBLE CAUSE
Engine Idles Rough	Ignition timing, idle mixture, vacuum leak or something amiss in the emission control system.
Hesitates on Acceleration	Dirty carburetor or fuel filter, improper accelerator pump setting, ignition timing or fouled spark plugs.
Starts Hard or Fails to Start	Worn spark plugs, improperly set automatic choke, ice (or water) in fuel system.
Stalls Frequently	Automatic choke improperly adjusted and possible dirty air filter or fuel filter.
Performs Sluggishly	Worn spark plugs, dirty fuel or air filter, ignition timing or automatic choke out of adjustment.

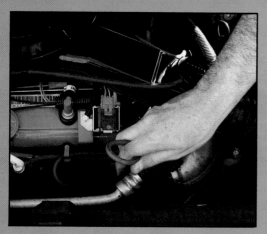

Check spark plug wires on conventional point type ignition for cracks by bending them in a loop around your finger.

Be sure that spark plug wires leading to adjacent cylinders do not run too close together. (Photo courtesy Champion Spark Plug Co.)

7. If your vehicle does not have electronic ignition, check the points, rotor and cap as specified.

8. Check the spark plug wires (used with conventional point-type ignitions) for cracks and burned or broken insulation by bending them in a loop around your finger. Cracked wires decrease fuel efficiency by failing to deliver full voltage to the spark plugs. One misfiring spark plug can cost you as much as 2 mpg.

9. Check the routing of the plug wires. Misfiring can be the result of spark plug leads to adjacent cylinders running parallel to each other and too close together. One wire tends to pick up voltage from the other causing it to fire "out of time".

10. Check all electrical and ignition circuits for voltage drop and resistance.

11. Check the distributor mechanical and/or vacuum advance mechanisms for proper functioning. The vacuum advance can be checked by twisting the distributor plate in the opposite direction of rotation. It should spring back when released.

12. Check and adjust the valve clearance on engines with mechanical lifters. The clearance should be slightly loose rather than too tight.

SPARK PLUG DIAGNOSIS

Normal

APPEARANCE: This plug is typical of one operating normally. The insulator nose varies from a light tan to grayish color with slight electrode wear. The presence of slight deposits is normal on used plugs and will have no adverse effect on engine performance. The spark plug heat range is correct for the engine and the engine is running normally.

CAUSE: Properly running engine.

RECOMMENDATION: Before reinstalling this plug, the electrodes should be cleaned and filed square. Set the gap to specifications. If the plug has been in service for more than 10-12,000 miles, the entire set should probably be replaced with a fresh set of the same heat range.

Oil Deposits

APPEARANCE: The firing end of the plug is covered with a wet, oily coating.

CAUSE: The problem is poor oil control. On high mileage engines, oil is leaking past the rings or valve guides into the combustion chamber. A common cause is also a plugged PCV valve, and a ruptured fuel pump diaphragm can also cause this condition. Oil fouled plugs such as these are often found in new or recently overhauled engines, before normal oil control is achieved, and can be cleaned and reinstalled.

RECOMMENDATION: A hotter spark plug may temporarily relieve the problem, but the engine is probably in need of work.

Incorrect Heat Range

APPEARANCE: The effects of high temperature on a spark plug are indicated by clean white, often blistered insulator. This can also be accompanied by excessive wear of the electrode, and the absence of deposits.

CAUSE: Check for the correct spark plug heat range. A plug which is too hot for the engine can result in overheating. A car operated mostly at high speeds can require a colder plug. Also check ignition timing, cooling system level, fuel mixture and leaking intake manifold.

RECOMMENDATION: If all ignition and engine adjustments are known to be correct, and no other malfunction exists, install spark plugs one heat range colder.

Carbon Deposits

APPEARANCE: Carbon fouling is easily identified by the presence of dry, soft, black, sooty deposits.

CAUSE: Changing the heat range can often lead to carbon fouling, as can prolonged slow, stop-and-start driving. If the heat range is correct, carbon fouling can be attributed to a rich fuel mixture, sticking choke, clogged air cleaner, worn breaker points, retarded timing or low compression. If only one or two plugs are carbon fouled, check for corroded or cracked wires on the affected plugs. Also look for cracks in the distributor cap between the towers of affected cylinders.

RECOMMENDATION: After the problem is corrected, these plugs can be cleaned and reinstalled if not worn severely.

MMT Fouled

APPEARANCE: Spark plugs fouled by MMT (Methycyclopentadienyl Maganese Tricarbonyl) have reddish, rusty appearance on the insulator and side electrode.

CAUSE: MMT is an anti-knock additive in gasoline used to replace lead. During the combustion process, the MMT leaves a reddish deposit on the insulator and side electrode.

RECOMMENDATION: No engine malfunction is indicated and the deposits will not affect plug performance any more than lead deposits (see Ash Deposits). MMT fouled plugs can be cleaned, regapped and reinstalled.

High Speed Glazing

APPEARANCE: Glazing appears as shiny coating on the plug, either yellow or tan in color.

CAUSE: During hard, fast acceleration, plug temperatures rise suddenly. Deposits from normal combustion have no chance to fluff-off; instead, they melt on the insulator forming an electrically conductive coating which causes misfiring.

RECOMMENDATION: Glazed plugs are not easily cleaned. They should be replaced with a fresh set of plugs of the correct heat range. If the condition recurs, using plugs with a heat range one step colder may cure the problem.

Ash (Lead) Deposits

APPEARANCE: Ash deposits are characterized by light brown or white colored deposits crusted on the side or center electrodes. In some cases it may give the plug a rusty appearance.

CAUSE: Ash deposits are normally derived from oil or fuel additives burned during normal combustion. Normally they are harmless, though excessive amounts can cause misfiring. If deposits are excessive in short mileage, the valve guides may be worn.

RECOMMENDATION: Ash-fouled plugs can be cleaned, gapped and reinstalled.

Detonation

APPEARANCE: Detonation is usually characterized by a broken plug insulator.

CAUSE: A portion of the fuel charge will begin to burn spontaneously, from the increased heat following ignition. The explosion that results applies extreme pressure to engine components, frequently damaging spark plugs and pistons.

Detonation can result by over-advanced ignition timing, inferior gasoline (low octane) lean air/fuel mixture, poor carburetion, engine lugging or an increase in compression ratio due to combustion chamber deposits or engine modification.

RECOMMENDATION: Replace the plugs after correcting the problem.

Photos Courtesy Champion Spark Plug Co.

EMISSION CONTROLS

13. Be aware of the general condition of the emission control system. It contributes to reduced pollution and should be serviced regularly to maintain efficient engine operation.

14. Check all vacuum lines for dried, cracked or brittle conditions. Something as simple as a leaking vacuum hose can cause poor performance and loss of economy.

15. Avoid tampering with the emission control system. Attempting to improve fuel econ-

FUEL SYSTEM

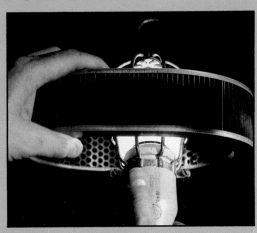

Check the air filter with a light behind it. If you can see light through the filter it can be reused.

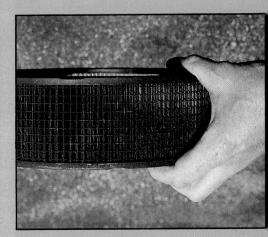

Extremely clogged filters should be discarded and replaced with a new one.

18. Replace the air filter regularly. A dirty air filter richens the air/fuel mixture and can increase fuel consumption as much as 10%. Tests show that ⅓ of all vehicles have air filters in need of replacement.

19. Replace the fuel filter at least as often as recommended.

20. Set the idle speed and carburetor mixture to specifications.

21. Check the automatic choke. A sticking or malfunctioning choke wastes gas.

22. During the summer months, adjust the automatic choke for a leaner mixture which will produce faster engine warm-ups.

COOLING SYSTEM

29. Be sure all accessory drive belts are in good condition. Check for cracks or wear.

30. Adjust all accessory drive belts to proper tension.

31. Check all hoses for swollen areas, worn spots, or loose clamps.

32. Check coolant level in the radiator or ex-pansion tank.

33. Be sure the thermostat is operating properly. A stuck thermostat delays engine warm-up and a cold engine uses nearly twice as much fuel as a warm engine.

34. Drain and replace the engine coolant at least as often as recommended. Rust and scale

TIRES & WHEELS

38. Check the tire pressure often with a pencil type gauge. Tests by a major tire manufacturer show that 90% of all vehicles have at least 1 tire improperly inflated. Better mileage can be achieved by over-inflating tires, but never exceed the maximum inflation pressure on the side of the tire.

39. If possible, install radial tires. Radial tires deliver as much as ½ mpg more than bias belted tires.

40. Avoid installing super-wide tires. They only create extra rolling resistance and decrease fuel mileage. Stick to the manufacturer's recommendations.

41. Have the wheels properly balanced.

omy by tampering with emission controls is more likely to worsen fuel economy than improve it. Emission control changes on modern engines are not readily reversible.

16. Clean (or replace) the EGR valve and lines as recommended.

17. Be sure that all vacuum lines and hoses are reconnected properly after working under the hood. An unconnected or misrouted vacuum line can wreak havoc with engine performance.

---

23. Check for fuel leaks at the carburetor, fuel pump, fuel lines and fuel tank. Be sure all lines and connections are tight.

24. Periodically check the tightness of the carburetor and intake manifold attaching nuts and bolts. These are a common place for vacuum leaks to occur.

25. Clean the carburetor periodically and lubricate the linkage.

26. The condition of the tailpipe can be an excellent indicator of proper engine combustion. After a long drive at highway speeds, the inside of the tailpipe should be a light grey in color. Black or soot on the insides indicates an overly rich mixture.

27. Check the fuel pump pressure. The fuel pump may be supplying more fuel than the engine needs.

28. Use the proper grade of gasoline for your engine. Don't try to compensate for knocking or "pinging" by advancing the ignition timing. This practice will only increase plug temperature and the chances of detonation or pre-ignition with relatively little performance gain.

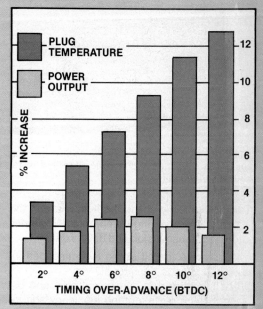

Increasing ignition timing past the specified setting results in a drastic increase in spark plug temperature with increased chance of detonation or preignition. Performance increase is considerably less. (Photo courtesy Champion Spark Plug Co.)

---

that form in the engine should be flushed out to allow the engine to operate at peak efficiency.

35. Clean the radiator of debris that can decrease cooling efficiency.

36. Install a flex-type or electric cooling fan, if you don't have a clutch type fan. Flex fans use curved plastic blades to push more air at low speeds when more cooling is needed; at high speeds the blades flatten out for less resistance. Electric fans only run when the engine temperature reaches a predetermined level.

37. Check the radiator cap for a worn or cracked gasket. If the cap does not seal properly, the cooling system will not function properly.

---

42. Be sure the front end is correctly aligned. A misaligned front end actually has wheels going in differed directions. The increased drag can reduce fuel economy by .3 mpg.

43. Correctly adjust the wheel bearings. Wheel bearings that are adjusted too tight increase rolling resistance.

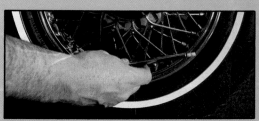

Check tire pressures regularly with a reliable pocket type gauge. Be sure to check the pressure on a cold tire.

GENERAL MAINTENANCE

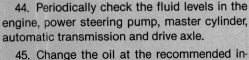

Check the fluid levels (particularly engine oil) on a regular basis. Be sure to check the oil for grit, water or other contamination.

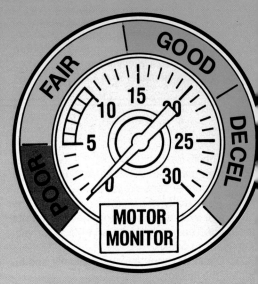

A vacuum gauge is another excellent indicator of internal engine condition and can also be installed in the dash as a mileage indicator.

44. Periodically check the fluid levels in the engine, power steering pump, master cylinder, automatic transmission and drive axle.

45. Change the oil at the recommended interval and change the filter at every oil change. Dirty oil is thick and causes extra friction between moving parts, cutting efficiency and increasing wear. A worn engine requires more frequent tune-ups and gets progressively worse fuel economy. In general, use the lightest viscosity oil for the driving conditions you will encounter.

46. Use the recommended viscosity fluids in the transmission and axle.

47. Be sure the battery is fully charged for fast starts. A slow starting engine wastes fuel.

48. Be sure battery terminals are clean and tight.

49. Check the battery electrolyte level and add distilled water if necessary.

50. Check the exhaust system for crushed pipes, blockages and leaks.

51. Adjust the brakes. Dragging brakes or brakes that are not releasing create increased drag on the engine.

52. Install a vacuum gauge or miles-per gallon gauge. These gauges visually indicate engine vacuum in the intake manifold. High vacuum = good mileage and low vacuum = poorer mileage. The gauge can also be an excellent indicator of internal engine conditions.

53. Be sure the clutch is properly adjusted. A slipping clutch wastes fuel.

54. Check and periodically lubricate the heat control valve in the exhaust manifold. A sticking or inoperative valve prevents engine warm-up and wastes gas.

55. Keep accurate records to check fuel economy over a period of time. A sudden drop in fuel economy may signal a need for tune-up or other maintenance.

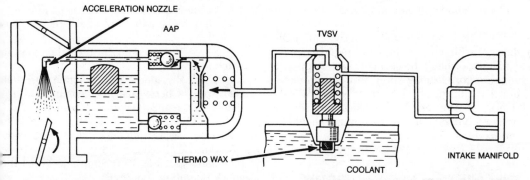

In this cross section view of the AAP system, the intake manifold vacuum has dropped enough to allow the AAP diaphragm to move in the direction of the arrow, forcing gasoline past the upper check valve into the acceleration nozzle

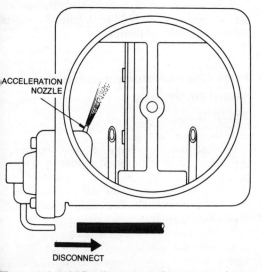

To test the AAP, disconnect the vacuum hose while looking down into the carburetor for a squirt of gas from the acceleration nozzle

heat. This spring is connected by mechanical linkage to the choke plate, and heated by the engine coolant. When the engine is cold, the spring expands and closes the choke. As the

engine heats, the spring contracts opening the choke.

1975, and 1977, and later engines have a Choke Breaker (CB) system (called Choke Opener in 1975) attached to the choke plate by mechanical linkage. The CB is essentially a diaphragm actuated by intake manifold vacuum. The vacuum causes the diaphragm to pull back on the linkage, opening the choke plate slightly against the force of the automatic choke spring.

The purpose of the CB system is to prevent the cold engine from receiving an overrich mixture, caused by the closed choke plate, because rich mixtures are higher in HC and CO emissions.

INSPECTION

Check the vacuum hose first for leaks, kinks, and improper connections.

1. With the engine cold and idling (parking brake set, front wheels blocked, and transmission in neutral), remove the lid from the air cleaner. Disconnect the vacuum hose from the CB diaphragm, while watching to see if the link is pulled out of the diaphragm by the force of the automatic choke spring.

2. When the hose is reconnected, the dia-

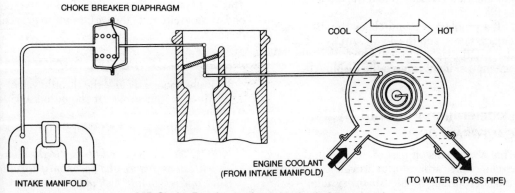

20R Choke Breaker and automatic choke systems

phragm should pull the link back in toward itself.

If CB does not operate properly, either the linkage is binding or the diaphragm is faulty. The linkage should be cleaned thoroughly with a carburetor cleaning spray and a clean cloth, but it should not be lubricated with any substance whatsoever. If this does not restore proper CB operation, the diaphragm should be replaced.

Fast Idle Cam Breaker (FICB)

After warm-up this system forcibly releases the fast idle cam which lowers the engine speed.

1. Connect the vacuum gauge between the fast idle cam breaker and the three way connector using enough hose to allow the gauge to rest on the truck fender.

2. Jack up the front and rear of the truck and support it with jack stands.

3. Start the engine, and with the coolant temperature below 122°F check that the vacuum is zero regardless of the driving speed.

NOTE: *Do not run the truck at high speeds while supported by the jack stands.*

4. Run the engine to normal temperature.

5. Check that the vacuum is high at 7 mph.

6. Check that the vacuum is lower (than the step 4 reading) above 16 mph. If a problem is found inspect the speed sensor, VSV, and the TSVS.

7. Check the diaphragm and linkage operation.

8. Disconnect the vacuum gauge and reconnect the hose to the proper location.

9. Stop the engine.

10. Remove the hose from the fast idle cam breaker.

11. Set the idle cam. While holding the throttle valve slightly open, pull up on the fast idle cam linkage and release the throttle.

12. Start the engine but do not touch the accelerator.

13. Reconnect the hose and check that the fast idle cam is released and the engine returns to idle.

If a problem is found check the diaphragm, linkage hoses, and the TVSV. Apply vacuum to the FICB diaphragm and check that the linkage moves, if not replace the diaphragm.

Deceleration Fuel Cut System
CALIFORNIA ONLY

This system cuts off part of the fuel in the slow circuit of the carburetor to prevent overheating and afterburning of the exhaust system.

1. Connect a tachometer to the engine.

2. Start the engine and check that it runs normally.

3. Pinch the vacuum hose to the vacuum switch.

4. Gradually increase the engine speed to 3000 rpm. Check that the engine misfires slightly between 2400 and 3000 rpm.

CAUTION: *Perform this procedure quickly to avoid overheating the catalytic converter.*

5. Release the hose and gradually increase the engine speed to 3000 rpm. Check that the engine operation is normal.

6. With the engine at idle unplug the solenoid valve. Check that the engine misfires or stalls.

7. If a problem is found check the switch and solenoid. If everything is normal connect the vacuum line and wiring.

Fuel Cut Solenoid Valve and Vacuum Switch
TESTING

1. Remove the solenoid.

2. Test that the solenoid is operating properly. This can be done by connecting two wires to the battery terminals, one negative, one positive. By attaching these wires to the switch you will hear it click. The click indicates it is operating properly.

3. Check the O-ring for damage.

4. Reinstall the solenoid, if no problem is found.

5. Use an ohmmeter to check that there is continuity between the switch terminal and the body.

6. Start the engine.

7. Check now for no continuity between the switch terminal and the body.

Secondary Slow Circuit Fuel Cut System

This system cuts off part of the fuel in the secondary slow circuit of the carburetor to prevent dieseling.

INSPECTION OF THE FUEL CUT VALVE

1. Fully open and close the throttle valve.

2. Measure the stroke. It should be 0.059–0.079 in.

3. If adjustment is necessary bend the lever.

NOTE: *The stroke should be set to the above specifications before the secondary throttle valve opens. (Before kick up).*

High Altitude Compensation (HAC)

At high altitudes, air/fuel mixtures become richer, due to the thinner air available. The High Altitude Compensation (HAC) system installed on 1977 and later trucks sold in federally designated areas insures a proper air/fuel mix by supplying additional air to the low and/or high speed circuits at high altitude (above 4000 feet) to minimize HC and CO emissions. The system also advances the ignition timing to improve driveability at high altitudes.

The HAC system consists of an HAC valve, a dual diaphragm distributor, and a check valve.

HIGH ALTITUDE OPERATION

Low atmospheric pressure allows the bellows in the HAC valve to expand and close port A. Intake manifold vacuum acts on the diaphragm in the HAC valve through the check valve, opening the passages between the carburetor and the atmosphere via the HAC valve. These open passages allow air to flow into the low and/or high speed circuits in the carburetor. As a result, the air/fuel mixture becomes leaner.

The intake manifold vacuum also acts on the subdiaphragm in the distributor. This vacuum is maintained by the check valve, except in the following instance: a vacuum in the main dia-

phragm of the distributor rises above 5.0 in. of mercury (Hg), the vacuum advance will revert to normal.

LOW ALTITUDE OPERATION

High atmospheric pressure, entering through the bottom of the HAC valve acts on the bellows and opens port A. Since the intake manifold vacuum does not act on the diaphragm in the HAC valve, the air passage from the carburetor to the atmosphere is closed by the diaphragm. This prevents a lean mixture at lower altitudes.

The intake manifold vacuum also cannot act on the distributor subdiaphragm, so the distributor advance in normal.

INSPECTION

NOTE: *Before checking the HAC system at altitudes near 4000 feet, determine the position of the HAC valve. This can be done by blowing into any one of the three ports on top of the HAC valve when the engine is idling. If the passage is open, the valve is in the high altitude position. If it is closed, the valve is in the low altitude position. When the position is determined, proceed with the appropriate high altitude or low altitude inspection.*

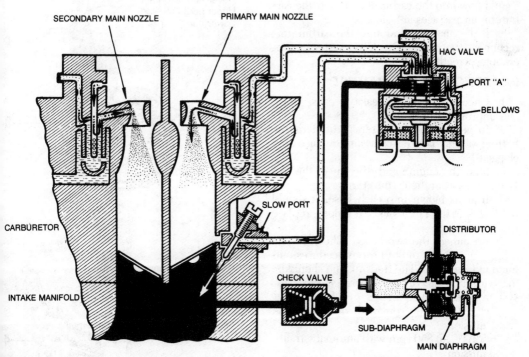

SECONDARY MAIN NOZZLE   PRIMARY MAIN NOZZLE   HAC VALVE   PORT "A"   BELLOWS   SLOW PORT   CARBURETOR   DISTRIBUTOR   CHECK VALVE   INTAKE MANIFOLD   SUB-DIAPHRAGM   MAIN DIAPHRAGM

Operation of the HAC system at high altitudes. The check valve is shown here in the closed position, but as the carburetor throttle plates are opened, the check valve will also open due to higher intake manifold vacuum

INSPECTION AT HIGH ALTITUDE

1. Check all vacuum hoses for leaks, breaks, kinks, or improper connections.

2. Visually inspect the HAC filter and replace it if clogged. It is located at the bottom of the HAC valve.

3. Start the engine and check the ignition timing as outlined in /chapter Two. If it is about 13°BTC, go on with the procedure. If it is only slightly out of adjustment, adjust the timing. If the hose between the HAC valve and the three way connector is pinched, does the ignition timing become about 13°BTC? If so, the HAC valve should be replaced. If not, the check valve must be inspected. It should be possible to blow air through it from the HAC side, and not from the intake manifold side. If faulty, replace. If not, the distributor vacuum advance is faulty and must be repaired or replaced.

4. If the hose between the white side of the check valve and the three way connector is pinched, the ignition timing should stay at 13°BTC for a minute or more. If not, replace the HAC valve.

5. If the hose is disconnected from the black side of the check valve and the hose end blocked, the ignition timing should stay at 13°BTC for one minute or more. If not, replace the check valve.

6. Disconnect the two HAC hoses from the carburetor. If air is blown into each hose, it should flow into the carburetor. If not, the carburetor air passages are blocked.

8. If the air does flow into the carburetor, reconnect the hoses. The HAC system is operating correctly.

INSPECTION AT LOW ALTITUDE

1. Check all hoses for leaks, breaks, kinks, and improper connections.

2. Inspect the HAC filter, located in the bottom of the HAC valve, and replace it if clogged.

3. Start the engine and disconnect the two HAC hoses from the carburetor.

4. If air is blown into each hose, it should not flow into the HAC valve. If it does, replace the valve.

5. Reconnect the two hoses. Check the ignition timing according to the procedures outlined in Chapter 2. The transmission should be in Neutral. If the timing is correct, the HAC system is okay. It should be:

- 8°BTC @ 800 rpm with manual transmission
- 8°BTC @ 850 rpm with automatic transmission

6. If the timing is incorrect, disconnect the vacuum hose from the distributor subdiaphragm. If the timing does not change, adjust the ignition timing. If the timing changes, replace the HAC valve.

GASOLINE ENGINE FUEL SYSTEM

Mechanical Fuel Pump

All engines, except the 1978 and earlier 20R are equipped with single action mechanical fuel pumps. The pump is located on the right side of the engine just in front of the oil filter.

TESTING

Disconnect the outlet line from the fuel pump and connect a pressure gauge. Fuel pump pressure should measure 2.8–4.3 psi at 2500 rpm. There is normally enough gasoline in the carburetor float bowl to perform this test.

Discharge rate of the pump should also be checked. The 8R-C pump should deliver over 800cc of gasoline per minute; the rate for all others should be 1500cc per minute.

The fuel pump should not be replaced until both of those tests have been performed. If gasoline is not being delivered to the carburetor, the fuel filter, fuel tank, and all fuel lines should be checked for blockage. The carbu-

1. Diaphragm and spring
2. Cover and diaphragm
3. Upper body
4. Lower body

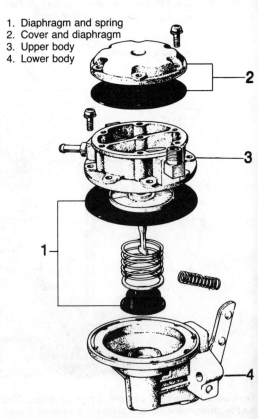

F series engine fuel pump

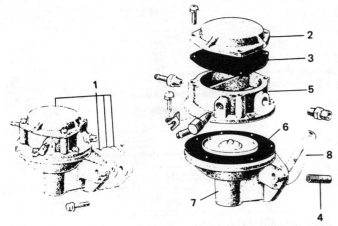

1. Fuel pump assembly
2. Fuel pump cover
3. Fuel pump cover gasket
4. Rocker arm spring
5. Fuel pump upper body
6. Diaphragm
7. Fuel pump lower body
8. Rocker arm

8R-C and 18R-C fuel pump disassembled

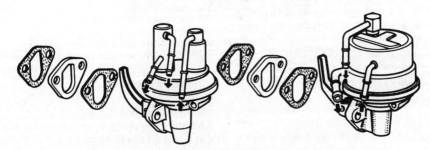

Mechanical fuel pump used on 20R and 22R engines

retor float and needle should also be inspected for proper operation. These sources should be checked before replacing the fuel pump.

REMOVAL AND INSTALLATION

1970–78

To remove the fuel pump simply disconnect and plug the fuel lines and remove the two bolts which hold the pump to the clock.

When installing a new pump always use a new gasket between the pump and the clock to prevent oil leakage. If any new rubber hose must be used to repair the fuel line, be sure that it is gasoline resistant.

1979 and Later

1. Disconnect the negative battery terminal.

CAUTION: *When working on the fuel system, do not smoke or work near any fire hazard. Keep gasoline off rubber or leather parts.*

2. Drain the radiator.
3. Remove the upper radiator hose.
4. Remove all three lines from the fuel pump.
5. Remove the two bolts, the fuel pump, and gasket.

NOTE: *The fuel pump is not repairable. It must be replaced as a complete unit.*

6. Installation is the reverse of removal.

Electric Fuel Pump

All 20R engined trucks 1975–78 are equipped with an electric fuel pump, located in the gas tank. The pump is serviced as a unit; if it breaks, replace it.

TESTING

Before performing pressure and discharge rate tests, pump operation should be checked with the oil pressure switch disconnected. The reason for this is that the electric fuel pump is wired into the oil pressure warning light and pressure switch wiring, so that it operates only when the engine has sufficient oil pressure. The fuel pump also runs when the ignition switch is turned to Start.

1. Disconnect the electrical clip from the oil pressure switch.
2. Turn the ignition switch to On.
3. Check for a smooth flow of gasoline from the fuel filter outlet. If the pump is noisy, it is probably defective. If the pump does not run, check the pump resistor and relay.
4. With the oil pressure switch electrical clip still off, check the discharge rate of the pump. Connect a line to the outlet of the fuel filter, turn the ignition switch to On, and measure the discharge capacity. It should be over 1.3 quarts per minute.

5. Turn the key off, and connect a pressure gauge to the filter outlet. Turn the ignition switch to On and measure to fuel pump pressure. It should be between 2.1 and 4.3 psi.

As with the mechanical pump, all tests should be performed, and all lines and the filter should be checked, before replacing the pump.

REMOVAL AND INSTALLATION

1. Remove the nagative (–) cable from the battery.

2. Remove the fuel tank, after disconnecting the fuel lines. See Chapter 10 for fuel tank removal and installation.

3. Remove the bolts which secure the access plate to the tank. Remove the plate and its gasket, and remove the pump.

CAUTION: *Do not operate the fuel pump unless it is immersed in gasoline and connected to its resistor.*

4. Installation is the reverse of removal. Use a new gasket on the access plate, and check for leaks after installation.

FUEL PUMP RESISTOR

Check the resistor for continuity between the two terminals. If there is no continuity, replace the resistor and check the fuel pump operation.

Carburetor

Two barrel carburetors are used on all engines to provide an adequate air/fuel mixture under all operating conditions. The carburetors are equipped with an automatic choke, vacuum operated secondary barrels, a thermostatic valve to prevent overrich mixtures in hot weather, and, on 18R-C and 20R engines, an electric solenoid valve for positive shut off of the fuel supply when the ignition is turned off.

OPERATION

All carburetors are similar in design having basic systems which enable them to perform their primary function of providing the correct air/fuel mixture for the engine.

These systems are float, starting, idle, progression, main feed, acceleration, and enrichment. Familiarity with these systems is helpful in the diagnosis and correction of carburetor malfunctions.

Float Circuit

The float mechanism maintains a constant fuel level so that atomization at all discharge jets will be uniform under varying condition.

Operation of the system is simple. As the float drops, a needle valve is released which admits fuel from the fuel supply (pump). The

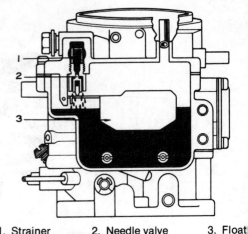

1. Strainer   2. Needle valve   3. Float

The float circuit

rising fuel level in the float chamber lifts the valves which are operated by the float wear quickly and should be replaced an any major carburetor overhaul.

Starting Circuit

An automatic choke is used to increase the vacuum of a cranking engine. A choke consists of a plate which covers the throat of the carburetor. When this plate closes over the throat of the carburetor, blocking the airflow, a rich mixture of fuel and air is drawn into the jets to the carburetor throat.

The automatic choke mechanism of the 8R-C and 18R-C two-barrel carburetor operates via a thermostatic spring and a vacuum chamber. The thermostatic spring is set to fully close the choke valve at 77°F.

As the engine is cranked vacuum in the intake manifold draws the vacuum piston down closing the choke valve. The pressure of the air

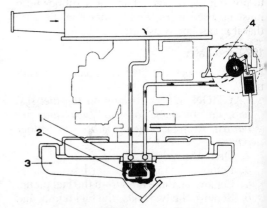

1. Intake manifold   4. Coil housing
2. Stove pipe   5. Vacuum piston
3. Exhaust manifold

The automatic choke system—8R-C and 18R-C

being drawn through the carburetor causes the choke valve to open. As the engine warms the bimetal spring releases the choke valve. Intake pressure and manifold vacuum balance each other causing the choke valve to remain open.

Operation of the 20R choke system is quite different from the earlier system, but the principle of an enriched mixture for cold engine operation remains the same. The 20R choke system is covered in the emission control section earlier in this chapter.

Idling Circuit

The idling system provides fuel for the engine when the throttle plate is closed or only slightly open. The system provides a rich mixture below the throttle plate by providing a passage for fuel to tenter and mix with the small quantity of air which can pass through the throttle plates. The idle speed screw, located below the lever of the throttle plate, provides the fuel metering device for the idle circuit.

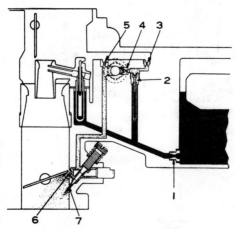

1. First main jet
2. Slow speed jet
3. Air bleed
4. Economizer jet
5. Air bleed
6. Throttle plate
7. Idle port

The idling circuit

Progression Circuit

As the throttle valve is opened, vacuum at the idle adjustment orifice is lessened because more air is passing around the throttle plate. With the lower vacuum, less mixture is drawn into the throat at the moment that more air is passing into the manifold. To provide more fuel, one or more orifices are drilled in the carburetor idle passage at points which are in line with the angled throttle plate. These hoes, comprising the progression circuit, ensure a smooth transfer from idling to main jet operation. These hoses are easily clogged if dirt en-

ters the carburetor. Clogging of the circuit creates flat spots in acceleration.

Main Jet Circuit

This circuit supplies the air/fuel mixture for normal engine operation. This circuit is in full operation when the throttle valve is opened and there is sufficient vacuum present in the air horn to draw fuel from the main jet circuit outlet centered in the venturi.

Acceleration Circuit

When the throttle valve is opened, an immediate need for an enriched air/fuel mixture is created. The accelerator pump supplies the engine with an extra squirt of gasoline for this demand period.

As the plunger moves upward, fuel is drawn into the plunger chamber through the strainer and the inlet check valve. When the throttle plate is opened the accelerator pump plunger is pushed downward discharging fuel through the accelerator jet and into the carburetor.

Power Circuit

This circuit is used to enrich the air/fuel mixture automatically when there are great columns of air being drawn into the intake manifold. This is the state of the intake system when the engine is under a heavy load or at high speed. When vacuum in the air horn is low, a vacuum piston is released which allows fuel from the float bowl to by-pass the main jet and raises the level in the main well of the carburetor. This allows a richer air/fuel mixture to be drawn into the venturi.

REMOVAL AND INSTALLATION

1. Remove the air cleaner.
2. Disconnect the fuel line at the carburetor.
3. Disconnect the automatic choke stove and the distributor vacuum line. On 20R engines, drain approximately two quarts of coolant from the cooling system, then disconnect the choke heater hoses from the choke housing.

CAUTION: *When draining the coolant, keep in mind that cats and dogs are attracted by the ethelyne glycol antifreeze, and are quite likely to drink any that is left in an uncovered container or in puddles on the ground. This will prove fatal in sufficient quantity. Always drain the coolant into a sealable container. Coolant should be reused unless it is contaminated or several years old.*

4. On models with an automatic transmission, remove the transmission throttle rod.
5. Remove the accelerator linkage.
6. Remove the four bolts holding the carburetor to the intake manifold. On the the 2F

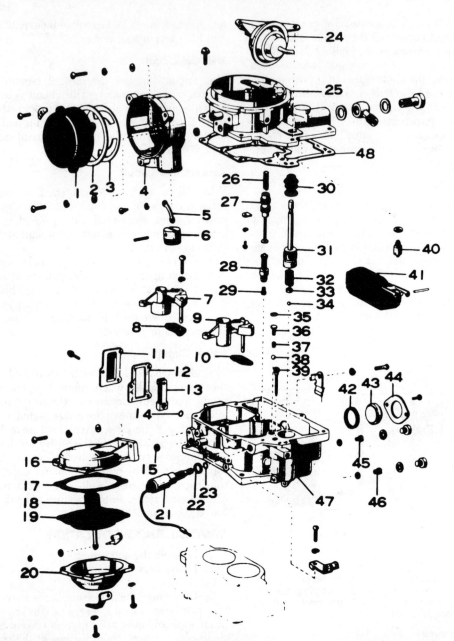

1. Choke coil housing	17. Diaphragm gasket	33. Ball retainer
2. Coil housing gasket	18. Diaphragm spring	34. Check ball
3. Coil housing plate	19. Diaphragm	35. Gasket
4. Thermostat case	20. Diaphragm housing	36. Discharge weight stopper
5. Connecting link	21. Solenoid valve	37. Pump discharge weight
6. Choke piston	22. Gasket	38. Check ball
7. Secondary venturi	23. O-ring	39. Slow jet
8. Venturi gasket	24. Diaphragm	40. Float needle valve
9. Primary venturi	25. Air horn	41. Float
10. Venturi gasket	26. Power piston spring	42. O-ring
11. Thermostatic valve cover	27. Power piston	43. Sight glass
12. Gasket	28. Power valve	44. Sight glass plate
13. Thermostatic valve	29. Power jet	45. Secondary main jet
14. O-ring	30. Boot	46. Primary main jet
15. Gasket	31. Pump plunger	47. Carburetor body
16. Diaphragm housing cap	32. Damping spring	48. Air horn gasket

18R-C carburetor body components

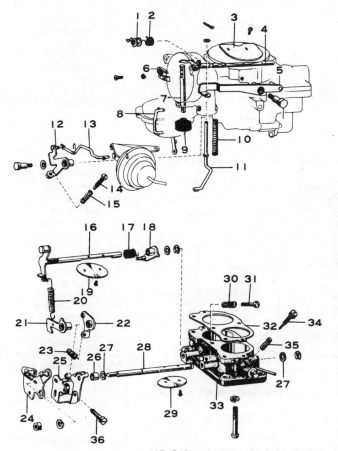

1. Fast idle cam
2. Fast idle cam spring
3. Choke valve
4. Choke shaft
5. Pump lever
6. Fast idle cam follower
7. Sliding rod
8. Connecting link
9. Boot
10. Pump spring
11. Pump connecting link
12. Lever
13. Connector
14. Screw (for T.P.)
15. Spring
16. Second throttle shaft
17. Diaphragm relief spring
18. Diaphragm relief lever
19. Second throttle valve
20. Back spring
21. Second kick lever
22. Fast idle adjusting lever
23. Fast idle adjust spring
24. First throttle lever
25. First throttle shaft arm
26. Collar
27. First throttle shaft shim
28. First throttle shaft
29. First throttle valve
30. Spring
31. Screw
32. Body flange gasket
33. Flange
34. Idle adjusting screw
35. Idle adjusting spring
36. Fast idle adjusting screw

18R-C throttle valve body exploded view

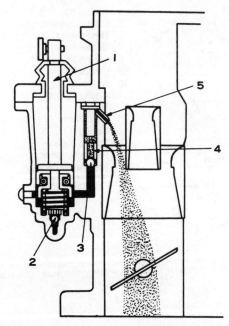

1. Pump plunger
2. Steel ball; inlet
3. Steel ball; outlet
4. Pump discharge weight
5. Accelerator pump jet

Acceleration circuit

engine, disconnect the magnetic valve wire from the coil terminal and the choke cable from the carburetor.

7. Remove the carburetor and gasket. Cover the intake manifold with a clean rag so that nothing will fall into the intake manifold.

8. Installation is the reverse of removal.

NOTE: *Be certain that the carburetor mounting gasket is intact and that it is not cracked or peeling. Leakage of air under the carburetor will cause a rough idle, flooding, stalling, and poor engine operation at higher speeds.*

FLOAT LEVEL ADJUSTMENT

All Except 2F Engines

With the engine idling, check the fuel level in the carburetor sight glass. If it is even with the line, no adjustment is necessary. If it is not, adjust the float as follows:

1. Remove and invert the air horn so that the float hangs by its own weight against the air horn. The distance from the tip of the float to the air horn should be 0.37 in. for 8R-C engines, 0.20 in. for 18R-Cs, and 0.197 for 20R engines, 1975–77. The measurement should be

1. Pump jet
2. Spring
3. Outlet check ball
4. Secondary venturi

5. Primary venturi
6. Pump plunger
7. Spring
8. Ball retainer
9. Inlet check ball
10. Plug
11. Spring
12. AAP outlet check ball
13. Plug
14. AAP inlet check ball
15. Throttle positioner
16. Thermostatic valve cover
17. Thermostatic valve
18. Primary slow jet
19. Power valve
20. Power jet
21. Sight glass
22. Glass retainer
23. Diaphragm housing cap
24. Spring
25. Diaphragm
26. Housing
27. Fast idle cam
28. Solenoid valve
29. Carburetor body
30. Diaphragm
31. Spring
32. AAP housing
33. Secondary main jet
34. Primary main jet

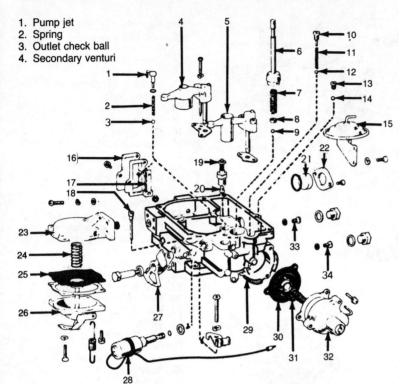

Carburetor main body on 20R engines

1. Choke coil water housing
2. Choke housing plate
3. Choke lever
4. Choke housing body
5. Choke breaker
6. Relief lever
7. Choke shaft
8. Connecting lever
9. Choke valve
10. Air horn
11. Choke opener
12. Union
13. Pump arm
14. Spring
15. Power piston
16. Piston retainer
17. Needle valve set
18. Float

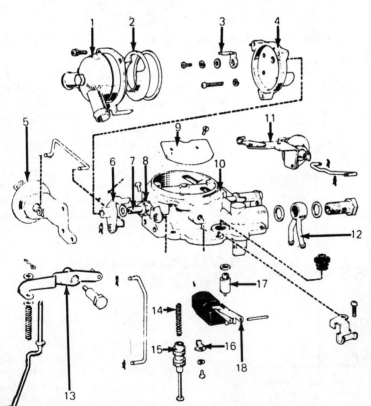

Carburetor air horn on 20R engines

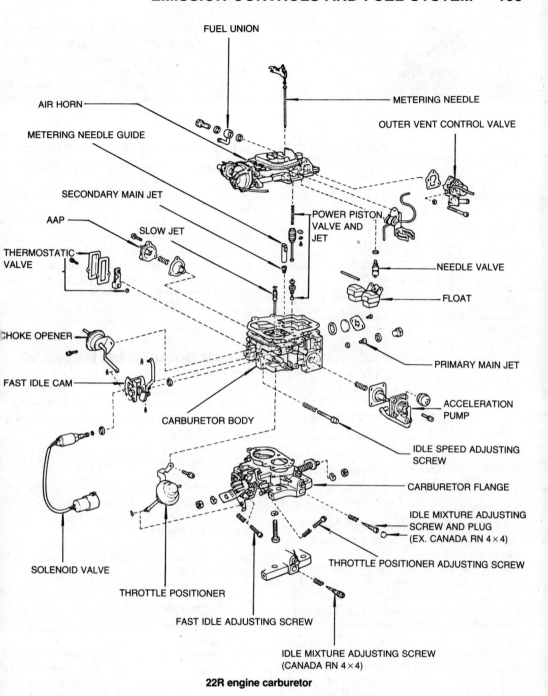

FUEL UNION

AIR HORN

METERING NEEDLE GUIDE

SECONDARY MAIN JET

AAP

SLOW JET

THERMOSTATIC VALVE

CHOKE OPENER

FAST IDLE CAM

CARBURETOR BODY

SOLENOID VALVE

THROTTLE POSITIONER

FAST IDLE ADJUSTING SCREW

IDLE MIXTURE ADJUSTING SCREW
(CANADA RN 4 × 4)

METERING NEEDLE

OUTER VENT CONTROL VALVE

POWER PISTON VALVE AND JET

NEEDLE VALVE

FLOAT

PRIMARY MAIN JET

ACCELERATION PUMP

IDLE SPEED ADJUSTING SCREW

CARBURETOR FLANGE

IDLE MIXTURE ADJUSTING SCREW AND PLUG
(EX. CANADA RN 4 × 4)

THROTTLE POSITIONER ADJUSTING SCREW

22R engine carburetor

0.276 in. for 1978, and 0.28 in. for 1979–80. The 1981 and later 22R float level is 0.413 in. (raised position) 1.89 in. (lowered position). In all cases, the air horn gasket should be removed before measuring. If the distance is incorrect, adjust the float by bending the center tab, marked A in the illustration, on all models except 1978. On 1978 floats only, adjust by bending the metal tab across the two slots and one hole right next to where it enters the float.

2. Raise the float away from the air horn and measure the distance from the needle valve push pin and the float lip. It should measure 0.04 in. Adjust by bending the portion of the float lip marked B in the illustration through 1977. On 1978 floats, there is a single center tab resembling the tab marked A in the illustration which must be bent to adjust the distance to 0.039 in.

3. Reinstall the air horn.

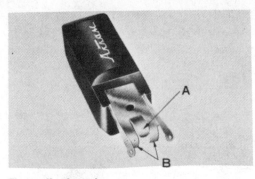

Float adjusting tabs

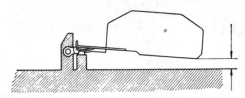

Measuring float lever—raised position

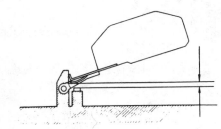

Measuring float lever—lowered position

2F Engines

1. Remove the carburetor air horn. Invert the air horn and allow the float to hang towards the air horn.

2. With the air horn gasket removed, measure the distance between the float and the air horn, at the end of the float opposite the needle valve. The distance should be 0.295 in. If adjustment is necessary, remove the float and bend the tab which is centered between the hinge pivot points. After the adjustment is completed, reinstall the float and recheck the setting.

3. Lift upward on the float and measure the distance between the needle valve push pin and the lip of the float. The distance should be 0.043 in. If adjustment is necessary, remove the float and bend the tabs located just inside of the hinge points. After the adjustment is completed, reinstall the float and recheck the setting.

FAST IDLE ADJUSTMENT

8R-C & 18R-C

This adjustment can only be made with the carburetor removed from the truck. With the carburetor inverted and the choke fully closed, measure the distance from the primary throttle plate to the throttle bore using a wire gauge. It should measure 0.029 in. on 8R-C carburetors, 0.040 in. on 18R-Cs, and 0.047 in. on 20Rs. Adjust the clearance to specifications by turning the fast idle adjustment screw.

20R Engines through 1979 and 2F Engines

1. Remove the carburetor as previously outlined.

2. Close the choke valve completely and invert the carburetor.

3. Using a wire type feeler gauge, check the clearance between the upper half of the primary throttle blade and the throttle bore. The clearance should be 0.047 for 20R engines; 0.051 for 2F engines. If necessary, adjust the clearance by turning the fast idle screw.

4. Install the carburetor as previously outlined.

1980 20R Engines and 1981 and Later 22R Engines

NOTE: *A special blade angle tool must be obtained to properly make this adjustment.*

1. Remove the carburetor as previously outlined.

2. Close the choke valve completely and set the throttle shaft lever to the first seep of the fast idle cam.

3. Attach the blade angle tool to the primary throttle blade. Adjust the primary throttle blade angle to 24° from horizontal by turning the fast idle screw.

4. Remove the angle tool from the carburetor and install the carburetor as previously outlined.

20R Engines through 1979

1. Start the engine and allow it to reach normal operating temperature.

2. Stop the engine and disconnect the vacuum hose from the EGR valve. Connect a tachometer to the engine as previously outlined.

3. Open the throttle valve slightly and close the choke plate, which will set the fast idle cam.

4. Disconnect the vacuum hose(s) from the distributor vacuum unit. Plug the vacuum hose end(s).

5. Without touching the accelerator pedal start the engine and read the tachometer. If necessary, adjust the fast idle speed to 2400 rpm by turning the fast idle screw.

6. Reconnect the vacuum hoses to both the EGR valve and the distributor vacuum unit. Disconnect the tachometer from the engine.

1980 20R Engines and 1981 and later 22R Engines

1. Start the engine and allow it to reach normal operating temperature.

2. Stop the engine and connect a tachometer to the engine as previously outlined.

3. Remove the air cleaner assembly.

4. Disconnect the vacuum hose at the fast idle cam breaker (if so equipped) and plug the hose end.

5. Disconnect the vacuum hose(s) from the distributor vacuum unit.

6. Disconnect the vacuum hose from the EGR valve.

7. Open the throttle valve slightly and fully pull up on the fast idle linkage. Release the throttle.

8. Without touching the accelerator pedal, start the engine and read the tachometer. If necessary, adjust the fast idle speed to 2400 rpm by turning the fast idle screw.

9. Reconnect the vacuum hoses, disconnect the tachometer and reinstall the air cleaner.

2F Engines

1. Start the engine and allow it to reach normal operating temperature.

2. Stop the engine and connect a tachometer to the engine as previously outlined.

3. Remove the air cleaner assembly.

4. Disconnect the vacuum hoses from both the EGR valve and the distributor vacuum unit.

5. Pull the dash mounted choke control knob fully outward.

6. Open the choke plate and prevent it from closing using a screwdriver. Do not jam the screwdriver into place.

7. Start the engine and read the tachometer. If necessary, adjust the fast idle speed to 1800 rpm by turning the fast idle screw.

8. Remove the screwdriver from the choke, disconnect the tachometer and reconnect the vacuum hoses.

9. Install the air cleaner assembly.

IDLE SPEED SCREW ADJUSTMENT

Before installing a freshly assembled carburetor make a preliminary idle speed adjustment. Turn the idle speed screw in all the way (until it just contacts the seat) and back it out two turns for the 8R-C, 2½ turns from fully closed for the 18R-C engine, and 1¾ turns from fully closed for the 20R and 2F and 2½ turns for the 22R.

CAUTION: *Do not overtighten the idle speed screw as you will damage the tip.*

AUTOMATIC CHOKE INSPECTION AND ADJUSTMENT

NOTE: *Steps 1–4 must be performed with the engine cold and turned OFF.*

1. Remove the air cleaner lid.

2. Depress the accelerator pedal. The choke plate should close. If the choke plate closes, proceed to step 5.

3. If the choke plate does not close, loosen the three screws around the thermostat case.

CAUTION: *Do not loosen the center housing screw, coolant leakage will occur.*

4. Rotate the case just until the choke plate closes and tighten the case screws.

5. Start the engine and allow it to reach normal operating temperature. If the choke plate opens fully, the choke adjustment is correct. If it does not, loosen the three case screws and rotate the case until the choke is fully open. Tighten the case screws.

CHOKE UNLOADER ADJUSTMENT

With the choke closed, fully open the throttle valve. The choke should open 51° on the 8RC engine and, 47° on the 18R-C, 45° for U.S. 22R, 50° for Canadian 22R, and 50° on the 20R and 2F. The total angle of choke opening can be measured with a special angle gauge, or with a gauge of the proper angle cut from cardboard.

To adjust the amount of choke opening on 8R-C and 18R-C engines, bend either the fast idle cam follower or the choke shaft tab. On 2F and 20R engines, bend the fast idle lever, and on 22R engines bend the first throttle arm.

CHOKE RELOADER ADJUSTMENT

A reloader is used on the 8R-C engine to prevent the throttle valve from opening during automatic choke operation.

1. When the choke valve is 50° from the closed position, the reloader lever should disengage from its stop.

NOTE: *Angle A in the illustration should be 20° when measured with a gauge.*

2. To adjust, bend the portion of the linkage indicated by the letter B.

3. When the primary throttle valve is fully opened, with the reloader in operating position, the clearance between the secondary throttle valve edge and the bore should be 0.014–0.030 in. Measure the clearance with a wire gauge, and bend the reloader tab to adjust.

4. Fully open the choke valve hand. The reloader lever should be disengaged from its stop by the weight on its link.

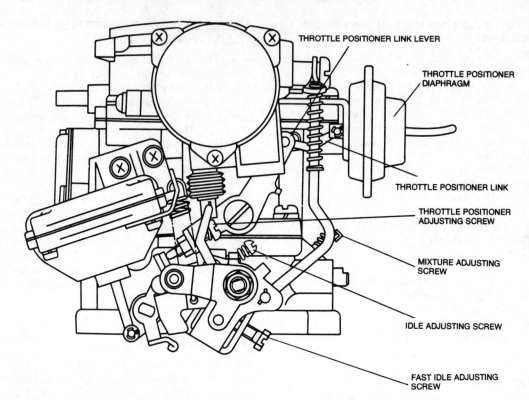

THROTTLE POSITIONER LINK LEVER

THROTTLE POSITIONER
DIAPHRAGM

THROTTLE POSITIONER LINK

THROTTLE POSITIONER
ADJUSTING SCREW

MIXTURE ADJUSTING
SCREW

IDLE ADJUSTING SCREW

FAST IDLE ADJUSTING
SCREW

Carburetor adjustments—18R-C. The 8R-C is identical, except that the idle speed screw is opposite the fast idle screw, instead of above it as shown here

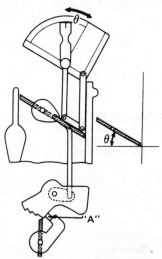

The choke angle can be measured with an angle gauge, as shown here, or with a piece of cardboard cut to the proper angle. On the 20R, bend the fast idle lever at "A" to adjust the unloader angle

CHOKE BREAKER ADJUSTMENT

20R and 22R Only

Push in the choke breaker rod fully to open the choke plate. The choke plate angle should

Bend the choke shaft tab to adjust the unloader angle on 8R-C and 18R-C carburetors

measure 40° (1975–78), 38° (1979 and later). To adjust, bend the relief lever (to the right of the thermostatic index mark).

KICK-UP ADJUSTMENT

18R-C and 20R

This adjustment must be made with the carburetor removed. With the primary throttle fully opened, check the clearance between the secondary plate and the throttle bore. It should measure 0.008 in. on both 18R-C and 20R engines. Adjust if necessary by bending the secondary throttle lever.

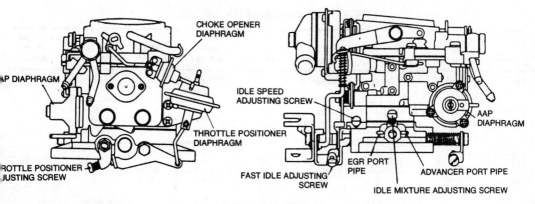

CHOKE OPENER DIAPHRAGM

AP DIAPHRAGM

IDLE SPEED ADJUSTING SCREW

THROTTLE POSITIONER DIAPHRAGM

AAP DIAPHRAGM

ROTTLE POSITIONER JUSTING SCREW

FAST IDLE ADJUSTING SCREW

EGR PORT PIPE

ADVANCER PORT PIPE

IDLE MIXTURE ADJUSTING SCREW

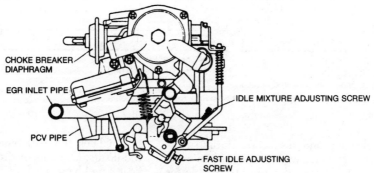

CHOKE BREAKER DIAPHRAGM

EGR INLET PIPE

PCV PIPE

IDLE MIXTURE ADJUSTING SCREW

FAST IDLE ADJUSTING SCREW

20R carburetor adjustments

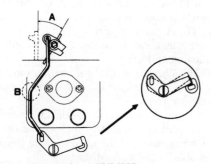

Measure the angle at "A" (20°)

2F Engines

NOTE: *A special blade angle gauge is needed for this adjustment.*

1. Remove the carburetor as previously outlined.

2. Attach the blade angle gauge to the secondary throttle blade.

3. Open the primary throttle blade fully and read the blade angle gauge. The secondary throttle blade should open slightly to an angle of 28° (except California) or 25° (California). If adjustment is necessary, bend the secondary throttle lever as required to attain the proper angle.

4. Detach the blade angle gauge and install the carburetor as previously outlined.

ACCELERATOR PUMP ADJUSTMENT

18R-C, 20R and 2F

Adjust the amount of pump stroke to 0.177 in. on 18R-C and 1975–79 20R carburetors by bending the pump rod at point A. The 1980 20R adjustment should be 0.154 in. The 2F is 0.374 in.

OVERHAUL

To overhaul the carburetor, you must first purchase the proper rebuilding kit by knowing the exact year and model of your carburetor and by making note of any identifying numbers on the casting. This will make it easier for you to get the right parts. Read the rebuilding instructions carefully and study the exploded drawings. Then proceed to remove the carburetor and disassemble it.

Efficient carburetion depends greatly on

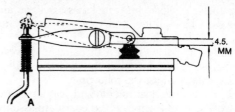

4.5. MM

A

Adjust the pump stroke at point "A"

Carburetor Specifications

Year	Engine	Float Level Adjustment	Fast Idle Adjustment	Choke Unloader	Choke Reloader	Choke Breaker	Kick Up Adjustment	Accelerator Pump Adjustment
1970–71	8R-C	0.37 in.	o.029 in.	51°	0.014–0.030 in.	—	—	—
1972–74	18R-C	0.20 in.	0.040 in.	47°	—	—	0.008 in.	0.177 in.
1975–78	20R	0.197 in.①	0.047 in.	50°	—	40°	0.008 in.	0.177 in.
1979–80	20R	0.28 in.	0.047 in.	50°	—	38°	0.008 in.	0.177 in.②
1981–82	22R	0.413 in.③	24°	45°④	—	38°	—	—
1970–82	2F	0.295 in.⑤	—	50°	—	38°	28°⑥	0.374 in.
1983–85	22R	0.386③	22°	45°④	—	38°–42°	—	—

① 1978 20R 0.276 in.
② 1980 20R 0.154 in.
③ Raised position; 1.89 lowered position
④ Canada: 50°
⑤ Float lowered: 0.043 in.
⑥ Calif.: 25°

NOTE: Some 84 & 85 models have Electronic Fuel Injection Systems.

careful cleaning and inspection during overhaul since dirt, gum, water, or varnish in or on the carburetor parts are often responsible for poor performance.

Overhaul your carburetor in a clean, dust free area. Carefully disassemble the carburetor, referring often to the exploded views. Keep all similar and look-alike parts segregated during disassembly and cleaning to avoid accidental interchange during assembly. Make a note of all jet sizes.

When the carburetor is disassembled, wash all parts (except diaphragms, electric choke units, pump plunger, and any other plastic, leather, fiber, or rubber parts) in clean carburetor solvent. Do not leave parts in the solvent any longer than necessary to sufficiently loosen the deposits. Excessive cleaning may remove the special finish from the float bowl and choke valve bodies, leaving these parts unfit for service. Rinse all parts in clean solvent and blow them dry with compressed air or allow them to air dry. Wipe clean all cork, plastic, leather, and fiber parts with a clean lint free cloth.

Blow out all passages and jets with compressed air and be sure that there are no restrictions or blockages. Never use wire or similar tools to clean jets, fuel passages, or air bleeds. Clean all jets and valves separately to avoid accidental interchange.

Check all parts for wear or damage. If wear or damage is found, replace the defective parts.

Especially check the following:

1. Check the float needle and seat for wear. If wear is found, replace the complete assembly.

2. Check the float hinge pin for wear and the float(s) for dents or distortion. Replace the float if fuel has leaked into it.

3. Check the throttle and choke shaft bores for wear or an out of round condition. Damage or wear to the throttle arm, shaft, or shaft bore will often require replacement of the throttle body. These parts require a close tolerance of fit; wear may allow air leakage, which could affect starting and idling.

NOTE: *Throttle shafts and bushings are not included in overhaul kits. They can be purchased separately.*

4. Inspect the idle mixture adjusting needles for burrs and grooves. Any such condition requires replacement of the needle, since you will not be able to obtain a satisfactory idle.

5. Test the accelerator pump check valves. They should pass air one way but not the other. Test for proper seating by blowing and sucking on the valve. Replace the valve if necessary. If the valve is satisfactory, wash the valve again to remove breath moisture.

6. Check the bowl cover for warped surface with a straightedge.

7. Closely inspect the valves and seats for wear and damage, replacing if necessary.

8. After the carburetor is assembled, check the choke valve for freedom of operation.

Carburetor overhaul kits are recommended for each overhaul. These kits contain all gaskets and new parts to replace those which deteriorate most rapidly. Failure to replace all parts supplied with the kit (especially the gasket) can result in poor performance later.

After cleaning and checking all components,

reassemble the carburetor, using new parts and referring to the exploded view. When reassembling, make sure that all screws and jets are tight in their seats, but do not overtighten as tips will be distorted. Tighten all screws gradually, in rotation. Do not tighten needle valves into their seats; uneven jetting will result. Always use new gaskets. Be sure to adjust the float level when assembling.

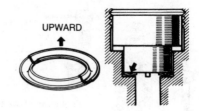

Injection nozzle installation

DIESEL ENGINE FUEL SYSTEM

Injection Pump

REMOVAL AND INSTALLATION

1. Disconnect the cables which are positioned above the valve cover and move the cables aside. Remove the valve cover.

2. Disconnect the cables from both batteries.

3. Using a wrench on the center crankshaft pulley bolt, rotate the engine (clockwise only) until the TDC mark on the pulley is aligned with the pointer. Check that the valves of the number one cylinder are closed (rocker arms loose). If the valves are not closed, rotate the engine 360° and again align the TDC mark with the pointer.

4. Disconnect the fuel injection lines at the injection pump and the injectors. Remove the injection lines.

Diesel fuel system priming pump. Pump the handle 30–40 times after any fuel system work to purge air from the system

5. Disconnect the fuel feed line at the injection pump and plug the line.

6. Remove the engine cooling fan, belts, and water pump pulley.

7. Remove the crankshaft pulley, using an appropriate puller.

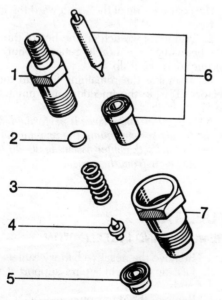

1. Nozzle holder retaining nut
2. Adjusting shim
3. Pressure spring
4. Pressure pin
5. Distance piece
6. Nozzle assembly
7. Nozzle holder body

Diesel fuel injection nozzle

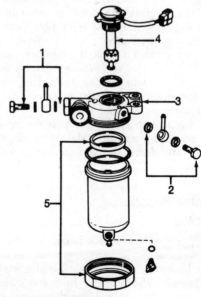

1. Fuel pipe follow screw
2. Fuel pipe follow screw
3. Fuel filter body
4. Level warning switch
5. Fuel sedimenter case and nut

Diesel fuel sediment bowl

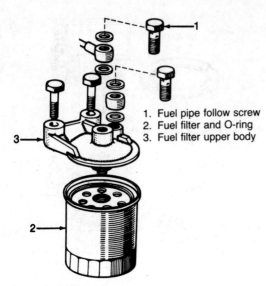

1. Fuel pipe follow screw
2. Fuel filter and O-ring
3. Fuel filter upper body

Diesel fuel filter

8. Remove the timing belt cover.

9. Using a piece of chalk or crayon, mark the relationships between each of the timing gears and the timing belt.

10. Remove the timing belt idler pulley, then remove the timing belt.

11. Remove the injection pump drive gear, using an appropriate puller.

12. Note the factory made alignment mark next to the outer pump fastener. This mark signifies the required relationship between the pump and the timing case assembly. Align this mark during installation.

13. Unbolt and remove the injection pump. CAUTION: *DO NOT disassemble the injection pump; only factory authorized repair centers have the facilities to do so. No adjustments are possible.*

14. Installation of the pump is the reverse of the removal procedure. Make sure all gasket surfaces are clean, and replace any damaged gaskets.

Injector Nozzle

REMOVAL

1. Remove the injection lines.

2. Remove the leakage pipe from the injectors and note the location of each sealing washer.

3. Remove the nozzle(s) from the cylinder head, noting the positions of the nozzle seats and seat gaskets.
   CAUTION: *DO NOT allow dirt to enter the engine through the nozzle holes.*
   NOTE: *Remove accumulations of carbon from the nozzle hoses.*

4. Keep the injectors in order so that they may be installed in their original positions.

5. If the engine exhibited any type of severe miss, excessive smoking, or drastic decrease in power, it is best to have the nozzles professionally tested for opening pressure, leakage, and spray pattern.

CLEANING

1. Remove the nozzle holder retaining nut from the nozzle holder body.

2. Disassemble the injector, following the accompanying illustration.

3. Wash the nozzles in clean diesel fuel.

4. Remove carbon from the nozzle needle tip with a small, wooden stick. Do not use any metallic object to clean the nozzle tip.

5. Remove carbon from the exterior of the nozzle body with a brass bristled brush. Don't use a brush having regular, steel bristles.

6. Inspect all parts for damage and/or corrosion. If either of these conditions exist, the entire injector assembly must be replaced.

7. Assemble the injector, using the illustration as a guide. Torque the nozzle holder retaining nut to 44–57 ft.lb.

INSTALLATION

1. Install the injector assembly, noting that:
   a. The nozzle seat is installed between the injector and the seat gasket, and
   b. The nozzle seat must be positioned with the concave side of the seat toward the injector.

2. Position a wrench on the hex of the nozzle body (not the nozzle retaining nut) and torque to 51–65 ft. lb.

3. Assemble the remaining lines to the injectors. Torque the injection pipe union nuts to 15–21 ft. lb.
   NOTE: *After any service is performed to the diesel fuel system, pump the priming handle on the fuel sedimenter assembly 30–40 times to purge air from the system.*

FUEL TANK

REMOVAL AND INSTALLATION

1. Remove the negative battery cable.

2. Jack up the vehicle and support it with jack stands.

3. Remove the drain plug and drain into a suitable container.
   NOTE: *It is best to run the tank as low on fuel as possible before removing it.*

4. Disconnect the plug from the sanding unit.

5. Disconnect the three fuel lines. Plug the outlet line to prevent fuel from leaking.

6. Disconnect the filler neck and vent line.

7. Remove the fuel tank protector.

8. Remove the six bolts from the tank and carefully lower the tank.

9. Installation is the reverse of removal. Tighten the six tank bolts to 11–16 ft. lb. This procedure is basically the same on all models.

Chassis Electrical

5

HEATER

NOTE: *On models equipped with air conditioning, the heater and air conditioner are completely separate units. The heater removal procedure is the same as outlined here. However, be certain when working under the dashboard that only the heater hoses are disconnected. The air conditioning hoses are under pressure. If disconnected, the escaping refrigerant will freeze any surface with which it comes in contact, including your skin and eyes. Refer all air conditioning work to a qualified mechanic.*

Heater Core
REMOVAL AND INSTALLATION
1970–78 Pick-Up

The heater core and blower motor are assembled into one unit which is centrally located in the passenger compartment. To effect repairs on either the core or blower motor, remove the entire assembly from the truck and separate the components with the unit removed.

1. Drain the cooling system completely.
2. Remove the package tray from under the dashboard.
3. Unfasten the hose clamps holding the heater hoses to the core.

NOTE: *Hold a shallow pan under the hoses so that any water left in them will not run on the floor of the truck.*

4. Remove the defroster hoses from the heater case.
5. Disconnect the heater control cables from the heater case.
6. Remove the fresh air intake duct.
7. Remove the electrical connector feeding the heater blower motor.
8. There are four bolts holding the assembly to the inside of the cowl. Remove the bolts and withdraw the heater assembly from the passenger compartment.

9. To remove the blower motor, tap the fan retaining nut slightly and then remove the nut from the shaft. Withdraw the fan. Remove the blower motor-to-heater case attaching screws and remove the motor.

10. To remove the core, remove the heater control panel and heater lower case cover as a unit. The core may then be taken out of the heater case.

11. Upon reassembly of the unit be sure to tighten all clamps to prevent leaks. Fill the cooling system with the correct mixture of coolant. With the heater off, run the engine to operating temperature. Open the heater control valve and see if the system is functioning properly.

1979 and Later Pick-Up and 1985 4Runner

The heater removal is basically the same with the following exceptions.

1. Remove the glove box from the dashboard.
2. Remove the heater controls from the dashboard.
3. Remove the 3 bolts holding the unit in place.
4. To remove the blower motor, remove the three screws on the blower housing and remove the motor.

1979 and Earlier Land Cruiser
FRONT CORE

1. Turn off the water valve.
2. Detach both hoses from the heater core.
3. Unfasten the air duct clamp.
4. Detach the defroster hoses from the heater box.
5. Unfasten its attachment bolts and withdraw the core.
6. Installation is the reverse of removal.

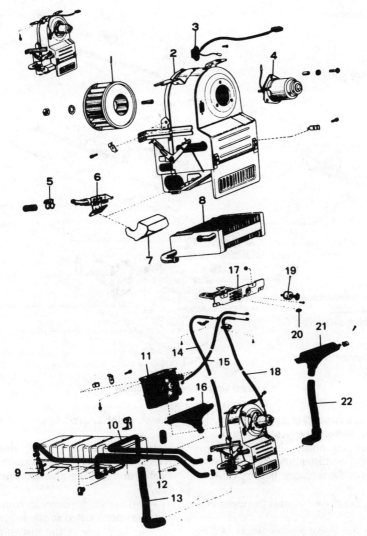

1. Heater blower fan subassembly
2. Heater case
3. Heater blower resistor
4. Heater blower motor subassembly
5. Heater radiator unit hose clamp
6. Heater water valve assembly
7. Heater water valve protector
8. Heater radiator unit subassembly
9. Water hose joint
10. Heater outlet water hose
11. Cowl ventilator duct assembly
12. Heater inlet water hose
13. Defroster hose, left
14. Heater control cable subassembly
15. Heater air inlet butterfly cable subassembly
16. Defroster nozzle subassembly, left
17. Heater control base subassembly
18. Defroster control cable subassembly
19. Heater blower switch assembly
20. Heater control knob
21. Defroster nozzle subassembly, right
22. Defroster hose, right

Heater for all except Land Cruiser

1980 and Later Land Cruiser

FRONT CORE

NOTE: *The entire heater unit must be removed to gain access to the heater core. This procedure requires almost complete disassembly of the instrument panel and lowering of the steering column. If you decide to perform this operation, note the following points before proceeding.*

a. Be sure to tag any wiring which must be disconnected so that it may be correctly installed.

b. As fasteners are removed, arrange them so that they may be installed in their original locations.

c. Do not force any parts to remove them; if a part cannot easily be removed, remove any additional fasteners which may have been initially overlooked.

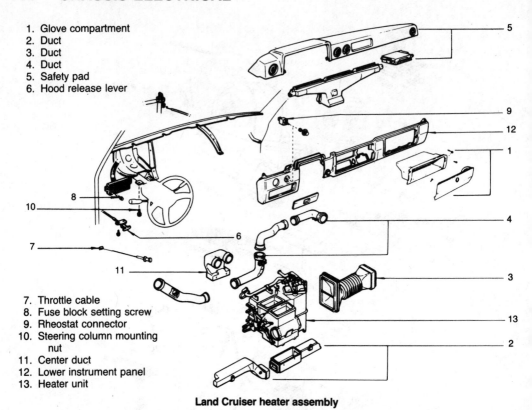

1. Glove compartment
2. Duct
3. Duct
4. Duct
5. Safety pad
6. Hood release lever

7. Throttle cable
8. Fuse block setting screw
9. Rheostat connector
10. Steering column mounting nut
11. Center duct
12. Lower instrument panel
13. Heater unit

Land Cruiser heater assembly

d. When disconnecting coolant hoses, be careful not to damage the heater core tubes. Place a drain pan under the coolant hose connections before disconnecting the hoses.

1. Disconnect the negative battery cable at the battery.

2. Remove the glove box and the glove box door.

3. Remove the lower heater ducts (#2 in the accompanying illustration).

4. Remove the large heater duct from the passenger side of the heater unit (#3 in the accompanying illustration).

5. Remove the ductwork from behind the instrument panel (#4 in the accompanying illustration).

6. Remove the radio, if so equipped.

7. Disconnect the wiring connector from the right side inner portion of the glove opening.

8. Remove the instrument panel pad (8 fasteners).

9. Remove the hood release lever.

10. Disconnect the hand throttle control cable.

11. Remove the retaining screw from the left side of the fuse block.

12. Remove the steering column-to-instrument panel attaching nuts and carefully lower the steering column. Tag and disconnect the wiring as necessary in order to lower the column assembly.

13. Disconnect the electrical connector from the rheostat located to the left of the steering column opening.

14. Remove the center duel outlet duct which is attached to the upper portion of the heater unit (#11 in the accompanying illustration).

15. Remove the lower instrument panel. The fasteners are located in the following places:

a. Left side of the instrument panel: two at the left side end and two at the left lower end.

b. Above the steering column: two.

c. To the right of the steering column opening: two.

d. Left upper corner of the glove box opening: two.

e. Left lower corner of the glove box opening: one.

f. Right side of the instrument panel: two at the right side end and two at the right lower end.

16. Tag and disconnect the hoses from the heater unit.

17. Remove the heater unit-to-firewall fasteners and remove the heater unit.

18. Remove the heater core pipe clamps from the heater unit. Also remove the heater core retaining clamp.

19. Withdraw the heater core from the heater unit.

20. Installation of the heater core and heater unit is the reverse of the previous steps. Torque

the steering column-to-instrument panel fasteners to 14–15 ft.lb. Replenish the cooling system and check for leaks.

Land Cruiser
REAR CORE

1. Shut the water valve.
2. Detach both of the hoses from the rear heater core.
3. Detach the wiring from the rear heater.
4. Unfasten the bolts and lift out the core.
5. Installation is the reverse of removal.

Heater Blower Motor

NOTE: *To service the blower motor of pick-up models, refer to the previous Heater Core Removal and Installation procedure.*

REMOVAL AND INSTALLATION
Land Cruiser
1979 AND EARLIER

1. Loosen the air duct clamping screws and remove the ducts.
2. Remove the air duct screen.
3. Unfasten the mounting bolts and remove the blower motor complete with fan.
4. Installation is the reverse of removal.

1980 AND LATER

1. Disconnect the electrical connector from the blower motor.
2. Disconnect the flexible tube from the side of the blower motor.
3. Remove the blower motor fasteners and lower the blower motor out of the air inlet duct.
4. Installation is the reverse of the previous steps. During installation, be sure to position the motor so that the flexible tube can be attached to the motor.

RADIO

CAUTION: *Never operate the radio without a speaker; severe damage to the output transistors will result. If the speaker must be replaced, use a speaker of the correct impedance (ohms) or else the output transistors will be damaged and require replacement.*

REMOVAL AND INSTALLATION
1978 and Earlier

1. Remove the knobs from the radio.
2. Remove the nuts from the radio control shafts.
3. Detach the antenna lead from the jack on the radio case.
4. Detach the power and speaker leads.
5. Remove the radio support nuts and bolts.

6. Remove the radio from beneath the dashboard.
7. Installation is the reverse of removal.

1979 and Later

1. Disconnect the negative battery cable from the battery.
2. Remove the steering column upper and lower covers.
3. Remove the five screws holding the instrument cluster trim panel and remove trim panel.
4. Remove the knobs from the radio and remove the securing nuts from the control shafts.
5. Remove the heater/air conditioner knobs from their control arms. Do not remove the blower fan control knob.
6. Remove the two screws holding the heater control dash light. Remove the ashtray and remove all of the screws holding the center dash facade onto the dash.
7. Pull the facade out, and carefully disconnect the cigarette lighter and the blower fan control at their plugs.
8. Unscrew any remaining screws holding the radio and pull it out part way. Disconnect the power source, speaker coupling and antenna from the radio and remove through the dash.
9. Installation is the reverse of removal.

WINDSHIELD WIPERS

Motor
REMOVAL AND INSTALLATION
Pick-Up and 4Runner

1. Disconnect the wiring from the wiper motor and unbolt it from the fire wall.
2. On 1978 and earlier models, remove the arm nut and crank arm from the wiper motor. On 1979 and later models, pry the wiper link from the crank arm.
3. Remove the motor.
4. Installation is the reverse of removal.

Land Cruiser
EXCEPT 1980 AND LATER STATION WAGON

1. Detach the wiper link from the motor with a screwdriver.
2. Unfasten the two bracket bolts at the rear of the motor.
3. Disconnect the wiper motor wiring.
4. Unfasten the wiper motor screws and withdraw the motor.
5. Installation is the reverse of removal.

1980 AND LATER STATION WAGON

NOTE: *On these models, the wiper motor is removed with the linkage assembly.*

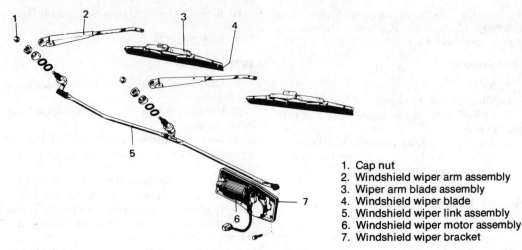

1. Cap nut
2. Windshield wiper arm assembly
3. Wiper arm blade assembly
4. Windshield wiper blade
5. Windshield wiper link assembly
6. Windshield wiper motor assembly
7. Windshield wiper bracket

Windshield wiper components

Installed position of crank arm on wiper motor

1. Remove the wiper arm retaining nuts and remove the wiper arm and blade assemblies.
2. Remove both wiper arm pivot covers.
3. Remove the pivot-to-cowl attaching screws.
4. Remove the two service hole covers from the cowl area of the engine compartment.
5. Disconnect the wiring from the wiper motor.
6. From the engine compartment, remove the wiper motor plate-to-cowl retaining screws.
7. Withdraw the wiper motor and linkage from the cowl panel as an assembly.
8. Pry the linkage off of the wiper motor and linkage from the cowl panel as an assembly.
9. Pry the linkage off of the wiper motor and disconnect the linkage from the motor.
10. Installation is the reverse of the previous steps.

Linkage

REMOVAL AND INSTALLATION

Pick-Up and 4Runner

1. Remove the wiper motor as described above.

2. Remove the wiper arms by removing their retaining nuts and working them off their shafts.
3. Remove the nuts and spacers holding the wiper shafts and push the shafts down into the body cavity. Pull the linkage out of the cavity through the wiper motor hole.
4. Installation is the reverse of removal.

2-Door Land Cruiser

1. Remove the wiper arm assemblies.
2. Remove the end plate from the pivot housing.
3. Remove the wiper motor complete with the linkage cable.
4. Separate the wiper motor and transmission.
5. Remove the linkage cable.
6. Installation is performed in the reverse order of removal.

Land Cruiser Station Wagon

1979 AND EARLIER

1. Perform the wiper motor removal procedures above.
2. Remove the wiper arm assemblies.
3. Remove the instrument cluster, as detailed below.
4. Loosen the throttle cable to improve access to the wiper linkage.
5. Remove the linkage attachment bolts and withdraw the linkage.
6. Installation is the reverse of removal.

1980 AND LATER

Refer to the Blower Motor Removal and Installation procedure.

INSTRUMENT CLUSTER

REMOVAL AND INSTALLATION

Pick-Up

1978 AND EARLIER

1. Loosen the steering column clamp bolts at the base of the instrument panel. This will allow the steering column to drop slightly.
2. Remove the three retaining screws on the instrument group and pull out gently on the hood of the cluster.
3. Disconnect the speedometer cable and the wiring connector and withdraw the cluster.
4. Installation is the reverse of removal.

1980 AND LATER PICK-UP AND 4RUNNER

1. Disconnect the negative battery cable at the battery.
2. Remove the upper and lower steering column covers.
3. Remove the five screws holding the instrument trim panel and remove the panel.
4. Disconnect the speedometer cable from the back of the speedometer.
5. Remove the four screws holding the instrument panel in place and pull the panel forward. Unplug the two connectors from the back of the panel and remove the panel.
6. Installation is the reverse of removal.

Land Cruiser

1. Disconnect the speedometer cable.
2. Remove the instrument panel attaching screws.
3. Loosen the steering column clamp by removing the attaching bolts.
4. Pull out the instrument panel and the speedometer, disconnect the wiring connectors, and remove the panel.

Location of cluster retaining screws

5. Install the panel in the reverse order from removal.

Speedometer Cable

REPLACEMENT

1. Remove the instrument cluster and disconnect the cable at the speedometer.
2. Disconnect the other end of the speedometer cable at the transmission extension housing and pull the cable from its jacket at the transmission end. If you are replacing the cable because it is broken, don't forget to remove both pieces of broken cable.
3. Lubricate the new cable with graphite speedometer cable lubricant, and feed it into the cable jacket from the lower end.
4. Connect the cable to the transmission, then to the speedometer. Plug the electrical connector into the instrument cluster, and replace the cluster.

LIGHTING

Head Lights

REMOVAL AND INSTALLATION

1. On 1970–72 models, remove the three

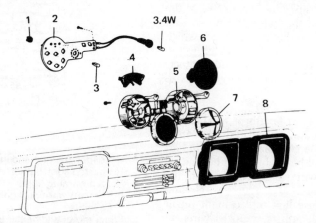

1. Meter bulb socket subassembly
2. Meter circuit plate subassembly
3. Bulb (3.4W)
4. Fuel level gauge assembly
5. Combination meter body
6. Speedometer assembly
7. Combination meter lens
8. Meter front hoood

Instrument cluster—1973 and later

Bulb Replacement Chart

Bulb Location	Bulb Trade Number
Sealed beam—outer	4002
Sealed beam—inner	4001
Front turn signal and parking	1157
Side markers—front and rear	67
Rear turn signal	1073
Stop and taillight combination	1157
Back-up lights	1073
License Plate	89
Interior	12V-5W-3CP

trim cover retaining screws, and remove the cover. On later models, the half of the grille covering the affected unit must be removed. There are seven retaining screws on 1973–74 trucks, and six screws on 1975 and later (one is hidden behind the grille emblem).

2. Loosen the three headlight ring retaining screws, but do not remove them. Turn the retaining ring clockwise and pull out the headlight with the ring.

3. Unplug the electrical connector from the rear of the headlight, and remove the headlight from the ring.

NOTE: *Do not interchange the inner and outer headlights. Do not disturb the headlight aiming screws located on the retaining ring mounting plate.*

All other bulbs on the vehicle are replaced by removing the screws retaining the lens and twisting out the defective bulb.

CIRCUIT PROTECTION

Fusible Links

All electrical circuits, except for the starter, are protected by two fusible links connected to the positive terminal of the battery. One is used exclusively for the headlight circuit, for which no fuse is used. The other is connected to the main electrical wiring harness, and protects those circuits from high current surges.

FUSE LINK

The fuse link is a short length of special, Hypalon (high temperature) insulated wire, integral with the engine compartment wiring harness and should not be confused with standard wire. It is several wire gauges smaller than the circuit which protects. Under no circumstances should a fuse link replacement repair be made using a length of standard wire out from bulk stock or from another wiring harness.

To repair any blown fuse link use the following procedure:

1. Determine which circuit is damaged, its location and the cause of the open fuse link. If the damaged fuse link is one of three fed by a common No. 10 or 12 gauge feed wire, determine the specific affected circuit.

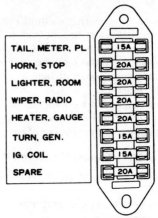

Fuse box connections—1973 and later

2. Disconnect the negative battery cable.

3. Cut the damaged fuse link from the wiring harness and discard it. If the fuse link is one of three circuits fed by a single feed wire, cut it out of the harness at each splice end and discard it.

4. Identify and procure the proper fuse link and butt connectors for attaching the fuse link to the harness.

5. To repair any fuse link in a 3-link ground with one feed:

a. After cutting the open link out of the harness, cut each of the remaining undamaged fuse links closed to the feed wire weld.

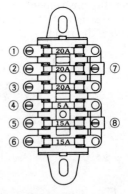

1. Headlight, parking and interior lights
2. Horn, stop light, lighter
3. Hazard warning lights
4. Instrument warning lights, gauges, and back-up lights
5. Wiper motor and heater blower
6. Turn signals
7. From battery
8. From ignition switch

Fuse block—1970–72

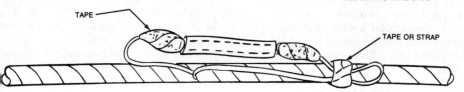

REMOVE EXISTING VINYL TUBE SHIELDING
REINSTALL OVER FUSE LINK BEFORE CRIMPING
FUSE LINK TO WIRE ENDS

TAPE

TAPE OR STRAP

TYPICAL REPAIR USING THE SPECIAL #17 GA. (9.00" LONG-YELLOW) FUSE LINK REQUIRED FOR THE AIR/COND.
CIRCUITS (2) #687E and #261A LOCATED IN THE ENGINE COMPARTMENT

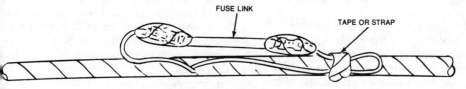

FUSE LINK

TAPE OR STRAP

TYPICAL REPAIR FOR ANY IN-LINE FUSE LINK USING THE SPECIFIED GAUGE FUSE LINK FOR THE SPECIFIC CIRCUIT

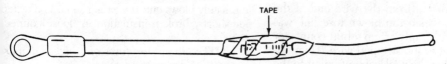

TAPE

TYPICAL REPAIR USING THE EYELET TERMINAL FUSE LINK OF THE SPECIFIED GAUGE FOR ATTACHMENT TO A CIRCUIT WIRE END

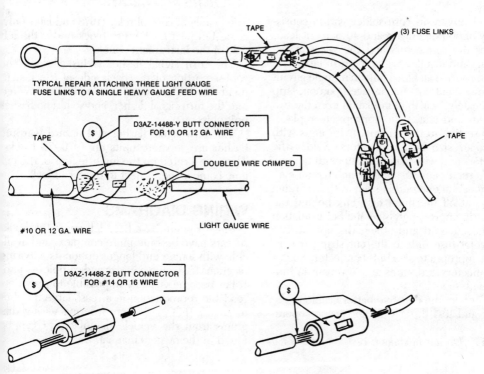

TAPE

(3) FUSE LINKS

TYPICAL REPAIR ATTACHING THREE LIGHT GAUGE
FUSE LINKS TO A SINGLE HEAVY GAUGE FEED WIRE

TAPE

$

D3AZ-14488-Y BUTT CONNECTOR
FOR 10 OR 12 GA. WIRE

DOUBLED WIRE CRIMPED

TAPE

#10 OR 12 GA. WIRE

LIGHT GAUGE WIRE

$

D3AZ-14488-Z BUTT CONNECTOR
FOR #14 OR 16 WIRE

$

FUSIBLE LINK REPAIR PROCEDURE

General fuse link repair procedure

b. Strip approximately ½ inch of insulation from the detached ends of the two good fuse links. Then insert two wire ends into one end of a butt connector and carefully push one strip end of the replacement fuse link into the same end of the butt connector and crimp all three firmly together.

NOTE: *Care must be taken when fitting the three fuse links into the butt connector as the internal diameter is a snug fit for three wires. Make sure to use a proper crimping tool. Pliers, side cutters, etc., will not apply the proper crimp to retain the wires and withstand a pull test.*

c. After crimping the butt connector to the three fuse links, cut the weld portion from the feed wire and strip approximately ½ inch of insulation from the end cut. Insert the stripped end into the open end of the butt connector and crimp very firmly.

d. To attach the remaining end of the replacement fuse link, strip approximately ½ inch of insulation from the wire end of the circuit from which the blown fuse link was removed, and firmly crimp a butt connector or equivalent to the stripped wire. Then, insert the end of the replacement link into the other end of the butt connector and crimp firmly.

e. Using resin core solder with a consistency of 60 percent tin and 40 percent lead, solder the connectors and the wires at the repairs and insulate with electrical tape.

6. To replace any fuse link on a single circuit in a harness, cut out the damaged portion, strip approximately ½ inch of insulation from the two wire ends and attach the appropriate replacement fuse link to the stripped wire ends with two proper size butt connectors. Solder the connectors and wires and insulate with tape.

7. To repair any fuse link which has an eyelet terminal on one end of such as the charging circuit, cut off the open fuse link behind the weld, strip approximately ½ inch of insulation from the cut end and attach the appropriate new eyelet fuse link to the cut stripped wire with an appropriate size butt connector. Solder the connectors and wires at the repair and insulate with tape.

8. Connect the negative battery cable to the battery and test the system for proper operation.

NOTE: *Do not mistake a resistor wire for a fuse link. The resistor wire is generally longer and has print stating, resistor—don't cut or splice. When attaching a single No. 16, 17, 18, or 20 gauge fuse link to a heavy gauge wire, always double the stripped wire end of the fuse link before inserting and crimping it into the butt connector for positive wire retention.*

Fuses and Flashers

FUSES

The fuse block is located on the inner fender well on 1970–72 trucks, and below the left side of the instrument panel on 1973 and later. In addition, the radio is protected by a separate fuse located in the wire between the radio and the fuse block.

If a fuse should blow, turn off the ignition switch and also the circuit involved. Replace the fuse with one of the same amperage rating, and turn on the switches. If the new fuse immediately blows out, the circuit should be tested for shorts, broken insulation, or loose connections.

NOTE: *Do not use fuses of a higher amperage than recommended.*

FLASHERS AND RELAYS

The headlight control relay (1973 and later only) is located next to the fuse block under the left side of the instrument panel.

The turn signal flasher is installed on the center portion of the back side of the instrument panel. The hazard warning flasher is wired into the turn signal flasher, and so has no flasher unit of its own.

The turn signal flasher and hazard warning flasher are separate units on 1970–72 trucks. They are located on the inner fender of the engine compartment, next to the fuse block.

WIRING DIAGRAMS

Wiring diagrams have been left out of this book. As cars have become more complex, and available with longer and longer option lists, wiring diagrams have grown in size and complexity also. It has become virtually impossible to provide a readable reproduction in a reasonable number of pages. Information on ordering wiring diagrams from the vehicle manufacturer can be found in the owners manual.

Clutch and Transmission

6

MANUAL TRANSMISSION

Transmission Case
REMOVAL AND INSTALLATION

2WD Pick-Up

1. Remove the console box or floor mat, and remove the shift lever boot retainer. Raise the boot and remove the shift lever assembly using a pair of channel lock pliers as outlined in Chapter 3 under Engine Removal and Installation.

2. Disconnect the negative battery cable.

3. Drain the coolant from the engine and disconnect the upper radiator hose.

CAUTION: *When draining the coolant, keep in mind that cats and dogs are attracted by the ethylene glycol antifreeze, and are quite likely to drink any that is left in an uncovered container or in puddles on the ground. This will prove fatal in sufficient quantity. Always drain the coolant into a sealable container. Coolant should be reused unless it is contaminated or several years old.*

4. On 8R-C and 18R-C engines, there is a bracket which supports the flexible line from the clutch master cylinder to the slave cylinder. Unbolt the bracket from the engine.

NOTE: *Do not separate the tubes. Just remove the bracket.*

5. Disconnect the accelerator torque rod, which runs from the gas pedal to the carburetor, at the firewall.

6. Remove the starter upper mounting nut on 8R-C and 18R-C engines.

7. Jack up the truck and support it on jackstands.

8. On 8R-C and 18R-C engines, remove the starter lower mounting bolt and the starter wiring, and remove the starter. On 20Rs, 22Rs and 22R-Es disconnect the starter wiring, remove the mounting nut and bolt, and remove the starter.

9. Remove the clamp holding the clutch slave cylinder in position.

NOTE: *Do not disconnect the hydraulic line from the cylinder.*

10. Disconnect the exhaust pipe from the manifold flange, and remove the pipe clamp closest to the manifold. On 20Rs and 22Rs, also remove the heat insulator, transmission mounting bolts, and bracket on that side.

11. Disconnect the clutch slave cylinder to clutch fork link at the clutch fork.

12. Remove the parking brake cable from the lever. It is not necessary to remove the entire equalizer assembly, as it will drop out of the way when the frame crossmember is removed.

13. Disconnect the speedometer cable.

14. Disconnect the back-up light wiring.

15. Matchmark the driveshaft flange and the transmission flange, then unbolt the driveshaft and move it out of the way. Plug the transmission output shaft opening to prevent oil leakage.

16. Support the transmission on a jack and remove the rear engine support/frame crossmember.

17. Loosen, but do not remove, the clutch housing-to-engine block bolts. Drop the transmission down slightly and then remove the bolts completely. The transmission must be drawn to the rear of the truck while lowering so that it will clear the clutch assembly.

CAUTION: *The clutch driven disc contains asbestos, which has been determined to be a cancer causing agent. Never clean clutch surfaces with compressed air! Avoid inhaling any dust from any clutch surface! When cleaning clutch surfaces, use a commercially available brake cleaning fluid.*

NOTE: *To prevent the oil pan from striking the suspension in 8R-C and 18R-Cs, and to*

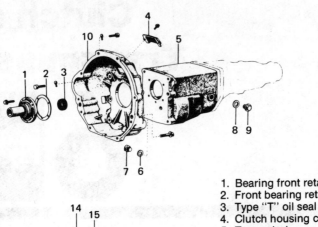

1. Bearing front retainer
2. Front bearing retainer gasket
3. Type "T" oil seal
4. Clutch housing cover No. 1
5. Transmission case
6. Drain plug gasket
7. Plug subassembly w/straight screw
8. Drain plug gasket
9. Transmission case cover plug
10. Clutch housing
11. Extension housing gasket
12. Extension housing subassembly
13. Breather plug
14. Transmission case cover plug
15. Drain plug gasket
16. Bimetal formed bushing

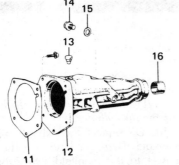

The external components of the four speed transmission

prevent the EGR valve from striking the firewall on 20Rs, place a wood block under the oil pan and support it with a jack.

18. Before installing the transmission, apply a thin coating of multipurpose grease on the input shaft end and splines, the clutch release bearing, and the clutch diaphragm spring contact surfaces.

When installing the transmission, it is necessary to use an alignment tool to center the clutch disc. These are available at auto parts stores.

After aligning the clutch, insert the transmission input shaft, being certain that its splines are properly meshed with those on the clutch. Use a jack to support the transmission while aligning the mounting bolts of the clutch housing. Tighten the clutch housing-to-engine block bolts to 36–51 ft.lb.

After installing all the components removed earlier, adjust the parking brake if necessary and the clutch release fork end play to 0.08–0.14 in. Apply gear oil to the shift lever ball, and the multipurpose grease to the shift lever bushing. Be certain that the driveshaft matchmarks are aligned. Fill the engine cooling system and check the level of transmission oil before road testing the truck.

NOTE: *If the clutch master cylinder hydraulic system has been separated at one of its connections, the system will have to be bled.*

4WD Pick-Up and 4Runner

NOTE: *A special service tool, Toyota #09305 20012 or its equivalent, is needed to remov the transmission shift lever.*

1. Disconnect the battery cables at th battery.

2. Remove the shift lever handles. Re move the front floor mat or carpet along wit both shift lever boots to gain access to the shi levers.

3. Using a special shift lever removal too mentioned previously, remove the transmis sion shift lever.

4. Using needle nose pliers, remove th transfer case shift lever retainer, then remov the shift lever.

5. Raise the vehicle and support it se curely with jackstands.

NOTE: *Because of space limitations, it ma be necessary to raise both the front and re of the vehicle. If this is done, place jac stands under both axles as follows: On t outside of the U-bolts at the front axle; the inside of the U-bolts at the rear axle.*

6. Drain the lubricant from both the tran mission and the transfer case.

7. Chalk matchmarks on the drivesh flanges and the differential pinion flanges to i dicate their relationships. These marks must aligned during installation.

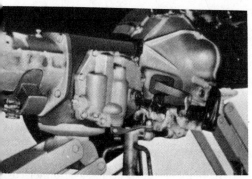

Removing the transmission

8. Remove the four bolts from each end of the front driveshaft and remove the driveshaft assembly.

NOTE: *Do not disassemble the front driveshaft to remove it.*

9. Chalk matchmarks on the rear driveshaft and the slip yoke to indicate their relationships. These marks must be aligned during installation.

10. Remove the four bolts from the rearward flange of the rear driveshaft. Lower the driveshaft out of the vehicle. Remove the four bolts from the slip yoke flange, then remove the flange and yoke assembly.

11. Unbolt the clutch release cylinder and tie it out of the way.

NOTE: *It is not necessary to disconnect the hydraulic line from the clutch release cylinder.*

12. Disconnect the positive battery cable at the starter motor switch.

13. Disconnect the remaining wire at the starter.

14. Remove the two starter retaining bolts and lower the starter out of the vehicle.

15. Disconnect the speedometer cable at the transfer case and tie it out of the way.

16. Disconnect the exhaust pipe clamp at the transmission housing.

17. Disconnect the wiring for the back-up lamp switch and the 4WD indicator switch.

18. Remove the crossmember-to-transfer case adaptor mounting bolts. Using a jack, raise the transmission and transfer case assembly SLIGHTLY off of the crossmember, just enough to take the weight off of the crossmember.

19. Remove the crossmember-to-frame attaching bolts and remove the crossmember.

20. Place a support under the engine with a wooden block between the support and the engine.

CAUTION: *The wooden block and support should be no more than about ¼" away from the engine so that when the engine is low-*

ered, *damage will not occur to any underhood components. If possible, shim and support so that the wooden block touches the engine.*

21. Lower the jack until the engine rests on the support.

NOTE: *For the next step, it is recommended that you have an assistant help you guide the transmission and transfer case assembly out of the vehicle.*

22. Remove the transmission-to-engine attaching bolts and draw the transmission and transfer case assembly rearward and down away from the engine.

CAUTION: *The clutch driven disc contains asbestos, which has been determined to be a cancer causing agent. Never clean clutch surfaces with compressed air! Avoid inhaling any dust from any clutch surface! When cleaning clutch surfaces, use a commercially available brake cleaning fluid.*

23. To separate the transmission and transfer case, stand the transmission on its front face with the tailshaft pointing upward. Remove the transfer case-to-adapter mounting bolts and lift the transfer case off of the transmission assembly.

24. To install the transmission, reverse the previous steps. Refer to the end of the 2WD procedure for installation points.

Land Cruiser

1979 AND EARLIER MODELS

NOTE: *Steps 2–4 pertain to 2 door models.*

1. Disconnect the battery cables at the battery.

2. Remove the front seats, seat tracks, and the console box, if so equipped.

3. Remove the heater pipe clamp which is located on the transmission tunnel to the right of the transfer case shift lever.

4. If the fuel tank is mounted beneath the passenger seat, drain the fuel, remove the fuel tank cover, disconnect the lines, etc., and remove the fuel tank.

5. Remove the shift lever knobs and the shift lever boots.

6. Using Toyota special service tool #09305-60010 or its equivalent, remove the transmission shift lever.

7. Remove the transmission tunnel cover.

8. Raise the vehicle and support it safely with jack stands.

9. Drain the lubricant from both the transmission and the transfer case.

10. Remove the undercover located beneath the front driveshaft.

11. Chalk matchmarks on the driveshaft

flanges and the differential pinion flanges to indicate their relationships. These marks must be aligned during installation.

12. Unbolt the driveshaft flanges and remove both the front and rear driveshafts.

13. Disconnect the speedometer cable from the transfer case and tie it out of the way.

14. Disconnect the parking brake cable at the parking brake lever. Leave the cable attached at the drum end; the cable will be removed with the transmission and transfer case assembly.

15. If the vehicle is equipped with a vacuum 4WD engagement system, mark and disconnect the following items at the transfer case.

- Wiring for the indicator
- Wiring for the transfer switch
- Vacuum hoses

16. Disconnect the wiring for the back-up lamp switch. Unbolt the back-up lamp wiring harness clamp from the transfer case, if so equipped.

17. On column shift models, disconnect the shift linkage at the transmission.

18. Remove the power take-off (PTO) lever, if so equipped.

19. Follow steps 18–22 of the 4WD pick-up procedure to remove the transmission and transfer case assembly.

20. To separate the transmission from the transfer case:

a. Remove the 4WD engagement lever guide.

b. Remove the 4WD lever and rod as an assembly.

c. Remove the back-up lamp switch.

d. If the vehicle is equipped with a PTO, remove the PTO unit from the transmission. If the vehicle does not have a PTO, remove the cover from the left side of the transfer case.

e. Remove the rear transfer case cover (six bolts) from the transfer case. Remove the shaft nut located behind the cover.

NOTE: *This nut is staked at the factory. To remove it, you must tap the staked portions outward to clear the shaft. Restake the nut after installation.*

f. Remove the five transfer case-to-transmission bolts.

NOTE: *Two of these bolts are located inside the left side of the transfer case, where the PTO or cover was previously removed.*

g. Using a puller assembled to the transfer case and the transmission output shaft, separate the transfer case from the transmission.

21. Installation is the reverse of the previous steps. Refer to the installation points at the end of the 2WD pick-up procedure.

1. Disconnect the battery cables at the battery.

2. Remove the entrance scuff plates from the floor of the interior.

3. Remove both side trim panels from beneath the instrument panel.

4. Remove the center heater duct.

5. Remove the floor mat or carpet.

6. Remove the handles from both shift levers.

7. Remove the transmission tunnel cover along with the shift lever boots.

8. Disconnect the wiring from both the back-up lamp switch and the 4WD indicator (if so equipped).

9. Using Toyota special service tool #09305 55010 or its equivalent, remove the transmission shift lever.

10. Raise the vehicle and support it safely with jackstands.

11. Remove the transfer case skid plate.

12. Disconnect the speedometer cable at the transfer case and tie it out of the way.

13. Chalk matchmarks on the driveshaft flanges and the differential pinion flanges to indicate their relationships. These marks must be aligned during installation.

14. Remove the mounting bolts from the driveshaft flanges and remove the driveshaft assemblies.

15. Disconnect the starter wire. Remove the starter mounting bolts and remove the starter from the vehicle.

16. Unbolt the clutch release cylinder and move it out of the way.

NOTE: *It is not necessary to disconnect the hydraulic line from the release cylinder.*

17. Drain the lubricant from both the transmission and the transfer case.

18. Remove the tachometer sensor, if so equipped.

19. Follow steps 18–22 of the 2WD pick-up procedure to remove the transmission and transfer case assembly.

20. To separate the transfer case from the transmission, remove the transfer case mounting bolts and slide the transfer case off of the transmission.

21. Installation is the reverse of the previous steps. Refer to the installation points at the end of the 2WD pick-up procedure.

CLUTCH

REMOVAL AND INSTALLATION

CAUTION: *The clutch driven disc contains asbestos, which has been determined to be*

1. Clutch disc
2. Pressure plate
3. Clutch cover
4. Throwout bearing

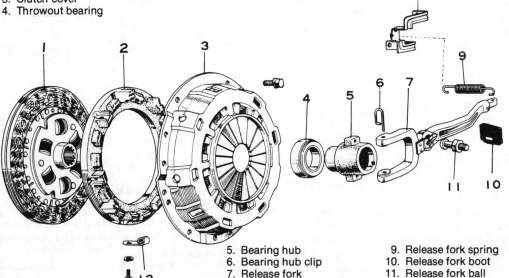

5. Bearing hub
6. Bearing hub clip
7. Release fork
8. Release fork spring hanger

9. Release fork spring
10. Release fork boot
11. Release fork ball
12. Clutch retracting spring

Clutch components

cancer causing agent. Never clean clutch surfaces with compressed air! Avoid inhaling any dust from any clutch surface! When cleaning clutch surfaces, use a commercially available brake cleaning fluid.

1. Remove the transmission according to the procedure following the clutch section.

2. Stamp or chalk matchmarks on the clutch cover and flywheel, indicating their relationship.

3. Loosen the clutch cover-to-flywheel retaining bolts one turn at a time. The pressure on the clutch disc must be released GRADUALLY.

4. Remove the clutch cover-to-flywheel bolts. Remove the clutch cover and the clutch disc.

5. If the clutch release bearing is to be replaced, do so at this time as follows:

a. Remove the bearing retaining clip(s) and remove the bearing hub.

b. Remove the release fork and the boot.

c. The bearing is press fitted to the hub. In some cases, the bearing is available with the hub from automotive suppliers. If this is not the case with your model, contact a machine shop and have the bearing replaced using a hydraulic press. Using other means to replace the bearing could result in personal injury.

d. Clean all parts and lightly grease the input shaft splines and all of the contact points.

e. Install the bearing/hub assembly, fork, boot, and retaining clip(s) in their original locations.

6. Inspect the flywheel surface for cracks, heat scoring (blue marks), and warpage. If oil

Centering the clutch disc

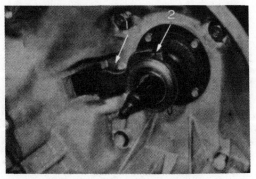

1. Release fork ball   2. Hub clip

Clutch release fork and bearing installed

is present on the flywheel surface, this indicates that either the engine rear oil seal or the transmission front oil seal is leaking. If necessary, refer to the appropriate section for seal replacement. If in doubt concerning the condition of the flywheel, consult an automotive machine shop.

7. Before installing any new parts, make sure that they are clean. During installation, do not get grease or oil on any of the components, as this will shorten clutch life considerably.

8. Position the clutch disc against the flywheel. On pick-ups, the short side of the splined section faces the flywheel. On Land Cruisers, the long side of the splined section faces the flywheel.

9. Install the clutch cover over the disc and install the bolts loosely. Align the matchmarks made during Step 2. If a new or rebuilt clutch cover assembly is installed, use the matchmark on the old cover assembly as a reference.

10. Align the clutch disc with the flywheel using a clutch aligning tool, which is available in most auto stores at a reasonable price.

11. With the clutch aligning tool installed, tighten the clutch cover bolts gradually in a star pattern, as is done with lug nuts. Finally torque the bolts to 11–16 ft.lb.

12. Install the transmission using the procedure following the clutch section.

CLUTCH PEDAL HEIGHT ADJUSTMENT

The pedal height measurement is gauged from the angle section of the floorboard to the center of the clutch pedal pad. Refer to the accompanying specification chart to determine the recommended pedal height.

If necessary, adjust the pedal height by loosening the locknut and turning the pedal stop bolt which is located above the pedal towards the drivers seat. Tighten the locknut after the adjustment.

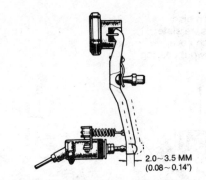

Measuring the play at the release fork tip

2.0~3.5 MM (0.08~0.14″)

CLUTCH PEDAL PUSHROD PLAY ADJUSTMENT

The pedal pushrod play is the distance between the clutch master cylinder piston and the pedal pushrod located above the pedal towards the firewall. Since it is nearly impossible to measure this distance at the source, it must be measured at the pedal pad, preferably with a dial indicator gauge. Refer to the accompanying specification chart to determine the recommended play.

If necessary, adjust the pedal play by loosening the pedal pushrod locknut and turning the pushrod. Tighten the locknut after the adjustment.

CLUTCH FORK TIP PLAY ADJUSTMENT

The fork tip play is the total amount of travel evident at the outer end of the clutch release fork where the fork comes in contact with the release cylinder pushrod. Refer to the accompanying specification chart to determine the recommended fork tip play.

The fork tip play is adjusted by loosening the release cylinder pushrod locknut and effectively increasing or decreasing the pushrod length as required.

NOTE: *Some models do not have adjustable release cylinder pushrods. These models are*

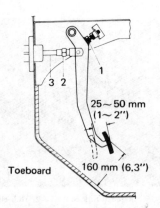

25~50 mm (1~2″)

160 mm (6.3″)

Toeboard

Clutch pedal adjustment

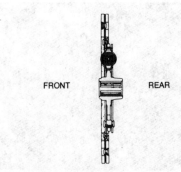

FRONT   REAR

Proper placement of the clutch disc

identified by having no adjustment nuts on the pushrod.

CLUTCH PEDAL FREE-PLAY ADJUSTMENT

The free-play measurement is the total travel of the clutch pedal from the fully released position to where resistance is felt as the pedal is pushed downward. Refer to the accompanying specification chart to determine the recommended pedal free play.

If the clutch pedal free play is incorrect, perform the previous clutch adjustments then bleed the system according to the procedure which follows. If a pedal free-play dimension is not listed for your model, perform the previous clutch adjustments and disregard the pedal free-play measurement.

Clutch Master Cylinder

REMOVAL

1. Disconnect the master cylinder pushrod from the clutch pedal.

2. Remove the hydraulic line from the master cylinder being careful not to damage the compression fitting.

3. Remove the two bolts holding the master cylinder to the engine compartment.

CAUTION: *Brake fluid dissolves paint. Do not allow it to drip onto the body when removing the master cylinder.*

OVERHAUL AND INSTALLATION

1. Disassemble the master cylinder by unscrewing the clutch pedal clevis from the pushrod. Also remove the locknut.

2. Pull off the rubber boot to expose an internal snapring. Remove the snapring and withdraw the piston and compression spring.

3. Take a clean rag and wipe out the inside of the cylinder. Inspect the inside of the cylinder for scoring and deposits. Use crocus cloth or a small hone to refinish the inside of the cylinder. If light honing will not remove score marks replace the cylinder.

NOTE: *Be careful not to remove too much from the cylinder walls as the cups will not be able to seal the cylinder if the diameter is enlarged excessively.*

4. Wash all metal parts in solvent.

5. Further disassembly should be avoided unless the reservoir is leaking. If the reservoir needs to be replaced, remove the cap and remove the master cylinder reservoir bolt located at the bottom of the reservoir. Tighten the bolt upon reassembly.

6. With new parts from the rebuilding kit assemble the master cylinder. Coat the cylinder wall with brake fluid so that the edges of the new cups will not be damaged.

7. Reinstall the master cylinder. Partially tighten the hydraulic line before tightening the master cylinder mounting bolts. Adjust the pushrod play clearance as outlined earlier, after bleeding the system.

1. Reservoir filler cap assembly
2. Master cylinder reservoir float
3. Master cylinder reservoir bolt
4. Reservoir bolt washer
5. Master cylinder reservoir
10. Compression spring
11. Master cylinder body
12. Master cylinder piston
13. Cylinder cup
14. Plate washer
15. Hole snap-ring
16. Master cylinder boot
17. Master cylinder pushrod
18. Nut
19. Master cylinder pushrod clevis

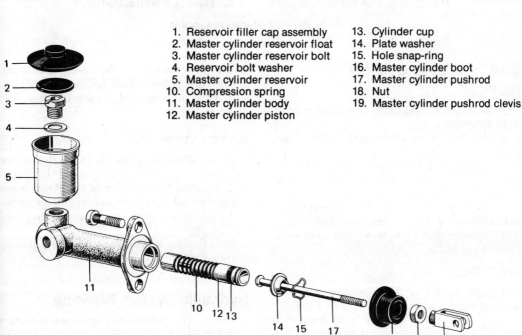

Clutch master cylinder—exploded view

Clutch Adjustment Specifications
(All measurements in inches)

Year	Model	Pedal			
		Height	Push Rod Play	Free-Play	Fork Tip Play
'79 and earlier	Pickup	6.0–6.4	0.020–0.200	0.200–0.600	—
'80 and later	Pickup & 4 Runner	6.0–6.4	0.040–0.200	0.200–0.600 ①	— ②
'79 and earlier	Land Cruiser 2 dr.				
	w/P.B.③	8.5	0.020–0.120	—	0.120–0.160
	wo/P.B.④	7.9	0.020–0.120	—	0.120–0.160
'80 and later	Land Cruiser 2 dr.	8.5	0.040–0.200	—	0.157–0.197
'79 and earlier	Land Cruiser Wagon				
	w/P.B.③	7.3	0.020–0.200	—	0.120–0.160
	wo/P.B.④	6.8	0.020–0.200	—	0.120–0.160
'80 and later	Land Cruiser Wagon	7.7	0.040–0.200	—	0.160–0.197

① '80 4WD models—0.980–1.770   ③ With power brakes
② '80 4WD models—0.079–0.118   ④ Without power brakes

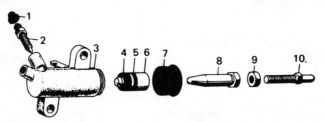

1. Bleeder plug cap
2. Bleeder plug
3. Slave cylinder body
4. Cylinder cup
5. Cylinder cup
6. Slave cylinder piston
7. Slave cylinder boot
8. Slave cylinder pushrod No. 1
9. Nut
10. Slave cylinder pushrod No. 2

Clutch slave cylinder disassembled

Clutch Release Cylinder

REMOVAL

1. Jack up the front of the truck and support it on jackstands.
2. Remove the tension spring on the clutch fork.
3. Remove the hydraulic line from the release cylinder. Be careful not to damage the fitting.
4. Turn the release cylinder pushrod in sufficiently to gain clearance from the fork.
5. Remove the mounting bolts and withdraw the cylinder.

OVERHAUL

1. Remove the pushrod, rubber boot, piston and cups from the cylinder.
2. Clean the inside of the cylinder with a rag and inspect for scoring. If there is no serious damage, hone the cylinder just enough to remove deposits. Replace the cylinder if light honing does not remove the score marks. Wash all the parts in brake fluid before assembly.
3. Coat the new rubber parts in brake fluid and reassemble.

INSTALLATION

1. Install the hydraulic line from the master cylinder.
2. Position the cylinder on the clutch housing and install the clamp and retaining screws.
3. Adjust the fork tip clearance as previously outlined.
NOTE: *The system must be bled after the cylinder is reinstalled.*

Hydraulic System Bleeding

NOTE: *This procedure may be utilized when either the clutch master or release cylinder has been removed or if any of the hydraulic lines have been disturbed.*

CAUTION: *Do not spill brake fluid on the body of the vehicle as it will destroy the paint.*

1. Fill the master cylinder reservoir with brake fluid.

2. Remove the cap and loosen the bleeder screw on the clutch release cylinder. Cover the hole with your finger.

3. Have an assistant pump the clutch pedal several times. Take your finger off the hole while the pedal is being depressed so that the air in the system can be released. Put your finger back on the hole and release the pedal.

4. After fluid pressure can be felt (with your finger) tighten the bleeder screw.

5. Put a short length of hose over the bleeder screw and place the other end into a jar half full of clean brake fluid.

6. Depress the clutch pedal and loosen the bleeder screw. Allow the fluid to flow into the jar.

7. Tighten the plug and then release the clutch pedal.

8. Repeat steps 6 and 7 until no air bubbles are visible in the bleeder tube.

9. When there are not more air bubbles in the system, tighten the plug fully with the pedal depressed. Replace the plastic cap.

10. Fill the master cylinder to the correct level with brake fluid.

11. Check the system for leaks.

AUTOMATIC TRANSMISSION

Description

The A-30 Toyoglide transmission is used in all 1977 and earlier models. The A-30 is a fully automatic three speed transmission using a combination of multiple disc clutches and front and rear bands to accomplish gear ratio changes. Internal adjustments necessary on this transmission include only the front and rear bands.

The A-40 transmission is used in 1978–79 models. The A-40 is also a fully automatic three speed, but it does not use bands for gear changes, thus internal adjustments are not possible.

In 1980, the A-40 was replaced by the A-43 three speed, which is used through the current model year. Internal adjustments are not required on this transmission.

The A-43D is a fully automatic four speed transmission first offered as an option on 1981 models and is available through the current model year. The fourth speed of this transmission is an overdrive ratio of 0.688 to 1, which offers improved gasoline mileage by lowering the engine rpm at highway speeds. The hydraulic circuit of the overdrive mode is electri-

cally controlled. The main electrical components include the following:

1. A dash mounted overdrive control switch.

2. A dash mounted OVERDRIVE-OFF indicator lamp.

3. A transmission mounted solenoid.

4. An engine mounted thermo switch which prevents overdrive engagement until the engine coolant temperature reaches 131°F.

Transmission

REMOVAL

A-30 and A-40 Transmissions

1. Disconnect the battery cables at the battery.

2. Disconnect the transmission throttle linkage at the carburetor.

3. Raise the vehicle and support it with jackstands.

4. Drain the transmission fluid.

5. Disconnect the wiring from the starter.

6. Unbolt the starter and lower it out of the vehicle.

7. Disconnect the exhaust pipe from the exhaust manifold. Remove the exhaust clamp from the exhaust pipe.

8. Disconnect the linkage from the drivers side of the transmission.

9. Disconnect the speedometer cable and tie it out of the way.

10. Disconnect the parking brake cable from the parking brake control lever.

11. Chalk matchmarks on the rear driveshaft flange and the differential pinion flange. These marks must be aligned during installation.

12. Unbolt the rear driveshaft flange. If the vehicle has a two piece driveshaft, remove the center bearing bracket-to-frame bolts. Remove the driveshaft from the vehicle.

13. Support the transmission using a jack with a wooden block placed between the jack and the transmission pan. Do not raise the transmission, just raise the jack until the wooden block touches the transmission pan.

14. Place a support under the engine with a wooden block between the support and the engine.

CAUTION: *The wooden block and support should be no more than about ¼" away from the engine so that when the engine is lowered, damage will not occur to any underhood components.*

15. Remove the transmission mount-to-crossmember bolts.

16. Raise the transmission SLIGHTLY, just enough to take the weight of the transmission off of the crossmember. Remove the cross-

member-to-frame mounting bolts and remove the crossmember from the vehicle.

17. Slowly lower the transmission until the engine rests on the support placed during step 14.

18. Disconnect the two fluid cooler lines at the transmission. Plug the lines and the holes in the transmission to prevent the entry of dirt.

NOTE: *Before performing step 19, place a drain pan under the torque convertor area of the transmission. Fluid leakage will occur as the transmission is uncoupled.*

19. Remove the transmission-to-engine mounting bolts. Carefully pull the transmission to the rear and after the transmission uncouples from the engine, lower the transmission out of the vehicle.

20. Remove the torque convertor from the flywheel.

A-43 and A-43D Transmissions

1. Disconnect the battery cables at the battery.

2. Remove the air cleaner assembly.

3. Disconnect the transmission throttle cable at the carburetor.

4. Raise the vehicle and support it safely with jack stands.

5. Disconnect the wiring connectors (near the starter) for the neutral start switch and the back-up light switch. Also, on A-43D transmission equipped models, disconnect the solenoid switch wiring at the same location.

6. Disconnect the starter wiring at the starter. Unbolt the starter and remove it from the vehicle.

7. Drain the transmission fluid.

8. Chalk matchmarks on the rear driveshaft flange and the differential pinion flange. These marks must be aligned during installation.

9. Unbolt the rear driveshaft flange. If the vehicle has a two piece driveshaft, remove the center bearing bracket-to-frame bolts. Remove the driveshaft from the vehicle.

10. Disconnect the speedometer cable from the transmission and tie it out of the way.

11. Disconnect the shift linkage at the transmission.

12. Disconnect the exhaust pipe clamp at the bellhousing and remove the oil filler tube.

13. Disconnect the transmission oil cooler lines at the transmission.

14. Support the transmission using a jack with a wooden block placed between the jack and the transmission pan. Do not raise the transmission, just raise the jack until the wooden block touches the transmission pan.

15. Place a wooden block (or blocks) between the engine oil pan and the front frame crossmember.

CAUTION: *The wooden block(s) should be no more than about ¼" away from the engine so that when the engine is lowered, damage will not occur to any underhood components.*

16. Remove the transmission mount-to-crossmember bolts.

17. Raise the transmission SLIGHTLY, just enough to take the weight of the transmission off of the crossmember. Remove the crossmember-to-frame mounting bolts and remove the crossmember from the vehicle.

18. Slowly lower the transmission until the engine rests on the wooden block placed during step 15.

19. Remove the engine undercover in order to gain access to the engine crankshaft pulley.

20. Remove the two rubber plugs from the service holes located at the rear of the engine in order to gain access to the torque convertor bolts.

21. Rotate the crankshaft as necessary to remove the torque converter bolt (6). Access to these bolts is through the service holes mentioned in step 20.

22. Obtain a bolt of the same dimensions as the torque converter bolts. Cut the head off of the bolt and hacksaw a screwdriver slot in the bolt opposite the threaded end.

NOTE: *This modified bolt is used as a guide pin. Two guide pins are needed to properly install the transmission.*

23. Thread the guide pin into one of the torque converter bolt holes. The guide pin will help keep the converter with the transmission.

24. Remove the transmission-to-engine mounting bolts.

25. Carefully move the transmission rearward by prying on the guide pin through the service hole.

NOTE: *As soon as the transmission is away from the engine about ⅛", feed wire through the front of the transmission and secure the wire in order to keep the converter attached to the transmission. Also, try to keep the nose of the transmission pointed upward SLIGHTLY to help keep the converter in place.*

26. Pull the transmission rearward and lower it out of the vehicle.

NOTE: *Do not allow the attached cables to catch on any components during removal.*

27. With the transmission out of the vehicle, remove the torque converter as follows:

a. Place a drain pan under the front of the transmission.

b. Pull the converter straight off of the transmission and allow the fluid to drain.

TORQUE CONVERTER AND FLYWHEEL RUNOUT

Testing

Prior to installation of the transmission, Toyota recommends to check the torque converter and flywheel runout dimensions. If either of these runout limits are beyond the maximum allowable limits, excessive wear of the front transmission seal will occur.

Refer to the accompanying chart to assist in performing and interpreting this procedure. A dial indicator gauge is needed to perform the runout checks.

1. Mount the torque converter on the flywheel and torque the converter bolts to 11–16 ft. lb.

2. Mount the dial indicator so that the indicator probe touches the outer surface of the converter extension sleeve (90° to the converter centerline).

3. Adjust the dial indicator to zero.

4. Slowly rotate the converter and read the dial indicator. The indicator needle should not deviate more than the following amounts:
   - 1980 and earlier transmissions: 0.008 in.
   - 1981 and later transmissions: 0.012 in.

5. Remove the torque converter from the flywheel.

6. Except A-43 and A-43D transmissions: Mount the dial indicator so that the indicator probe touches the flywheel drive plate (converter mounting) surface. A-43 and A-43D transmissions: Mount the dial indicator so that the indicator probe touches the flywheel ring gear just inside of the gear teeth (surface faces the rear of the vehicle).

7. Zero the indicator needle and slowly rotate the flywheel. The indicator needle should not deviate more than the following amounts:
   - A-30 transmissions: 0.005 in.
   - A-40 transmissions: 0.012 in.
   - A-43 and A-43D transmissions: 0.008 in.

INSTALLATION

A-30 and A-40 Transmissions

1. Apply a coat of multipurpose grease to the torque converter stub shaft and the pilot hole of the flywheel.

2. Assemble the torque converter into the transmission, so that its output shaft and the transmission input shaft are aligned. Rotate the torque converter until the dowel pin is at the bottom.

3. Install a guide pin into the bottom bolt hole next to the dowel pin. Align the flywheel and the torque converter.

4. Tighten the torque converter bolts to 11–16 ft.lb. Rotate the crankshaft half a turn to reach all the bolts, and tighten them evenly.

5. Bolt the transmission to the engine. Tighten the bolts to 37–51 ft.lb.

6. Replace the frame crossmember and the driveshaft. Attach the parking brake cable.

7. Replace the starter and its wiring. Attach the transmission cooler lines. Attach the speedometer cable.

8. Replace the exhaust pipe clamp and bolt the exhaust pipe to the manifold.

9. Install and adjust the throttle linkage rod. Attach the connecting rod to the transmission and adjust the shift lever linkage.

10. Fill the transmission with the specified type fluid. If the torque converter was completely drained, the transmission will need about 7 quarts of fluid.

11. Connect the battery cables. Road test and check for leaks.

A-43 and A-43D Transmissions

1. Apply a coat of multi-purpose grease to the torque converter stub shaft and the corresponding pilot hole in the flywheel.

2. Install the torque converter into the front if the transmission. Push inward on the torque converter while rotating it to completely couple the torque converter to the transmission.

3. To make sure that the converter is properly installed, measure the distance between the torque converter mounting lugs and the front mounting face of the transmission. The proper distance is 0.080 in.

4. Install the guide pins into two opposite mounting lugs of the torque converter.

5. Raise the transmission to the engine and align the transmission with the engine alignment dowels. Also, position the converter guide pins into the mounting holes of the flywheel.

6. Install and tighten the transmission-to-engine mounting bolts. Torque the bolts to 37–57 ft. lb.

7. Remove the converter guide pins and install the converter mounting bolts. Rotate the crankshaft as necessary to gain access to the guide pins and bolts through the service holes.

8. Evenly tighten the converter mounting bolts to 11–15 ft. lb. Install the rubber plugs into the access holes.

9. Install the engine undercover.

10. Raise the transmission slightly and remove the wood block(s) from beneath the engine oil pan.

11. Install the transmission crossmember. Torque the crossmember-to-frame bolts to 26–36 ft.lb.

12. Lower the transmission onto the crossmember and install the transmission mounting bolts. Torque the bolts to 14–22 ft.lb.

13. Install the oil filler tube and connect the exhaust pipe clamp.

14. Connect the oil cooler lines to the transmission and torque the fittings to 15–21 ft.lb.

15. Connect the shift linkage and the speedometer cable.

16. Install the driveshaft and the starter.

17. Connect the wiring which was disconnected during removal of the transmission.

18. Connect and adjust the transmission throttle cable (adjustment covered in a later procedure).

19. Install the air cleaner assembly and connect the battery cables.

20. Fill the transmission with the specified type of fluid. If the torque converter was completely drained, the transmission will need about 7 quarts of fluid.

21. Road test the vehicle and check for leaks.

Transmission Pan and Filter

REMOVAL AND INSTALLATION

1. Jack up the front end of the vehicle and support it on jackstands.

2. Place a container under the transmission drain plug and drain the transmission fluid.

3. Remove the pan securing bolts and remove the pan and gasket.

4. The pan may be washed in solvent for cleaning but must be absolutely dry when it is reinstalled. Do not wipe it out with a rag, or you will risk leaving bits of lint inside the transmission.

5. Remove all traces of the old gasket from the pan and from the transmission. Install a new gasket on the pan using small quantities of sealer around the bolt holes.

6. Replace the transmission filter at this time, if necessary.

7. Install the pan, tightening the securing bolts to 11–14 ft.lb.

CAUTION: *The pan bolts break easily if overtightened.*

8. Fill the transmission to the correct level with the specified fluid.

ADJUSTMENTS

Front Band

A-30 TRANSMISSION

1. Remove the pan as previously outlined.

2. Pry the band engagement lever toward the band with a screwdriver.

3. The gap between the end of the piston rod and the engagement bolt should be 0.118 in.

4. Turn the engagement bolt until the proper clearance is obtained.

5. Install the pan and refill the transmission.

Rear Band

A-30 TRANSMISSION

The rear band adjusting bolt is located on the outside of the transmission case so that it is not necessary to remove the pan in order to perform the adjustment.

1. Loosen the adjusting bolt locknut and turn the screw all the way in.

2. Back off the adjusting screw one full turn.

3. Lock the adjustment by tightening the adjusting screw locknut.

Shift Linkage

1979 AND EARLIER

1. Check all of the shift linkage bushings for wear. Replace any that are excessively worn.

2. Set the manual valve lever on the transmission in the Neutral position.

3. Lock the connecting rod swivel with the locknut so that the pointer, selector, and manual valve lever are all in the Neutral position.

4. Check the operation by moving the selector through all the gears.

1980 AND LATER

1. Loosen the adjustment nut on the transmission connecting rod.

2. Push the manual lever of the transmission fully forward.

3. Move the manual lever back three notches, which is the NEUTRAL position.

4. Set the gearshift selector lever in its NEUTRAL position.

5. Apply a slight amount of forward pressure on the selector lever (towards the reverse position) and tighten the connecting rod adjustment nut.

1. Shift lever
2. Connecting rod
3. Control rod
4. Manual valve lever
5. Manual valve lever shaft

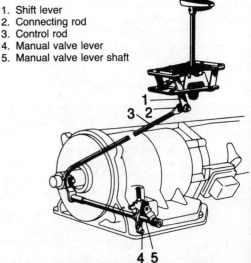

1979 and earlier automatic transmission floor shift. Adjustment is made at point 2

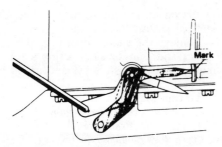

1979 and earlier floor shift alignment marks

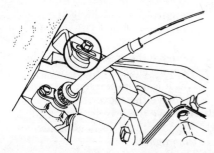

1980 and later automatic transmission adjustment point

Transmission Throttle Control

1977 AND EARLIER

When the carburetor throttle is wide open, the throttle linkage pointer should line up with the mark stamped on the transmission case. To adjust:

1. Loosen the locknuts on either end of the linkage adjusting turnbuckle located midway between the carburetor and the transmission.

2. Detach the throttle linkage connecting rod from the carburetor.

3. Align the pointer on the throttle valve lever with the mark stamped on the transmission case.

4. Rotate the turnbuckle so that the end of the throttle linkage rod and the carburetor throttle lever are aligned.

NOTE: *The throttle valve of the carburetor must be fully open during this adjustment.*

5. Tighten the turnbuckle locknuts and connect the throttle rod to the carburetor.

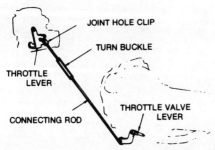

1977 and earlier throttle control linkage adjustment

6. Open the throttle valve and check to see that the pointer and the mark are aligned on the transmission.

7. Road test the truck. If the transmission keeps shifting rapidly back and forth between gears at certain speeds or if it fails to downshift properly when going up hills, repeat the throttle linkage adjustment.

1978 AND LATER

1. Remove the air cleaner assembly.

2. Push the accelerator to the floor and check that the throttle opens fully. If not, adjust the accelerator link so that it does.

3. Push back the rubber boot from the throttle cable which runs down to the transmission. Loosen the throttle cable adjustment nuts so that the cable housing can be adjusted.

4. Fully open the carburetor throttle by having an assistant press the accelerator all the way to the floor.

5. Adjust the cable housing so that, with the throttle wide open, the distance between the outer cable end rubber cap to the inner cable stopper is 2.05 in.

NOTE: *1979 and later distance is 0–0.04 in.*

6. Tighten the nuts and double check the adjustment. Install the rubber boot and the air cleaner.

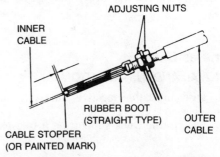

1978 and later throttle control linkage adjustment

Neutral Safety Switch

The neutral safety switch prevents the vehicle from starting unless the gearshift selector is in either the PARK or NEUTRAL positions. If

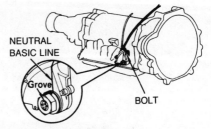

1980 and later neutral safety switch

the vehicle will start in these positions, adjustment of the switch is required.

ADJUSTMENT

1979 and Earlier Transmissions

1. Remove the screws which hold the center console in place.
2. Remove the electrical connector and remove the console from the vehicle.
3. Loosen the switch securing bolts.
4. Set the selector in the Drive position.
5. Move the switch so that the arm just contacts the control shaft lever.
6. Tighten the switch retaining bolts.
7. Check the operation of the switch; the truck should start only in Neutral or in Park. The back-up lamps should only operate in the Reverse position.
8. If the switch cannot be adjusted so that it functions properly, replace it with a new one.
9. Reinstall the console.

1980 and Later Transmissions

1. Loosen the neutral start switch bolt.
2. Place the gearshift selector lever in the Neutral position.
3. Align the shaft groove of the switch with the neutral Basic line. Hold the switch in this position and tighten the switch bolts to 35–60 in. lbs.

Transfer Case

REMOVAL AND INSTALLATION

1. Disconnect the negative battery terminal.
2. Jack up the truck supporting it by jack-stands placed on the front rear housing. Use the same procedure for the rear.
3. Remove the rubber boot from the gear shift lever and transfer case. Using a pair of channel lock pliers push down and turn at the same time to remove the gear shift lever. Remove the transfer case lever by using a pair of snap ring pliers to remove the ring.
4. Remove the front propeller shaft.

NOTE: *Before removing the bolts in this shaft mark each flange for proper alignment during assembly.*

5. Remove the back-up light wiring.
6. Remove 4 Wheel Drive Light indicator wire.
7. Remove the speedometer cable.
8. Remove clutch cylinder but do not break the line as it is not necessary.
9. Remove the starter.
10. Remove the exhaust pipe clamp.
11. Remove the bolts holding the bell housing to the engine.

NOTE: *Before attempting to remove the rear cross member support the transmission with a jack.*

12. Remove the rear cross member.
13. Support the engine with a wooden block and jack in the oil pan area.
14. Release the tension on the transmission jack and at the same time pull backwards on the transmission. You may have to lower the jack holding the engine to allow the transmission to come out of the clutch assembly.
15. Move the transmission from underneath the truck.

NOTE: *Using this procedure may necessitate having a helper.*

16. If you intend to disassemble the transfer case drain the oil at this time.
17. Installation is the reverse of removal.

DRIVELINE

Driveshaft and U-Joints
REMOVAL AND INSTALLATION
2WD Standard Bed

1. Jack up the rear of the truck and support the rear axle housing with jackstands.
2. Paint a mating mark on the two halves of the rear universal joint flange.
3. Remove the bolts which hold the rear flange together.
4. Remove the splined end of the driveshaft from the transmission.
   NOTE: *If you don't want to lose a lot of gear oil, plug the end of the transmission with a rag.*
5. Remove the driveshaft from under the truck.

Installation is performed in the following sequence:
1. Apply multipurpose grease to the splined end of the shaft.
2. Insert the driveshaft sleeve into the transmission.

NOTE: *Be careful not to damage the extension housing grease seal.*
3. Align the mating marks on the rear flange and replace the bolts. Tighten to 22–36 ft.lb.
4. Remove the jackstands and lower the vehicle.

2WD Long Bed

1. Jack up the rear of the truck and support the rear axle housing on jackstands.
2. Before you begin to disassemble the driveshaft components, you must first paint accurate alignment marks on the mating flanges. Do this on the rear universal joint flange, the center flange, and on the transmission flange.
3. Remove the bolts attaching the rear universal joint flange to the drive pinion flange.
4. Drop the rear section of the shaft slightly and pull the unit out of the center bearing sleeve yoke.
5. Remove the center bearing support from the crossmember.
6. Separate the transmission output flange and remove the front half of the driveshaft together with the center bearing assembly.

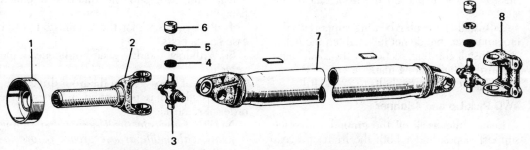

1. Sliding shaft dust cover
2. Universal joint yoke sleeve
3. Universal joint spider
4. Spider bearing seal
5. Snap-ring
6. Spider bearing
7. Driveshaft
8. Universal joint yoke flange

Components of the one-piece driveshaft used in the standard bed models

1. Intermediate driveshaft
2. Dust deflector No. 1
3. Dust deflector No. 2
4. Hole snap-ring
5. Dust deflector No. 3
6. Radial ball bearing
7. Dust deflector No. 4
8. Center support bearing cushion
9. Set ring
10. Hole snap-ring
11. Dust deflector No. 2
12. Center support bearing housing No. 1
13. Center support bearing housing No. 2
14. Dust deflector No. 1
15. Universal joint flange
16. Plate washer
17. Castle nut
18. Cotter pin
19. Universal joint flange yoke
20. Universal joint spider
21. Universal joint spider bearing seal
22. Universal joint spider bearing
23. Hole snap-ring
24. Grease fitting
25. Universal joint sleeve yoke
26. Sliding shaft dust cover
27. Balance piece
28. Driveshaft

Two-piece driveshaft used in the long bed truck

Removing the driveshaft

To install proceed in this manner:

1. Connect the output flange of the transmission to the flange on the front half of the shaft.

2. Install the center bearing support to the crossmember, but do not fully tighten the bolts.

3. Install the rear section of the shaft making sure that all mating marks are aligned.

4. Tighten all flange bolts to 22–36 ft.lb.

4WD Pick-Up and 4Runner

1. Jack the truck off the ground and place support stands under both the front and rear axles.

2. Matchmark all driveshaft flanges BE-FORE removing the bolts.

3. Unbolt the rear driveshaft flange from the rear pinion flange.

4. Unbolt the rear driveshaft flange from the rear transfer case flange and remove the driveshaft.

5. Repeat steps 3 and 4 on the front driveshaft.

6. Reverse order for reassembly. Tighten flange bolts to 29–43 ft.lb.

NOTE: *For 4x4 long bed pick-ups, see above for rear driveshaft removal and installation.*

Land Cruiser

1. Raise the vehicle and support it with jackstands.

2. Matchmark all driveshaft flanges BE-FORE removing the bolts.

3. Unfasten the bolts which secure the universal joint flange to the differential pinion flange.

4. Perform step 2 for the U-joint-to-transfer case flange bolts.

5. Withdraw the driveshaft from beneath the vehicle.

6. Repeat steps 3–5 on the front driveshaft.

7. Installation is performed in the reverse order of removal.

NOTE: *Lubricate the U-joints and sliding joints with multipurpose grease before installation.*

CENTER BEARING REPLACEMENT

The center support bearing is a sealed unit which requires no periodic maintenance. The

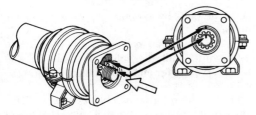

Make the same aligning mark on the propeller intermediate shaft as the flange on disassembly

following procedure should be used if it should become necessary to replace the bearing.

1. Remove the intermediate driveshaft and the center support bearing assembly.

2. Paint mating marks on the universal joint flange and the intermediate driveshaft.

3. Remove the cotter pin and castle nut from the intermediate driveshaft. Remove the universal joint flange from the driveshaft using a press.

4. Remove the center support bearing assembly from the driveshaft.

5. Remove the two bolts from the bearing housing and remove the housing.

6. Remove the dust deflectors (type #2) from both sides of the bearing cushion. Remove the dust deflectors type #3 and #4 from either side of the bearing.

7. Remove the snap rings from each side of the bearing. This is easy to do if you have a snap ring tool which fits the holes in the ring, and very difficult otherwise. Remove the bearing.

To assemble:

1. Install the new bearing into the cushion and fit a snap ring on each side.

2. Apply a coat of multipurpose grease to the dust deflectors type #3 and #4, and put them

in their respective places on each side of the bearing. Type #4, which has a slightly larger diameter, goes on the rear of the bearing.

3. Press the type #2 dust deflector onto each side of the cushion. The water drain holes in the deflectors should be in the same position on each side of the cushion. The water drain holes should face the bottom of the housing.

4. Press the support bearing assembly firmly onto the intermediate driveshaft, with the #3 type seal facing front.

5. Match the mating marks painted earlier, and install the universal joint flange to the driveshaft. Tighten the castle nut to about 130 ft. lb., and use a new cotter pin to lock it in place. Tighten the nut to align the holes for the cotter pin, but do not loosen it. It is okay to tighten it up to 150 lbs.

NOTE: *Check to see if the center support bearing assembly will rotate smoothly around the driveshaft.*

6. When reinstalling the driveshaft, be certain to match up the marks on both the front transmission flange and the flange on the sleeve yoke of the rear driveshaft.

FRONT DRIVE AXLE

Axleshaft

REMOVAL AND INSTALLATION

4WD Pick-Up and 4Runner

1. Set the control handle in the free position.

2. Remove the bolts in the hub and remove the hub and gasket.

3. Remove the nuts, spring washers, and cone washers.

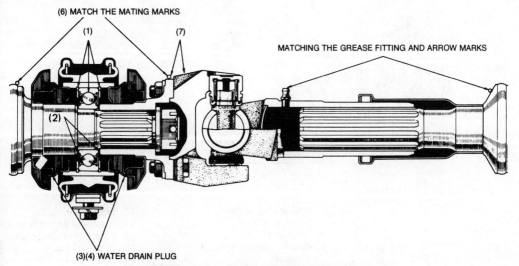

(6) MATCH THE MATING MARKS

(1)　　　　(7)

MATCHING THE GREASE FITTING AND ARROW MARKS

(2)

(3)(4) WATER DRAIN PLUG

Assembled relationship of the driveshaft components

NOTE: *Cone washers can be removed by using a tapered punch.*

4. Remove hub body and gasket.

5. Remove snapring from free wheel hub body.

6. Remove hub ring, spacer and inner hub.

7. Remove compression spring, follower, tension spring, and clutch.

8. Remove snapring, free wheel hub cover ball and spring, seal, and control handle.

NOTE: *Check inner hub and free wheel hub ring oil clearance. Clearance should be 0.012 in.*

9. Disconnect the brake line and the two bolts holding the brake caliper.

10. Remove the dust cap and snapring.

11. Remove the cone washers with a tapered punch.

12. Remove the flange by installing two bolts in the special holes for flange removal. Tighten these bolts until the flange comes loose. Remove the bolts by loosening them and remove the flange.

13. Remove the locknut, washer, and adjusting nut. Pull the rotor assembly off the spindle. The outer and inner bearings and seal will come apart as a unit.

14. Set the rotor on two blocks of wood. Using a drift pin drive the seal out. The inner bearing will drop out at this time. Using this pin drive the front and rear race from the rotor.

15. Place the rotor in a vice and remove the front axle hub.

16. Inspect the rotor, spindle and hub for damage.

17. Remove the dust seal, gasket, and dust cover.

18. Remove the spindle and gasket.

19. Position the flat part of the outer shaft up and pull out the shaft.

20. Remove the oil seal retainer.

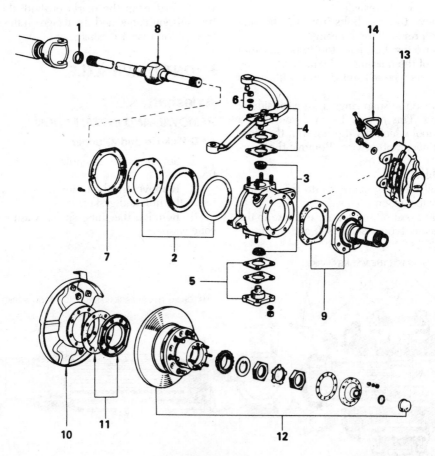

1. Oil seal
2. Oil seal set
3. Bearings
4. Steering knuckle
5. Bearing cup and shim
6. Nut, washer dowel
7. Oil seal retainer
8. Front axle shaft
9. Knuckle spindle and gasket
10. Dust cover
11. Dust seal and gasket
12. Front axle hub with disc
13. Brake caliper
14. Brake line

Later type front drive axle knuckle, hub and spindle

21. Remove the cone type washers from the drag link with a tapered punch.

22. Remove the drag link and tie rod.

23. Remove the bottom bearing cap and shim.

24. Remove the upper and lower bearings with the proper tool.

NOTE: *The steering knuckle bearing remover is available from your Toyota dealer. Part #09606-60010. Remember to mark the bearings in order to reassemble them in their proper place.*

25. Remove the upper and lower races with a brass drift pin.

26. Remove the steering knuckle and inspect for damage or wear.

27. Place the inner shaft in a vice. Using a drift pin drive the outer shaft apart and remove six ball bearings.

NOTE: *Tilt the inner race and cage. Take the balls out one at a time.*

28. Remove the cage and race from the shaft.

NOTE: *Turn the large opening in the cage against the protruding portion of the shaft, pull the race and cage out.*

29. Remove the inner race from the cage through the large opening.

30. Remove the inner oil seal. Thoroughly wash and inspect all parts for wear or damage.

31. Installation is the reversal of removal with the following suggestions:

    a. Replace all oil and grease seals.

    b. Pack the hub interior, inner and outer bearings with a multipurpose grease.

Land Cruiser

1. Raise and support the vehicle securely and remove the wheel/tire assembly.

2. Plug the brake master cylinder reservoir to prevent brake fluid leakage from the disconnected brake flexible hose.

3. Remove the outer axleshaft flange cap, and then remove the shaft snapring on the outer shaft. If equipped with free wheel locking hubs, complete steps 1–4 under 4WD pick-up axleshaft removal.

4. Remove the bolts retaining the outer axleshaft flange onto the front axle hub, and then, screw service bolts into the shaft flange alternately, and remove the shaft flange with its gasket.

5. Remove the brake drum set screws and remove the brake drum. If equipped with disc brakes, remove the caliper and disc.

6. Straighten the lockwasher, and remove the front wheel bearing adjusting nuts with front wheel adjusting nut wrench or similar tool.

7. Remove the front axle hub together with its claw washer, bearings, and oil seal.

8. Remove the clip and disconnect the brake flexible hose from the brake tube.

9. Cut and remove the lock wire and remove the bolts retaining the brake backing plate onto the steering knuckle. Remove the brake backing plate together with the brake shoes, tension spring, and the wheel cylinder still assembled to the backing plate.

10. Tap the steering knuckle spindle lightly with a soft mallet, and remove the spindle with its gasket.

NOTE: *When removing the steering knuckle spindle on a vehicle equipped with the ball joint type axleshaft joint, be prepared for the disconnection of the outer axleshaft from the joint. The joint ball will fall from the joint. Try to cushion its fall or catch it if you can.*

11. On those models equipped with the ball type axleshaft joint, slide the inner front axleshaft out of the axle housing. On those models equipped with the Birfield constant velocity joint type of axle joint, remove the entire axleshaft assembly from the axle housing.

12. Remove bushing from inside of knuckle spindle with a bearing puller. Install new bushing using a metal tube as a seating tool.

13. Remove axle housing oil seal with a bearing puller. To install, use a metal tube as a seating tool.

14. Install the axleshaft in the reverse order of removal. On those models equipped with the ball joint type axle joint, install the inner axle with its proper spacer in position until the splines are fully meshed with the differential side gear splines. Next, fill the steering knuckle three quarters full with grease and place the joint ball on the inner shaft end. Install the outer shaft and the front axleshaft spacer into the steering knuckle spindle and install the spindle with its gasket onto the steering knuckle.

15. On those models equipped with the Birfield constant velocity joint axle joint, install the axle into the housing and rotate the axleshaft until its splines mesh with the splines in the differential. Fill the steering knuckle housing three quarters full with grease and install the steering knuckle spindle.

16. Install and assemble the remaining components in the reverse order of removal. Adjust the wheel bearing preload.

NOTE: *See brake drum or disc removal section for wheel bearing preload instructions.*

Locking Hubs
REMOVAL AND INSTALLATION

1. Set the hub control handle to the FREE position.

2. Remove the hub bolts which retain the

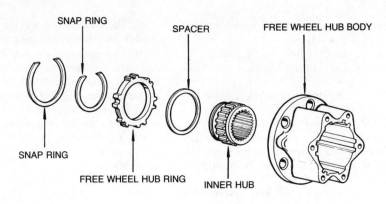

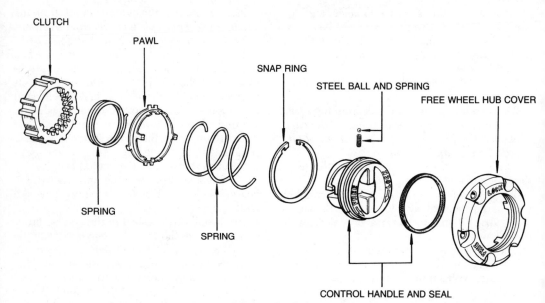

Free running hub

front cover and handle assembly and remove the assembly.

3. Remove the snapring from the axleshaft using snapring pliers.

4. Remove the hub body mounting nuts.

5. Remove the cone washers from the hub body mounting studs by tapping on the washer slits with a tapered punch.

6. Remove the hub body from the axle hub.

7. Installation is the reverse of the previous steps. Use a new gasket when installing the hub.

DISASSEMBLY

1. Remove the snapring which attaches the control handle to the hub cover. Remove the control handle.

2. Remove the ball and spring from the control handle.

3. Remove the snapring which holds the free wheel hub ring and the inner hub into the hub body.

4. Remove the inner hub and the free wheel hub ring from the hub body.

5. Remove the snapring from the inner hub and remove the free wheel hub and spacer from the inner hub.

INSPECTION

1. Check all parts for damage or excessive wear.

2. Temporarily install the control handle into the hub cover and make sure the handle operates freely.

3. Check that the clutch slides freely within the hub body.

4. Measure the inner diameter of the hub ring and the outer diameter (smooth surface) of the inner hub. The difference between these measurements should be no greater than 0.012 in.

ASSEMBLY

1. Apply a coat of multipurpose grease to the sliding service of each part.
2. Install the seal, spring, and ball into the control handle.
3. Install the control handle and snapring.
4. Install the tension spring into the clutch with the end of the spring aligned with the initial groove of the clutch.
5. Install the follower pawl as follows:

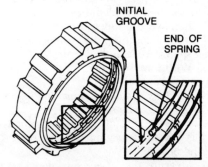

Aligning the end of the tension spring with the initial groove of the clutch

a. Place the pawl on the tension spring with one of the large tabs (of the pawl) against the bent end of the tension spring.
b. Place the top ring of the tension spring on the small tabs of the pawl.
6. Position the hub cover into the large end of the tension spring. Compress the spring and install the clutch with the pawl tab of the clutch fit to the control handle.
7. Install the inner hub and hub ring into the hub body. Install the snapring.
8. Temporarily install the cover and handle assembly into the hub body. Adjust the control handle to the FREE position and check that the inner hub turns smoothly.
9. Remove the cover and handle assembly from the hub body and install these components as previously outlined.

Differential

Overhaul of the differential carrier is a complex operation requiring special tools and technical knowledge. If either of these is not available, it may be wise (economically) to remove the car-

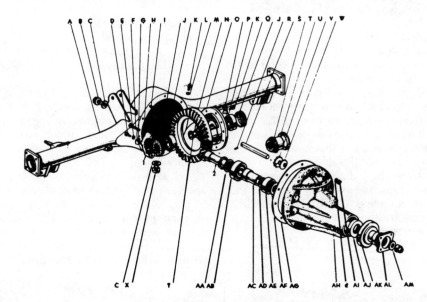

a. Housing assembly	n. Ring gear and drive pinion 1 and 2
b. Filler plug	o. Case
c. Gasket	p. Lockplate
d. Bolt	q. Bolt
e. Lock washer	r. Lockpin
f. Hexagon bolt	s. Pinion shaft
g. Bearing adjusting nut lock	t. Side gear
h. Lockwasher	u. Thrust washer
i. Stud	v. Pinion
j. Bearing adjusting nut	w. Thrust washer
k. Bearing	x. Drain plug
l. Breather plug	y. Oil reservoir
m. Lockwasher	

aa. Shim
ab. Bearing
ac. Spacer
ad. Shim
ae. Bearing
af. Oil slinger
ag. Gasket
ah. Carrier
ai. Nut
aj. Oil seal
ak. Dust deflector
al. Universal joint flange
am. Flat washer

Differential components

rier yourself and have a professional perform the overhaul, rather than purchase special (and expensive) tools or take the vehicle to a shop.

REMOVAL AND INSTALLATION

1. Drain the lubricant from the differential.
2. Remove the axleshafts as previously outlined.
3. Remove the driveshaft as previously outlined.
4. Remove the carrier retaining nuts and pull the carrier assembly out of the differential housing.
5. Installation is performed in the reverse of the previous steps. Apply a thin coat of liquid or silicone sealer to the new carrier to the housing gasket before installing the carrier. Also apply sealer to the carrier side of the face of each carrier retaining nut before installing these nuts.

OVERHAUL

1. Thoroughly wash and rinse the carrier and blow dry with compressed air.
2. Securely clamp the carrier in a vise or suitable stand.
3. Apply a light coating of mechanic's blue to the teeth of the ring gear.
4. Applying a slight drag on the ring gear to avoid backlash, rotate the pinion in a smooth and continuous manner to obtain a good tooth pattern on the ring gear.
5. Next, attach a dial indicator gauge to the carrier base and check the ring gear backlash.
6. Also, check ring gear runout at this time. If the tooth pattern obtained is correct, and the backlash and runout are within limits, any gear noise must come from the side gear.
7. With the dial indicator gauge set up on the carrier, check the backlash between the pinion gears and side gears. Excessive backlash usually is due to either worn thrust washers or a worn pinion shaft.
8. Check the side gear thrust clearance with a feeler gauge.

9. If everything is within specifications, test the preload on the differential drive pinion nut. Punch mark both pinion and nut in their original positions, then loosen the pinion nut about ½ turn and torque to specifications. If the punch marks line up again (within 60°) the pinion preload was correct.
10. Punch mark both the carrier and the side bearing caps for identification, remove the locknuts and take off the caps.
11. Remove the differential case assembly from the carrier. Do not mix the bearing cups; paint mark them for identification.
12. Remove the differential pinion nut (do not let the pinion drop out), then remove the pinion spacer, yoke and oil seal.
13. With a brass punch, drive out the pinion bearing cups.
NOTE: *This should be done only when the bearings are to be replaced.*
14. Press or pull off the drive pinion rear bearing. Avoid damaging the flat spacer behind the bearing.
15. Measure the spacer thickness and note the measurement for future use. Remove both side bearings from the differential case and mark them L and R for identification.
NOTE: *Remove the side bearings only if they must be replaced.*
16. Punch mark the differential case and cover, then remove the cover bolts and the cover (where fitted).
17. Remove the shaft and pinions, the side gears and all thrust washers.
NOTE: *Some differential types have four spider pinion gears; punch mark the gears before removal so they can be correctly reinstalled.*
Check all bearing cones and cups for wear. Inspect the tooth surface of all gears carefully and inspect all thrust washers for wear and signs of slipping in their seats. Check all gear shafts for scoring, wear or distortion. Finally, inspect the case and carrier housing for cracks or other damage. Also check the case for signs of wear

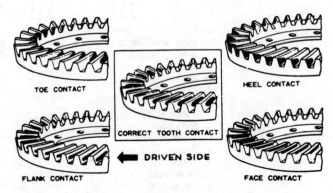

TOE CONTACT

HEEL CONTACT

CORRECT TOOTH CONTACT

FLANK CONTACT

◀ DRIVEN SIDE

FACE CONTACT

Ring gear tooth contact patterns

at the side gear bores, bearing cap and mounting hubs.

Assembly is performed in the following order:

1. Wash and clean all parts before installation.

2. Lightly oil all bearings and gear shafts, except the ring gear and drive pinion teeth.

3. Place the side gears and pinion gears, with their thrust washers, into the differential case.

4. Insert the shaft and align the lock pin holes in the case and shaft.

5. Install the case cover in place and install the lock pin (bolt) and tighten the cover bolts to specifications; check the play.

6. If the side bearings were removed, install them now. If the ring gear was removed, install it now. Tighten the bolts in symmetrical sequence to avoid distortion and runout.

7. Install the drive pinion bearing cups into the carrier housing, using a suitable installing tool. Make sure the cups are seated solidly.

8. Assemble the drive pinion rear bearing to the drive pinion and insert it into the carrier housing. Install the spacer and front bearing to the drive pinion; install the yoke and tighten the nut to specifications.

NOTE: *The drive pinion oil seal is NOT installed at this point.*

9. The drive pinion preload is measured in in.lb. (not ft.lb.). Adjust the preload by changing the length of the bearing spacer (between the front and rear bearings) until the required preload is obtained.

10. Place the previously assembled differential case into position in the bearing hubs and put the caps into position as marked (L and R).

11. Set the case so that there will be the least amount of backlash between the ring gear and pinion (in order to save time adjusting).

12. Install the adjusting nuts (also marked L and R) and take care not to crossthread them.

13. Finger-tighten the bearing caps until the threads are lined up correctly, then tighten slowly.

14. Back off the right hand adjusting nut (ring gear teeth side) and screw in the other nut until almost no backlash is felt.

15. Attach a dial indicator gauge so that it reads at right angles to the back of the ring gear, then screw in the right hand adjusting nut until the gauge indicates that all side play has been eliminated.

16. Tighten the adjusting nut another 1 or 1½ notches (depending on the fit of the lock tabs).

17. Recheck the preload on the drive pinion as before; this time the specifications are different.

18. If too loose, readjust the side bearing preload; if too tight, adjust the ring gear backlash.

19. Install the dial indicator gauge so that it contacts the ring gear teeth at right angles. Adjust the backlash to specifications.

20. If too great, adjust by loosening the bearing cap bolts slightly and screwing the right hand adjusting nut (ring gear teeth side) out about two notches.

21. Tighten the left hand adjusting nut the same amount.

NOTE: *One notch of the adjusting nut equals about 0.002 in. of backlash.*

22. Recheck the backlash, then tighten the bearing cap nuts.

23. Using a dial indicator recheck all runout dimensions (ring gear back, ring gear outer circumference and differential case).

24. Apply a thin coat of mechanic's blue, red lead or even lipstick to the ring gear teeth. Rotate the gear several times, applying a light drag

Differential Specifications

Model	Backlash (in.)		Runout (in.) Ring Gear	Torque (ft. lbs.)		Pinion Bearing Preload ④ (in. lbs.)	
	Ring Gear and Pinion	Side Gears		Side Bearing Cap	Differential Pinion Nut	New	Used
Pick-up (all) & 4 Runner	0.005–0.007	0.002–0.008	①	51–65	②	③	③
Land Cruiser (all)	0.006–0.008	0.001–0.008	0.004	65–80	145–175	16–23	8–11

① '75–0.002 in.
'76–'77—0.004 in.
'78–'85.
  w/7½" ring gear—0.003 in.
  w/8" ring gear—0.004 in.
② w/7.5" ring gear—80–173 ft. lbs.
  w/8.0" ring gear—123–151 ft. lbs.
③ '75—8.5–11.5 new
  2.2–6.6 used

'76–'85 except '81–'82 2WD w/7.5" ring gear:
  16.5–22.5 new
  7.8–11.3 used
'81–'85 2WD w/7.5" ring gear:
  10.4–16.5 new
  5.2–8.7 used
④ Without oil seal or differential gears installed

to the ring gear. Rotate the gear in both directions.

25. Inspect the tooth pattern. There are four basic tooth patterns: heel, toe, flank and face. Most often the tooth pattern obtained will be a combination of two of these patterns and the adjustments must be made accordingly.

   a. Heel contact: Move the drive pinion in by increasing the thickness of the spacer (between the pinion head and rear bearing). Readjust backlash by moving the ring gear away from the pinion.

   b. Face contact: Adjust same as above.

   c. Toe contact: Adjust by moving the drive pinion out by reducing the thickness of the spacer.

   d. Readjust backlash.

   e. Flank contact: Adjust same as toe contact.

Continue assembling as follows:

26. Remove the drive pinion nut and install the seal into the differential carrier housing, then install the oil slinger, dust shield and yoke and retorque the pinion nut as specified.

27. Install the differential carrier assembly into the axle housing.

Steering Knuckle
REMOVAL AND INSTALLATION
2WD Pick-Up

NOTE: *On pick-ups with coil springs, it will be necessary to obtain a spring compressor for installation.*

1. Jack up front of vehicle and support on stands.

2. Remove wheel.

3. If vehicle has front disc brakes, remove brake caliper.

4. Remove axle hub dust cap. Remove cotter key, lock, front nut and front nut washer from axle hub. Remove front bearing and remove brake disc or drum.

5. On drum brakes, remove brake line and plug.

6. Remove cotter keys and four bolts holding the brake backing plate and brake shoes on drum and the rotor dust cover on disk brakes. Remove the plate or cover.

7. Remove steering link from back of knuckle.

8. Support the lower arm with a jack and raise to put pressure on spring.

CAUTION: *Be careful not to unbalance vehicle support stands when jacking up lower arm.*

9. Remove cotter key and large lower ball

joint nut and separate the ball joint from the steering knuckle with a gear puller.

10. Repeat step 9 on upper ball joint.

NOTE: *Do not let the steering knuckle fall after removing upper ball joint.*

11. Installation is the reverse of removal. On pick-ups with coil springs, use a spring compressor when reassembling. Observe the following torques:

Large nut on upper ball joint: 66–94 ft.lb.

Large nut on lower ball joint: 87–123 ft.lb.

Rotor dust cover or drum backing plate to steering knuckle: 66–99 ft.lb.

NOTE: *See Chapter 9 for hub nut installation procedures.*

CAUTION: *Be sure to bleed brakes.*

4WD Pick-Up, Land Cruiser and 4Runner

1. Complete front axleshaft removal procedures in drive axle section, above.

2. Unbolt and remove the tie rod from the knuckle arm with a gear puller. On the pickup, if removing the driver's side knuckle see section on steering adjustment below for removal of the steering drag link.

3. Remove the oil seal retainer at the back of the steering knuckle.

4. Remove the four nuts on the top steering knuckle cap along with the cone washers. See section on axleshaft removal for procedures in removing cone washers.

5. Remove the four nuts on the bottom steering knuckle cap along with cone washers.

6. Using a small drift and hammer, tap the knuckle bearing caps out from inside the steering knuckle.

NOTE: *Do not tap on the bearings! Do not mix or lose the upper and lower bearing cap shims.*

7. Installation is the reverse of removal. To test the knuckle bearing preload, attach a spring scale to the end hole in the steering knuckle at a right angle to the arm. The force required to move the knuckle from side to side should be 4–8 lbs. 4WD pick-ups; 4–5 lbs. (Land Cruiser) If the preload is not correct, adjust by replacing shims.

REAR DRIVE AXLE

Axleshaft
REMOVAL AND INSTALLATION
Pick-Ups and 4Runner

1. Loosen the lug nuts on the wheel, then raise the truck and support it on jackstands.

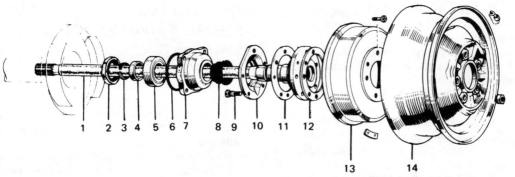

1. Rear axle shaft
2. Type "S" oil seal
3. Shaft snap-ring
4. Rear axle bearing retainer
5. Bearing

6. O-ring
7. Rear axle bearing case
8. Type "K" oil seal
9. Hub bolt
10. Brake drum oil deflector

11. Brake drum oil deflector gasket
12. Brake drum gasket
13. Brake drum
14. Disc wheel subassembly

Rear axle—exploded view

Pull the backing plate and axle shaft from the axle housing

09515-30010

You must support the inner race of the bearing when you press the axle shaft into the bearing case

2. Drain the axle housing.

3. Remove the lug nuts and remove the wheel.

4. Remove the brake drum securing screw and remove the drum.

5. Remove the brake springs and the retracting spring clamp bolt. Remove the lower springs and shoe strut. Remove the brake shoes, screws, and the parking brake lever. Disengage the parking brake cable from the lever and the backing plate.

6. Plug the master cylinder reservoir inlet to prevent the fluid from running out. Disconnect the brake line from the wheel cylinder, being careful not to damage the fitting. Plug the brake line.

7. Remove the four nuts retaining the brake backing plate to the axle housing.

8. Pull the backing plate and axle from the axle housing.

Install the axle in the following manner:

1. Install a new O-ring onto the axle housing.

2. Install the axleshaft and brake backing plate assembly into the axle housing. Be careful not to damage the oil seal with the axle splines. Rotate the axle back and forth until the shaft splines mesh with the differential gear splines.

3. Install the brake backing plate nuts and tighten to 44–58 ft.lb.

4. Install the brake shoes and lever assembly. Connect the parking brake cable and the brake shoe springs.

5. After installing the brake drum, bleed the brakes and adjust the brake shoe clearance.

6. Refill the axle housing with SAE 90W GL-5 gear oil.

Land Cruiser

SEMI-FLOATING TYPE DIFFERENTIAL

1. Remove the hub cap and loosen the wheel nuts.

2. Raise the rear axle housing with a jack and support the rear of the vehicle with jack stands.

3. Drain the oil from the differential.

4. Remove the wheel nuts and take off the wheels.

5. Remove the brake drum and related parts, as detailed below.

6. Remove the cover from the back of the differential housing.

7. Remove the pin from the differential pinion shaft.

8. Withdraw the pinion shaft and its spacer from the case.

9. Use a mallet to tap the rear shaft toward the differential, to aid in the removal of the axleshaft C-lock.

10. Remove the C-lock.

11. Withdraw the axleshaft from the housing.

12. Repeat the removal procedure for the opposite side.

13. To remove oil seal and bearing, use a bearing puller and remove the axle bearing and oil seal together. To replace, use a metal tube to drive bearing and seal into seat.

NOTE: *Do not mix the parts of the left and the right axleshaft assemblies.*

14. Installation is performed in the reverse order of removal. After installing the axleshaft, C-lock, spacer and pinion shaft, measure the clearance between the axleshaft and the pinion shaft spacer with a feeler gauge. The clearance should fall between 0.0024–0.0181 in. If the clearance is not within specifications, use one of the following spacers to adjust it.

- 1.172–1.173 in.
- 1.188–1.189 in.
- 1.204–1.205 in.

15. The rest of the axleshaft installation is the reverse of removal. Remember to fill the axle with lubricant.

FULL FLOATING TYPE DIFFERENTIAL

1. Remove the nuts from the rear axleshaft plate.

2. Remove the cone washers from the mounting studs by tapping the slits of the washers with a tapered punch.

3. Install bolts into the two unused holes of the axleshaft plate.

4. Tighten the bolts to draw the axleshaft assembly out of the housing.

5. Installation is the reverse of the previous steps. Install the axle using a new gasket and torque the axleshaft nuts to 21–25 ft.lb.

Rear Axle Hub

REMOVAL AND INSTALLATION

Land Cruiser

FULL FLOATING TYPE DIFFERENTIAL

1. Raise the vehicle and support it safely with jack stands.

2. Remove the rear wheels.

3. Remove the rear axleshaft as previously outlined.

4. Loosen the lock screws and remove the adjusting nut from inside the hub using Toyota special tool #09509-25011 or its equivalent.

5. Remove the hub from the axle housing. Inspect all parts for damage or excessive wear. If the seal needs to be replaced, pry the seal out of the hub with an appropriate tool. The seal is installed by tapping it into the hub until it is firmly seated. If the bearing race(s) needs replacement, drive the race(s) from the hub using a brass drift. Use the brass drift to install the race(s). Drive the new race(s) into the hub until firmly seated.

Install the hub in the following manner:

1. Place the hub on the axle housing and install the outer bearing.

2. Install the lock plate with the lock plate tab positioned into the groove of the axle housing.

3. Install and tighten the adjusting nut with the special tool used during removal.

4. Torque the nut to 43 ft.lb. Rotate the hub a few times and retorque the adjusting nut to 43 ft.lb.

5. Loosen the adjusting nut until the hub can be turned by hand.

6. Tighten the nut a small amount and check the amount of pressure required to rotate the hub using a spring tension gauge.

7. The recommended rational torque is 5.7 to 12.6 ft.lb. Tighten or loosen the adjusting nut as required to obtain this reading.

8. Align one of the axle housing slots with one of the adjusting nut slots. Install the lock screws into the holes of the adjusting nut which are at right angles to the aligned slots. Torque the lock screws to 35–60 in.lb.

9. Recheck the rational torque and install the axleshaft using a new gasket. Tighten the axleshaft nuts to 21–25 ft.lb.

10. Install the wheels and lower the vehicle.

DIFFERENTIAL

REMOVAL AND INSTALLATION, AND OVERHAUL

Refer to the procedures listed with the Front Drive Axle section.

Suspension and Steering

FRONT SUSPENSION

Springs

REMOVAL AND INSTALLATION

1978 and Earlier 2WD Pick-Up

1. Remove the hub cap and loosen the lug nuts.

2. Raise the front end of the truck and support the front suspension crossmember with jackstands.

3. Remove the lug nuts and the wheel.

4. Remove the stabilizer bar connecting bolts and remove the bracket parts, being careful to note their removal sequence in order to aid in installation.

5. Remove the tie rod cotter pin and nut. Use a puller to remove the end of the tie rod from the knuckle arm.

6. Remove the shock absorber, as detailed in the appropriate section. Detach the brake hose.

7. Raise the lower control arm, using a jack, so that the arm is free of the steering knuckle.

8. Loosen the ball joint attachment nut and remove the ball joint.

9. Slowly lower the jack underneath the control arm.

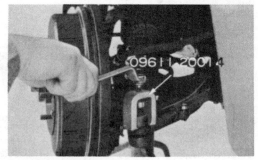

Separating the tie-rod end

CAUTION: *If the jack is lowered too fast, the spring could suddenly release, causing damage and/or injury.*

10. Remove the coil spring and its insulator from beneath the truck.

11. Inspect the coil spring, its insulator, and bumper for cracks, wear or damage. Replace parts as necessary.

12. Installation is basically performed in the reverse order of removal. However a coil spring compressor should be used to install the spring, rather than the method for removing it.

13. Torque the suspension components to the following specifications:

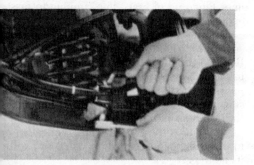

Removing the stabilizer bar

Removing the lower ball joint

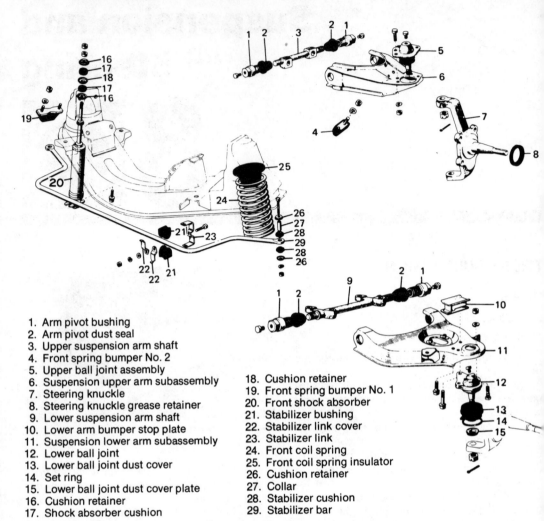

1. Arm pivot bushing
2. Arm pivot dust seal
3. Upper suspension arm shaft
4. Front spring bumper No. 2
5. Upper ball joint assembly
6. Suspension upper arm subassembly
7. Steering knuckle
8. Steering knuckle grease retainer
9. Lower suspension arm shaft
10. Lower arm bumper stop plate
11. Suspension lower arm subassembly
12. Lower ball joint
13. Lower ball joint dust cover
14. Set ring
15. Lower ball joint dust cover plate
16. Cushion retainer
17. Shock absorber cushion

18. Cushion retainer
19. Front spring bumper No. 1
20. Front shock absorber
21. Stabilizer bushing
22. Stabilizer link cover
23. Stabilizer link
24. Front coil spring
25. Front coil spring insulator
26. Cushion retainer
27. Collar
28. Stabilizer cushion
29. Stabilizer bar

Components of the 1970–78 front suspension

- Lower control arm: 51–65 ft.lb. (1976–78 33–43 ft. lbs.).
- Ball joint: 87–123 ft.lbs.

4WD Pick-Up and 4Runner

1. Jack up the front of vehicle and place support stands under the chassis frame.

NOTE: *Do not place supports under front axle housing.*

2. Remove wheel.

3. Remove the bolt from the bottom of the shock absorber and raise shock up out of the way.

4. If removing driver's side front leaf spring, remove the cotter pin from the end of the steering drag link at the axle housing. Unscrew the slotted bolt in the end of the drag link and remove the bolt, spring holder, spring, and outer socket holder. Remove drag link from steering knuckle arm.

NOTE: *Be careful not to lose inner socke[holder.*

5. Remove stabilizer bar bolt and spacer an washer assembly.

6. Disconnect brake line at the holder be hind the brake assembly. Drive out shim hold ing brake line to holder and withdraw brak line. Plug end of brake line running to maste cylinder to prevent fluid loss.

7. Place a jack under the front axle housin and raise to put pressure on the leaf spring Remove the four nuts holding the two U-bol to the axle housing and remove the U-bolts.

8. Lower the jack enough to take the pre sure off the leaf spring but so it still suppor the axle housing.

9. Remove the bolts holding the leaf sprin to its hangers and carefully pry the spring fro its holders.

NOTE: *It may be necessary to lower the jac*

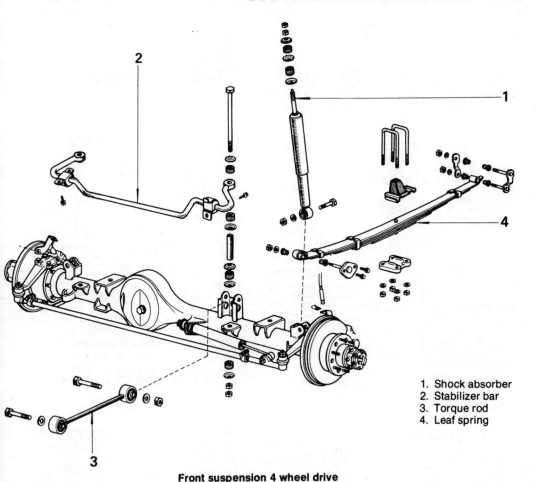

1. Shock absorber
2. Stabilizer bar
3. Torque rod
4. Leaf spring

Front suspension 4 wheel drive

under the axle housing to remove spring. Installation is the reverse of removal.

CAUTION: *Be sure to refill the brake master cylinder reservoir and bleed the brakes.*

NOTE: *Finger tighten the front and rear leaf spring hanger pin nuts. After the spring is attached to the axle housing and chassis, jack up the axle housing until the vehicle clears its support stands and then torque the pin nuts.*

Observe the following torques:
- U-bolt nuts: 73–108 ft.lb.
- Front hanger pin placer bolts: 8–11 ft.lb.
- Front hanger pin nut: 55–79 ft.lb.
- Rear shackle pin nuts: 55–79 ft.lb.

Land Cruiser

Land Cruiser models are equipped with leaf springs in the front and rear. Thus, front spring removal is performed in almost the same manner as rear spring removal. Follow the procedure outlined in the rear suspension section, below.

CAUTION: *Be careful when raising or lowering the front suspension with a jack so as*

not to damage any of the steering system components.

Torsion Bars
REMOVAL AND INSTALLATION
1979 And Later 2WD Pick-Up

CAUTION: *Great care must be taken to make sure springs are not mixed after removal, it is strongly suggested that before removal, each spring be marked with paint, showing front and rear of spring and from which side of the truck it was taken. If springs are installed backward or on the wrong sides of the truck, they could fracture. If replacing springs, it is not necessary to mark them.*

1. Jack up the truck and support the frame on stands.

2. Slide the boot from the rear of torsion bar spring housing and onto spring.

3. Follow the same procedure on the front of the spring.

NOTE: *Be sure to make a mark showing front of spring from back of spring.*

4. On the rear torsion bar spring holder,

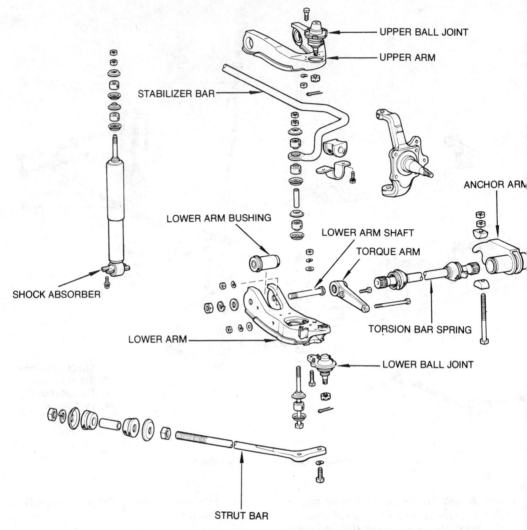

Front suspension components 1979 and later

there is a long bolt that passes through the arm of the holder and up through the frame crossmember. REMOVE THE LOCKING NUT ONLY, FROM THE BOLT.

5. Using a small ruler, measure the length

from the bottom of the remaining nut to the threaded tip of the bolt and record this measurement.

NOTE: *Be sure to complete step five accurately.*

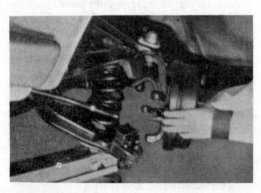

Coil spring removal

Installing the coil spring using a compressor

Removing the front shock absorber and disconnecting the flexible brake line

6. Place a jack under the rear torsion bar spring holder arm and jack up the arm to remove the spring pressure from the long bolt. Remove the adjusting nut from the long bolt.

7. Slowly lower the jack.

8. Remove the long bolt and its spacer and remove rear holder. You should be able to pull the torsion bar out of the front and rear holders.

9. Inspect all parts for wear, damage or cracks. Check the boot for rips and wear. Inspect the splined ends of the torsion bar spring and the splined holes in the rear holder and the front torque arm for damage. Replace as

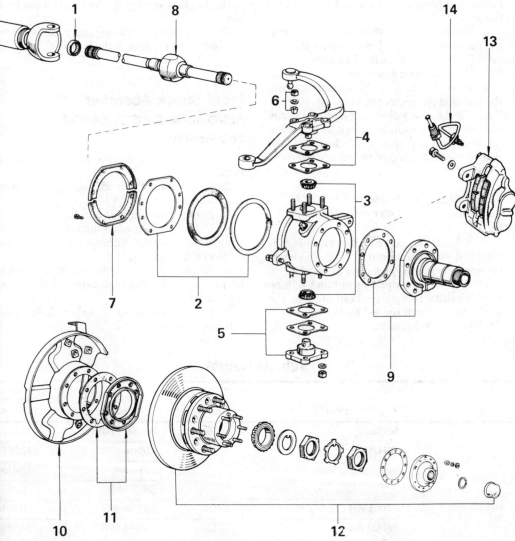

1. Oil seal	6. Nut, washer, dowel	11. Dust seal and gasket
2. Oil seal set	7. Oil seal retainer	12. Front axle hub with disc
3. Bearings	8. Front axle shaft	13. Brake caliper
4. Steering knuckle	9. Knuckle spindle and gasket	14. Brake line
5. Bearing cup and shim	10. Dust cover	

Steering knuckle and axle shaft

necessary. On the rear end of the torsion bar springs, there are markings to show which is right and which is the left bar. Do not confuse them.

10. Coat the splined ends of the torsion bar with multipurpose grease.

11. If fitting old torsion bars:

a. Slide the front of the bar into the opening on the torque arm, making sure you line up the marks you made earlier on the torsion bar spring and the torque arm.

b. Repeat the above step with the rear spring holder and replace the long bolt and its spacers.

c. Place a pipe that will fit in the notch on the rear holder arm on a jack and jack up the arm.

d. Tighten the adjusting nut so that it is the same length it was before removal.

NOTE: *Do not replace the lock nut yet.*

12. When installing a new torsion bar spring:

a. Slide the front of the torsion bar into the opening on the torque arm.

b. Fit the rear holder in place and install the rear of the torsion bar into it so that when the long bolt and spacers are installed, the distance from the top of the upper spacer to the tip of the threader end of the bolt is 0.7–1.0 in.

NOTE: *Make sure the bolt and bottom spacer are snugly in the holder arm while measuring.*

c. When the correct measurement is achieved, fit a pipe or round bar in the notch on rear holder arm. Jack up arm on pipe.

d. Replace the adjusting nut and tighten until the distance from the bottom of the nut to the top of the threaded end of the bolt is 71–89mm (2.8–3.5 in.).

NOTE: *Do not install the lock nut yet.*

13. Apply multipurpose grease to the boot lips and refit the boots over splines.

14. Replace the wheel and lower the truck.

15. With the wheels on the ground, measure the distance from the ground to the center of the lower arm shaft (See Chart). Adjust vehicle height with the adjusting nut on the rear spring holder.

NOTE: *If, after achieving the correct vehicle height, the distance from the bottom of the adjusting nut to the top of the threaded end of the long bolt is more than 3.8 in., change the position of the rear spring holder arm spline and reassemble.*

16. Replace and tighten lock nut on the long bolt.

NOTE: *Make sure the adjusting nut does not move when tightening the lock nut.*

Front Shock Absorber

REMOVAL AND INSTALLATION

2WD Pick-Up

1. Remove the hubcap and loosen the lug nuts.

2. Raise front of the truck and support it with jack stands.

3. Remove the lug nuts and the wheel.

4. Unfasten the double nuts at the top end of the shock absorber. Remove the cushions and cushion retainers.

5. Remove the two bolts which secure the lower end of the shock absorber to the lower control arm.

6. Remove the shock absorber. Installation is the reverse of removal.

Vehicle Height

Yr.	Model	Pay Load	Tire Size	Front Height in. (Unloaded)
79–80	RN32L	½ Ton	185 SR 14-4PR	9.827
	RN42L		7.00-14-6PR	10.291
			E78-14(B)	10.016
			ER78-14(B)	9.866
	RN42L-KH	¾ Ton	7.50-14-6PR	10.961
	RN421-3W C & C	¾ Ton	7.50-14-6PR	10.961
81–83	RN34	½ Ton	7.00-14-6PR	10.291
	RN44		E78-14(B)	10.016
			ER78-14(B)	9.866
			205/70 SR 14	9.512

Vehicle Height (cont.)

Yr.	Model	Pay Load	Tire Size	Front Height in. (Unloaded)
81–83	RN44L-KH	¾ Ton	7.50-14-6PR	10.961
	RN44L-3W C & C		7.50-14-6PR	10.961
84	Short Bed (Std)		7.00-14-6PR	10.59
			ER78-14	10.04
	Long Bed (Std)		7.00-14-6PR	10.75
			ER78-14	10.20
	Long Bed (Soft Ride)		ER78-14	10.20
	Extra Cab (Soft Ride)		ER78-14	9.80
	Extra Cab (Std)		ER78-14	9.80
	¾ Ton		7.50-14-6PR	10.71
	C & C		7.50-14-6PR	10.83
	SR-5 (Short)		P195/75R 14	9.76
			205/70 R 14	10.00
			ER78-14	10.00
	SR-5 (Long)		P195/75 R 14	9.96
			205/70 SR 14	10.20
			ER 78-14	10.12
	Extra Cab SR5 (Long Bed)		P195/75 R 14	9.80
			205/70 SR 14	10.04
			ER78-14	9.96
85–86	Short Bed (Std)		7.00-14-6PR	10.63
	Long Bed (Std)		7.00-14-6PR	10.83
	Long Bed (Soft Ride)		P195/75 R 14	10.24
	Extra Cab (Soft Ride)		P195/75 R 14	9.84
	Extra Cab (Std)		P195/75 R 14	9.84
	1 Ton		185 R 14-LT8PR	10.31
	C & C		185 R 14-LT8PR	10.20
	Short Bed (SR-5)		P195/75 R 14	9.80
			205/70 SR 14	10.04
	Long Bed (SR-5)		P195/75 R 14	9.96
			205/70 SR 14	10.20
	Extra Cab SR-5 (Long Bed)		P195/75 R 14	9.84
			205/70 SR 14	10.08
85–86 (Diesel)	Short Bed (Std)		7.00-14-6PR	10.59
	Long Bed (Soft Ride)		P195/75 R 14	9.96
	Extra Cab (Soft Ride)		P195/75 R 14	9.80
	Extra Cab (Std)		P195/75 R 14	9.80
83–86	Van		P185/75 R 14	9.57

4WD Pick-Up and 4Runner

Removal and installation is the same as the 2WD pick-up, except there is only one through-bolt holding the bottom of the shock in place.

Land Cruiser

Complete steps 1–3 of the 2WD pick-up shock absorber removal. Remove the bolts holding the top and bottom of the shock in place and remove the shock. Installation is the reverse of removal.

> CAUTION: *Be careful not to damage the steering assembly when jacking up front of the vehicle.*

Stabilizer Bar

REMOVAL AND INSTALLATION

2WD Pick-Up

1. Remove one torsion bar spring according to the previous spring removal and installation procedure.
2. Remove the stabilizer bar attachment hardware from the ends of the stabilizer bar. During installation, be sure to arrange the spacers, bushings, and washers as originally installed.
3. Remove the stabilizer bar-to-frame brackets and bushings and lower the stabilizer bar from the vehicle.
4. Installation is the reverse of the previous steps. Be sure to carefully inspect each bushing for damage and replace the bushing(s) if necessary. Retorque all stabilizer bar fasteners to 8–11 ft.lb.

4WD Pick-Up, 4Runner and Land Cruiser

Follow steps 2–4 of the previous 2WD pick-up procedure. Removal of a spring is not necessary on these models.

Upper Control Arm

REMOVAL AND INSTALLATION

2WD Pick-Up

1. Raise and support the truck under the frame.
2. Remove the wheel.
3. Raise the lower control arm with a jack.
4. Remove the nut from the upper ball joint stud.
5. Separate the ball joint from the steering knuckle.
6. Unbolt and remove the upper arm at the two bolts holding the inner shaft to the frame, taking note of the number and size of the aligning shims.
7. Installation is the reverse of removal. Re-

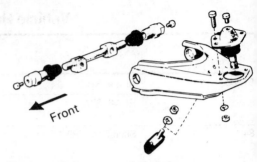

Front

Upper control arm—exploded view

place the shims as found. Tighten fasteners, but do not torque them until the truck is on the ground.

8. Lower the truck and torque the upper arm mounting bolts to 95–153 ft.lb.

Lower Control Arm

REMOVAL AND INSTALLATION

2WD Pick-Up

1. Raise and support the front end.
2. On 1978 and earlier pick-ups, remove the coil spring as previously outlined. On 1979 and later pick-ups, remove the torsion bar spring as previously outlined.
3. Remove the stabilizer bar and the strut bar from the lower arm, if so equipped.
4. On 1979 and later pick-ups, remove the bottom of the shock absorber from the lower arm.
5. Unbolt and remove lower ball joint.

> NOTE: *If the lower ball joint is not to be replaced, simply unbolt it from the lower control arm. It is not necessary to separate the ball joint from the steering knuckle.*

6. On 1978 and earlier pick-ups, unbolt and remove the lower control arm at the four bolts mounting the lower control arm on the frame. On 1979 and later pick-ups, unbolt and remove the nut from the lower arm shaft. Remove the nut from the lower arm shaft. Remove the spring torque arm from the other side.
7. Installation is the reverse of removal.

Removing the lower control arm

	Ft. Lbs.
Ball joint retainer bolts (1978 and earlier):	
Large bolts	21–32
Small bolts	21–28
Ball joint retainer bolts (1979 and later):	
Large bolts	29–39
Small bolts	15–21
Strut bar (1979 and later):	55–75
Torque arm (1979 and later):	29–39

Tighten the bolt(s) holding the lower control arm to the frame but do not torque them until the vehicle is on level ground. Observe the following torques during installation:

8. Lower the truck and torque the lower arm mounting bolt(s) to the following values:

- 1978 and earlier: 33–43 ft. lb.
- 1979 and later: 145–217 ft. lb.

CAUTION: *Do not tighten the control arm bolts fully until the vehicle is lowered. If the bolts are tightened with the control arm(s) hanging, excessive bushing wear will result.*

Ball Joints

INSPECTION

To check the lower ball joint for wear, jack up the lower suspension arm, after removing all excess play from the other suspension parts (wheel bearings, tie rods, etc.). The bottom of the tire should not move more than 0.2 in. when the tire is pushed and pulled inward and outward. The tire should not move more than 0.09 in. up and down. If the play is greater than these figures, replace the ball joint. The upper ball joint should be replaced if a distinct looseness is felt when turning the ball joint stud with the steering knuckle removed.

REMOVAL AND INSTALLATION

1978 and Earlier

1. Remove the wheel and tire.
2. Support the front suspension crossmember with jackstands.
3. Place a jack under the lower control arm and raise the control arm until the spring bumper is off the frame.
4. Disconnect the flexible brake hose.
5. Disconnect the tie rod end from the steering knuckle using a puller.
6. Using a suitable puller remove the ball joint from the steering knuckle.
7. Remove the ball joint from the lower arm.
8. From this position the upper ball joint may also be removed in a similar manner. Removal and installation will be easier if the lower removed first.
9. Install the new ball joints and reassemble the steering components. Due to the fact that the shock absorber is not removed in this

procedure the coil spring may be positioned with the jack and no compressor is necessary.

NOTE: *Be sure to grease the new ball joints before using the vehicle.*

10. Tighten the upper ball joint nuts to 15–22 ft.lb., the lower to 22–29 ft.lb. Tighten the steering knuckle to the upper joint to 65–94 ft. lbs; the knuckle to the lower joint to 87–123 ft.lb. Bleed the brakes before driving the truck.

1979 and Later

1. Jack up the vehicle and support it with jackstands.
2. Remove the front wheel.
3. Support the lower control arm with a jack.
4. Remove the brake caliper and tie it out of the way, as outlined later in this section.
5. Remove the tie rod end.
6. Remove the ball joint from the steering knuckle.

NOTE: *You can also remove the upper ball joint now if needed. Removal and installation will be easier if the bottom joint is removed first.*

7. Installation is the reverse of removal.

NOTE: *Be sure to grease the ball joints before moving the vehicle.*

The following torque figures should be observed:

- Upper mounting bolts: 15–21 ft. lb.
- Upper ball joint: 66–94 ft. lb.
- Lower mounting bolts: 15–39 ft. lb.
- Lower ball joint: 87–122 ft. lb.

Front End Alignment

Front end alignment measurements require the use of special equipment. Before measuring alignment or attempting to adjust it, always check the following points:

1. Be sure that the tires are properly inflated.
2. See that the wheels are properly balanced.
3. Check the ball joints to determine if they are worn or loose.
4. Check the front bearing adjustment.
5. Be sure that the car is on a level surface.
6. Check all suspension parts for tightness.

CASTER AND CAMBER ADJUSTMENTS

Measure the caster and camber angles. If they are not within specifications, adjust them by adding or subtracting the shims on the mounting bolts between the upper control arm and the suspension member:

1. To increase camber, remove shims equally from both of the control shaft mounting bolts. Do the reverse to decrease camber.
2. To increase caster, add camber adjusting shims to the rear mounting bolt, or remove them

from the front mounting bolt. Do the reverse to decrease caster.

NOTE: *Caster and camber adjustments should always be performed in a single operation.*

TOE-IN ADJUSTMENT

Measure the toe-in. Adjust it, if necessary, by loosening the tie rod end clamping bolts and rotating the tie rod adjusting tubes. Tighten the clamping bolts when finished.

NOTE: *Both tie rod ends should be the same length. If they are not, perform the adjustment until the toe-in is within specifications and the tie rod ends are equal in length.*

REAR SUSPENSION

Springs

REMOVAL AND INSTALLATION

1. Loosen the rear wheel lug nuts.
2. Raise the rear of the vehicle. Support the frame and rear axle housing with stands.

3. Remove the lug nuts and the wheel.
4. Remove the cotter pin, nut, and washer from the lower end of the shock absorber.
5. On Land Cruiser models, perform the following:
   a. Remove the cotter pins and nuts from the lower end of the stabilizer link.
   b. Detach the link from the axle housing.
6. Detach the shock absorber from the spring seat pivot pin.
7. Remove the parking brake cable clamp (except Land Cruiser).

NOTE: *Remove the parking brake equalizer, if necessary.*

8. Unfasten the U-bolt nuts and remove the spring seat assemblies.
9. Adjust the height of the rear axle housing so that the weight of the rear axle is removed from the rear springs.
10. Unfasten the spring shackle retaining nuts. Withdraw the spring shackle inner plate. Carefully pry out the spring shackle with bar.
11. Remove the spring bracket pin from the

Wheel Alignment Specifications

Year	Model	Caster		Camber		Toe-in (in.)	Steering Axis Inclination (deg)
		Range (deg)	Preferred Setting (deg)	Range (deg)	Preferred Setting (deg)		
1970–71	Pick-up	—	⅓ N	—	1 P	¼	—
1972–74	Pick-up	¼ P–1¼ N	½ N	¼–1¾ P	1 P	³⁄₁₆	7¼
1975–78	Pick up	0–1 P	½ P	½–1½ P	1 P	0.24	—
1979–82	Pick-up 2-WD	½ P–½ N	½ P	¹⁄₁₂–½ P	1 P	0.20– + 0.04 in.① 0.08– + 0.04 in.②	7
1983	Pick-up 2-WD ½ ton	¼ P–1¾ P	1P	½ P–½ P	1P	⑤	7°10′
	¾ ton	¼ N–1¼ P	½ P	0–1P	½ P	⑤	7°10′
1979–82	Pick-up 4-WD	—	3½	—	1 P 9½ ①	0.16– + 0.04 in.① 0.04∓ 0.04 in.②	—
1983–85	Pick-up 4-WD & 4 Runner	2¾ P–4¼ P	3½	¼ P–1¾ P	¾ P	⑥	9°30′
1970–78	Land Cruiser	½ P–1½ P	1P	½ P–1½ P	1P	0.12–0.21	9½
1979–85	Land Cruiser	½ P–1½ P	1P	½–1½ P	1P	④	9½

① Bias Ply Tire
② Radial Ply tire
③ King Pin Inclination (4WD only)
④ Non Radial tires: 0.10–0.20
　Radial tires: 0.04 out–0.04 in

⑤ Bias ply tires: 0.16–0.24 in.
　Radial tires: 0.04–0.12
⑥ Bias ply tires: 0.12–0.20 in.
　Radial tires: 0–0.08 in.

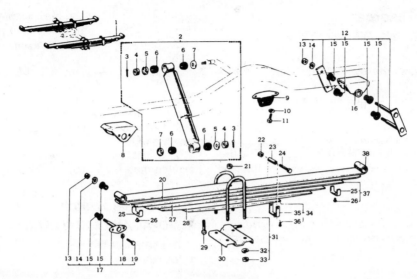

1. Rear spring
2. Rear shock absorber
3. Cotter pin
4. Castle pin
5. Shock absorber cushion washer
6. Bushing
7. Shock absorber cushion washer
8. Spring bracket
9. Rear spring bumper
10. Spring washer
11. Bolt
12. Rear spring shackle
13. Nut

14. Spring washer
15. Bushing
16. Spring bracket
17. Rear spring hanger pin
18. Spring washer
19. Bolt
20. Rear spring leaf
21. Nut
22. Nut
23. Rear spring clip bolt
24. Clip bolt
25. Rear spring clip
26. Round rivet

27. Rear spring leaf
28. Rear spring leaf No. 5
29. Rear spring center bolt
30. U-bolt seat
31. U-bolt
32. Spring washer
33. Nut
34. Rear spring leaf
35. Rear spring clip
36. Round rivet
37. Rear spring leaf
38. Rear spring leaf

Rear spring and shock absorber

front end of the spring hanger and remove the rubber bushing.

12. Remove the spring.

CAUTION: *Use care not to damage the hydraulic brake line or the parking brake cable.*

Installation is performed in the following order:

1. Install the rubber bushing in the eye of the spring.

2. Align the eye of the spring with the spring hanger bracket and drive the pin through the bracket holes and rubber bushings.

NOTE: *Use soapy water as lubricant, if necessary, to aid in pin installation. Never use oil or grease.*

3. Finger-tighten the spring hanger nuts and/or bolts.

4. Install the rubber bushing in the spring eye at the opposite end of the spring.

5. Raise the free end of the spring. Install the spring shackle through the bushing and the bracket.

6. Install the shackle inner plate and finger-tighten the retaining nuts.

7. Center the bolt head in the hole which is provided in the spring seat on the axle housing.

8. Fit the U-bolts over the axle housing. Install the lower spring seat.

9. Tighten the U-bolt nuts.

NOTE: *Some models have two sets of nuts, while others have a nut and lockwasher.*

10. Install the parking brake cable clamp. Install the equalizer, if it was removed.

11. Pick-up, 4Runner and Land Cruiser:

a. Raise the rear axle with the jack so that the stands no longer support the frame.

b. Tighten the hanger pin and shackle nuts.

c. Install the shock absorber bushings and washers. Tighten, and install the cotter pins.

d. Install the stabilizer link and hand tighten its retaining nuts (Land Cruiser).

e. Install the wheels, remove the stands, and lower the vehicle to the ground.

f. Tighten the stabilizer link bolts, bounce the vehicle, and tighten them again (Land Cruiser).

Shock Absorbers

REMOVAL AND INSTALLATION

1. Jack up the rear of the vehicle.
2. Support the rear axle housing with jack stands.
3. Unfasten the upper shock absorber retaining nuts and/or bolts from the upper frame member.
4. Depending upon the type of rear spring used, either disconnect the lower end of the shock absorber from the spring seat, or the rear axle housing, by removing its cotter pins, nuts and/or bolts.
5. Remove the shock absorber. Inspect the shock for wear, leaks, or other signs of damage. Installation is performed in the reverse order of removal.

STEERING

Steering Wheel

REMOVAL AND INSTALLATION

Three Spoke

CAUTION: *Do not attempt to remove or install the steering wheel by hammering on it. Damage to the energy absorbing steering column may result.*

1. Unfasten the horn and turn signal multi-connector(s) at the base of the steering column shroud.
2. Loosen the trim pad retaining screws from the back side of the steering wheel.
3. Lift the trim pad and horn button assembly(ies) from the wheel.
4. Remove the steering wheel hub retaining nut.
5. Scratch match marks in the hub and shaft to aid in correct installation.
6. Use a steering wheel puller to remove the steering wheel.
7. Installation is the reverse of removal. Tighten the wheel retaining nut to 22–29 ft.lb.

Two Spoke

The two spoke steering wheel is removed in the same manner as the three spoke, except that the trim pad should be pried off with a screwdriver. Remove the pad by lifting it toward the top of the wheel.

Four Spoke

CAUTION: *Do not attempt to remove or install the steering wheel by hammering on it. Damage to the energy absorbing steering column may result.*

1. Unfasten the horn and turn signal connectors at the base of the steering column shroud, underneath the instrument panel.
2. Gently pry the center emblem off the front of the steering wheel.
3. Insert a wrench through the hole and remove the steering wheel retaining nut.
4. Scratch matchmarks in the hub and shaft to aid in correct installation.
5. Use a steering wheel puller to remove the steering wheel.
6. Installation is the reverse of removal. Tighten the wheel retaining nut to 15–22 ft.lb.

Turn Signal Switch

REMOVAL AND INSTALLATION

1. Diconnect the negative (–) battery cable at the battery.
2. Remove the steering wheel, as outlined in the appropriate section above.
3. Unfasten the screws which secure the upper and lower steering column shroud halves.
4. Unfasten the screws which retain the turn signal switch and remove the switch from the column. On 1979 and later pick-ups, the windshield wiper switch is part of the assembly, and will be removed as well.
5. Installation is the reverse of removal.

Ignition Lock/Switch

REMOVAL AND INSTALLATION

1. Diconnect the negative (–) battery cable at the battery.
2. Unfasten the ignition switch connector underneath the instrument panel.
3. Remove the screws which secure the upper and lower halves of the steering column cover.
4. Turn the lock cylinder to the ACC position with the ignition key.
5. Push the lock cylinder stop in with a small round object (cotter pin, punch, etc.).

NOTE: *On some models it may be necessary to remove the steering wheel and turn signal switch first.*

6. Withdraw the lock cylinder from the lock housing while depressing the lock tab.
7. To remove the ignition switch, unfasten its securing screws and withdraw the switch from the lock housing.

Installation is performed in the following order:

1. Align the locking cam with the hole in the ignition switch and insert the switch in the lock housing.
2. Secure the switch with its screws.
3. Make sure that both the lock cylinder and the column lock are in the ACC position. Slide

the cylinder into the lock housing until the stop tab engages the hole in the lock.

4. The rest of installation is performed in the reverse order of removal.

Power Steering Pump

REMOVAL AND INSTALLATION

1. Remove the fan shroud.
2. Unfasten the nut from the center of the pump pulley.

NOTE: *Use the drive belt as a brake to keep the pulley from rotating.*

3. Withdraw the drive belt.
4. Remove the pulley and the Woodruff key from the pump shaft.
5. Detach the intake and outlet hoses from the pump reservoir.

NOTE: *Tie the hose ends up high so the fluid cannot flow out of them. Drain or plug the pump to prevent fluid leakage.*

6. Remove the bolt from the rear mounting brace.
7. Remove the front bracket bolts and withdraw the pump.

Installation is performed in the reverse order of removal. Note the following however:

1. Tighten the pump pulley mounting bolt to 25–39 ft.lb.
2. Adjust the pump drive belt tension. The belt should deflect 0.31–0.39 in. under thumb pressure applied midway between the air pump and power steering pump.
3. Fill the reservoir with Dexron®II automatic transmission fluid. Bleed the air from the system.

BLEEDING

1. Raise the front of the truck and support it securely with jackstands.
2. Fill the pump reservoir with Dexron®II automatic transmission fluid.
3. Rotate the steering wheel from lock to lock several times. Add fluid as necessary.
4. With the steering wheel turned fully to one lock, crank the starter while watching the fluid level in the reservoir.

NOTE: *Do not start the engine. Operate the starter with a remote starter switch or have an assistant do it from inside the car. Do not run the starter for prolonged periods.*

5. Repeat step 4 with the steering wheel turned to the opposite lock.
6. Start the engine. With the engine idling, turn the steering wheel from lock to lock several times.
7. Lower the front of the car and repeat step 6.
8. Center the wheel at the midpoint of its travel. Stop the engine.

9. The fluid level should not have risen more than 0.2 in. If it does, repeat step 7.
10. Check for fluid leakage.

Manual Steering Gear

REMOVAL AND INSTALLATION

2WD Pick-Up

1. Remove the pitman arm from the sector shaft with a puller.
2. Matchmark the flexible coupling and the wormshaft and remove the lock bolt.
3. Unbolt and remove the steering gear housing.
4. Install in reverse of removal. Torque the housing bolts to 26–36 ft.lb., and the pitman arm to 80–90 ft.lb. Tighten the coupling yoke to 15–20 ft.lb.

4WD Pick-Up and 4Runner

1. Remove the pitman arm from the sector shaft with a puller.
2. Matchmark and then loosen the intermediate shaft coupling at the steering gear wormshaft.
3. Loosen the bolt holding the intermediate shaft at the coupling near the fire wall and slide the shaft up off the steering gear wormshaft.
4. Remove the four bolts on the steering gear base and remove the steering gear.
5. Installation is the reverse of removal.
Observe the following torques:
- Steering gear housing to frame: 37–47 ft. lb.
- Pitman arm to sector shaft: 116–137 ft. lb.
- Wormshaft coupling bolt: 22–32 ft. lb.

Land Cruiser

55 SERIES

1. Remove the worm yoke from the worm and main shaft.
2. Remove the intermediate shaft assembly.
3. Remove the pitman arm from the sector shaft.
4. Unbolt and remove the gear housing.
5. Install in reverse of removal. Torque the pitman arm to 119–141 ft.lb.

NOTE: *The intermediate shaft must be installed with the wheels in a straight ahead position and the steering wheel straight ahead.*

40 SERIES

1. Remove the horn button assembly and, using a puller, remove the steering wheel.
2. Remove the steering column jacket lower clamp.
3. Remove the turn signal switch assembly.

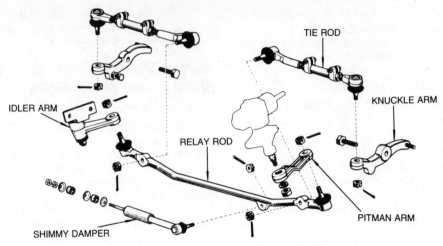

TIE ROD

KNUCKLE ARM

IDLER ARM

RELAY ROD

PITMAN ARM

SHIMMY DAMPER

2-WD steering gear linkage; 1979 and later shown

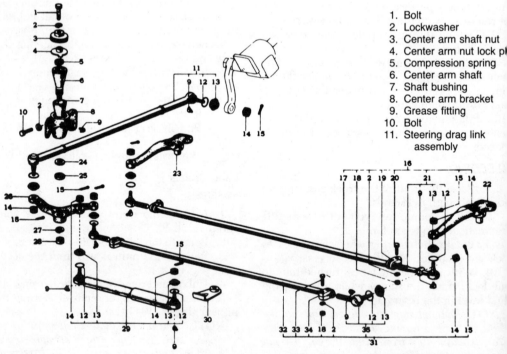

1. Bolt
2. Lockwasher
3. Center arm shaft nut
4. Center arm nut lock pl
5. Compression spring
6. Center arm shaft
7. Shaft bushing
8. Center arm bracket
9. Grease fitting
10. Bolt
11. Steering drag link assembly

12. Set ring
13. Joint dust seal
14. Lock nut
15. Cotter pin
16. Tie-rod assembly
17. Steering tie-rod
18. Lock nut
19. Tie-rod end clamp
20. Bolt

21. Tie-rod end assembly
22. Steering knuckle arm
23. Steering knuckle arm
24. Dust seal
25. Center arm dust lower seal
26. Steering center arm
27. Lock washer
28. Nut

29. Steering damper
30. Damper brakcet
31. Steering relay rod assembly
32. Steering relay rod
33. Bolt
34. Tie-rod end clamp
35. Relay rod end assemb

Land Cruiser steering gear linkage

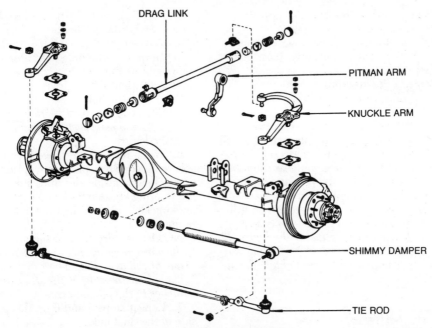

DRAG LINK — PITMAN ARM — KNUCKLE ARM — SHIMMY DAMPER — TIE ROD

4-WD pick-up steering gear linkage

4. Remove the steering column access plate.

5. Remove the carburetor and oil filter (not necessary on 1975–76).

6. Disconnect the #1 shift rod and select rod at the ends of the shift controls and select levers.

7. Remove the lower shift control and bracket clamp.

8. Remove the shift control lever, select lever, control shaft lower bracket, control shaft lower speed lever, and control shaft lower bracket.

9. Pull the control shaft out toward the driver's side.

10. Remove the pitman arm with a puller.

11. Remove the steering gear box bracket cap and lift out the gear box.

12. Installation is the reverse of removal. Torque the gear box bracket cap to 75–90 ft.lb. (30–40 for 1975–76); the pitman arm to 120–140 ft.lb., the steering wheel nut to 30–50 ft.lb.

ADJUSTMENTS

Adjustments to the manual steering gear are not necessary during normal service. Adjustments are performed only as part of overhaul.

Power Steering Gear

REMOVAL AND INSTALLATION

Pick-Up and 4Runner

1. Disconnect the hydraulic lines from the steering gear.

2. Mark the relationship between the intermediate shaft U-joint yoke and the steering gear wormshaft.

3. Loosen the set bolt of the intermediate shaft U-joint yoke and disconnect the intermediate shaft from the steering gear wormshaft.

4. Using a puller, remove the pitman arm from the steering gear.

5. Remove the steering gear mounting bolts and remove the steering gear through the engine compartment.

6. Installation is the reverse of the previous steps. Be sure to align the marks made during step 2. Torque the steering gear mounting bolts to 37–47 ft.lb.; the pitman arm nut to 116–137 ft. lb.; the U-joint yoke bolt to 22–32 ft.lb.; the pressure hose fitting to 29–36 ft.lb.; the return line fitting to 24–30 ft.lb.

NOTE: *During installation of the hydraulic lines, position each line clear of any surrounding components then tighten the fittings.*

Land Cruiser

1. Disconnect the hydraulic lines from the steering gear.

2. Remove the steering shaft coupling set bolt.

3. Remove the steering column-to-firewall bolts.

4. Loosen the steering column-to-dash bolts.

5. Using a puller, disconnect the relay rod from the pitman shaft.

6. Using a puller, remove the pitman arm from the steering gear.

7. Pull the steering column towards the passenger compartment to uncouple the steering shaft from the steering gear.

8. Remove the steering gear mounting fasteners and remove the steering gear from the vehicle.

9. Installation is the reverse of the previous steps. Be sure to align the marks on the pitman arm with the corresponding marks on the pitman shaft. Torque the steering gear mounting fasteners to 40–63 ft.lb.; the pitman arm nut to 120–141 ft.lb.; the coupling set bolt to 22–32 ft.lb.; the pressure hose fitting to 29–36 ft.lb.; and the return hose fitting to 24–30 ft.lb.

NOTE: *During installation of the hydraulic lines, position each line clear of any surrounding components then tighten the fittings.*

Steering Linkage

REMOVAL AND INSTALLATION

2WD Pick-Up

1. Raise the front of the vehicle and support it with jack stands.

2. Remove the front wheels.

3. Remove the nut on the pitman arm and using a puller remove it from the steering sector shaft.

4. Unfasten the idler arm support securing bolts and remove the support from the frame.

5. Remove the castle nuts and cotter pins from the tie rod ends and separate them from the steering knuckle arms with a puller.

6. Remove the relay rod complete with the tie rods, pitman arm and idler arm.

Installation is the reverse of removal with the following notes.

7. Align the marks on the pitman arm and sector shaft before installing the pitman arm.

8. Torque all of the following to 55–79 ft. lb.; tie rod ends to steering knuckles and relay rod; relay rod to pitman arm. Torque the relay rod to the idler arm to 37–50 ft.lb. Torque the pitman arm to the sector shaft to 80–90 ft.lb.

4WD Pick-Up and 4Runner

1. Jack up the vehicle and support it on stands.

2. Remove the front wheels.

3. Remove cotter pin and nut from the shimmy damper at the tie rod and remove shimmy damper from the tie rod with a puller. Remove the lock nut from the other other end of the damper. Be sure to note the order of the rubber spacers and washers, and remove damper.

4. Repeat the above precedure where the tie rod ends connect to the steering knuckles. Remove the tie rod.

5. To remove the drag link, remove the cotter pin from the steering knuckle end of the drag, and, using a screwdriver, unscrew the cap at the end of the link.

NOTE: *The cap may be tight, so you may have to use a wrench or pliers to turn the screwdriver.*

6. When the cap is removed, you should be able to dislodge the spring seat, spring and outer socket holder inside the drag link by working the steering knuckle back and forth. The steering knuckle socket in the drag link can now be removed.

NOTE: *Be sure to note the order in which the spring seat, spring and outer socket come out of the drag link. Their order will be reversed on the side of the drag link that attaches to the pitman arm.*

7. Repeat steps 5 and 6 on the pitman arm side of the drag link.

8. Installation is the reverse of removal. Be sure to insert the assemblies in the drag link in their correct orders. On drag links, screw on the caps completely then loosen them 1⅓ turns Observe the following torques:

- Shimmy damper-to-axle housing mount 8–11 ft. lb.
- Tie rod end-to-steering knuckle arm: 55–79 ft. lb.
- Shimmy damper-to-tie rod end: 37–50 ft. lb.

NOTE: *Be sure to grease the drag link ends at their grease nipples, and, when installing*

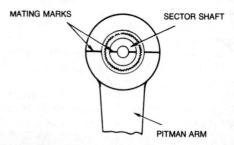

Aligning the mating marks on the pitman arm and the sector shaft

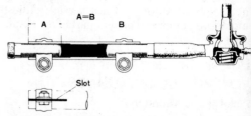

Adjust the tie-rod ends equally within the tube and the clamp bolt at the tube slot

the drag link end caps, tighten them completely and then loosen them 1⅓ turns.

Land Cruiser

1. Remove the hub caps and loosen the lug nuts.
2. Jack up the front of the vehicle and support it on jackstands. Remove the wheels.
3. Unfasten the pitman arm retaining nut.
4. Punch matchmarks on the pitman arm and the sector shaft to aid reinstallation.
5. Remove the pitman arm from the sector shaft with a puller.
6. Detach the drag link from the center arm with a tie rod puller. Remove the link together with the pitman arm.
7. Detach the tie rod ends from the steering knuckle arm with a puller.
8. Detach the relay rod ends from the cen-ter arm. Remove the tie rod/relay rod assembly.
9. Disconnect the end of the steering damper from its brackets on the front crossmember.
10. Remove the center arm attaching nut and use a puller to remove the arm, complete with damper.
11. Remove the skid plate and then remove the center arm bracket from the frame.
12. Installation is the reverse of removal.
13. Be sure to align the matchmarks, which were made during removal, on the pitman arm and the sector shaft. Tighten the mounting bolt to 120–140 ft.lb.
14. Lubricate all of the rod ends and damper ends with multipurpose grease.
15. After the linkage is installed, adjust the toe-in to the proper specifications.

Brakes

BRAKE SYSTEM

CAUTION: *Brake shoes contain asbestos, which has been determined to be a cancer causing agent. Never clean thebrake surfaces with compressed air! Avoid inhaling any dust from any brake surface! When cleaning brake surfaces, use a commercially available brake cleaning fluid.*

ADJUSTMENT

Front 1970–74

The front wheels are equipped with two wheel cylinders and two sets of adjusters. Each brake shoe must be adjusted separately to achieve the correct adjustment. The procedure outlined is for the adjustment of one shoe; repeat the procedure on all four shoes of the front wheel brakes.

1. Jack up the front end of the truck and support the crossmember with jackstands.

CAUTION: *You will be working under the truck so be absolutely certain that it is firmly supported.*

2. Remove the adjusting hole plug from the backing plate.

3. Expand the brake shoe with a starwheel adjusting wrench or a screwdriver.

4. Pump the brake pedal several times while doing this to center the brake shoe.

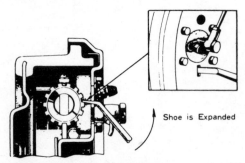

Shoe is Expanded

Adjusting brake shoe clearance

5. Back off the adjuster just enough so that the wheel will turn with a slight drag. Then back off the adjuster another five notches. The wheel should turn smoothly.

6. If the wheel does not turn smoothly, back off one or two more notches. If the wheel is still dragging, check for worn or defective parts.

7. Pump the brake pedal again to center the shoe.

8. Proceed to the next shoe and repeat the procedure.

1975 and Later

Front disc brakes require no adjustment, as hydraulic pressure maintains proper pad-to-disc clearance.

Rear (All)

NOTE: *This procedure is necessary on 1975 and later self-adjusting brakes only after the brake shoes have been changed.*

1. Place blocks under the front wheels so that the truck will not roll forward when it is jacked up at the rear.

2. Fully release the emergency brake.

3. Jack up the rear end of the truck and support the differential housing with jackstands.

4. Remove the plug from the adjusting hole at the bottom of the backing plate.

NOTE: *Unlike the front wheels, the rear brakes have only one wheel cylinder and therefore both shoes on the wheel are adjusted at the same time.*

5. Turn the adjusting starwheel to expand the shoes fully. While doing this, step on the brake pedal occasionally to center the shoes.

6. Tighten the shoes until the wheel will not turn when you release the brake pedal.

7. From this position back off the adjuster until the wheel turns with just a slight drag.

8. Back off the adjuster an additional five notches. The wheel should turn smoothly. If it does not, back off another two or three notches.

Should this fail, check for worn or defective parts.

9. Adjust the other wheel in the same manner.

Master Cylinder

REMOVAL AND INSTALLATION

1. Remove the hydraulic lines from the master cylinder. Be careful not to damage the nuts on the compression fittings. On 1970–72 models, also disconnect the brake fluid hoses from the reservoir at the master cylinder.

CAUTION: *Brake fluid will ruin paint. Avoid getting it on the body.*

2. Detach the brake fluid warning switch wiring.

3. Remove the bolts attaching the master cylinder to the booster unit.

4. Installation of the unit is performed in the reverse order. Screw the hydraulic lines into the cylinder a few turns before bolting the unit to the booster assembly. After installation, bleed the system.

NOTE: *To accurately install the master cylinder the clearance between the booster piston rod and the master cylinder piston should be 0.12–0.24 in. This can be done after the master cylinder is installed. The brake pedal should move the specified distance with just a slight touch. Remember, you are only checking the distance in which the rod is traveling to connect the pistons, not to depress it. See the Brake Pedal Adjustment section in this Chapter.*

OVERHAUL

1. On all 1973 and later models, remove the reservoir cap, floats, and strainers. Remove the reservoir mounting bolts and the reservoirs, being careful not to damage the rubber rings beneath them. On 1970–72 models, remove the two reservoir hose fittings and washers.

2. Unbolt the pressure warning switches.

3. Remove the bolt and gasket from the side of the cylinder.

4. Remove the bolt and snapring from the rear of the cylinder, then remove piston #1,

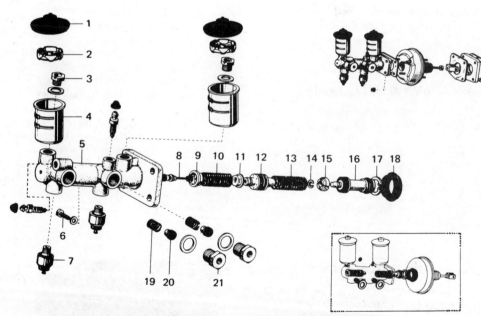

1. Reservoir filler cap subassembly
2. Master cylinder reservoir strainer
3. Master cylinder reservoir set bolt
4. Master cylinder reservoir
5. Tandem master cylinder body
6. Bolt
7. Brake warning switch assembly
8. Inlet valve connecting rod
9. Inlet valve case
10. Compression spring
11. Piston return spring retainer No. 2
12. Master cylinder piston No. 2
13. Compression spring
14. Shaft snap-ring
15. Piston return spring retainer
16. Master cylinder piston No. 1
17. Hole snap-ring
18. Master cylinder boot
19. Compression spring
20. Master cylinder outlet check valve assembly
21. Master cylinder fluid outlet plug

1973–74 master cylinder—exploded view

the compression spring, piston #2, spring, and the inlet valve seat and rod.

5. Remove the outlet plugs, gaskets, check valves, and springs from the side of the cylinder.

6. Wash all of the parts in brake fluid and allow to air dry. Inspect the cylinder bore and piston surfaces for wear and concentricity. The cylinder may be honed slightly if necessary, but the piston-to-cylinder clearance limit is 0.006 in.

7. Rubber parts deteriorate over time, and disassembly usually causes them to deform. Therefore, all rubber parts should be replaced. They are available as a kit from your dealer. Wash them in brake fluid before use.

8. Replace the parts in reverse order of removal. All parts must be absolutely clean. Lubricate all the parts with brake fluid before assembly.

9. Tighten the outlet plugs over the gaskets, check valves, and springs, to 80–95 ft.lb. tighten the warning switches to 22–30 ft.lb. On 1973 and later models, tighten the master cylinder reservoirs to 14–22 ft.lb., making certain that the markings are towards the front. The front reservoir is the larger of the two on 1975 and later models.

10. After installation, bleed the master cylinder and check all lines for leaks. Adjust the brake pedal clearance if necessary.

Brake Booster

REMOVAL AND INSTALLATION

1. Remove the master cylinder.
2. Remove the clip and clevis pin from the brake pedal.
3. Remove the vacuum hose from the booster.
4. Remove the brake booster nuts and gaskets, and remove the booster.

NOTE: *The 4x4 has two extra brackets that must be removed when removing the brake booster.*

Load Sensing Proportioning Valve

The purpose of this valve is to control the fluid pressure applied to the brakes to prevent rear wheel lock-up during weight transfer at high speed stops.

REMOVAL AND INSTALLATION

1. Disconnect the brake lines going to the valve.
2. Remove the mounting bolt, if used, and remove the valve.

NOTE: *This valve cannot be rebuilt. It must be replaced.*

3. Installation is the reverse of removal.
4. Bleed the brake system.

ADJUSTMENT

1. Pull down the load sensing spring to determine that the piston moves slowly.
2. Set the valve body so that the piston lightly touches the load sensing spring.
3. Tighten the mounting bolts.

BLEEDING

Never reuse brake fluid that has been bled from the brake system.

1. On 1973–74 models, if the master cylinder has been overhauled, start the bleeding procedure with the master cylinder. On all other models (and after bleeding the master cylinder on 1973–74) start with the wheel cylinder farthest from the master cylinder (right rear) and work toward it.

2. Clean the bleeder screw at each wheel.

3. Fill the master cylinder with DOT 3 brake fluid.

NOTE: *Brake fluid picks up moisture from the air. Don't leave the master cylinder or the fluid container uncovered any longer than necessary. Be careful, brake fluid eats paint. Check the level of the fluid often when bleeding, and refill the reservoirs as necessary. Don't let them run dry or you will have to repeat the process.*

4. Attach a length of clear vinyl tubing to the bleeder screw on the wheel cylinder (or master cylinder). Insert the other end of the tube into a clear, clean jar half filled with brake fluid.

5. Have your helper slowly depress the brake pedal. As this is done, open the bleeder screw ⅓–½ of a turn, and allow the fluid to run through the tube. Then close the bleeder screw before the pedal reaches the end of its travel. Have your assistant slowly release the pedal. Repeat this process until no air bubbles appear in the expelled fluid.

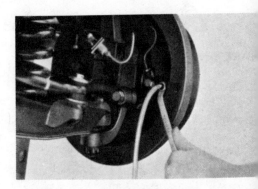

Air bleeding the wheel cylinder

NOTE: *If the brake pedal is depressed too quickly, small air bubbles will form in the brake fluid.*

6. Repeat the procedure on the other three brakes, checking the level of fluid in the cylinder reservoirs often.

Brake Pedal Adjustment

There are two adjustments possible on the break pedal: pedal height and master cylinder piston/pushrod clearance.

1. To adjust the distance between the pedal and toeboard, loosen the lock nut on the tail light stop switch and adjust the pedal to a height of 6.18–6.57 in. above the toe board by turning the switch body.

NOTE: *If the pedal cannot be adjusted properly with the switch body, loosen the pushrod locknut and turn the pushrod.*

2. After adjusting the pedal, tighten the stop switch locknut.

3. Loosen the pushrod locknut and turn the pushrod to provide 0.12–0.24 in. clearance between the master cylinder piston and the pushrod.

4. After tightening the pushrod locknut, check to see if the pedal has about 2½ in. of reserve travel when depressed.

5. Check the brake light (tail light) operation after all adjustments have been made.

FRONT DRUM BRAKES

Brake Drums

REMOVAL AND INSTALLATION

CAUTION: *Brake shoes contain asbestos, which has been determined to be a cancer causing agent. Never clean the brake surfaces with compressed air! Avoid inhaling any dust from any brake surface! When cleaning*

Removing the front brake drum

brake surfaces, use a commercially available brake cleaning fluid.*

1. Remove the hub cap and loosen the lug nuts.

2. Raise the front of the vehicle and support it on jackstands.

3. Remove the lug nuts, tire and wheel.

4. Remove the axle hub grease cap.

5. Remove the cotter pin, and then loosen the hub nut. When the nut is close to the end of the spindle, pull the drum and hub assembly toward you. If it does not slide off the brake shoes, loosen the brake shoe adjuster star wheels. Remove the spindle nut, brake drum and hub, the washer, and the wheel bearings.

NOTE: *Be careful not to get foreign matter in the wheel bearings. The heavy coating of grease will hold many particles. These will damage the bearings.*

6. Inspect the brake drum as outlined below.

CAUTION: *Do not depress the brake pedal with the brake drum removed.*

7. Install the drum in the reverse order. For instructions on preloading the front wheel bearings, see the appropriate section in chapter 1.

INSPECTION

1. Clean the drum with a rag and a little paint thinner.

CAUTION: *Do not blow the brake dust out of the drum with compressed air or lung power. Brake linings contain asbestos, a known cancer causing agent.*

2. Inspect the drum for cracks, grooves, scoring and out-of-roundness.

3. Light scoring may be removed with fine emery paper, Heavy scores or grooves will have to be removed by having the drum turned on a lathe. This can be done at many automotive machine shops and some service stations.

4. Before cutting the drum it must be measured to determine whether or not the inside dimension of the drum is within limitations after removing the score marks. The service limits of the brake drums are as follows:

1970–71 9 inch drum: 9.134 in.

1972 and later 10 inch drum: 10.08 in.

5. Check the drum for concentricity. An inside micrometer is necessary for an exact measurement, so unless this tool is available, the drum should be taken to a machine shop to be checked. Any drum which measures more than 0.006 in. out of round will result in an inaccurate brake adjustment and other problems, and must be refinished or replaced.

NOTE: *Make all measurements at right angles to each other and at the open and closed edges of the drum machined surface.*

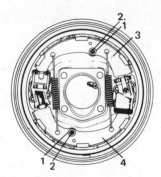

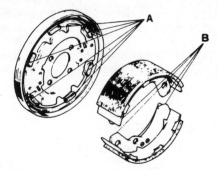

1. Hold down spring   3. Upper brake shoe
2. Spring pin   4. Lower brake shoe

Remove these parts in the order shown here, after removing the long shoe tension springs

Lightly coat points A and B with grease

Brake Shoes

REMOVAL AND INSTALLATION

CAUTION: *Brake shoes contain asbestos, which has been determined to be a cancer causing agent. Never clean the brake surfaces with compressed air! Avoid inhaling any dust from any brake surface! When cleaning brake surfaces, use a commercially available brake cleaning fluid.*

1. Remove the brake drum.

2. Remove the long brake tension (retracting) springs. These have hooks on each end, but you should be able to get them off with a pair of needlenosed pliers. Remove the holddown springs with a brake tool. You can make due with some other tool, but it won't be easy.

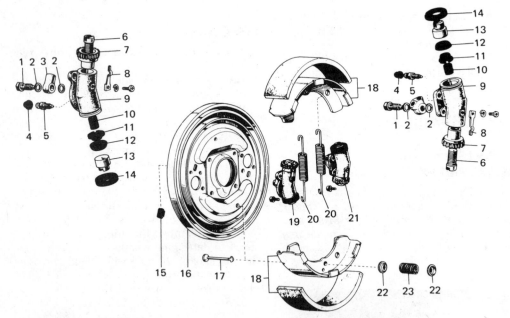

1. Union bolt
2. Gasket
3. Union
4. Bleeder plug cap
5. Bleeder plug
6. Wheel cylinder adjusting bolt
7. Wheel cylinder adjusting nut
8. Adjuster lock spring
9. Front brake wheel cylinder body
10. Compression spring
11. Wheel cylinder piston spring seat
12. Cylinder cup
13. Wheel brake cylinder piston
14. Wheel cylinder boot
15. Shoe adjusting hole plug
16. Brake backing front plate subassembly
17. Shoe hold-down spring pin
18. Brake shoe assembly
19. Front brake No. 1 wheel cylinder assembly
20. Tension spring
21. Front brake No. 2 wheel cylinder assembly
22. Shoe hold-down spring cup
23. Spring

Front brake components—1970–74

Pull out the spring pin from the rear, and remove the shoes.

NOTE: *If the brake shoes are to be reused, mark them so that they may be returned to their original locations.*

3. Clean the backing plate with a wire brush.

4. Inspect the brake springs for deformation and weakness; replace any parts found to be defective.

5. Check the brake linings for wear. The factory limit is 0.04 in. measured at both ends and middle of the shoe. If the limit is exceeded, replace both brake shoes.

NOTE: *This measurement may disagree with your state inspection laws.*

6. Check to see that no grease or break fluid is leaking onto the backing plate or the shoes. Fresh grease on the backing plate may indicate a faulty seal in the hub. Break fluid leakage can be traced to the wheel cylinder or brake line. If there is any leakage, rebuild the wheel cylinders or replace the brake lines. DO NOT DELAY, as a brake failure may result.

NOTE: *A small trace of fluid may be present to act as a lubricant for the wheel cylinder pistons.*

7. Before proceeding to the installation of the brake shoes, coat all the points of contact on the backing plate with a film of multipurpose grease.

CAUTION: *Do not get grease or oil on the brake shoes.*

Install the shoes in the following manner:

1. Fit the upper and lower shoes onto the grooves on the wheel cylinders and adjusting bolts. Install the spring pins and the retaining springs with the aid of a brake spring tool.

2. Hook the brake shoe tension springs on the upper and lower shoes.

3. Install the drum and adjust the brakes as outlined earlier.

Wheel Cylinders
REMOVAL AND INSTALLATION

CAUTION: *Brake shoes contain asbestos, which has been determined to be a cancer causing agent. Never clean the brake surfaces with compressed air! Avoid inhaling any dust from any brake surface! When cleaning brake surfaces, use a commercially available brake cleaning fluid.*

1. Perform the brake drum and brake shoe removal procedures, as outlined above.

2. Plug the master cylinder reservoir inlet, to prevent fluid from leaking out.

3. Remove the hydraulic lines from the wheel cylinders by unfastening the union bolt.

4. Remove the wheel cylinder attachment screws and remove the wheel cylinders.

NOTE: *Do not mix the right and left wheel cylinders.*

To install the wheel cylinders, proceed in the following manner:

1. Use the attaching screws to install the wheel cylinder on the backing plate.

NOTE: *The wheel cylinder adjusting nut and bolt on the right side of the brake have left hand threads; those on the left side have right hand threads. Be careful not to mix them.*

2. Connect the hydraulic lines to the wheel cylinders.

CAUTION: *Use care to ensure that the hydraulic line is not twisted.*

3. Install the brake drum and shoes, as outlined above. Bleed the brake system.

OVERHAUL

Remove the boots, pistons and the cups and closely inspect the bores for signs of wear, scoring and/or scuffing. When in doubt, replace or hone the wheel cylinders with a special brake hone, using clean brake fluid as lubricant. Wash residue from the bores using clean fluid; never use oil or any other solvent on any brake components. Blow dry with air and install with fresh brake fluid. The The general limit for a honed cylinder is 0.005 in. oversize. Wheel cylinder rebuilding kits are available which include new boots and cups. Never reuse these parts. The adjuster screws should be taken apart and all dirt and rust removed with a wire brush. Lightly coat with Lubriplate® before assemble; components should turn freely.

FRONT DISC BRAKES

Brake Pads
REMOVAL AND INSTALLATION

The front pads must be removed for wear inspection. It is not necessary to remove the caliper.

CAUTION: *Brake shoes contain asbestos, which has been determined to be a cancer causing agent. Never clean the brake surfaces with compressed air! Avoid inhaling any dust from any brake surface! When cleaning brake surfaces, use a commercially available brake cleaning fluid.*

1. Jack up the front of the truck, support it on jackstands, and remove the front wheel.

2. Pull out the two wire clips at the ends of the pad pins.

3. Pull out the pads and anti-squeal shims.

4. Check the pad thickness and replace the

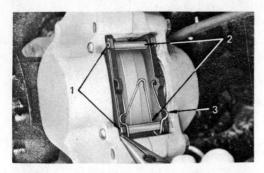

Remove the pin clips (1), pins (2) and anti-rattle spring (3) to get at the pads

pads if they are less than 0.04 in. thick. New pads measure approximately 0.38 in. thick.

NOTE: *This minimum thickness measurement may disagree with your state inspection laws.*

5. Check the pins for straightness and wear, and replace if necessary.

6. To install, position the anti-squeal shims so that the folded part will face the pad, and the arrows will face the direction of forward rotation. Lightly coat both sides of the shims with anti-squeak lubricant before installation.

7. Install the shims and pads.

8. Install the anti-rattle spring, the pad pins, and the pin clips.

Caliper
REMOVAL AND INSTALLATION

CAUTION: *Brake shoes contain asbestos, which has been determined to be a cancer causing agent. Never clean the brake surfaces with compressed air! Avoid inhaling any dust from any brake surface! When cleaning brake surfaces, use a commercially available brake cleaning fluid.*

2-Wheel Drive

1. Perform the first three steps of the pad removal procedure.

2. Plug the vent hole on the master cylinder cap to prevent fluid leak. Unbolt the brake line from the caliper, being careful not to deform the fittings.

3. Remove the two caliper mounting bolts, and remove the caliper.

4. To install, reverse the removal procedure. Tighten the caliper mounting bolts to 67–87 ft.lb. Be certain to position the shims cor-

1. Brake backing plate
2. Caliper
3. Anti-squeal shim
4. Brake pad
5. Seal ring
6. Piston
7. Piston boot
8. Set ring
9. Pad pin
10. Anti-rattle spring

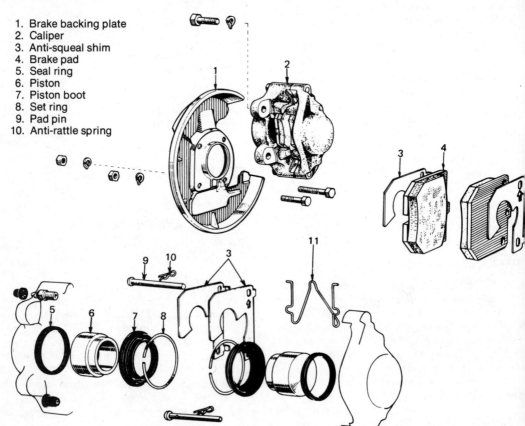

2-wheel drive caliper components

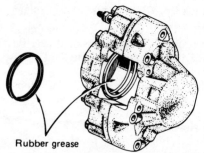

Rubber grease

Coat the seal rings and the piston bores with rubber grease

rectly, and bleed the system after all parts are installed.

OVERHAUL

1. Remove the caliper.
2. Remove the set ring and the piston boot from the caliper.
3. Place a thin wooden slat between the pistons. Remove the pistons by blowing compressed air through the brake line hole.
4. Remove the seal rings from the piston seat.
CAUTION: *Do not loosen the four bolts holding the two halves of the caliper together.*

5. Inspect the caliper for cracks or deformation. Check the piston bores and pistons for wear, scoring, and corrosion. Replace any worn or defective parts.
6. To assemble, coat the piston walls and seal rings with rubber grease. Insert the rings into the piston seats.
7. Coat the pistons with rubber grease and push them into the bores.
8. Install the piston boots, and replace the set rings.
9. Install the caliper, and bleed the system.

4-Wheel Drive and 4Runner

1. Disconnect the brake line.
2. Unbolt the caliper from the backing plate.
3. Insert a thin piece of wood in the caliper.
4. Apply compressed air to one piston at a time through the brake line hole.
CAUTION: *Don't loosen the caliper bolts or separate the caliper.*

5. Inspect the pistons for wear or damage. Replace the parts if necessary.
NOTE: *Clean the piston and cylinder with brake fluid. Do not reuse the piston ring and cylinder boot.*

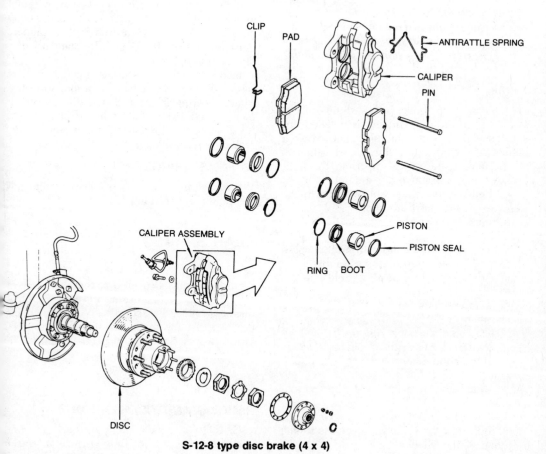

S-12-8 type disc brake (4 x 4)

6. Check the disc for thickness. Standard is 0.49 in. Limit is 0.45 in. This must be done with a caliper.

7. Check the disc runout. Limit 0.006 in.

NOTE: *Before checking disc runout, check the wheel bearing looseness. You will need a dial indicator to check disc runout.*

8. Apply rubber grease to the new seal and piston.

9. Do not pry the piston into the cylinder.

10. Apply disc brake grease on the cylinder that the pads slide on.

11. Install the pads.

12. Install the anti-rattle spring, caliper pins and pin clip.

13. Tighten the caliper bolts 55–75 ft.lb.

14. Connect the brake line to the caliper. Tighten to 10–13 ft.lb.

15. Bleed the system.

16. Refill the master cylinder to the maximum line.

Brake Disc

REMOVAL AND INSTALLATION

CAUTION: *Brake shoes contain asbestos, which has been determined to be a cancer causing agent. Never clean the brake surfaces with compressed air! Avoid inhaling any dust from any brake surface! When cleaning brake surfaces, use a commercially available brake cleaning fluid.*

Pick-Up

1. Remove the brake pads and the caliper.

2. Check the disc runout, as detailed under Inspection, below, at this point. Make a note of the results for use during installation.

3. Remove the grease cap from the hub. Remove the cotter pin and castle nut.

4. Remove the wheel hub with the brake rotor attached, inspect the rotor.

5. Installation is performed in the following order:

6. Coat the hub seal lip with multipurpose grease and install the rotor/hub assembly.

7. Adjust the wheel bearing preload as detailed below.

8. Measure rotor runout. Check it against specification.

NOTE: *If the wheel bearing nut is improperly tightened, rotor runout will be affected.*

9. Tighten the caliper securing bolts to 65–87 ft.lb.

10. Install the remainder of the components.

11. Bleed the brake system.

12. Road test the vehicle. Check the rolling resistance of the wheel.

4WD Pick-Up, 4Runner and Land Cruiser

1. For 4WD pick-up, complete steps 1–8 under front drive axle removal, above. Be sure to check rotor runout, as described in Inspection section, below.

2. For Land Cruiser, complete steps 1–7 under front drive axle removal, above. Be sure to check rotor runout, as described in Inspection, below.

NOTE: *Runout limit for Land Cruiser is 0.005 in.*

3. For all three vehicles, complete steps 5–12 under Pick-Up Rotor Removal and Installation, above, with the following notes:

4. When replacing the adjusting nut on the 4WD pick-up and 4Runner, tighten the nut to 43 ft.lb. and then loosen it again. Tighten the nut to 3–5 ft.lb. and test preload. Lock the adjusting nut and tighten the lock nut over it to 58–72 ft.lb.

NOTE: *Reverse steps taken from other sections to complete assembly procedures. Tighten Land Cruiser caliper securing bolts to 54–76 ft.lb.*

INSPECTION

The disc does not need to be removed for inspection. Runout can be checked with a dial indicator, and should measure less than 0.0059 in. Disc thickness, measured with a caliper, must be at least 0.453 in. The standard disc thickness in 0.492 in.

Inspect the disc for scoring or corrosion. If it is scored, it should be taken to a shop for refinishing, bearing in mind that it must measure more than 0.453 in. thick when all marks have been removed. Runout can sometimes be corrected by refinishing.

WHEEL BEARINGS

Wheel bearing removal, installation, and adjustment is covered in Chapter 1.

REAR BRAKES

Non self-adjusting brakes were used from 1970–74. Adjustment is covered at the beginning of this Chapter. Self-adjusting brakes were introduced in 1975. Procedures are combined for the two systems in this section for drum removal, installation, and inspection, and brake shoe removal.

Brake Drum

REMOVAL AND INSTALLATION

CAUTION: *Brake shoes contain asbestos, which has been determined to be a cancer* causing agent. Never clean the brake sur- faces with compressed air! Avoid inhaling any dust from any brake surface! When cleaning brake surfaces, use a commercially available brake cleaning fluid.

1. Block the front wheels so that the truck cannot roll forward.

2. Raise the rear of the truck and support it on jackstands.

3. Remove the wheel and tire.

4. Fully release the emergency brake.

NOTE: *Be absolutely certain that the emergency brake is released completely.*

5. Unfasten the brake drum retaining screw and remove the screw from the drum.

6. Tap the drum with a soft mallet and remove the drum. If the drum does not come off, back off the starwheel adjuster for the brake shoes.

NOTE: *Do not strike the brake drum with a regular hammer.*

7. To install the drum simply replace the drum on the axle and tighten the retaining screw.

NOTE: *Don't forget to adjust the brake shoes.*

CAUTION: *Do not step on the brake pedal with the drum removed.*

INSPECTION

The inspection procedure and measurements are the same for the rear drums as for the front drums and linings. See the appropriate section in this Chapter.

Brake Shoes
REMOVAL

CAUTION: *Brake shoes contain asbestos, which has been determined to be a cancer causing agent. Never clean the brake sur- faces with compressed air! Avoid inhaling any dust from any brake surface! When cleaning brake surfaces, use a commercially available brake cleaning fluid.*

1. Remove the drum as outlined earlier.

2. Loosen the retracting spring clamp bolt on non self-adjusting brakes. On self-adjusters, remove the adjusting spring and lever at the bottom.

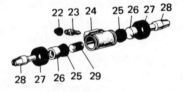

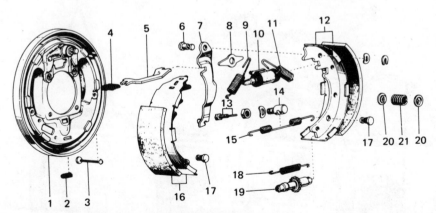

1. Brake backing plate subassembly	11. Tension spring	21. Spring
2. Shoe adjusting hole plug	12. Brake shoe assembly	22. Bleeder plug cap
3. Shoe hold-down spring pin	13. Retracting spring clamp bolt subassembly	23. Bleeder plug
4. Compression spring	14. Shoe retracting clamp holder	24. Wheel brake cylinder rear body
5. Parking brake shoe strut	15. Tension spring	25. Cylinder cup
6. Parking lever pin	16. Brake shoe assembly	26. Wheel brake cylinder piston
7. Parking brake shoe lever	17. Tension spring pin	27. Wheel cylinder boot
8. Rear brake shoe guide plate	18. Tension spring	28. Wheel cylinder connecting link
9. Tension spring	19. Adjuster assembly	29. Compression spring
10. Wheel brake rear cylinder assembly	20. Shoe hold-down spring cup	

Rear brake components on 1970–74 pick-ups

3. Using a brake spring tool, remove the return springs. On self-adjusters, also remove the adjusting cable, shoe guide plate, and the cable guide.

4. Remove the holddown springs and the holddown spring pins. On self-adjusters, first remove the parking brake shoe strut and spring, and the lower retracting spring and adjusting screw set. Then remove the hold down springs and pins.

5. Remove the parking brake shoe strut along with the spring on non self-adjusters only.

6. Grip the brake shoes at the top near the wheel cylinder, spread the shoes apart and draw the shoes, adjusting mechanism, and spring away from the backing plate. On self-adjusters, simply remove the brake shoes, as there should be no spring tension left. If the shoes are hard to remove, check for an obstructing part.

7. Remove the rear shoe and the parking brake shoe lever from the parking brake cable.

8. Remove the shoe lever from the shoe by removing the horseshoe clip from the pin.

INSTALLATION

Non Self-Adjusting

1. Assemble the rear shoe to the parking brake shoe lever, install a new clip.

NOTE: *Coat all contact points for the shoes*

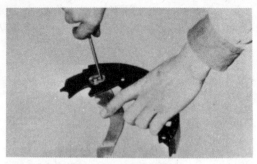

Removing the horseshoe clip and the parking brake shoe lever

and the parking brake mechanism with grease.

CAUTION: *Do not get grease on the linings or the inside of the brake drum.*

2. Assemble the adjusting mechanism between the shoes and install the adjusting spring. The adjuster with left hand threads goes on the left wheel, right hand threads on the right wheel. Install the shoes onto the wheel cylinder and backing plate.

3. Install the holddown pins and springs.

4. Install the parking brake strut arm and make the necessary connection of the emergency brake cable.

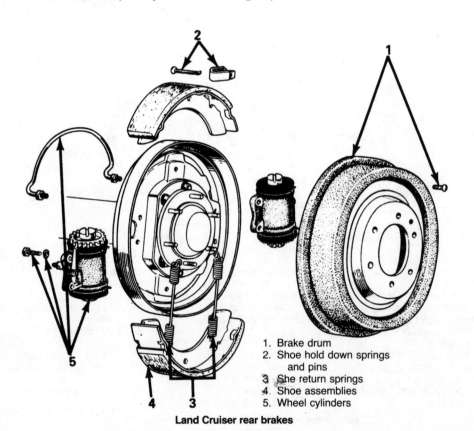

1. Brake drum
2. Shoe hold down springs and pins
3. Shoe return springs
4. Shoe assemblies
5. Wheel cylinders

Land Cruiser rear brakes

Brake Specifications

All measurements given are (in.) unless noted

Year	Model	Lug Nut Torque (ft/lb)	Brake Disc		Brake Drum			Minimum lining Thickness	
			Minimum Thickness	Maximum Run-Out	Diameter	Max. Machine O/S	Max. Wear Limit	Front	Rear
1970–72	Pick-up	65–86	—	—	9.1	9.13	9.15	0.06	0.06
1973–77	Pick-up	65–86	0.45	0.006	10.0	10.07	10.08	0.27	0.06
1978	Pick-up	65–86	0.45 ①	0.006	10.08	—	10.08	0.04	0.04
1979–80	Pick-up	65–86	0.453 ②	0.0059	10.079	—	10.079	0.039	0.039
1981–85	Pick-up & 4 Runner	65–86	0.453 ②	0.0059	10.0 ③	—	10.079	0.039	0.039
1970–83	Land Cruiser	65–86	0.750	0.005	11.70	—	11.90	④	0.06

① 0.79 in. "K" Type Disc Brake (Limit 0.75 in.)
Some 78 Hi-Lux Models have front drum brakes; Diameter 10.00 in. (limit 10.08 in.) Lining thickness 0.04 in.
② RN ½ & ¾ Ton, RN 4x4 0.453 in.—RN C + C Cab/Chassis 0.748 in.
③ Front Power Disc 10.4 in. ½ Ton—11.8 in. Power disc 4x4—9.8 in. Power disc Cap/Chassis
④ Disc Pads: 0.04; Drum Shoes 0.06

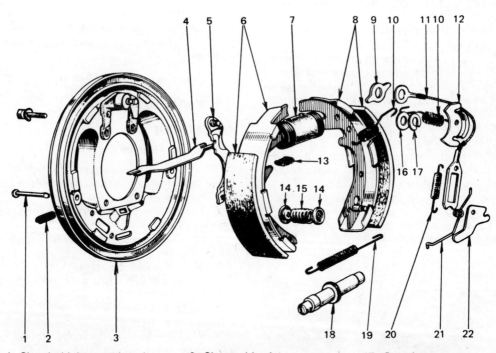

1. Shoe hold down spring pin
2. Adjusting hole plug
3. Backing plate
4. Parking brake shoe strut
5. Parking brake shoe lever
6. Front brake shoe
7. Wheel cylinder
8. Rear brake shoe
9. Shoe guide plate
10. Return spring
11. Automatic adjuster cable
12. Cable guide
13. Parking brake strut spring
14. Hold down spring seat
15. Shoe hold down spring
16. Washer
17. C washer
18. Adjusting screw set
19. Retracting spring
20. Adjusting cable spring
21. Adjusting lever spring
22. Adjusting lever

1975 and later self-adjusting brake components

5. Install the return springs.

6. Install the brake drum and adjust the brake shoes.

Self-Adjusting

1. Assemble the parking brake shoe lever and brake shoe.

2. Connect the parking brake shoe lever to the parking brake cable.

3. Apply a thin coat of grease to the backing plate and shoe contacting surfaces, and anchor pin and shoe end surfaces. Install the brake shoes, shorter lining shoe on the front, and the hold down springs and pins.

4. Install the spring onto the front of the parking brake shoe strut, and install the strut between the brake shoes.

5. Fit the shoe guide plate and automatic adjusting cable onto the anchor pin, and using a brake tool install the brake shoe return spring to the front side.

6. Apply a thin coat of grease to the cable guide sliding surface, and fit the cable guide to the rear shoe. Install the return spring to the rear shoe with a brake tool.

7. Install the adjusting screw set, right hand threads on the right wheel. Apply a coat of grease to the threads, washer, and slots.

NOTE: *Make sure that the threaded portion faces the front.*

8. Install the brake shoe retracting spring at the bottom, longer hook to the rear shoe.

9. Hook the adjusting lever to the adjusting cable spring. Insert the lever slot onto the pivot pin, and hook the adjusting lever spring onto the end of the lever.

10. With the parts assembled, test the auto-adjust mechanism. Insert a screw driver between the anchor pin and the rear shoe end, and move the shoe away from the pin. The adjuster should turn the adjusting screw set to expand slightly.

11. If the adjuster is OK, measure the maximum diameter of the brake drum, and adjust

Hook the adjusting lever (1) to the adjusting cable spring (2), then insert the lever slot onto the pin (4) and hook up the adjusting lever spring (3)

the shoes via the adjusting screw to be 0.012–0.024 in. smaller to diameter.

12. Install the brake drum.

Wheel Cylinders
REMOVAL AND INSTALLATION

CAUTION: *Brake shoes contain asbestos, which has been determined to be a cancer causing agent. Never clean the brake surfaces with compressed air! Avoid inhaling any dust from any brake surface! When cleaning brake surfaces, use a commercially available brake cleaning fluid.*

1. Plug the master cylinder inlet to prevent hydraulic fluid from leaking.

2. Remove the brake drum and shoes.

3. Working from behind the backing plate, disconnect the brake fluid line.

4. Remove the wheel cylinder-to-backing plate attaching bolts and withdraw the wheel cylinder.

5. Installation is the reverse of removal. Be sure to bleed the system throughly and to readjust the brake shoes.

OVERHAUL

Overhaul procedures are the same as for the front wheel cylinders, found earlier in this Chapter.

PARKING BRAKE

ADJUSTMENT
Pick-Up and 4Runner

NOTE: *Before attempting to adjust the parking brake, adjust the rear brake shoes as outlined earlier.*

1. Loosen the parking brake warning light switch bracket.

2. Push the parking brake lever in until it is stopped by the pawl.

3. Move the switch so that it will be OFF at this position, but ON when the handle is pulled out.

4. Tighten the switch bracket and push the bracket lever in again.

5. Working from underneath the vehicle, loosen the locknut on the parking brake cable equalizer.

6. Screw the adjusting nut in, just enough that the brake cables have no slack.

7. Hold the adjusting nut in this position while tightening the locknut.

8. Check the rotation of the rear wheels to make sure that the brakes are not dragging.

9. Pull out the parking lever and count the

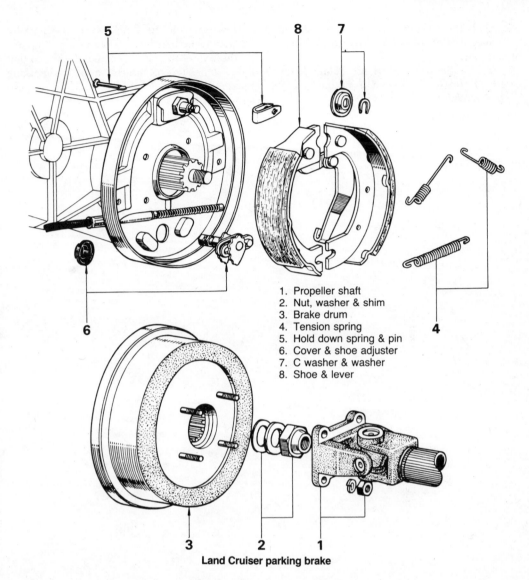

1. Propeller shaft
2. Nut, washer & shim
3. Brake drum
4. Tension spring
5. Hold down spring & pin
6. Cover & shoe adjuster
7. C washer & washer
8. Shoe & lever

Land Cruiser parking brake

number of notches needed to apply the brake. If it is between 6 and 9 notches, the brake is properly adjusted.

Land Cruiser

Land Cruiser models use a separate drum brake assembly, operating on the drive shaft, to serve as a parking brake. Adjust it as follows:

1. Push the parking brake lever all the way in, so that the brake is released.

2. Raise the rear of the vehicle and support it with jackstands.

3. Turn the parking brake adjustment shaft, which is located at the bottom of the parking brake backing plate, counterclockwise until the shoes seat against the drum.

4. Back the adjuster off one notch.

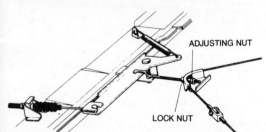

Parking brake adjustment from under the truck

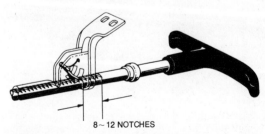

Parking brake handle—specified travel

5. Apply the parking brake; the drum should be locked. Release the brake; the drum should rotate freely.

NOTE: *If the drum does not rotate freely with the brake off, loosen the adjuster one more notch.*

6. Adjust the turnbuckles on the parking brake intermediate levers and the adjusting nuts on the end of the parking brake cables, so that 6–9 notches are required to apply the parking brake (1975). Set it for 7–12 notches for 1976 and later.

Troubleshooting
10

This section is designed to aid in the quick, accurate diagnosis of automotive problems. While automotive repairs can be made by many people, accurate troubleshooting is a rare skill for the amateur and professional alike.

In its simplest state, troubleshooting is an exercise in logic. It is essential to realize that an automobile is really composed of a series of systems. Some of these systems are interrelated; others are not. Automobiles operate within a framework of logical rules and physical laws, and the key to troubleshooting is a good understanding of all the automotive systems.

This section breaks the car or truck down into its component systems, allowing the problem to be isolated. The charts and diagnostic road maps list the most common problems and the most probable causes of trouble. Obviously it would be impossible to list every possible problem that could happen along with every possible cause, but it will locate MOST problems and eliminate a lot of unnecessary guesswork. The systematic format will locate problems within a given system, but, because many automotive systems are interrelated, the solution to your particular problem may be found in a number of systems on the car or truck.

USING THE TROUBLESHOOTING CHARTS

This book contains all of the specific information that the average do-it-yourself mechanic needs to repair and maintain his or her car or truck. The troubleshooting charts are designed to be used in conjunction with the specific procedures and information in the text. For instance, troubleshooting a point-type ignition system is fairly standard for all models, but you may be directed to the text to find procedures for troubleshooting an individual type of electronic ignition. You will also have to refer to the specification charts throughout the book for specifications applicable to your car or truck.

TOOLS AND EQUIPMENT

The tools illustrated in Chapter 1 (plus two more diagnostic pieces) will be adequate to troubleshoot most problems. The two other tools needed are a voltmeter and an ohmmeter. These can be purchased separately or in combination, known as a VOM meter.

In the event that other tools are required, they will be noted in the procedures.

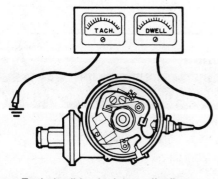

Tach-dwell hooked-up to distributor

Troubleshooting Engine Problems

See Chapters 2, 3, 4 for more information and service procedures.

Index to Systems

System	To Test	Group
Battery	Engine need not be running	1
Starting system	Engine need not be running	2
Primary electrical system	Engine need not be running	3
Secondary electrical system	Engine need not be running	4
Fuel system	Engine need not be running	5
Engine compression	Engine need not be running	6
Engine vacuum	Engine must be running	7
Secondary electrical system	Engine must be running	8
Valve train	Engine must be running	9
Exhaust system	Engine must be running	10
Cooling system	Engine must be running	11
Engine lubrication	Engine must be running	12

Index to Problems

Problem: Symptom	Begin at Specific Diagnosis, Number
Engine Won't Start:	
Starter doesn't turn	1.1, 2.1
Starter turns, engine doesn't	2.1
Starter turns engine very slowly	1.1, 2.4
Starter turns engine normally	3.1, 4.1
Starter turns engine very quickly	6.1
Engine fires intermittently	4.1
Engine fires consistently	5.1, 6.1
Engine Runs Poorly:	
Hard starting	3.1, 4.1, 5.1, 8.1
Rough idle	4.1, 5.1, 8.1
Stalling	3.1, 4.1, 5.1, 8.1
Engine dies at high speeds	4.1, 5.1
Hesitation (on acceleration from standing stop)	5.1, 8.1
Poor pickup	4.1, 5.1, 8.1
Lack of power	3.1, 4.1, 5.1, 8.1
Backfire through the carburetor	4.1, 8.1, 9.1
Backfire through the exhaust	4.1, 8.1, 9.1
Blue exhaust gases	6.1, 7.1
Black exhaust gases	5.1
Running on (after the ignition is shut off)	3.1, 8.1
Susceptible to moisture	4.1
Engine misfires under load	4.1, 7.1, 8.4, 9.1
Engine misfires at speed	4.1, 8.4
Engine misfires at idle	3.1, 4.1, 5.1, 7.1, 8.4

Sample Section

Test and Procedure	Results and Indications	Proceed to
4.1—Check for spark: Hold each spark plug wire approximately ¼" from ground with gloves or a heavy, dry rag. Crank the engine and observe the spark.	→ If no spark is evident:	→ 4.2
	→ If spark is good in some cases:	→ 4.3
	→ If spark is good in all cases:	→ 4.6

Specific Diagnosis

This section is arranged so that following each test, instructions are given to proceed to another, until a problem is diagnosed.

Section 1—Battery

Test and Procedure	Results and Indications	Proceed to
1.1—Inspect the battery visually for case condition (corrosion, cracks) and water level. 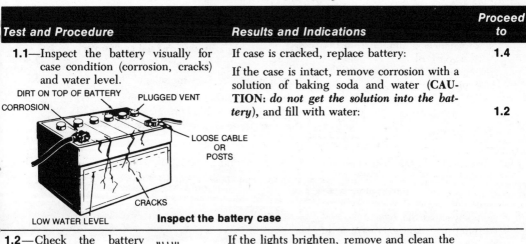	If case is cracked, replace battery:	**1.4**
	If the case is intact, remove corrosion with a solution of baking soda and water (**CAUTION**: *do not get the solution into the battery*), and fill with water:	**1.2**
1.2—Check the battery cable connections: Insert a screwdriver between the battery post and the cable clamp. Turn the headlights on high beam, and observe them as the screwdriver is gently twisted to ensure good metal to metal contact. 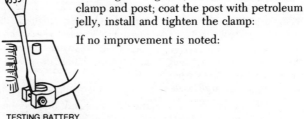	If the lights brighten, remove and clean the clamp and post; coat the post with petroleum jelly, install and tighten the clamp:	**1.4**
	If no improvement is noted:	**1.3**
1.3—Test the state of charge of the battery using an individual cell tester or hydrometer.	If indicated, charge the battery. **NOTE:** *If no obvious reason exists for the low state of charge (i.e., battery age, prolonged storage), proceed to:*	**1.4**

DIRT ON TOP OF BATTERY
CORROSION
PLUGGED VENT
LOOSE CABLE OR POSTS
CRACKS
LOW WATER LEVEL

Inspect the battery case

TESTING BATTERY CABLE CONNECTIONS USING A SCREWDRIVER

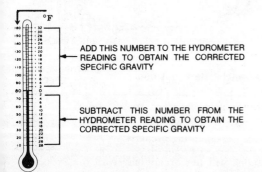

°F

ADD THIS NUMBER TO THE HYDROMETER READING TO OBTAIN THE CORRECTED SPECIFIC GRAVITY

SUBTRACT THIS NUMBER FROM THE HYDROMETER READING TO OBTAIN THE CORRECTED SPECIFIC GRAVITY

Specific Gravity (@ 80° F.)

Minimum	Battery Charge
1.260	100% Charged
1.230	75% Charged
1.200	50% Charged
1.170	25% Charged
1.140	Very Little Power Left
1.110	Completely Discharged

The effects of temperature on battery specific gravity (left) and amount of battery charge in relation to specific gravity (right)

Test and Procedure	Results and Indications	Proceed to
1.4—Visually inspect battery cables for cracking, bad connection to ground, or bad connection to starter.	If necessary, tighten connections or replace the cables:	**2.1**

Section 2—Starting System
See Chapter 3 for service procedures

Test and Procedure	Results and Indications	Proceed to
Note: Tests in Group 2 are performed with coil high tension lead disconnected to prevent accidental starting.		
2.1—Test the starter motor and solenoid: Connect a jumper from the battery post of the solenoid (or relay) to the starter post of the solenoid (or relay).	If starter turns the engine normally:	2.2
	If the starter buzzes, or turns the engine very slowly:	2.4
	If no response, replace the solenoid (or relay).	3.1
	If the starter turns, but the engine doesn't, ensure that the flywheel ring gear is intact. If the gear is undamaged, replace the starter drive.	3.1
2.2—Determine whether ignition override switches are functioning properly (clutch start switch, neutral safety switch), by connecting a jumper across the switch(es), and turning the ignition switch to "start".	If starter operates, adjust or replace switch:	3.1
	If the starter doesn't operate:	2.3
2.3—Check the ignition switch "start" position: Connect a 12V test lamp or voltmeter between the starter post of the solenoid (or relay) and ground. Turn the ignition switch to the "start" position, and jiggle the key.	If the lamp doesn't light or the meter needle doesn't move when the switch is turned, check the ignition switch for loose connections, cracked insulation, or broken wires. Repair or replace as necessary:	3.1
	If the lamp flickers or needle moves when the key is jiggled, replace the ignition switch.	3.3

Checking the ignition switch "start" position

STARTER RELAY (IF EQUIPPED)

Test and Procedure	Results and Indications	Proceed to
2.4—Remove and bench test the starter, according to specifications in the engine electrical section.	If the starter does not meet specifications, repair or replace as needed:	3.1
	If the starter is operating properly:	2.5
2.5—Determine whether the engine can turn freely: Remove the spark plugs, and check for water in the cylinders. Check for water on the dipstick, or oil in the radiator. Attempt to turn the engine using an 18″ flex drive and socket on the crankshaft pulley nut or bolt.	If the engine will turn freely only with the spark plugs out, and hydrostatic lock (water in the cylinders) is ruled out, check valve timing:	9.2
	If engine will not turn freely, and it is known that the clutch and transmission are free, the engine must be disassembled for further evaluation:	Chapter 3

Section 3—Primary Electrical System

Test and Procedure	Results and Indications	Proceed to
3.1—Check the ignition switch "on" position: Connect a jumper wire between the distributor side of the coil and ground, and a 12V test lamp between the switch side of the coil and ground. Remove the high tension lead from the coil. Turn the ignition switch on and jiggle the key.	If the lamp lights:	**3.2**
	If the lamp flickers when the key is jiggled, replace the ignition switch:	**3.3**
	If the lamp doesn't light, check for loose or open connections. If none are found, remove the ignition switch and check for continuity. If the switch is faulty, replace it:	**3.3**

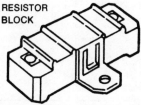

Checking the ignition switch "on" position

3.2—Check the ballast resistor or resistance wire for an open circuit, using an ohmmeter. See Chapter 3 for specific tests.	Replace the resistor or resistance wire if the resistance is zero. **NOTE:** *Some ignition systems have no ballast resistor.*	**3.3**

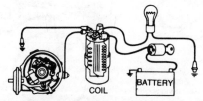

Two types of resistors

3.3—On point-type ignition systems, visually inspect the breaker points for burning, pitting or excessive wear. Gray coloring of the point contact surfaces is normal. Rotate the crankshaft until the contact heel rests on a high point of the distributor cam and adjust the point gap to specifications. On electronic ignition models, remove the distributor cap and visually inspect the armature. Ensure that the armature pin is in place, and that the armature is on tight and rotates when the engine is cranked. Make sure there are no cracks, chips or rounded edges on the armature.	If the breaker points are intact, clean the contact surfaces with fine emery cloth, and adjust the point gap to specifications. If the points are worn, replace them. On electronic systems, replace any parts which appear defective. If condition persists:	**3.4**

Test and Procedure	Results and Indications	Proceed to
3.4—On point-type ignition systems, connect a dwell-meter between the distributor primary lead and ground. Crank the engine and observe the point dwell angle. On electronic ignition systems, conduct a stator (magnetic pickup assembly) test. See Chapter 3.	On point-type systems, adjust the dwell angle if necessary. **NOTE:** *Increasing the point gap decreases the dwell angle and vice-versa.*	**3.6**
	If the dwell meter shows little or no reading;	**3.5**
	On electronic ignition systems, if the stator is bad, replace the stator. If the stator is good, proceed to the other tests in Chapter 3.	

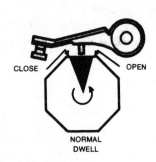
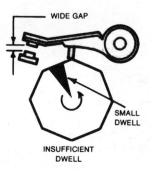
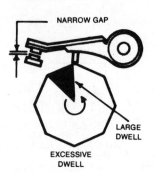

Dwell is a function of point gap

3.5—On the point-type ignition systems, check the condenser for short: connect an ohmeter across the condenser body and the pigtail lead.	If any reading other than infinite is noted, replace the condenser	**3.6**

Checking the condenser for short

3.6—Test the coil primary resistance: On point-type ignition systems, connect an ohmmeter across the coil primary terminals, and read the resistance on the low scale. Note whether an external ballast resistor or resistance wire is used. On electronic ignition systems, test the coil primary resistance as in Chapter 3.	Point-type ignition coils utilizing ballast resistors or resistance wires should have approximately 1.0 ohms resistance. Coils with internal resistors should have approximately 4.0 ohms resistance. If values far from the above are noted, replace the coil.	**4.1**

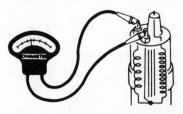

Check the coil primary resistance

Section 4—Secondary Electrical System
See Chapters 2–3 for service procedures

Test and Procedure	Results and Indications	Proceed to
4.1—Check for spark: Hold each spark plug wire approximately ¼″ from ground with gloves or a heavy, dry rag. Crank the engine, and observe the spark.	If no spark is evident:	**4.2**
	If spark is good in some cylinders:	**4.3**
	If spark is good in all cylinders:	**4.6**

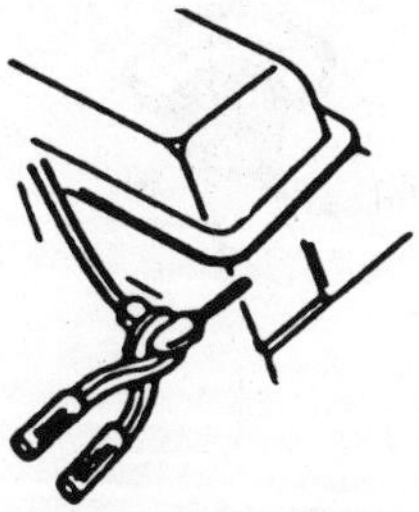

Check for spark at the plugs

Test and Procedure	Results and Indications	Proceed to
4.2—Check for spark at the coil high tension lead: Remove the coil high tension lead from the distributor and position it approximately ¼″ from ground. Crank the engine and observe spark. **CAUTION:** *This test should not be performed on engines equipped with electronic ignition.*	If the spark is good and consistent:	**4.3**
	If the spark is good but intermittent, test the primary electrical system starting at 3.3:	**3.3**
	If the spark is weak or non-existent, replace the coil high tension lead, clean and tighten all connections and retest. If no improvement is noted:	**4.4**
4.3—Visually inspect the distributor cap and rotor for burned or corroded contacts, cracks, carbon tracks, or moisture. Also check the fit of the rotor on the distributor shaft (where applicable).	If moisture is present, dry thoroughly, and retest per 4.1:	**4.1**
	If burned or excessively corroded contacts, cracks, or carbon tracks are noted, replace the defective part(s) and retest per 4.1:	**4.1**
	If the rotor and cap appear intact, or are only slightly corroded, clean the contacts thoroughly (including the cap towers and spark plug wire ends) and retest per 4.1:	
	If the spark is good in all cases:	**4.6**
	If the spark is poor in all cases:	**4.5**

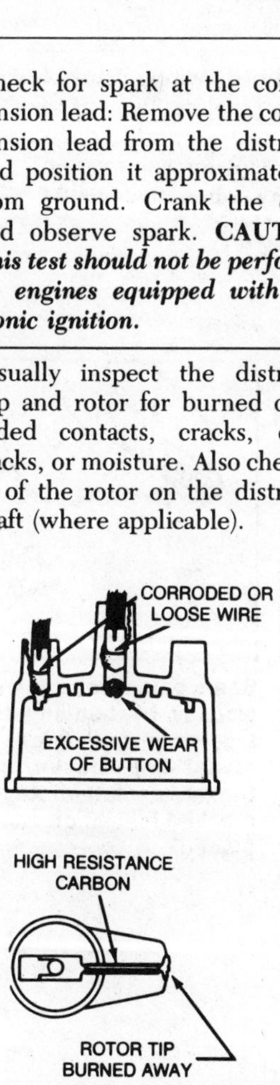

CORRODED OR LOOSE WIRE

EXCESSIVE WEAR OF BUTTON

HIGH RESISTANCE CARBON

ROTOR TIP BURNED AWAY

Inspect the distributor cap and rotor

Test and Procedure	Results and Indications	Proceed to
4.4—Check the coil secondary resistance: On point-type systems connect an ohmmeter across the distributor side of the coil and the coil tower. Read the resistance on the high scale of the ohmmeter. On electronic ignition systems, see Chapter 3 for specific tests.	The resistance of a satisfactory coil should be between 4,000 and 10,000 ohms. If resistance is considerably higher (i.e., 40,000 ohms) replace the coil and retest per 4.1. **NOTE: *This does not apply to high performance coils.***	

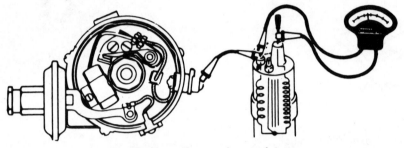

Testing the coil secondary resistance

4.5—Visually inspect the spark plug wires for cracking or brittleness. Ensure that no two wires are positioned so as to cause induction firing (adjacent and parallel). Remove each wire, one by one, and check resistance with an ohmmeter.	Replace any cracked or brittle wires. If any of the wires are defective, replace the entire set. Replace any wires with excessive resistance (over $8000\,\Omega$ per foot for suppression wire), and separate any wires that might cause induction firing.	**4.6**

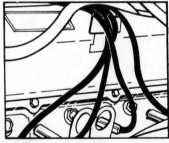

Misfiring can be the result of spark plug leads to adjacent, consecutively firing cylinders running parallel and too close together

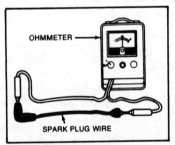

On point-type ignition systems, check the spark plug wires as shown. On electronic ignitions, do not remove the wire from the distributor cap terminal; instead, test through the cap

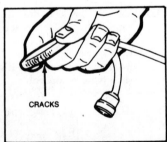

Spark plug wires can be checked visually by bending them in a loop over your finger. This will reveal any cracks, burned or broken insulation. Any wire with cracked insulation should be replaced

4.6—Remove the spark plugs, noting the cylinders from which they were removed, and evaluate according to the color photos in the middle of this book.	See following.	**See following.**

Test and Procedure	Results and Indications	Proceed to
4.7—Examine the location of all the plugs.	The following diagrams illustrate some of the conditions that the location of plugs will reveal.	**4.8**

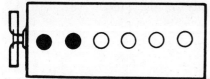

Two adjacent plugs are fouled in a 6-cylinder engine, 4-cylinder engine or either bank of a V-8. This is probably due to a blown head gasket between the two cylinders

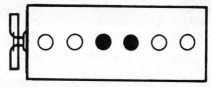

The two center plugs in a 6-cylinder engine are fouled. Raw fuel may be "boiled" out of the carburetor into the intake manifold after the engine is shut-off. Stop-start driving can also foul the center plugs, due to overly rich mixture. Proper float level, a new float needle and seat or use of an insulating spacer may help this problem

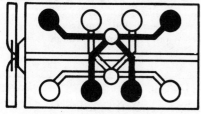

An unbalanced carburetor is indicated. Following the fuel flow on this particular design shows that the cylinders fed by the right-hand barrel are fouled from overly rich mixture, while the cylinders fed by the left-hand barrel are normal

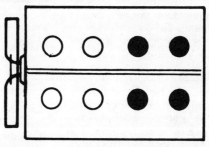

If the four rear plugs are overheated, a cooling system problem is suggested. A thorough cleaning of the cooling system may restore coolant circulation and cure the problem

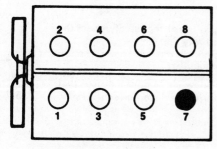

Finding one plug overheated may indicate an intake manifold leak near the affected cylinder. If the overheated plug is the second of two adjacent, consecutively firing plugs, it could be the result of ignition cross-firing. Separating the leads to these two plugs will eliminate cross-fire

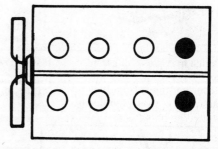

Occasionally, the two rear plugs in large, lightly used V-8's will become oil fouled. High oil consumption and smoky exhaust may also be noticed. It is probably due to plugged oil drain holes in the rear of the cylinder head, causing oil to be sucked in around the valve stems. This usually occurs in the rear cylinders first, because the engine slants that way

Test and Procedure	Results and Indications	Proceed to
4.8—Determine the static ignition timing. Using the crankshaft pulley timing marks as a guide, locate top dead center on the compression stroke of the number one cylinder.	The rotor should be pointing toward the No. 1 tower in the distributor cap, and, on electronic ignitions, the armature spoke for that cylinder should be lined up with the stator.	4.8
4.9—Check coil polarity: Connect a voltmeter negative lead to the coil high tension lead, and the positive lead to ground (**NOTE: Reverse the hook-up for positive ground systems**). Crank the engine momentarily. **Checking coil polarity**	If the voltmeter reads up-scale, the polarity is correct: If the voltmeter reads down-scale, reverse the coil polarity (switch the primary leads):	5.1 5.1

Section 5—Fuel System
See Chapter 4 for service procedures

Test and Procedure	Results and Indications	Proceed to
5.1—Determine that the air filter is functioning efficiently: Hold paper elements up to a strong light, and attempt to see light through the filter.	Clean permanent air filters in solvent (or manufacturer's recommendation), and allow to dry. Replace paper elements through which light cannot be seen:	5.2
5.2—Determine whether a flooding condition exists: Flooding is identified by a strong gasoline odor, and excessive gasoline present in the throttle bore(s) of the carburetor.	If flooding is not evident: If flooding is evident, permit the gasoline to dry for a few moments and restart. If flooding doesn't recur: If flooding is persistent:	5.3 5.7 5.5

If the engine floods repeatedly, check the choke butterfly flap

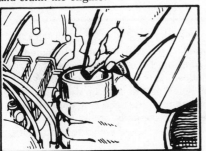

5.3—Check that fuel is reaching the carburetor: Detach the fuel line at the carburetor inlet. Hold the end of the line in a cup (not styrofoam), and crank the engine.	If fuel flows smoothly: If fuel doesn't flow (**NOTE: Make sure that there is fuel in the tank**), or flows erratically:	5.7 5.4

Check the fuel pump by disconnecting the output line (fuel pump-to-carburetor) at the carburetor and operating the starter briefly

CHILTON'S
AUTO BODY
REPAIR TIPS

Tools and Materials • Step-by-Step Illustrated Procedures
How To Repair Dents, Scratches and Rust Holes
Spray Painting and Refinishing Tips

With a little practice, basic body repair procedures can be mastered by any do-it-yourself mechanic. The step-by-step repairs shown here can be applied to almost any type of auto body repair.

TOOLS & MATERIALS

You may already have basic tools, such as hammers and electric drills. Other tools unique to body repair — body hammers, grinding attachments, sanding blocks, dent puller, half-round plastic file and plastic spreaders — are relatively inexpensive and can be obtained wherever auto parts or auto body repair parts are sold. Portable air compressors and paint spray guns can be purchased or rented.

Auto Body Repair Kits

The best and most often used products are available to the do-it-yourselfer in kit form, from major manufacturers of auto body repair products. The same manufacturers also merchandise the individual products for use by pros.

Kits are available to make a wide variety of repairs, including holes, dents and scratches and fiberglass, and offer the advantage of buying the materials you'll need for the job. There is little waste or chance of materials going bad from not being used. Many kits may also contain basic body-working tools such as body files, sanding blocks and spreaders. Check the contents of the kit before buying your tools.

BODY REPAIR TIPS

Safety

Many of the products associated with auto body repair and refinishing contain toxic chemicals. Read all labels before opening containers and store them in a safe place and manner.

• Wear eye protection (safety goggles) when using power tools or when performing any operation that involves

the removal of any type of material.

• Wear lung protection (disposa mask or respirator) when grinding, s ing or painting.

Sanding

1 Sand off paint before using a d puller. When using a non-adhes sanding disc, cover the back of the c with an overlapping layer or two masking tape and trim the edges. disc will last considerably longer.

2 Use the circular motion of the sa ing disc to grind *into* the edge of repair. Grinding or sanding away fi the jagged edge will only tear the sa paper.

3 Use the palm of your ha flat on the panel to det high and low spots. Do not use y fingertips. Slide your hand slowly b and forth.

WORKING WITH BODY FILLER

Mixing The Filler

leanliness and proper mixing and application are extremely impor-
nt. Use a clean piece of plastic or ass or a disposable artist's palette to ix body filler.

Allow plenty of time and follow directions. No useful purpose will be rved by adding more hardener to ake it cure (set-up) faster. Less hard-er means more curing time, but the ixture dries harder; more hardener eans less curing time but a softer mix-re.

Both the hardener and the filler should be thoroughly kneaded or rred before mixing. Hardener should a solid paste and dispense like thin othpaste. Body filler should be ooth, and free of lumps or thick ots.

Getting the proper amount of hard-er in the filler is the trickiest part of eparing the filler. Use the same ount of hardener in cold or warm ather. For contour filler (thick coats), ead of hardener twice the diameter of filler is about right. There's about a % margin on either side, but, if in ubt use less hardener.

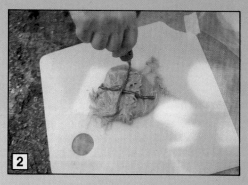

Mix the body filler and hardener by wiping across the mixing surface, picking the mixture up and wiping it again. Colder weather requires longer mixing times. Do not mix in a circular motion; this will trap air bubbles which will become holes in the cured filler.

Applying The Filler

For best results, filler should not be applied over 1/4" thick.

Apply the filler in several coats. Build it up to above the level of the repair surface so that it can be sanded or grated down.

The first coat of filler must be pressed on with a firm wiping motion.

Apply the filler in one direction only. Working the filler back and forth will either pull it off the metal or trap air bubbles.

REPAIRING DENTS

efore you start, take a few minutes to study the damaged area. Try to visualize the shape of the panel before it was damaged. If the damage is on the left fender, look at the right fender and use it as a guide. If there is access to the panel from behind, you can reshape it with a body hammer. If not, you'll have to use a dent puller. Go slowly and work the metal a little at a time. Get the panel as straight as possible before applying filler.

1 This dent is typical of one that can be pulled out or hammered out from behind. Remove the headlight cover, headlight assembly and turn signal housing.

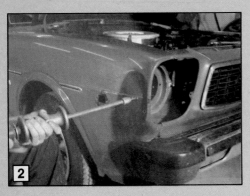

2 Drill a series of holes 1/2 the size of the end of the dent puller along the stress line. Make some trial pulls and assess the results. If necessary, drill more holes and try again. Do not hurry.

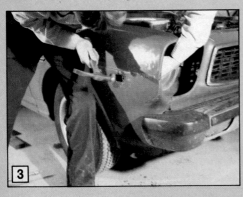

3 If possible, use a body hammer and block to shape the metal back to its original contours. Get the metal back as close to its original shape as possible. Don't depend on body filler to fill dents.

4 Using an 80-grit grinding disc on an electric drill, grind the paint from the surrounding area down to bare metal. Use a new grinding pad to prevent heat buildup that will warp metal.

5 The area should look like this when you're finished grinding. Knock the drill holes in and tape over small openings to keep plastic filler out.

6 Mix the body filler (see Body Repair Tips). Spread the body filler evenly over the entire area (see Body Repair Tips). Be sure to cover the area completely.

7 Let the body filler dry until the surface can just be scratched with your fingernail. Knock the high spots from the body filler with a body file ("Cheese grater"). Check frequently with the palm of your hand for high and low spots.

8 Check to be sure that trim pieces that will be installed later will fit exactly. Sand the area with 40-grit paper.

9 If you wind up with low spots, you may have to apply another layer of filler.

10 Knock the high spots off with 40-grit paper. When you are satisfied with the contours of the repair, apply a thin coat of filler to cover pin holes and scratches.

11 Block sand the area with 40-grit paper to a smooth finish. Pay particular attention to body lines and ridges that must be well-defined.

12 Sand the area with 400 paper and then finish with a scuff pad. The finished repair is ready for priming and painting (see Painting Tips).

Materials and photos courtesy of Ritt Jones Auto Body, Prospect Park, PA.

REPAIRING RUST HOLES

There are many ways to repair rust holes. The fiberglass cloth kit shown here is one of the most cost efficient for the owner because it provides a strong repair that resists cracking and moisture and is relatively easy to use. It can be used on large and small holes (with or without backing) and can be applied over contoured areas. Remember, however, that short of replacing an entire panel, no repair is a guarantee that the rust will not return.

1 Remove any trim that will be in the way. Clean away all loose debris. Cut away all the rusted metal. But be sure to leave enough metal to retain the contour or body shape.

2 Grind away all traces of rust with a 24-grit grinding disc. Be sure to grind back 3-4 inches from the edge of the hole down to bare metal and be sure all traces of paint, primer and rust are removed.

3 Block sand the area with 80 or 100 grit sandpaper to get a clear, shiny surface and feathered paint edge. Tap the edges of the hole inward with a ball peen hammer.

4 If you are going to use release film, cut a piece about 2-3" larger than the area you have sanded. Place the film over the repair and mark the sanded area on the film. Avoid any unnecessary wrinkling of the film.

5 Cut 2 pieces of fiberglass matte to match the shape of the repair. One piece should be about 1" smaller than the sanded area and the second piece should be 1" smaller than the first. Mix enough filler and hardener to saturate the fiberglass material (see Body Repair Tips).

6 Lay the release sheet on a flat su[r]face and spread an even layer [of] filler, large enough to cover the repa[ir.] Lay the smaller piece of fiberglass clot[h] in the center of the sheet and sprea[d] another layer of filler over the fibergla[ss] cloth. Repeat the operation for th[e] larger piece of cloth.

7 Place the repair material over th[e] repair area, with the release film fa[c]ing outward. Use a spreader and wo[rk] from the center outward to smooth th[e] material, following the body contour[s.] Be sure to remove all air bubbles.

8 Wait until the repair has dried tac[k] free and peel off the release shee[t.] The ideal working temperature is 6[0-] 90° F. Cooler or warmer temperatures [or] high humidity may require additio[nal] curing time. Wait longer, if in doubt.

9

Sand and feather-edge the entire area. The initial sanding can be done with a sanding disc on an electric drill if care is used. Finish the sanding with a block sander. Low spots can be filled with body filler; this may require several applications.

10 When the filler can just be scratched with a fingernail, knock the high spots down with a body file and smooth the entire area with 80-grit. Feather the filled areas into the surrounding areas.

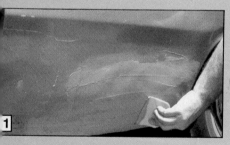

11 When the area is sanded smooth, mix some topcoat and hardener and apply it directly with a spreader. This will give a smooth finish and prevent the glass matte from showing through the paint.

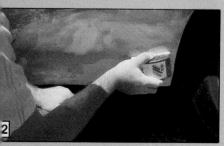

12 Block sand the topcoat smooth with finishing sandpaper (200 grit), and 400 grit. The repair is ready for masking, priming and painting (see Painting Tips).

Materials and photos courtesy Marson Corporation, Chelsea, Massachusetts

PAINTING TIPS

Preparation

1 SANDING — Use a 400 or 600 grit wet or dry sandpaper. Wet-sand the area with a 1/4 sheet of sandpaper soaked in clean water. Keep the paper wet while sanding. Sand the area until the repaired area tapers into the original finish.

2 CLEANING — Wash the area to be painted thoroughly with water and a clean rag. Rinse it thoroughly and wipe the surface dry until you're sure it's completely free of dirt, dust, fingerprints, wax, detergent or other foreign matter.

3 MASKING — Protect any areas you don't want to overspray by covering them with masking tape and newspaper. Be careful not get fingerprints on the area to be painted.

4 PRIMING — All exposed metal should be primed before painting. Primer protects the metal and provides an excellent surface for paint adhesion. When the primer is dry, wet-sand the area again with 600 grit wet-sandpaper. Clean the area again after sanding.

Painting Techniques

P aint applied from either a spray gun or a spray can (for small areas) will provide good results. Experiment on an old piece of metal to get the right combination before you begin painting.

SPRAYING VISCOSITY (SPRAY GUN ONLY) — Paint should be thinned to spraying viscosity according to the directions on the can. Use only the recommended thinner or reducer and the same amount of reduction regardless of temperature.

AIR PRESSURE (SPRAY GUN ONLY) — This is extremely important. Be sure you are using the proper recommended pressure.

TEMPERATURE — The surface to be painted should be approximately the same temperature as the surrounding air. Applying warm paint to a cold surface, or vice versa, will completely upset the paint characteristics.

THICKNESS — Spray with smooth strokes. In general, the thicker the coat of paint, the longer the drying time. Apply several thin coats about 30 seconds apart. The paint should remain wet long enough to flow out and no longer; heavier coats will only produce sags or wrinkles. Spray a light (fog) coat, followed by heavier color coats.

DISTANCE — The ideal spraying distance is 8″-12″ from the gun or can to the surface. Shorter distances will produce ripples, while greater distances will result in orange peel, dry film and poor color match and loss of material due to overspray.

OVERLAPPING — The gun or can should be kept at right angles to the surface at all times. Work to a wet edge at an even speed, using a 50% overlap and direct the center of the spray at the lower or nearest edge of the previous stroke.

RUBBING OUT (BLENDING) FRESH PAINT — Let the paint dry thoroughly. Runs or imperfections can be sanded out, primed and repainted.

Don't be in too big a hurry to remove the masking. This only produces paint ridges. When the finish has dried for at least a week, apply a small amount of fine grade rubbing compound with a clean, wet cloth. Use lots of water and blend the new paint with the surrounding area.

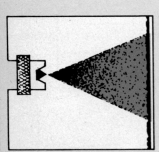

WRONG

Thin coat. Stroke too fast, not enough overlap, gun too far away.

CORRECT

Medium coat. Proper distance, good stroke, proper overlap.

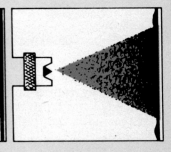

WRONG

Heavy coat. Stroke too slow, too much overlap, gun too close.

Test and Procedure	Results and Indications	Proceed to
5.4—Test the fuel pump: Disconnect all fuel lines from the fuel pump. Hold a finger over the input fitting, crank the engine (with electric pump, turn the ignition or pump on); and feel for suction.	If suction is evident, blow out the fuel line to the tank with low pressure compressed air until bubbling is heard from the fuel filler neck. Also blow out the carburetor fuel line (both ends disconnected):	5.7
	If no suction is evident, replace or repair the fuel pump: **NOTE:** *Repeated oil fouling of the spark plugs, or a no-start condition, could be the result of a ruptured vacuum booster pump diaphragm, through which oil or gasoline is being drawn into the intake manifold (where applicable).*	5.7
5.5—Occasionally, small specks of dirt will clog the small jets and orifices in the carburetor. With the engine cold, hold a flat piece of wood or similar material over the carburetor, where possible, and crank the engine.	If the engine starts, but runs roughly the engine is probably not run enough. If the engine won't start:	5.9
5.6—Check the needle and seat: Tap the carburetor in the area of the needle and seat.	If flooding stops, a gasoline additive (e.g., Gumout) will often cure the problem:	5.7
	If flooding continues, check the fuel pump for excessive pressure at the carburetor (according to specifications). If the pressure is normal, the needle and seat must be removed and checked, and/or the float level adjusted:	5.7
5.7—Test the accelerator pump by looking into the throttle bores while operating the throttle.	If the accelerator pump appears to be operating normally:	5.8
	If the accelerator pump is not operating, the pump must be reconditioned. Where possible, service the pump with the carburetor(s) installed on the engine. If necessary, remove the carburetor. Prior to removal:	5.8
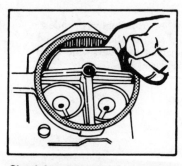 **Check for gas at the carburetor by looking down the carburetor throat while someone moves the accelerator**		
5.8—Determine whether the carburetor main fuel system is functioning: Spray a commercial starting fluid into the carburetor while attempting to start the engine.	If the engine starts, runs for a few seconds, and dies:	5.9
	If the engine doesn't start:	6.1

Test and Procedure	Results and Indications	Proceed to
5.9—Uncommon fuel system malfunctions: See below:	If the problem is solved: If the problem remains, remove and recondition the carburetor.	6.1

Condition	Indication	Test	Prevailing Weather Conditions	Remedy
Vapor lock	Engine will not restart shortly after running.	Cool the components of the fuel system until the engine starts. Vapor lock can be cured faster by draping a wet cloth over a mechanical fuel pump.	Hot to very hot	Ensure that the exhaust manifold heat control valve is operating. Check with the vehicle manufacturer for the recommended solution to vapor lock on the model in question.
Carburetor icing	Engine will not idle, stalls at low speeds.	Visually inspect the throttle plate area of the throttle bores for frost.	High humidity, 32–40° F.	Ensure that the exhaust manifold heat control valve is operating, and that the intake manifold heat riser is not blocked.
Water in the fuel	Engine sputters and stalls; may not start.	Pump a small amount of fuel into a glass jar. Allow to stand, and inspect for droplets or a layer of water.	High humidity, extreme temperature changes.	For droplets, use one or two cans of commercial gas line anti-freeze. For a layer of water, the tank must be drained, and the fuel lines blown out with compressed air.

Section 6—Engine Compression

See Chapter 3 for service procedures

6.1—Test engine compression: Remove all spark plugs. Block the throttle wide open. Insert a compression gauge into a spark plug port, crank the engine to obtain the maximum reading, and record.	If compression is within limits on all cylinders: If gauge reading is extremely low on all cylinders: If gauge reading is low on one or two cylinders: (If gauge readings are identical and low on two or more adjacent cylinders, the head gasket must be replaced.)	7.1 6.2 6.2

Checking compression

6.2—Test engine compression (wet): Squirt approximately 30 cc. of engine oil into each cylinder, and retest per 6.1.	If the readings improve, worn or cracked rings or broken pistons are indicated: If the readings do not improve, burned or excessively carboned valves or a jumped timing chain are indicated: NOTE: *A jumped timing chain is often indicated by difficult cranking.*	See Chapter 3 7.1

Section 7—Engine Vacuum
See Chapter 3 for service procedures

Test and Procedure	Results and Indications	Proceed to
7.1—Attach a vacuum gauge to the intake manifold beyond the throttle plate. Start the engine, and observe the action of the needle over the range of engine speeds.	See below.	**See below**

INDICATION: normal engine in good condition

Proceed to: 8.1

Normal engine
Gauge reading: steady, from 17–22 in./Hg.

INDICATION: sticking valves or ignition miss

Proceed to: 9.1, 8.3

Sticking valves
Gauge reading: intermittent fluctuation at idle

INDICATION: late ignition or valve timing, low compression, stuck throttle valve, leaking carburetor or manifold gasket

Proceed to: 6.1

Incorrect valve timing
Gauge reading: low (10–15 in./Hg) but steady

INDICATION: improper carburetor adjustment or minor intake leak.

Proceed to: 7.2

Carburetor requires adjustment
Gauge reading: drifting needle

INDICATION: ignition miss, blown cylinder head gasket, leaking valve or weak valve spring

Proceed to: 8.3, 6.1

Blown head gasket
Gauge reading: needle fluctuates as engine speed increases

INDICATION: burnt valve or faulty valve clearance. Needle will fall when defective valve operates

Proceed to: 9.1

Burnt or leaking valves
Gauge reading: steady needle, but drops regularly

INDICATION: choked muffler, excessive back pressure in system

Proceed to: 10.1

Clogged exhaust system
Gauge reading: gradual drop in reading at idle

INDICATION: worn valve guides

Proceed to: 9.1

Worn valve guides
Gauge reading: needle vibrates excessively at idle, but steadies as engine speed increases

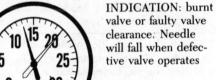

White pointer = steady gauge hand   Black pointer = fluctuating gauge hand

Test and Procedure	Results and Indications	Proceed to
7.2—Attach a vacuum gauge per 7.1, and test for an intake manifold leak. Squirt a small amount of oil around the intake manifold gaskets, carburetor gaskets, plugs and fittings. Observe the action of the vacuum gauge.	If the reading improves, replace the indicated gasket, or seal the indicated fitting or plug:	**8.1**
	If the reading remains low:	**7.3**
7.3—Test all vacuum hoses and accessories for leaks as described in 7.2. Also check the carburetor body (dashpots, automatic choke mechanism, throttle shafts) for leaks in the same manner.	If the reading improves, service or replace the offending part(s):	**8.1**
	If the reading remains low:	**6.1**

Section 8—Secondary Electrical System
See Chapter 2 for service procedures

Test and Procedure	Results and Indications	Proceed to
8.1—Remove the distributor cap and check to make sure that the rotor turns when the engine is cranked. Visually inspect the distributor components.	Clean, tighten or replace any components which appear defective.	**8.2**
8.2—Connect a timing light (per manufacturer's recommendation) and check the dynamic ignition timing. Disconnect and plug the vacuum hose(s) to the distributor if specified, start the engine, and observe the timing marks at the specified engine speed.	If the timing is not correct, adjust to specifications by rotating the distributor in the engine: (Advance timing by rotating distributor opposite normal direction of rotor rotation, retard timing by rotating distributor in same direction as rotor rotation.)	**8.3**
8.3—Check the operation of the distributor advance mechanism(s): To test the mechanical advance, disconnect the vacuum lines from the distributor advance unit and observe the timing marks with a timing light as the engine speed is increased from idle. If the mark moves smoothly, without hesitation, it may be assumed that the mechanical advance is functioning properly. To test vacuum advance and/or retard systems, alternately crimp and release the vacuum line, and observe the timing mark for movement. If movement is noted, the system is operating.	If the systems are functioning:	**8.4**
	If the systems are not functioning, remove the distributor, and test on a distributor tester:	**8.4**
8.4—Locate an ignition miss: With the engine running, remove each spark plug wire, one at a time, until one is found that doesn't cause the engine to roughen and slow down.	When the missing cylinder is identified:	**4.1**

Section 9—Valve Train
See Chapter 3 for service procedures

Test and Procedure	Results and Indications	Proceed to
9.1—Evaluate the valve train: Remove the valve cover, and ensure that the valves are adjusted to specifications. A mechanic's stethoscope may be used to aid in the diagnosis of the valve train. By pushing the probe on or near push rods or rockers, valve noise often can be isolated. A timing light also may be used to diagnose valve problems. Connect the light according to manufacturer's recommendations, and start the engine. Vary the firing moment of the light by increasing the engine speed (and therefore the ignition advance), and moving the trigger from cylinder to cylinder. Observe the movement of each valve.	Sticking valves or erratic valve train motion can be observed with the timing light. The cylinder head must be disassembled for repairs.	**See Chapter 3**
9.2—Check the valve timing: Locate top dead center of the No. 1 piston, and install a degree wheel or tape on the crankshaft pulley or damper with zero corresponding to an index mark on the engine. Rotate the crankshaft in its direction of rotation, and observe the opening of the No. 1 cylinder intake valve. The opening should correspond with the correct mark on the degree wheel according to specifications.	If the timing is not correct, the timing cover must be removed for further investigation.	**See Chapter 3**

Section 10—Exhaust System

Test and Procedure	Results and Indications	Proceed to
10.1—Determine whether the exhaust manifold heat control valve is operating: Operate the valve by hand to determine whether it is free to move. If the valve is free, run the engine to operating temperature and observe the action of the valve, to ensure that it is opening.	If the valve sticks, spray it with a suitable solvent, open and close the valve to free it, and retest. If the valve functions properly:	10.2
	If the valve does not free, or does not operate, replace the valve:	10.2
10.2—Ensure that there are no exhaust restrictions: Visually inspect the exhaust system for kinks, dents, or crushing. Also note that gases are flowing freely from the tailpipe at all engine speeds, indicating no restriction in the muffler or resonator.	Replace any damaged portion of the system:	11.1

Section 11—Cooling System
See Chapter 3 for service procedures

Test and Procedure	Results and Indications	Proceed to
11.1—Visually inspect the fan belt for glazing, cracks, and fraying, and replace if necessary. Tighten the belt so that the longest span has approximately ½″ play at its midpoint under thumb pressure (see Chapter 1).	Replace or tighten the fan belt as necessary:	**11.2**

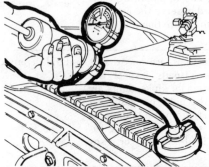

Checking belt tension

Test and Procedure	Results and Indications	Proceed to
11.2—Check the fluid level of the cooling system.	If full or slightly low, fill as necessary:	**11.5**
	If extremely low:	**11.3**
11.3—Visually inspect the external portions of the cooling system (radiator, radiator hoses, thermostat elbow, water pump seals, heater hoses, etc.) for leaks. If none are found, pressurize the cooling system to 14–15 psi.	If cooling system holds the pressure:	**11.5**
	If cooling system loses pressure rapidly, reinspect external parts of the system for leaks under pressure. If none are found, check dipstick for coolant in crankcase. If no coolant is present, but pressure loss continues:	**11.4**
	If coolant is evident in crankcase, remove cylinder head(s), and check gasket(s). If gaskets are intact, block and cylinder head(s) should be checked for cracks or holes.	
	If the gasket(s) is blown, replace, and purge the crankcase of coolant:	**12.6**
	NOTE: *Occasionally, due to atmospheric and driving conditions, condensation of water can occur in the crankcase. This causes the oil to appear milky white. To remedy, run the engine until hot, and change the oil and oil filter.*	
11.4—Check for combustion leaks into the cooling system: Pressurize the cooling system as above. Start the engine, and observe the pressure gauge. If the needle fluctuates, remove each spark plug wire, one at a time, noting which cylinder(s) reduce or eliminate the fluctuation.	Cylinders which reduce or eliminate the fluctuation, when the spark plug wire is removed, are leaking into the cooling system. Replace the head gasket on the affected cylinder bank(s).	

Pressurizing the cooling system

Test and Procedure	Results and Indications	Proceed to
11.5—Check the radiator pressure cap: Attach a radiator pressure tester to the radiator cap (wet the seal prior to installation). Quickly pump up the pressure, noting the point at which the cap releases.	If the cap releases within ± 1 psi of the specified rating, it is operating properly:	**11.6**
	If the cap releases at more than ± 1 psi of the specified rating, it should be replaced:	**11.6**

Checking radiator pressure cap

Test and Procedure	Results and Indications	Proceed to
11.6—Test the thermostat: Start the engine cold, remove the radiator cap, and insert a thermometer into the radiator. Allow the engine to idle. After a short while, there will be a sudden, rapid increase in coolant temperature. The temperature at which this sharp rise stops is the thermostat opening temperature.	If the thermostat opens at or about the specified temperature:	**11.7**
	If the temperature doesn't increase: (If the temperature increases slowly and gradually, replace the thermostat.)	**11.7**
11.7—Check the water pump: Remove the thermostat elbow and the thermostat, disconnect the coil high tension lead (to prevent starting), and crank the engine momentarily.	If coolant flows, replace the thermostat and retest per 11.6:	**11.6**
	If coolant doesn't flow, reverse flush the cooling system to alleviate any blockage that might exist. If system is not blocked, and coolant will not flow, replace the water pump.	

Section 12—Lubrication
See Chapter 3 for service procedures

Test and Procedure	Results and Indications	Proceed to
12.1—Check the oil pressure gauge or warning light: If the gauge shows low pressure, or the light is on for no obvious reason, remove the oil pressure sender. Install an accurate oil pressure gauge and run the engine momentarily.	If oil pressure builds normally, run engine for a few moments to determine that it is functioning normally, and replace the sender.	—
	If the pressure remains low:	**12.2**
	If the pressure surges:	**12.3**
	If the oil pressure is zero:	**12.3**
12.2—Visually inspect the oil: If the oil is watery or very thin, milky, or foamy, replace the oil and oil filter.	If the oil is normal:	**12.3**
	If after replacing oil the pressure remains low:	**12.3**
	If after replacing oil the pressure becomes normal:	—

Test and Procedure	Results and Indications	Proceed to
12.3—Inspect the oil pressure relief valve and spring, to ensure that it is not sticking or stuck. Remove and thoroughly clean the valve, spring, and the valve body.	If the oil pressure improves: If no improvement is noted:	— **12.4**
12.4—Check to ensure that the oil pump is not cavitating (sucking air instead of oil): See that the crankcase is neither over nor underfull, and that the pickup in the sump is in the proper position and free from sludge.	Fill or drain the crankcase to the proper capacity, and clean the pickup screen in solvent if necessary. If no improvement is noted:	**12.5**
12.5—Inspect the oil pump drive and the oil pump:	If the pump drive or the oil pump appear to be defective, service as necessary and retest per 12.1: If the pump drive and pump appear to be operating normally, the engine should be disassembled to determine where blockage exists:	**12.1** **See Chapter 3**
12.6—Purge the engine of ethylene glycol coolant: Completely drain the crankcase and the oil filter. Obtain a commercial butyl cellosolve base solvent, designated for this purpose, and follow the instructions precisely. Following this, install a new oil filter and refill the crankcase with the proper weight oil. The next oil and filter change should follow shortly thereafter (1000 miles).		

TROUBLESHOOTING EMISSION CONTROL SYSTEMS

See Chapter 4 for procedures applicable to individual emission control systems used on specific combinations of engine/transmission/model.

TROUBLESHOOTING THE CARBURETOR
See Chapter 4 for service procedures

Carburetor problems cannot be effectively isolated unless all other engine systems (particularly ignition and emission) are functioning properly and the engine is properly tuned.

Condition	Possible Cause
Engine cranks, but does not start	1. Improper starting procedure 2. No fuel in tank 3. Clogged fuel line or filter 4. Defective fuel pump 5. Choke valve not closing properly 6. Engine flooded 7. Choke valve not unloading 8. Throttle linkage not making full travel 9. Stuck needle or float 10. Leaking float needle or seat 11. Improper float adjustment
Engine stalls	1. Improperly adjusted idle speed or mixture **Engine hot** 2. Improperly adjusted dashpot 3. Defective or improperly adjusted solenoid 4. Incorrect fuel level in fuel bowl 5. Fuel pump pressure too high 6. Leaking float needle seat 7. Secondary throttle valve stuck open 8. Air or fuel leaks 9. Idle air bleeds plugged or missing 10. Idle passages plugged **Engine Cold** 11. Incorrectly adjusted choke 12. Improperly adjusted fast idle speed 13. Air leaks 14. Plugged idle or idle air passages 15. Stuck choke valve or binding linkage 16. Stuck secondary throttle valves 17. Engine flooding—high fuel level 18. Leaking or misaligned float
Engine hesitates on acceleration	1. Clogged fuel filter 2. Leaking fuel pump diaphragm 3. Low fuel pump pressure 4. Secondary throttle valves stuck, bent or misadjusted 5. Sticking or binding air valve 6. Defective accelerator pump 7. Vacuum leaks 8. Clogged air filter 9. Incorrect choke adjustment (engine cold)
Engine feels sluggish or flat on acceleration	1. Improperly adjusted idle speed or mixture 2. Clogged fuel filter 3. Defective accelerator pump 4. Dirty, plugged or incorrect main metering jets 5. Bent or sticking main metering rods 6. Sticking throttle valves 7. Stuck heat riser 8. Binding or stuck air valve 9. Dirty, plugged or incorrect secondary jets 10. Bent or sticking secondary metering rods. 11. Throttle body or manifold heat passages plugged 12. Improperly adjusted choke or choke vacuum break.
Carburetor floods	1. Defective fuel pump. Pressure too high. 2. Stuck choke valve 3. Dirty, worn or damaged float or needle valve/seat 4. Incorrect float/fuel level 5. Leaking float bowl

Condition	Possible Cause
Engine idles roughly and stalls	1. Incorrect idle speed 2. Clogged fuel filter 3. Dirt in fuel system or carburetor 4. Loose carburetor screws or attaching bolts 5. Broken carburetor gaskets 6. Air leaks 7. Dirty carburetor 8. Worn idle mixture needles 9. Throttle valves stuck open 10. Incorrectly adjusted float or fuel level 11. Clogged air filter
Engine runs unevenly or surges	1. Defective fuel pump 2. Dirty or clogged fuel filter 3. Plugged, loose or incorrect main metering jets or rods 4. Air leaks 5. Bent or sticking main metering rods 6. Stuck power piston 7. Incorrect float adjustment 8. Incorrect idle speed or mixture 9. Dirty or plugged idle system passages 10. Hard, brittle or broken gaskets 11. Loose attaching or mounting screws 12. Stuck or misaligned secondary throttle valves
Poor fuel economy	1. Poor driving habits 2. Stuck choke valve 3. Binding choke linkage 4. Stuck heat riser 5. Incorrect idle mixture 6. Defective accelerator pump 7. Air leaks 8. Plugged, loose or incorrect main metering jets 9. Improperly adjusted float or fuel level 10. Bent, misaligned or fuel-clogged float 11. Leaking float needle seat 12. Fuel leak 13. Accelerator pump discharge ball not seating properly 14. Incorrect main jets
Engine lacks high speed performance or power	1. Incorrect throttle linkage adjustment 2. Stuck or binding power piston 3. Defective accelerator pump 4. Air leaks 5. Incorrect float setting or fuel level 6. Dirty, plugged, worn or incorrect main metering jets or rods 7. Binding or sticking air valve 8. Brittle or cracked gaskets 9. Bent, incorrect or improperly adjusted secondary metering rods 10. Clogged fuel filter 11. Clogged air filter 12. Defective fuel pump

TROUBLESHOOTING FUEL INJECTION PROBLEMS

Each fuel injection system has its own unique components and test procedures, for which it is impossible to generalize. Refer to Chapter 4 of this Repair & Tune-Up Guide for specific test and repair procedures, if the vehicle is equipped with fuel injection.

TROUBLESHOOTING ELECTRICAL PROBLEMS

See Chapter 5 for service procedures

For any electrical system to operate, it must make a complete circuit. This simply means that the power flow from the battery must make a complete circle. When an electrical component is operating, power flows from the battery to the component, passes through the component causing it to perform its function (lighting a light bulb), and then returns to the battery through the ground of the circuit. This ground is usually (but not always) the metal part of the car or truck on which the electrical component is mounted.

Perhaps the easiest way to visualize this is to think of connecting a light bulb with two wires attached to it to the battery. If one of the two wires attached to the light bulb were attached to the negative post of the battery and the other were attached to the positive post of the battery, you would have a complete circuit. Current from the battery would flow to the light bulb, causing it to light, and return to the negative post of the battery.

The normal automotive circuit differs from this simple example in two ways. First, instead of having a return wire from the bulb to the battery, the light bulb returns the current to the battery through the chassis of the vehicle. Since the negative battery cable is attached to the chassis and the chassis is made of electrically conductive metal, the chassis of the vehicle can serve as a ground wire to complete the circuit. Secondly, most automotive circuits contain switches to turn components on and off as required.

Every complete circuit from a power source must include a component which is using the power from the power source. If you were to disconnect the light bulb from the wires and touch the two wires together (don't do this) the power supply wire to the component would be grounded before the normal ground connection for the circuit.

Because grounding a wire from a power source makes a complete circuit—less the required component to use the power—this phenomenon is called a short circuit. Common causes are: broken insulation (exposing the metal wire to a metal part of the car or truck), or a shorted switch.

Some electrical components which require a large amount of current to operate also have a relay in their circuit. Since these circuits carry a large amount of current, the thickness of the wire in the circuit (gauge size) is also greater. If this large wire were connected from the component to the control switch on the instrument panel, and then back to the component, a voltage drop would occur in the circuit. To prevent this potential drop in voltage, an electromagnetic switch (relay) is used. The large wires in the circuit are connected from the battery to one side of the relay, and from the opposite side of the relay to the component. The relay is normally open, preventing current from passing through the circuit. An additional, smaller, wire is connected from the relay to the control switch for the circuit. When the control switch is turned on, it grounds the smaller wire from the relay and completes the circuit. This closes the relay and allows current to flow from the battery to the component. The horn, headlight, and starter circuits are three which use relays.

It is possible for larger surges of current to pass through the electrical system of your car or truck. If this surge of current were to reach an electrical component, it could burn it out. To prevent this, fuses, circuit breakers or fusible links are connected into the current supply wires of most of the major electrical systems. When an electrical current of excessive power passes through the component's fuse, the fuse blows out and breaks the circuit, saving the component from destruction.

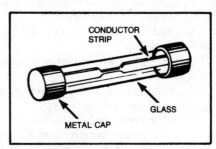

Typical automotive fuse

A circuit breaker is basically a self-repairing fuse. The circuit breaker opens the circuit the same way a fuse does. However, when either the short is removed from the circuit or the surge subsides, the circuit breaker resets itself and does not have to be replaced as a fuse does.

A fuse link is a wire that acts as a fuse. It is normally connected between the starter relay and the main wiring harness. This connection is usually under the hood. The fuse link (if installed) protects all the

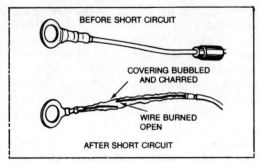

Most fusible links show a charred, melted insulation when they burn out

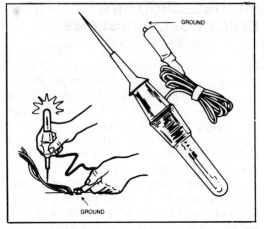

The test light will show the presence of current when touched to a hot wire and grounded at the other end

chassis electrical components, and is the probable cause of trouble when none of the electrical components function, unless the battery is disconnected or dead.

Electrical problems generally fall into one of three areas:

1. The component that is not functioning is not receiving current.

2. The component itself is not functioning.

3. The component is not properly grounded.

The electrical system can be checked with a test light and a jumper wire. A test light is a device that looks like a pointed screwdriver with a wire attached to it and has a light bulb in its handle. A jumper wire is a piece of insulated wire with an alligator clip attached to each end.

If a component is not working, you must follow a systematic plan to determine which of the three causes is the villain.

1. Turn on the switch that controls the inoperable component.

2. Disconnect the power supply wire from the component.

3. Attach the ground wire on the test light to a good metal ground.

4. Touch the probe end of the test light to the end of the power supply wire that was disconnected from the component. If the component is receiving current, the test light will go on.

NOTE: *Some components work only when the ignition switch is turned on.*

If the test light does not go on, then the problem is in the circuit between the battery and the component. This includes all the switches, fuses, and relays in the system. Follow the wire that runs back to the battery. The problem is an open circuit between the

battery and the component. If the fuse is blown and, when replaced, immediately blows again, there is a short circuit in the system which must be located and repaired. If there is a switch in the system, bypass it with a jumper wire. This is done by connecting one end of the jumper wire to the power supply wire into the switch and the other end of the jumper wire to the wire coming out of the switch. If the test light lights with the jumper wire installed, the switch or whatever was bypassed is defective.

NOTE: *Never substitute the jumper wire for the component, since it is required to use the power from the power source.*

5. If the bulb in the test light goes on, then the current is getting to the component that is not working. This eliminates the first of the three possible causes. Connect the power supply wire and connect a jumper wire from the component to a good metal ground. Do this with the switch which controls the component turned on, and also the ignition switch turned on if it is required for the component to work. If the component works with the jumper wire installed, then it has a bad ground. This is usually caused by the metal area on which the component mounts to the chassis being coated with some type of foreign matter.

6. If neither test located the source of the trouble, then the component itself is defective. Remember that for any electrical system to work, all connections must be clean and tight.

Troubleshooting Basic Turn Signal and Flasher Problems
See Chapter 5 for service procedures

Most problems in the turn signals or flasher system can be reduced to defective flashers or bulbs, which are easily replaced. Occasionally, the turn signal switch will prove defective.

F = Front   R = Rear   ● = Lights off   ○ = Lights on

Condition	Possible Cause
Turn signals light, but do not flash	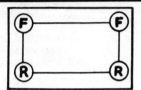 Defective flasher
No turn signals light on either side	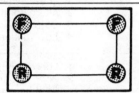 Blown fuse. Replace if defective. Defective flasher. Check by substitution. Open circuit, short circuit or poor ground.
Both turn signals on one side don't work	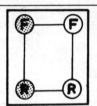 Bad bulbs. Bad ground in both (or either) housings.
One turn signal light on one side doesn't work	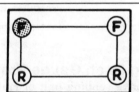 Defective bulb. Corrosion in socket. Clean contacts. Poor ground at socket.
Turn signal flashes too fast or too slowly	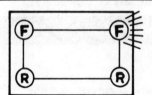 Check any bulb on the side flashing too fast. A heavy-duty bulb is probably installed in place of a regular bulb. Check the bulb flashing too slowly. A standard bulb was probably installed in place of a heavy-duty bulb. Loose connections or corrosion at the bulb socket.
Indicator lights don't work in either direction	 Check if the turn signals are working. Check the dash indicator lights. Check the flasher by substitution.
One indicator light doesn't light	 On systems with one dash indicator: See if the lights work on the same side. Often the filaments have been reversed in systems combining stoplights with taillights and turn signals. Check the flasher by substitution. On systems with two indicators: Check the bulbs on the same side. Check the indicator light bulb. Check the flasher by substitution.

Troubleshooting Lighting Problems
See Chapter 5 for service procedures

Condition	Possible Cause
One or more lights don't work, but others do	1. Defective bulb(s) 2. Blown fuse(s) 3. Dirty fuse clips or light sockets 4. Poor ground circuit
Lights burn out quickly	1. Incorrect voltage regulator setting or defective regulator 2. Poor battery/alternator connections
Lights go dim	1. Low/discharged battery 2. Alternator not charging 3. Corroded sockets or connections 4. Low voltage output
Lights flicker	1. Loose connection 2. Poor ground. (Run ground wire from light housing to frame) 3. Circuit breaker operating (short circuit)
Lights "flare"—Some flare is normal on acceleration—If excessive, see "Lights Burn Out Quickly"	High voltage setting
Lights glare—approaching drivers are blinded	1. Lights adjusted too high 2. Rear springs or shocks sagging 3. Rear tires soft

Troubleshooting Dash Gauge Problems

Most problems can be traced to a defective sending unit or faulty wiring. Occasionally, the gauge itself is at fault. See Chapter 5 for service procedures.

Condition	Possible Cause
COOLANT TEMPERATURE GAUGE	
Gauge reads erratically or not at all	1. Loose or dirty connections 2. Defective sending unit. 3. Defective gauge. To test a bi-metal gauge, remove the wire from the sending unit. Ground the wire for an instant. If the gauge registers, replace the sending unit. To test a magnetic gauge, disconnect the wire at the sending unit. With ignition ON gauge should register COLD. Ground the wire; gauge should register HOT.
AMMETER GAUGE—TURN HEADLIGHTS ON (DO NOT START ENGINE). NOTE REACTION	
Ammeter shows charge Ammeter shows discharge Ammeter does not move	1. Connections reversed on gauge 2. Ammeter is OK 3. Loose connections or faulty wiring 4. Defective gauge

Condition	Possible Cause

OIL PRESSURE GAUGE

Gauge does not register or is inaccurate	1. On mechanical gauge, Bourdon tube may be bent or kinked. 2. Low oil pressure. Remove sending unit. Idle the engine briefly. If no oil flows from sending unit hole, problem is in engine. 3. Defective gauge. Remove the wire from the sending unit and ground it for an instant with the ignition ON. A good gauge will go to the top of the scale. 4. Defective wiring. Check the wiring to the gauge. If it's OK and the gauge doesn't register when grounded, replace the gauge. 5. Defective sending unit.

ALL GAUGES

All gauges do not operate	1. Blown fuse 2. Defective instrument regulator
All gauges read low or erratically All gauges pegged	3. Defective or dirty instrument voltage regulator 4. Loss of ground between instrument voltage regulator and frame 5. Defective instrument regulator

WARNING LIGHTS

Light(s) do not come on when ignition is ON, but engine is not started	1. Defective bulb 2. Defective wire 3. Defective sending unit. Disconnect the wire from the sending unit and ground it. Replace the sending unit if the light comes on with the ignition ON.
Light comes on with engine running	4. Problem in individual system 5. Defective sending unit

Troubleshooting Clutch Problems

It is false economy to replace individual clutch components. The pressure plate, clutch plate and throwout bearing should be replaced as a set, and the flywheel face inspected, whenever the clutch is overhauled. See Chapter 6 for service procedures.

Condition	Possible Cause
Clutch chatter	1. Grease on driven plate (disc) facing 2. Binding clutch linkage or cable 3. Loose, damaged facings on driven plate (disc) 4. Engine mounts loose 5. Incorrect height adjustment of pressure plate release levers 6. Clutch housing or housing to transmission adapter misalignment 7. Loose driven plate hub
Clutch grabbing	1. Oil, grease on driven plate (disc) facing 2. Broken pressure plate 3. Warped or binding driven plate. Driven plate binding on clutch shaft
Clutch slips	1. Lack of lubrication in clutch linkage or cable (linkage or cable binds, causes incomplete engagement) 2. Incorrect pedal, or linkage adjustment 3. Broken pressure plate springs 4. Weak pressure plate springs 5. Grease on driven plate facings (disc)

Troubleshooting Clutch Problems (cont.)

Condition	Possible Cause
Incomplete clutch release	1. Incorrect pedal or linkage adjustment or linkage or cable binding 2. Incorrect height adjustment on pressure plate release levers 3. Loose, broken facings on driven plate (disc) 4. Bent, dished, warped driven plate caused by overheating
Grinding, whirring grating noise when pedal is depressed	1. Worn or defective throwout bearing 2. Starter drive teeth contacting flywheel ring gear teeth. Look for milled or polished teeth on ring gear.
Squeal, howl, trumpeting noise when pedal is being released (occurs during first inch to inch and one-half of pedal travel)	Pilot bushing worn or lack of lubricant. If bushing appears OK, polish bushing with emery cloth, soak lube wick in oil, lube bushing with oil, apply film of chassis grease to clutch shaft pilot hub, reassemble. NOTE: Bushing wear may be due to misalignment of clutch housing or housing to transmission adapter
Vibration or clutch pedal pulsation with clutch disengaged (pedal fully depressed)	1. Worn or defective engine transmission mounts 2. Flywheel run out. (Flywheel run out at face not to exceed 0.005") 3. Damaged or defective clutch components

Troubleshooting Manual Transmission Problems
See Chapter 6 for service procedures

Condition	Possible Cause
Transmission jumps out of gear	1. Misalignment of transmission case or clutch housing. 2. Worn pilot bearing in crankshaft. 3. Bent transmission shaft. 4. Worn high speed sliding gear. 5. Worn teeth or end-play in clutch shaft. 6. Insufficient spring tension on shifter rail plunger. 7. Bent or loose shifter fork. 8. Gears not engaging completely. 9. Loose or worn bearings on clutch shaft or mainshaft. 10. Worn gear teeth. 11. Worn or damaged detent balls.
Transmission sticks in gear	1. Clutch not releasing fully. 2. Burred or battered teeth on clutch shaft, or sliding sleeve. 3. Burred or battered transmission mainshaft. 4. Frozen synchronizing clutch. 5. Stuck shifter rail plunger. 6. Gearshift lever twisting and binding shifter rail. 7. Battered teeth on high speed sliding gear or on sleeve. 8. Improper lubrication, or lack of lubrication. 9. Corroded transmission parts. 10. Defective mainshaft pilot bearing. 11. Locked gear bearings will give same effect as stuck in gear.
Transmission gears will not synchronize	1. Binding pilot bearing on mainshaft, will synchronize in high gear only. 2. Clutch not releasing fully. 3. Detent spring weak or broken. 4. Weak or broken springs under balls in sliding gear sleeve. 5. Binding bearing on clutch shaft, or binding countershaft. 6. Binding pilot bearing in crankshaft. 7. Badly worn gear teeth. 8. Improper lubrication. 9. Constant mesh gear not turning freely on transmission mainshaft. Will synchronize in that gear only.

Condition	Possible Cause
Gears spinning when shifting into gear from neutral	1. Clutch not releasing fully. 2. In some cases an extremely light lubricant in transmission will cause gears to continue to spin for a short time after clutch is released. 3. Binding pilot bearing in crankshaft.
Transmission noisy in all gears	1. Insufficient lubricant, or improper lubricant. 2. Worn countergear bearings. 3. Worn or damaged main drive gear or countergear. 4. Damaged main drive gear or mainshaft bearings. 5. Worn or damaged countergear anti-lash plate.
Transmission noisy in neutral only	1. Damaged main drive gear bearing. 2. Damaged or loose mainshaft pilot bearing. 3. Worn or damaged countergear anti-lash plate. 4. Worn countergear bearings.
Transmission noisy in one gear only	1. Damaged or worn constant mesh gears. 2. Worn or damaged countergear bearings. 3. Damaged or worn synchronizer.
Transmission noisy in reverse only	1. Worn or damaged reverse idler gear or idler bushing. 2. Worn or damaged mainshaft reverse gear. 3. Worn or damaged reverse countergear. 4. Damaged shift mechanism.

TROUBLESHOOTING AUTOMATIC TRANSMISSION PROBLEMS

Keeping alert to changes in the operating characteristics of the transmission (changing shift points, noises, etc.) can prevent small problems from becoming large ones. If the problem cannot be traced to loose bolts, fluid level, misadjusted linkage, clogged filters or similar problems, you should probably seek professional service.

Transmission Fluid Indications

The appearance and odor of the transmission fluid can give valuable clues to the overall condition of the transmission. Always note the appearance of the fluid when you check the fluid level or change the fluid. Rub a small amount of fluid between your fingers to feel for grit and smell the fluid on the dipstick.

If the fluid appears:	It indicates:
Clear and red colored	Normal operation
Discolored (extremely dark red or brownish) or smells burned	Band or clutch pack failure, usually caused by an overheated transmission. Hauling very heavy loads with insufficient power or failure to change the fluid often result in overheating. Do not confuse this appearance with newer fluids that have a darker red color and a strong odor (though not a burned odor).
Foamy or aerated (light in color and full of bubbles)	1. The level is too high (gear train is churning oil) 2. An internal air leak (air is mixing with the fluid). Have the transmission checked professionally.
Solid residue in the fluid	Defective bands, clutch pack or bearings. Bits of band material or metal abrasives are clinging to the dipstick. Have the transmission checked professionally.
Varnish coating on the dipstick	The transmission fluid is overheating

TROUBLESHOOTING DRIVE AXLE PROBLEMS

First, determine when the noise is most noticeable.

Drive Noise: Produced under vehicle acceleration.

Coast Noise: Produced while coasting with a closed throttle.

Float Noise: Occurs while maintaining constant speed (just enough to keep speed constant) on a level road.

External Noise Elimination

It is advisable to make a thorough road test to determine whether the noise originates in the rear axle or whether it originates from the tires, engine, transmission, wheel bearings or road surface. Noise originating from other places cannot be corrected by servicing the rear axle.

ROAD NOISE

Brick or rough surfaced concrete roads produce noises that seem to come from the rear axle. Road noise is usually identical in Drive or Coast and driving on a different type of road will tell whether the road is the problem.

TIRE NOISE

Tire noise can be mistaken as rear axle noise, even though the tires on the front are at fault. Snow tread and mud tread tires or tires worn unevenly will frequently cause vibrations which seem to originate elsewhere; *temporarily, and for test purposes only,* inflate the tires to 40–50 lbs. This will significantly alter the noise produced by the tires, but will not alter noise from the rear axle. Noises from the rear axle will normally cease at speeds below 30 mph on coast, while tire noise will continue at lower tone as speed is decreased. The rear axle noise will usually change from drive conditions to coast conditions, while tire noise will not. Do not forget to lower the tire pressure to normal after the test is complete.

ENGINE/TRANSMISSION NOISE

Determine at what speed the noise is most pronounced, then stop in a quiet place. With the transmission in Neutral, run the engine through speeds corresponding to road speeds where the noise was noticed. Noises produced with the vehicle standing still are coming from the engine or transmission.

FRONT WHEEL BEARINGS

Front wheel bearing noises, sometimes confused with rear axle noises, will not change when comparing drive and coast conditions. While holding the speed steady, lightly apply the footbrake. This will often cause wheel bearing noise to lessen, as some of the weight is taken off the bearing. Front wheel bearings are easily checked by jacking up the wheels and spinning the wheels. Shaking the wheels will also determine if the wheel bearings are excessively loose.

REAR AXLE NOISES

Eliminating other possible sources can narrow the cause to the rear axle, which normally produces noise from worn gears or bearings. Gear noises tend to peak in a narrow speed range, while bearing noises will usually vary in pitch with engine speeds.

Noise Diagnosis

The Noise Is:	Most Probably Produced By:
1. Identical under Drive or Coast	Road surface, tires or front wheel bearings
2. Different depending on road surface	Road surface or tires
3. Lower as speed is lowered	Tires
4. Similar when standing or moving	Engine or transmission
5. A vibration	Unbalanced tires, rear wheel bearing, unbalanced driveshaft or worn U-joint
6. A knock or click about every two tire revolutions	Rear wheel bearing
7. Most pronounced on turns	Damaged differential gears
8. A steady low-pitched whirring or scraping, starting at low speeds	Damaged or worn pinion bearing
9. A chattering vibration on turns	Wrong differential lubricant or worn clutch plates (limited slip rear axle)
10. Noticed only in Drive, Coast or Float conditions	Worn ring gear and/or pinion gear

Troubleshooting Steering & Suspension Problems

Condition	Possible Cause
Hard steering (wheel is hard to turn)	1. Improper tire pressure 2. Loose or glazed pump drive belt 3. Low or incorrect fluid 4. Loose, bent or poorly lubricated front end parts 5. Improper front end alignment (excessive caster) 6. Bind in steering column or linkage 7. Kinked hydraulic hose 8. Air in hydraulic system 9. Low pump output or leaks in system 10. Obstruction in lines 11. Pump valves sticking or out of adjustment 12. Incorrect wheel alignment
Loose steering (too much play in steering wheel)	1. Loose wheel bearings 2. Faulty shocks 3. Worn linkage or suspension components 4. Loose steering gear mounting or linkage points 5. Steering mechanism worn or improperly adjusted 6. Valve spool improperly adjusted 7. Worn ball joints, tie-rod ends, etc.
Veers or wanders (pulls to one side with hands off steering wheel)	1. Improper tire pressure 2. Improper front end alignment 3. Dragging or improperly adjusted brakes 4. Bent frame 5. Improper rear end alignment 6. Faulty shocks or springs 7. Loose or bent front end components 8. Play in Pitman arm 9. Steering gear mountings loose 10. Loose wheel bearings 11. Binding Pitman arm 12. Spool valve sticking or improperly adjusted 13. Worn ball joints
Wheel oscillation or vibration transmitted through steering wheel	1. Low or uneven tire pressure 2. Loose wheel bearings 3. Improper front end alignment 4. Bent spindle 5. Worn, bent or broken front end components 6. Tires out of round or out of balance 7. Excessive lateral runout in disc brake rotor 8. Loose or bent shock absorber or strut
Noises (see also "Troubleshooting Drive Axle Problems")	1. Loose belts 2. Low fluid, air in system 3. Foreign matter in system 4. Improper lubrication 5. Interference or chafing in linkage 6. Steering gear mountings loose 7. Incorrect adjustment or wear in gear box 8. Faulty valves or wear in pump 9. Kinked hydraulic lines 10. Worn wheel bearings
Poor return of steering	1. Over-inflated tires 2. Improperly aligned front end (excessive caster) 3. Binding in steering column 4. No lubrication in front end 5. Steering gear adjusted too tight
Uneven tire wear (see "How To Read Tire Wear")	1. Incorrect tire pressure 2. Improperly aligned front end 3. Tires out-of-balance 4. Bent or worn suspension parts

HOW TO READ TIRE WEAR

The way your tires wear is a good indicator of other parts of the suspension. Abnormal wear patterns are often caused by the need for simple tire maintenance, or for front end alignment.

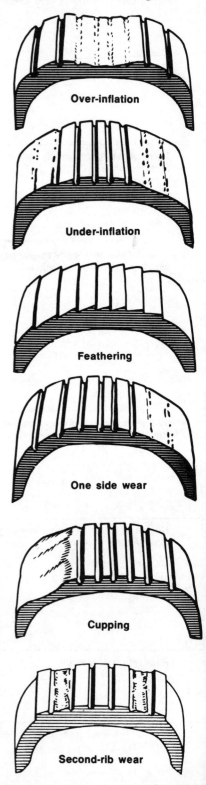

Excessive wear at the center of the tread indicates that the air pressure in the tire is consistently too high. The tire is riding on the center of the tread and wearing it prematurely. Occasionally, this wear pattern can result from outrageously wide tires on narrow rims. The cure for this is to replace either the tires or the wheels.

Over-inflation

This type of wear usually results from consistent under-inflation. When a tire is under-inflated, there is too much contact with the road by the outer treads, which wear prematurely. When this type of wear occurs, and the tire pressure is known to be consistently correct, a bent or worn steering component or the need for wheel alignment could be indicated.

Under-inflation

Feathering is a condition when the edge of each tread rib develops a slightly rounded edge on one side and a sharp edge on the other. By running your hand over the tire, you can usually feel the sharper edges before you'll be able to see them. The most common causes of feathering are incorrect toe-in setting or deteriorated bushings in the front suspension.

Feathering

When an inner or outer rib wears faster than the rest of the tire, the need for wheel alignment is indicated. There is excessive camber in the front suspension, causing the wheel to lean too much putting excessive load on one side of the tire. Misalignment could also be due to sagging springs, worn ball joints, or worn control arm bushings. Be sure the vehicle is loaded the way it's normally driven when you have the wheels aligned.

One side wear

Cups or scalloped dips appearing around the edge of the tread almost always indicate worn (sometimes bent) suspension parts. Adjustment of wheel alignment alone will seldom cure the problem. Any worn component that connects the wheel to the suspension can cause this type of wear. Occasionally, wheels that are out of balance will wear like this, but wheel imbalance usually shows up as bald spots between the outside edges and center of the tread.

Cupping

Second-rib wear is usually found only in radial tires, and appears where the steel belts end in relation to the tread. It can be kept to a minimum by paying careful attention to tire pressure and frequently rotating the tires. This is often considered normal wear but excessive amounts indicate that the tires are too wide for the wheels.

Second-rib wear

Troubleshooting Disc Brake Problems

Condition	Possible Cause
Noise—groan—brake noise emanating when slowly releasing brakes (creep-groan)	Not detrimental to function of disc brakes—no corrective action required. (This noise may be eliminated by slightly increasing or decreasing brake pedal efforts.)
Rattle—brake noise or rattle emanating at low speeds on rough roads, (front wheels only).	1. Shoe anti-rattle spring missing or not properly positioned. 2. Excessive clearance between shoe and caliper. 3. Soft or broken caliper seals. 4. Deformed or misaligned disc. 5. Loose caliper.
Scraping	1. Mounting bolts too long. 2. Loose wheel bearings. 3. Bent, loose, or misaligned splash shield.
Front brakes heat up during driving and fail to release	1. Operator riding brake pedal. 2. Stop light switch improperly adjusted. 3. Sticking pedal linkage. 4. Frozen or seized piston. 5. Residual pressure valve in master cylinder. 6. Power brake malfunction. 7. Proportioning valve malfunction.
Leaky brake caliper	1. Damaged or worn caliper piston seal. 2. Scores or corrosion on surface of cylinder bore.
Grabbing or uneven brake action—Brakes pull to one side	1. Causes listed under "Brakes Pull". 2. Power brake malfunction. 3. Low fluid level in master cylinder. 4. Air in hydraulic system. 5. Brake fluid, oil or grease on linings. 6. Unmatched linings. 7. Distorted brake pads. 8. Frozen or seized pistons. 9. Incorrect tire pressure. 10. Front end out of alignment. 11. Broken rear spring. 12. Brake caliper pistons sticking. 13. Restricted hose or line. 14. Caliper not in proper alignment to braking disc. 15. Stuck or malfunctioning metering valve. 16. Soft or broken caliper seals. 17. Loose caliper.
Brake pedal can be depressed without braking effect	1. Air in hydraulic system or improper bleeding procedure. 2. Leak past primary cup in master cylinder. 3. Leak in system. 4. Rear brakes out of adjustment. 5. Bleeder screw open.
Excessive pedal travel	1. Air, leak, or insufficient fluid in system or caliper. 2. Warped or excessively tapered shoe and lining assembly. 3. Excessive disc runout. 4. Rear brake adjustment required. 5. Loose wheel bearing adjustment. 6. Damaged caliper piston seal. 7. Improper brake fluid (boil). 8. Power brake malfunction. 9. Weak or soft hoses.

Troubleshooting Disc Brake Problems (cont.)

Condition	Possible Cause
Brake roughness or chatter (pedal pumping)	1. Excessive thickness variation of braking disc. 2. Excessive lateral runout of braking disc. 3. Rear brake drums out-of-round. 4. Excessive front bearing clearance.
Excessive pedal effort	1. Brake fluid, oil or grease on linings. 2. Incorrect lining. 3. Frozen or seized pistons. 4. Power brake malfunction. 5. Kinked or collapsed hose or line. 6. Stuck metering valve. 7. Scored caliper or master cylinder bore. 8. Seized caliper pistons.
Brake pedal fades (pedal travel increases with foot on brake)	1. Rough master cylinder or caliper bore. 2. Loose or broken hydraulic lines/connections. 3. Air in hydraulic system. 4. Fluid level low. 5. Weak or soft hoses. 6. Inferior quality brake shoes or fluid. 7. Worn master cylinder piston cups or seals.

Troubleshooting Drum Brakes

Condition	Possible Cause
Pedal goes to floor	1. Fluid low in reservoir. 2. Air in hydraulic system. 3. Improperly adjusted brake. 4. Leaking wheel cylinders. 5. Loose or broken brake lines. 6. Leaking or worn master cylinder. 7. Excessively worn brake lining.
Spongy brake pedal	1. Air in hydraulic system. 2. Improper brake fluid (low boiling point). 3. Excessively worn or cracked brake drums. 4. Broken pedal pivot bushing.
Brakes pulling	1. Contaminated lining. 2. Front end out of alignment. 3. Incorrect brake adjustment. 4. Unmatched brake lining. 5. Brake drums out of round. 6. Brake shoes distorted. 7. Restricted brake hose or line. 8. Broken rear spring. 9. Worn brake linings. 10. Uneven lining wear. 11. Glazed brake lining. 12. Excessive brake lining dust. 13. Heat spotted brake drums. 14. Weak brake return springs. 15. Faulty automatic adjusters. 16. Low or incorrect tire pressure.

Condition	Possible Cause
Squealing brakes	1. Glazed brake lining. 2. Saturated brake lining. 3. Weak or broken brake shoe retaining spring. 4. Broken or weak brake shoe return spring. 5. Incorrect brake lining. 6. Distorted brake shoes. 7. Bent support plate. 8. Dust in brakes or scored brake drums. 9. Linings worn below limit. 10. Uneven brake lining wear. 11. Heat spotted brake drums.
Chirping brakes	1. Out of round drum or eccentric axle flange pilot.
Dragging brakes	1. Incorrect wheel or parking brake adjustment. 2. Parking brakes engaged or improperly adjusted. 3. Weak or broken brake shoe return spring. 4. Brake pedal binding. 5. Master cylinder cup sticking. 6. Obstructed master cylinder relief port. 7. Saturated brake lining. 8. Bent or out of round brake drum. 9. Contaminated or improper brake fluid. 10. Sticking wheel cylinder pistons. 11. Driver riding brake pedal. 12. Defective proportioning valve. 13. Insufficient brake shoe lubricant.
Hard pedal	1. Brake booster inoperative. 2. Incorrect brake lining. 3. Restricted brake line or hose. 4. Frozen brake pedal linkage. 5. Stuck wheel cylinder. 6. Binding pedal linkage. 7. Faulty proportioning valve.
Wheel locks	1. Contaminated brake lining. 2. Loose or torn brake lining. 3. Wheel cylinder cups sticking. 4. Incorrect wheel bearing adjustment. 5. Faulty proportioning valve.
Brakes fade (high speed)	1. Incorrect lining. 2. Overheated brake drums. 3. Incorrect brake fluid (low boiling temperature). 4. Saturated brake lining. 5. Leak in hydraulic system. 6. Faulty automatic adjusters.
Pedal pulsates	1. Bent or out of round brake drum.
Brake chatter and shoe knock	1. Out of round brake drum. 2. Loose support plate. 3. Bent support plate. 4. Distorted brake shoes. 5. Machine grooves in contact face of brake drum (Shoe Knock). 6. Contaminated brake lining. 7. Missing or loose components. 8. Incorrect lining material. 9. Out-of-round brake drums. 10. Heat spotted or scored brake drums. 11. Out-of-balance wheels.

Troubleshooting Drum Brakes (cont.)

Condition	Possible Cause
Brakes do not self adjust	1. Adjuster screw frozen in thread. 2. Adjuster screw corroded at thrust washer. 3. Adjuster lever does not engage star wheel. 4. Adjuster installed on wrong wheel.
Brake light glows	1. Leak in the hydraulic system. 2. Air in the system. 3. Improperly adjusted master cylinder pushrod. 4. Uneven lining wear. 5. Failure to center combination valve or proportioning valve.

Mechanic's Data

General Conversion Table

Multiply By	To Convert	To	
LENGTH			
2.54	Inches	Centimeters	.3937
25.4	Inches	Millimeters	.03937
30.48	Feet	Centimeters	.0328
.304	Feet	Meters	3.28
.914	Yards	Meters	1.094
1.609	Miles	Kilometers	.621
VOLUME			
.473	Pints	Liters	2.11
.946	Quarts	Liters	1.06
3.785	Gallons	Liters	.264
.016	Cubic inches	Liters	61.02
16.39	Cubic inches	Cubic cms.	.061
28.3	Cubic feet	Liters	.0353
MASS (Weight)			
28.35	Ounces	Grams	.035
.4536	Pounds	Kilograms	2.20
—	To obtain	From	Multiply by

Multiply By	To Convert	To	
AREA			
.645	Square inches	Square cms.	.155
.836	Square yds.	Square meters	1.196
FORCE			
4.448	Pounds	Newtons	.225
.138	Ft./lbs.	Kilogram/meters	7.23
1.36	Ft./lbs.	Newton-meters	.737
.112	In./lbs.	Newton-meters	8.844
PRESSURE			
.068	Psi	Atmospheres	14.7
6.89	Psi	Kilopascals	.145
OTHER			
1.104	Horsepower (DIN)	Horsepower (SAE)	.9861
.746	Horsepower (SAE)	Kilowatts (KW)	1.34
1.60	Mph	Km/h	.625
.425	Mpg	Km/1	2.35
—	To obtain	From	Multiply by

Tap Drill Sizes

National Coarse or U.S.S.

Screw & Tap Size	Threads Per Inch	Use Drill Number
No. 5	40	39
No. 6	32	36
No. 8	32	29
No. 10	24	25
No. 12	24	17
1/4	20	8
5/16	18	F
3/8	16	5/16
7/16	14	U
1/2	13	27/64
9/16	12	31/64
5/8	11	17/32
3/4	10	21/32
7/8	9	49/64

National Coarse or U.S.S.

Screw & Tap Size	Threads Per Inch	Use Drill Number
1	8	7/8
1 1/8	7	63/64
1 1/4	7	1 7/64
1 1/2	6	1 11/32

National Fine or S.A.E.

Screw & Tap Size	Threads Per Inch	Use Drill Number
No. 5	44	37
No. 6	40	33
No. 8	36	29
No. 10	32	21

National Fine or S.A.E.

Screw & Tap Size	Threads Per Inch	Use Drill Number
No. 12	28	15
1/4	28	3
6/16	24	1
3/8	24	Q
7/16	20	W
1/2	20	29/64
9/16	18	33/64
5/8	18	37/64
3/4	16	11/16
7/8	14	13/16
1 1/8	12	1 3/64
1 1/4	12	1 11/64
1 1/2	12	1 27/64

Drill Sizes In Decimal Equivalents

Inch	Decimal	Wire	mm
1/64	.0156		.39
	.0157		.4
	.0160	78	
	.0165		.42
	.0173		.44
	.0177		.45
	.0180	77	
	.0181		.46
	.0189		.48
	.0197		.5
	.0200	76	
	.0210	75	
	.0217		.55
	.0225	74	
	.0236		.6
	.0240	73	
	.0250	72	
	.0256		.65
	.0260	71	
	.0276		.7
	.0280	70	
	.0292	69	
	.0295		.75
	.0310	68.	
1/32	.0312		.79
	.0315		.8
	.0320	67	
	.0330	66	
	.0335		.85
	.0350	65	
	.0354		.9
	.0360	64	
	.0370	63	
	.0374		.95
	.0380	62	
	.0390	61	
	.0394		1.0
	.0400	60	
	.0410	59	
	.0413		1.05
	.0420	58	
	.0430	57	
	.0433		1.1
	.0453		1.15
	.0465	56	
3/64	.0469		1.19
	.0472		1.2
	.0492		1.25
	.0512		1.3
	.0520	55	
	.0531		1.35
	.0550	54	
	.0551		1.4
	.0571		1.45
	.0591		1.5
	.0595	53	
	.0610		1.55
1/16	.0625		1.59
	.0630		1.6
	.0635	52	
	.0650		1.65
	.0669		1.7
	.0670	51	
	.0689		1.75
	.0700	50	
	.0709		1.8
	.0728		1.85

Inch	Decimal	Wire	mm
	.0730	49	
	.0748		1.9
	.0760	48	
	.0768		1.95
5/64	.0781		1.98
	.0785	47	
	.0787		2.0
	.0807		2.05
	.0810	46	
	.0820	45	
	.0827		2.1
	.0846		2.15
	.0860	44	
	.0866		2.2
	.0886		2.25
	.0890	43	
	.0906		2.3
	.0925		2.35
	.0935	42	
3/32	.0938		2.38
	.0945		2.4
	.0960	41	
	.0965		2.45
	.0980	40	
	.0981		2.5
	.0995	39	
	.1015	38	
	.1024		2.6
	.1040	37	
	.1063		2.7
	.1065	36	
	.1083		2.75
7/64	.1094		2.77
	.1100	35	
	.1102		2.8
	.1110	34	
	.1130	33	
	.1142		2.9
	.1160	32	
	.1181		3.0
	.1200	31	
	.1220		3.1
1/8	.1250		3.17
	.1260		3.2
	.1280		3.25
	.1285	30	
	.1299		3.3
	.1339		3.4
	.1360	29	
	.1378		3.5
	.1405	28	
9/64	.1406		3.57
	.1417		3.6
	.1440	27	
	.1457		3.7
	.1470	26	
	.1476		3.75
	.1495	25	
	.1496		3.8
	.1520	24	
	.1535		3.9
	.1540	23	
5/32	.1562		3.96
	.1570	22	
	.1575		4.0
	.1590	21	
	.1610	20	

Inch	Decimal	Wire & Letter	mm
	.1614		4.1
	.1654		4.2
	.1660	19	
	.1673		4.25
	.1693		4.3
	.1695	18	
11/64	.1719		4.36
	.1730	17	
	.1732		4.4
	.1770	16	
	.1772		4.5
	.1800	15	
	.1811		4.6
	.1820	14	
	.1850	13	
	.1850		4.7
	.1870		4.75
3/16	.1875		4.76
	.1890		4.8
	.1890	12	
	.1910	11	
	.1929		4.9
	.1935	10	
	.1960	9	
	.1969		5.0
	.1990	8	
	.2008		5.1
	.2010	7	
13/64	.2031		5.16
	.2040	6	
	.2047		5.2
	.2055	5	
	.2067		5.25
	.2087		5.3
	.2090	4	
	.2126		5.4
	.2130	3	
	.2165		5.5
7/32	.2188		5.55
	.2205		5.6
	.2210	2	
	.2244		5.7
	.2264		5.75
	.2280	1	
	.2283		5.8
	.2323		5.9
	.2340	A	
15/64	.2344		5.95
	.2362		6.0
	.2380	B	
	.2402		6.1
	.2420	C	
	.2441		6.2
	.2460	D	
	.2461		6.25
	.2480		6.3
1/4	.2500	E	6.35
	.2520		6.
	.2559		6.5
	.2570	F	
	.2598		6.6
	.2610	G	
	.2638		6.7
17/64	.2656		6.74
	.2657		6.75
	.2660	H	
	.2677		6.8

Inch	Decimal	Letter	mm
	.2717		6.9
	.2720	I	
	.2756		7.0
	.2770	J	
	.2795		7.1
	.2810	K	
9/32	.2812		7.14
	.2835		7.2
	.2854		7.25
	.2874		7.3
	.2900	L	
	.2913		7.4
	.2950	M	
	.2953		7.5
19/64	.2969		7.54
	.2992		7.6
	.3020	N	
	.3031		7.7
	.3051		7.75
	.3071		7.8
	.3110		7.9
5/16	.3125		7.93
	.3150		8.0
	.3160	O	
	.3189		8.1
	.3228		8.2
	.3230	P	
	.3248		8.25
	.3268		8.3
21/64	.3281		8.33
	.3307		8.4
	.3320	Q	
	.3346		8.5
	.3386		8.6
	.3390	R	
	.3425		8.7
11/32	.3438		8.73
	.3445		8.75
	.3465		8.8
	.3480	S	
	.3504		8.9
	.3543		9.0
	.3580	T	
	.3583		9.1
23/64	.3594		9.12
	.3622		9.2
	.3642		9.25
	.3661		9.3
	.3680	U	
	.3701		9.4
	.3740		9.5
3/8	.3750		9.52
	.3770	V	
	.3780		9.6
	.3819		9.7
	.3839		9.75
	.3858		9.8
	.3860	W	
	.3898		9.9
25/64	.3906		9.92
	.3937		10.0
	.3970	X	
	.4040	Y	
13/32	.4062		10.31
	.4130	Z	
	.4134		10.5
27/64	.4219		10.71

Inch	Decimal	mm
	.4331	11.0
7/16	.4375	11.11
	.4528	11.5
29/64	.4531	11.51
15/32	.4688	11.90
	.4724	12.0
31/64	.4844	12.30
	.4921	12.5
1/2	.5000	12.70
	.5118	13.0
33/64	.5156	13.09
17/32	.5312	13.49
	.5315	13.5
35/64	.5469	13.89
	.5512	14.0
9/16	.5625	14.28
	.5709	14.5
37/64	.5781	14.68
	.5906	15.0
19/32	.5938	15.08
39/64	.6094	15.47
	.6102	15.5
5/8	.6250	15.87
	.6299	16.0
41/64	.6406	16.27
	.6496	16.5
21/32	.6562	16.66
	.6693	17.0
43/64	.6719	17.06
11/16	.6875	17.46
	.6890	17.5
45/64	.7031	17.85
	.7087	18.0
23/32	.7188	18.25
	.7283	18.5
47/64	.7344	18.65
	.7480	19.0
3/4	.7500	19.05
49/64	.7656	19.44
	.7677	19.5
25/32	.7812	19.84
	.7874	20.0
51/64	.7969	20.24
	.8071	20.5
13/16	.8125	20.63
	.8268	21.0
53/64	.8281	21.03
27/32	.8438	21.43
	.8465	21.5
55/64	.8594	21.82
	.8661	22.0
7/8	.8750	22.22
	.8858	22.5
57/64	.8906	22.62
	.9055	23.0
29/32	.9062	23.01
59/64	.9219	23.41
	.9252	23.5
15/16	.9375	23.81
	.9449	24.0
61/64	.9531	24.2
	.9646	24.5
31/32	.9688	24.6
	.9843	25.0
63/64	.9844	25.0
1	1.0000	25.4

Index

A

Air cleaner, 4, 91
Air conditioning inspection, 8
Air pump, 87
Alternator, 41
Automatic transmission
   Adjustments, 132
   Filter change, 132
   Removal and installation, 129, 131
Axle
   Axle shaft, bearings and seals, 137

B

Ball joints, 155
Battery
   Fluid level, 9
   Jump starting, 23
   Removal and installation, 46
Brakes
   Adjustment, 164
   Bleeding, 166
   Disc brakes
      Caliper, 170
      Pads, 169
      Rotor (Disc), 172
   Drum brakes
      Drum, 172
      Shoes, 168, 173
      Wheel cylinder, 169, 176
   Fluid level, 9
   Master cylinder, 165
   Parking brake, 176
   Power booster, 166
   Proportioning valve, 166
Bulbs, 118

C

Calipers, 170
Camber, 155
Camshaft and bearings, 76
Capacities, 15
Carburetor
   Adjustments, 36, 98-107
   Overhaul, 107
   Replacement, 99
   Specifications, 108
Caster, 155
Choke, 92
Clutch, 121
Combination manifold, 70
Condenser, 26
Connecting rods and bearings, 80
Control arm, 154
Crankcase ventilation valve, 5
Cylinder head, 59

D

Diesel fuel system, 38, 109
Differential, 141
Disc brakes, 160
Distributor, 26
Drive axle
   Front, 137
   Rear, 144
Driveshaft, 135
Drum bakes, 167
Dwell angle, 29

E

Electrical
   Chassis, 112
   Engine, 40
Emission controls, 82
Engine
   Camshaft, 76
   Combination manifold, 70
   Cylinder head, 59
   Exhaust manifold, 68
   Fluids and lubricants, 9
   Front (timing) cover, 73
   Front seal, 73
   Identification, 5
   Intake manifold, 68
   Oil pan, 71
   Oil pump, 77, 79
   Pistons, 80
   Rear main seal, 77
   Removal and installation, 52
   Rings, 80
   Rocker arms and/or shafts, 68
   Specifications, 55-57
   Thermostat, 58
   Timing belt, 75
   Timing chain, 71
   Timing gears, 76
   Valves, 59
   Water pump, 58
Evaporative canister, 5, 82
Exhaust Manifold, 68

F

Firing orders, 41
Flashers, 120
Fluids and lubricants
   Automatic transmission, 9
   Battery, 11
   Coolant, 10
   Drive axle, 10
   Engine oil, 9
   Manual transmission, 9
   Steering gear, 11
   Transfer case, 9
Front axle, 137

Front brakes, 169
Front suspension
  Ball joints, 155
  Lower control arm, 154
  Shock absorbers, 152
  Springs, 147
  Torsion bars, 149
  Upper control arm, 154
  Wheel alignment, 156
Fuel injection (Gasoline), 38
Fuel filter, 12
Fuel pump, 96
Fuel system
  Diesel, 109
  Gasoline, 96
Fuel tank, 110
Fuses and circuit breakers, 118
Fusible links, 118

H

Headlights, 118
Heater
  Blower, 115
  Core, 112

I

Identification
  Engine, 4
  Vehicle, 3
Idle speed and mixture adjustment, 36, 105
Ignition lock cylinder, 158
Ignition switch, 158
Ignition timing, 30
Instrument cluster, 117
Intake manifold, 68

J

Jacking points, 24
Jump starting, 23

L

Lower control arm, 154
Lubrication, 13ff

M

Maintenance intervals, 14
Manifolds
  Combination, 70
  Intake, 68
  Exhaust, 68
Manual transmission, 121
Model identification, 3

N

Neutral safety switch, 133

O

Oil and fuel recommendations, 13
Oil and filter change (engine), 15
Oil level check
  Differential, 18
  Engine, 9
  Transfer case, 17
  Transmission, 17
Oil pan, 71
Oil pump, 77

P

Parking brake, 176
Pistons, 80
PCV valve, 5
Points, 26
Power steering pump, 159
Pushing, 22

R

Radiator, 51
Radio, 115
Rear axle, 144
Rear brakes, 164, 172
Rear suspension
  Shock absorbers, 158
  Springs, 156
Regulator, 43
Rings, 80
Rocker arms or shaft, 68
Routine maintenance, 4

S

Safety notice, ii
Serial number location, 3
Shock absorbers
  Front, 152
  Rear, 158
Spark plugs, 25
Special tools, 1
Specifications
  Brakes, 175
  Capacities, 15
  Carburetor, 108
  Crankshaft and connecting rod, 56
  General engine, 55
  Piston and ring, 56
  Starter, 51
  Torque, 55
  Tune-up, 27
  Valves, 57
  Wheel alignment, 156
Speedometer cable, 117
Springs
  Front, 147
  Rear, 156
Starter, 44
Steering gear

Manual, 159
  Power, 161
Steering knuckles, 144
Steering linkage, 162
Steering wheel, 158
Sway bar, 154

T

Thermostat, 58
Timing, 30
Timing belt, 75
Timing chain, 71
Timing gears, 76
Tires, 11
Tools, 1
Torsion bars, 149
Transfer Case, 134
Transmission
  Automatic, 129
  Manual, 121
Troubleshooting, 31
Tune-up

Procedures, 25
  Specifications, 27
Turn signal switch, 158

U

U-joints, 135
Upper control arm, 154

V

Vehicle identification, 3

W

Water pump, 58
Wheel alignment, 156
Wheel bearings, 19
Wheel cylinders, 169, 176
Windshield wipers
  Blade, 8
  Linkage, 116
  Motor, 115

Chilton's Repair & Tune-Up Guides

The Complete line covers domestic cars, imports, trucks, vans, RV's and 4-wheel drive vehicles.

RTUG Title	Part No.
AMC 1975-82	7199
Covers all U.S. and Canadian models	
Aspen/Volare 1976-80	6637
Covers all U.S. and Canadian models	
Audi 1970-73	5902
Covers all U.S. and Canadian models.	
Audi 4000/5000 1978-81	7028
Covers all U.S. and Canadian models including turbocharged and diesel engines	
Barracuda/Challenger 1965-72	5807
Covers all U.S. and Canadian models	
Blazer/Jimmy 1969-82	6931
Covers all U.S. and Canadian 2- and 4-wheel drive models, including diesel engines	
BMW 1970-82	6844
Covers U.S. and Canadian models	
Buick/Olds/Pontiac 1975-85	7308
Covers all U.S. and Canadian full size rear wheel drive models	
Cadillac 1967-84	7462
Covers all U.S. and Canadian rear wheel drive models	
Camaro 1967-81	6735
Covers all U.S. and Canadian models	
Camaro 1982-85	7317
Covers all U.S. and Canadian models	
Capri 1970-77	6695
Covers all U.S. and Canadian models	
Caravan/Voyager 1984-85	7482
Covers all U.S. and Canadian models	
Century/Regal 1975-85	7307
Covers all U.S. and Canadian rear wheel drive models, including turbocharged engines	
Champ/Arrow/Sapporo 1978-83	7041
Covers all U.S. and Canadian models	
Chevette/1000 1976-86	6836
Covers all U.S. and Canadian models	
Chevrolet 1968-85	7135
Covers all U.S. and Canadian models	
Chevrolet 1968-79 Spanish	7082
Chevrolet/GMC Pick-Ups 1970-82 Spanish	7468
Chevrolet/GMC Pick-Ups and Suburban 1970-86	6936
Covers all U.S. and Canadian 1/2, 3/4 and 1 ton models, including 4-wheel drive and diesel engines	
Chevrolet LUV 1972-81	6815
Covers all U.S. and Canadian models	
Chevrolet Mid-Size 1964-86	6840
Covers all U.S. and Canadian models of 1964-77 Chevelle, Malibu and Malibu SS; 1974-77 Laguna; 1978-85 Malibu; 1970-86 Monte Carlo; 1964-84 El Camino, including diesel engines	
Chevrolet Nova 1986	7658
Covers all U.S. and Canadian models	
Chevy/GMC Vans 1967-84	6930
Covers all U.S. and Canadian models of 1/2, 3/4, and 1 ton vans, cutaways, and motor home chassis, including diesel engines	
Chevy S-10 Blazer/GMC S-15 Jimmy 1982-85	7383
Covers all U.S. and Canadian models	
Chevy S-10/GMC S-15 Pick-Ups 1982-85	7310
Covers all U.S. and Canadian models	
Chevy II/Nova 1962-79	6841
Covers all U.S. and Canadian models	
Chrysler K- and E-Car 1981-85	7163
Covers all U.S. and Canadian front wheel drive models	
Colt/Challenger/Vista/Conquest 1971-85	7037
Corolla/Carina/Tercel/Starlet 1970-85	7036
Covers all U.S. and Canadian models	
Corona/Cressida/Crown/Mk.II/Camry/Van 1970-84	7044
Covers all U.S. and Canadian models	
Corvair 1960-69	6691
Covers all U.S. and Canadian models	
Corvette 1953-62	6576
Covers all U.S. and Canadian models	
Corvette 1963-84	6843
Covers all U.S. and Canadian models	
Cutlass 1970-85	6933
Covers all U.S. and Canadian models	
Dart/Demon 1968-76	6324
Covers all U.S. and Canadian models	
Datsun 1961-72	5790
Covers all U.S. and Canadian models of Nissan Patrol; 1500, 1600 and 2000 sports cars; Pick-Ups; 410, 411, 510, 1200 and 240Z	
Datsun 1973-80 Spanish	7083
Datsun/Nissan F-10, 310, Stanza, Pulsar 1977-86	7196
Covers all U.S. and Canadian models	
Datsun/Nissan Pick-Ups 1970-84	6816
Covers all U.S and Canadian models	
Datsun/Nissan Z & ZX 1970-86	6932
Covers all U.S. and Canadian models	
Datsun/Nissan 1200, 210, Sentra 1973-86	7197
Covers all U.S. and Canadian models	
Datsun/Nissan 200SX, 510, 610, 710, 810, Maxima 1973-84	7170
Covers all U.S. and Canadian models	
Dodge 1968-77	6554
Covers all U.S. and Canadian models	
Dodge Charger 1967-70	6486
Covers all U.S. and Canadian models	
Dodge/Plymouth Trucks 1967-84	7459
Covers all 1/2, 3/4, and 1 ton 2- and 4-wheel drive U.S. and Canadian models, including diesel engines	
Dodge/Plymouth Vans 1967-84	6934
Covers all 1/2, 3/4, and 1 ton U.S. and Canadian models of vans, cutaways and motor home chassis	
D-50/Arrow Pick-Up 1979-81	7032
Covers all U.S. and Canadian models	
Fairlane/Torino 1962-75	6320
Covers all U.S. and Canadian models	
Fairmont/Zephyr 1978-83	6965
Covers all U.S. and Canadian models	
Fiat 1969-81	7042
Covers all U.S. and Canadian models	
Fiesta 1978-80	6846
Covers all U.S. and Canadian models	
Firebird 1967-81	5996
Covers all U.S. and Canadian models	
Firebird 1982-85	7345
Covers all U.S. and Canadian models	
Ford 1968-79 Spanish	7084
Ford Bronco 1966-83	7140
Covers all U.S. and Canadian models	
Ford Bronco II 1984	7408
Covers all U.S. and Canadian models	
Ford Courier 1972-82	6983
Covers all U.S. and Canadian models	
Ford/Mercury Front Wheel Drive 1981-85	7055
Covers all U.S. and Canadian models Escort, EXP, Tempo, Lynx, LN-7 and Topaz	
Ford/Mercury/Lincoln 1968-85	6842
Covers all U.S. and Canadian models of FORD Country Sedan, Country Squire, Crown Victoria, Custom, Custom 500, Galaxie 500, LTD through 1982, Ranch Wagon, and XL; MERCURY Colony Park, Commuter, Marquis through 1982, Gran Marquis, Monterey and Park Lane; LINCOLN Continental and Towne Car	
Ford/Mercury/Lincoln Mid-Size 1971-85	6696
Covers all U.S. and Canadian models of FORD Elite, 1983-85 LTD, 1977-79 LTD II, Ranchero, Torino, Gran Torino, 1977-85 Thunderbird; MERCURY 1972-85 Cougar,	

continued on next page

RTUG Title	Part No.
1983-85 Marquis, Montego, 1980-85 XR-7; LINCOLN 1982-85 Continental, 1984-85 Mark VII, 1978-80 Versailles	
Ford Pick-Ups 1965-86 Covers all $^1/_2$, $^3/_4$ and 1 ton, 2- and 4-wheel drive U.S. and Canadian pick-up, chassis cab and camper models, including diesel engines	6913
Ford Pick-Ups 1965-82 Spanish	7469
Ford Ranger 1983-84 Covers all U.S. and Canadian models	7338
Ford Vans 1961-86 Covers all U.S. and Canadian $^1/_2$, $^3/_4$ and 1 ton van and cutaway chassis models, including diesel engines	6849
GM A-Body 1982-85 Covers all front wheel drive U.S. and Canadian models of BUICK Century, CHEVROLET Celebrity, OLDSMOBILE Cutlass Ciera and PONTIAC 6000	7309
GM C-Body 1985 Covers all front wheel drive U.S. and Canadian models of BUICK Electra Park Avenue and Electra T-Type, CADILLAC Fleetwood and deVille, OLDSMOBILE 98 Regency and Regency Brougham	7587
GM J-Car 1982-85 Covers all U.S. and Canadian models of BUICK Skyhawk, CHEVROLET Cavalier, CADILLAC Cimarron, OLDSMOBILE Firenza and PONTIAC 2000 and Sunbird	7059
GM N-Body 1985-86 Covers all U.S. and Canadian models of front wheel drive BUICK Somerset and Skylark, OLDSMOBILE Calais, and PONTIAC Grand Am	7657
GM X-Body 1980-85 Covers all U.S. and Canadian models of BUICK Skylark, CHEVROLET Citation, OLDSMOBILE Omega and PONTIAC Phoenix	7049
GM Subcompact 1971-80 Covers all U.S. and Canadian models of BUICK Skyhawk (1975-80), CHEVROLET Vega and Monza, OLDSMOBILE Starfire, and PONTIAC Astre and 1975-80 Sunbird	6935
Granada/Monarch 1975-82 Covers all U.S. and Canadian models	6937
Honda 1973-84 Covers all U.S. and Canadian models	6980
International Scout 1967-73 Covers all U.S. and Canadian models	5912
Jeep 1945-87 Covers all U.S. and Canadian CJ-2A, CJ-3A, CJ-3B, CJ-5, CJ-6, CJ-7, Scrambler and Wrangler models	6817
Jeep Wagoneer, Commando, Cherokee, Truck 1957-86 Covers all U.S. and Canadian models of Wagoneer, Cherokee, Grand Wagoneer, Jeepster, Jeepster Commando, J-100, J-200, J-300, J-10, J20, FC-150 and FC-170	6739
Laser/Daytona 1984-85 Covers all U.S. and Canadian models	7563
Maverick/Comet 1970-77 Covers all U.S. and Canadian models	6634
Mazda 1971-84 Covers all U.S. and Canadian models of RX-2, RX-3, RX-4, 808, 1300, 1600, Cosmo, GLC and 626	6981
Mazda Pick-Ups 1972-86 Covers all U.S. and Canadian models	7659
Mercedes-Benz 1959-70 Covers all U.S. and Canadian models	6065
Mereceds-Benz 1968-73 Covers all U.S. and Canadian models	5907

RTUG Title	Part No.
Mercedes-Benz 1974-84 Covers all U.S. and Canadian models	6809
Mitsubishi, Cordia, Tredia, Starlon, Galant 1983-85 Covers all U.S. and Canadian models	7583
MG 1961-81 Covers all U.S. and Canadian models	6780
Mustang/Capri/Merkur 1979-85 Covers all U.S. and Canadian models	6963
Mustang/Cougar 1965-73 Covers all U.S. and Canadian models	6542
Mustang II 1974-78 Covers all U.S. and Canadian models	6812
Omni/Horizon/Rampage 1978-84 Covers all U.S. and Canadian models of DODGE omni, Miser, 024, Charger 2.2; PLYMOUTH Horizon, Miser, TC3, TC3 Tourismo; Rampage	6845
Opel 1971-75 Covers all U.S. and Canadian models	6575
Peugeot 1970-74 Covers all U.S. and Canadian models	5982
Pinto/Bobcat 1971-80 Covers all U.S. and Canadian models	7027
Plymouth 1968-76 Covers all U.S. and Canadian models	6552
Pontiac Fiero 1984-85 Covers all U.S. and Canadian models	7571
Pontiac Mid-Size 1974-83 Covers all U.S. and Canadian models of Ventura, Grand Am, LeMans, Grand LeMans, GTO, Phoenix, and Grand Prix	7346
Porsche 924/928 1976-81 Covers all U.S. and Canadian models	7048
Renault 1975-85 Covers all U.S. and Canadian models	7165
Roadrunner/Satellite/Belvedere/GTX 1968-73 Covers all U.S. and Canadian models	5821
RX-7 1979-81 Covers all U.S. and Canadian models	7031
SAAB 99 1969-75 Covers all U.S. and Canadian models	5988
SAAB 900 1979-85 Covers all U.S. and Canadian models	7572
Snowmobiles 1976-80 Covers Arctic Cat, John Deere, Kawasaki, Polaris, Ski-Doo and Yamaha	6978
Subaru 1970-84 Covers all U.S. and Canadian models	6982
Tempest/GTO/LeMans 1968-73 Covers all U.S. and Canadian models	5905
Toyota 1966-70 Covers all U.S. and Canadian models of Corona, MkII, Corolla, Crown, Land Cruiser, Stout and Hi-Lux	5795
Toyota 1970-79 Spanish	7467
Toyota Celica/Supra 1971-85 Covers all U.S. and Canadian models	7043
Toyota Trucks 1970-85 Covers all U.S. and Canadian models of pick-ups, Land Cruiser and 4Runner	7035
Valiant/Duster 1968-76 Covers all U.S. and Canadian models	6326
Volvo 1956-69 Covers all U.S. and Canadian models	6529
Volvo 1970-83 Covers all U.S. and Canadian models	7040
VW Front Wheel Drive 1974-85 Covers all U.S. and Canadian models	6962
VW 1949-71 Covers all U.S. and Canadian models	5796
VW 1970-79 Spanish	7081
VW 1970-81 Covers all U.S. and Canadian Beetles, Karmann Ghia, Fastback, Squareback, Vans, 411 and 412	6837

Chilton's Repair & Tune-Up Guides are available at your local retailer or by mailing a check or money order for **$13.50** plus **$2.50** to cover postage and handling to:

Chilton Book Company
Dept. DM
Radnor, PA 19089

NOTE: When ordering be sure to include your name & address, book part No. & title.